JANE'S

WORLD AIRCRAFT
Recognition Handbook
Derek Wood

JANE'S

Contents

ACKNOWLEDGMENTS

PICTURE ACKNOWLEDGMENTS

In preparing this book I have received help from a number of sources: Mark Daly gave considerable assistance with the preparation of several sections, John Blake has prepared all the sketch drawings, and the silhouettes have been supplied by Pilot Press and Michael Badrocke. I am also grateful to Michael Taylor and *Jane's All the World's Aircraft* for the supply of many of the photographs and to Alan Hall for model photographs. Derek Ballington kindly produced the test sillographs. My son Jonathan also assisted with text and picture research.

RECOMMENDED FURTHER READING

Jane's All the World's Aircraft
Frederick Warne: *Observer's Book of Aircraft*
Ian Allan: *Civil Aircraft of the World*
   Military Aircraft of the World

INTRODUCTION

Aircraft recognition is as important today as it ever was, for military and civilian observers alike. This volume is intended as a primer for students of the subject, and is not a standard collection of aircraft types by country and manufacturer with full data. There are a number of excellent volumes of this type and a list is provided on page 4.

The aim has been to satisfy the needs of three types of recognition student:

Armed service or auxiliary personnel worldwide to whom recognition is vital for survival in war.

Those who have an interest in aviation and wish to learn how to recognise aircraft from scratch.

The knowledgeable enthusiast in service or civilian life who requires quick answers, either to check judgement or for revision.

The initial "teach-in" section provides an introduction to the subject and includes a glossary, without which the newcomer would be lost in a world that has built up its own exclusive jargon.

The essential elements of airframes are illustrated, together with an explanation of the breakdown of the book into fixed-wing aircraft and helicopters of various distinctive types. The emphasis throughout is on shapes and not manufacturers or designations, and all groups are assembled on the basis of similarity in general configuration. After all, when an airborne object comes into view, the observer on the ground wants to refer to a shape to find out what it is. Is it jet or propeller-driven? Are its wings straight or swept? Are the engines on the wings?

The 480+ aircraft shown in the reference part of the book have been selected as most likely to be seen round the world. There is a limit to the number of aircraft that can be illustrated and those omitted include several "one-offs", types not due to fly or appear in service for some time, aircraft of which only a handful are flying, and ultra-lights and homebuilts.

Both military and civil machines are included, as it is impossible, even for the serviceman, just to study warplanes. Confusion can always arise if the observer has not covered all the significant types. In the early stages of the Second World War an axiom was adopted by those who were either unable or willing to learn recognition. Aircraft were divided into three categories: receding and presumed friendly; approaching and presumed hostile; and Lysanders. That the ultra-distinctive Lysander should be regarded as the only readily recognisable type is an indication of the very low standards that prevailed until recognition was really taken seriously and proper teaching methods were evolved. Faulty recognition in war has led to untold casualties which could have been avoided.

Black-and-white silhouettes have been used throughout the reference section of this book, as the detailed three-view silhouette remains the best method of encapsulating the shape and main features of any aircraft. Line drawings just do not give the same emphasis to recognition outline, although they can be useful once the student has become reasonably proficient.

All sorts of so-called mnemonic aircraft-recognition systems have been invented; one such is "WETFUR", standing for Wings, Engine, Tail Unit, Fuselage, Undercarriage and Radiator. In practice these methods are completely useless, as recognition depends on the aircraft's total appearance and there is usually little enough time to look for individual features, let alone reciting sets of letters. Mnemonics have no place here.

Long-winded descriptions of the aircraft with a mass of complex data also leave little impression on the recognition student and only serve to confuse; they too have been omitted.

Additional information such as designation systems, code-name lists and general characteristics are very important, both for reference and to add to the general picture. They have therefore been included.

After the basic details on each type there is a list of the similar designs with which it might be confused. This has been done to stimulate interest and comparison. Some students may decide that aircraft X is much more like aircraft Y. If this comes after careful study of a number of silhouettes and photographs, then the individual's recognition knowledge will have been significantly extended.

Introduction to new edition
Since the second edition of *Jane's World Aircraft Recognition Handbook* a number of new aircraft have emerged and many others have moved from the prototype or pre-production stages to production and service.

The text has been revised throughout, and 46 new silhouettes and over 120 new photographs, together with additional features, have been incorporated. The question "should it go in or not?" has remained the same. Are there sufficient numbers of a particular type flying over a wide enough area of the globe to warrant inclusion? A number of old aircraft are still familiar to many people, although seen over limited areas. A few of these earlier types are included at the end of the book.

Over the past three years some well known types have virtually left the regular scene, including the Vulcan delta-wing bomber, the Super Mystère B.2, the F-105 Thunderchief, the Seahawk and the F-101 Voodoo. Others have been so reduced in numbers that they have to be excluded on the grounds of limited visibility.

The increasing range of airborne guided missiles available has led to the inclusion of side view weapon drawings to help identify the payload being carried on military aircraft.

Quick-reference symbols
At the top outside corner of each page in the following chapters you will find a quick-reference symbol. They are designed to show the main characteristics of each class of aircraft, so that the user can find his way immediately to the right chapter after catching a fleeting glimpse of, say, a delta shape in the sky. In some cases one symbol has had to stand for two classes of aircraft. It would have been difficult to suggest high or low wings with simple plan-views, just as the addition of something to indicate fixed or retractable undercarriage would have made those symbols unnecessarily complicated. One symbol has therefore been used for both high and low-wing twin-propeller aircraft, while all three classes of single propeller designs are represented by a single plan view.

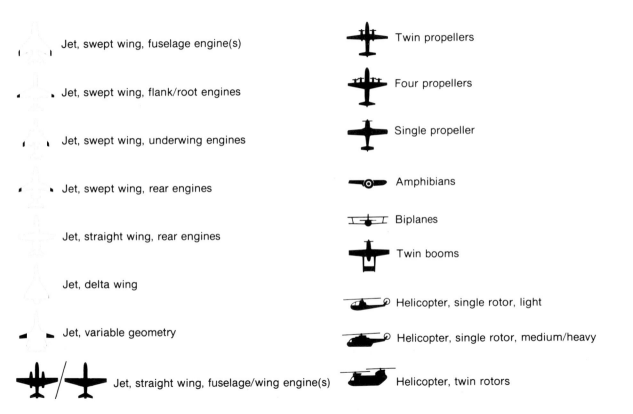

Jet, swept wing, fuselage engine(s)

Jet, swept wing, flank/root engines

Jet, swept wing, underwing engines

Jet, swept wing, rear engines

Jet, straight wing, rear engines

Jet, delta wing

Jet, variable geometry

Jet, straight wing, fuselage/wing engine(s)

Twin propellers

Four propellers

Single propeller

Amphibians

Biplanes

Twin booms

Helicopter, single rotor, light

Helicopter, single rotor, medium/heavy

Helicopter, twin rotors

A good example of a large military transport, the Lockheed C-141B Starlifter. This has a very long fuselage, swept wings, four under-wing pod-mounted turbofans and a T-tail.

The very unusual Edgley Optica observation aircraft, which looks like a jet but is in fact fitted with a piston engine driving a fan.

The General Dynamics F-16C has a distinctive shark's mouth intake under the nose and the wingtip outline is changed by the fitting of Sidewinder missiles.

THE BASICS OF RECOGNITION

The initial approach to aircraft recognition is daunting, confronting the student with a mass of shapes, hundreds of odd names, curious designations, incomprehensible specications and strange descriptive terms.

It is essential for any student to work in stages, gradually acquiring knowledge and storing it. Like people's faces and figures, every aircraft and helicopter has its own characteristics. It may have one engine and straight wings; four engines and swept wings; a fat fuselage; a triangular wing; a tailplane on top of the fin; or, in the case of a helicopter, one or two rotors.

The permutations are endless, but ultimately all powered flying machines can be sorted out into categories for detailed study. This book is divided into categories based on wing shape and engine layout in the case of fixed-wing aircraft, and size and number of rotors for helicopters.

The basic structure of an aircraft has to be studied from the outset. Every powered flying machine (other than helicopters) has some wing form, a fuselage and a tail structure, the last-mentioned having either a horizontal stabiliser and a fin, or a fin alone (as in the case of some delta-wing designs such as the Mirage and Concorde). Every wing, fuselage and tail structure differs in some respect from another, as do the engine installations and air intakes, be they for gas turbines or piston engines. It is the combination of these features with individual characteristics that makes up an aircraft's total shape. Knowledge of such shapes is the essence of recognition.

The same theory applies to helicopters, except that wings appear only occasionally in stub form, tail structures consist of rear rotors and some miniature tails, and the main rotor(s) dominate the shape.

The best way for the beginner to use this book is to look first at totally different types, say the Mirage fighter and the Boeing 747 airliner, or the Jaguar ground-attack aircraft and Chinook twin-rotor helicopter. In the first case, a single-engined delta wing fighter with the engine in the fuselage just cannot resemble a giant 385-seater with four jets slung under the wings. In the second case, the swept-wing Jaguar hardly compares with the Chinook, with its squat, boxlike fuselage and twin overhead rotors.

This process should be continued at random, selecting from the different sub-sections of the book. At the same time, the annotated drawings on pages 18–25 should be consulted to find out what the various parts of flying machines are and, in the case of flying controls, what they do. For an understanding of aviation terminology the glossary of terms and abbreviations at the end of this book can be used.

The second stage is for the reader to look at two of the aircraft in each sub-section which are similar in general layout but very different in detail characteristics. Take, for instance, the Corsair II and the Lightning in Section 1. The two wing shapes immediately strike the eye: that of the Corsair is broad in chord and moderately swept back, while the Lightning's resembles a triangle with two triangular notches cut out at the roots. The Corsair fuselage is dumpy, with a distinctive "pimple" above the nose intake. The Lightning, on the other hand, has a circular intake with a pointed centrebody. Unlike the Corsair, with its simple engine and exhaust arrangement, the Lightning has two engines mounted one above the other in the fuselage and exhausting through twin afterburning jetpipes. Finally, the fin of the Corsair tapers to what looks like a curved top, while the Lightning's fin is much broader and cut sharply across the top.

After several excursions through the pages to see how shapes differ markedly or are superficially similar, the student should select his basic first 30 aircraft. If he is a member of a military or paramilitary force, he can choose the friendly and unfriendly types which he is most likely to encounter.

A mixed first 30 could consist of the following:

Military	Civil
Dassault Mirage	Airbus A300
Vought Corsair II	Boeing 737
Tupolev Tu-20 Bear	Boeing 747
McDonnell Douglas Phantom	McDonnell Douglas DC-8
McDonnell Douglas F-15	McDonnell Douglas DC-9
Northrop F-5	McDonnell Douglas DC-10
SEPECAT Jaguar	BAe One-Eleven
Yakovlev Yak-28P Firebar	Lockheed TriStar
Panavia Tornado	Tupolev Tu-134
Saab Viggen	Piper Comanche
Mikoyan MiG-25 Foxbat	Yakovlev Yak-40 Codling
Lockheed F-104 Starfighter	Fokker F.27 Friendship
Mikoyan MiG-21 Fishbed	BAe 748

Military	Civil
Boeing B-52	Piper Cherokee
Tupolev Tu-22M/Tu-26	Beech Mentor
Backfire	

For helicopters an initial eight could be:

Military	Civil
Westland Lynx	Ka-26 Hoodlum
Ka-25 Hormone	Aérospatiale Alouette
Boeing Chinook	Hughes 500
Sikorsky S-61	MBB BO105

The student who wants to devise his own programme could well make his first selection from the types which fly from the nearest civil or military airfield, or both. After the first 30, a further 30 can be chosen, and so on. After the student has mastered his first 30 aircraft, he will be able to apply his self-acquired training to any types of his choice.

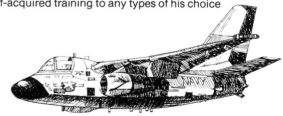

The Lockheed S-3A Viking carrier-borne anti-submarine aircraft. It has a shoulder-mounted swept wing, twin underwing turbofans and a swept fin.

The Nanchang Q-5, a Chinese development of the MiG-19 with flank intakes.

differentiate between types. Examples of similar outlines are the German MBB BO105 and the Hughes 500D helicopters.

The only way to progress in aircraft recognition is to "look and learn" as frequently as possible. This means not only scanning the skies but examining every photograph or drawing in newspapers and magazines and watching for aircraft on television. A scrapbook of picture cuttings and notes is an excellent way of improving the art.

A typical Soviet twin-turbine helicopter, the Mi-8 Hip with single main rotor and fixed tricycle undercarriage.

Throughout, the recognition of an aircraft must involve a total impression of the shape, but with certain distinctive elements borne in mind. When any aircraft appears it must be watched right across the sky so that it can be viewed from every angle.

In the air, the head-on view of an F-15 fighter looks very different to a side or plan view, possibly leading to confusion with the Soviet Foxbat. Aircraft viewed from the rear, going away, also often provide problems, as with the Mirage and Viggen. Particularly difficult are the head-on and retreating views of the transports with twin and triple rear-engine layouts, not least the Soviet Crusty and Careless airliners. The Soviet Badger and Bison bombers are easily confused at a distance, when the difference in size cannot be estimated.

Helicopters require special study as, at a distance and in poor weather, their shapes tend to be ill-defined. In certain cases very detailed knowledge of outlines is needed to

When an unknown aircraft flies over, or an uncaptioned photograph appears in a journal, note its main features and consult the appropriate section in this book. The more "mental images" of different types that can be stored away, the easier recognition becomes.

Radomes, tip tanks and tail-mounted Magnetic Anomality Detector (MAD) affect the outline of this twin-turboprop Atlantic maritime reconnaissance aircraft.

Really odd shapes. Top, the IAI 202 Arava high wing transport with twin booms, fixed undercarriage and winglets at the tips of the strut-braced wings. Below, the M-15 Belphegor agricultural biplane with twin booms, a turbofan engine and chemical hoppers between the wings.

Changing outline

Having learned the flying exterior of an aircraft, the effects of external items that may be attached to it require attention. Modern military aircraft carry a great variety of external "stores": missiles, rocket pods, bombs, reconnaissance pods, externally mounted guns, electronic jamming pods and auxiliary fuel tanks, to mention a few. As an example of the resulting outline change, the podded fuel tanks under the wings of a Hercules transport can, at a distance, give the impression of six engines instead of four. Radomes and other bumps or bulges on an aircraft also change the shape when viewed from different angles.

Variable-geometry or swing-wing aircraft present problems, as moving the wings from straight to fully swept changes the outline continuously.

Finally, an aircraft preparing to land can appear completely different from its normal cruising self. For instance, a Boeing 747 cruising across the sky is not the same as a 747 on the approach to an airfield with its multi-wheel undercarriage down and massive flaps extended.

To appreciate all the changing aspects of aircraft in the air, it is essential to keep watching with the eyes or, preferably, with binoculars. When there is cloud, watch where the aircraft enters and judge where it may reappear.

Viewed from above

For the military pilot, aircraft flying below or positioned on the ground are very important. The pilot's view can be very different from that of the ground observer. It takes a sharp eye to recognise a fleeting shape parked near a hangar, in a revetment, or with its nose sticking out of a shelter. Special study is needed to separate shapes on the ground from their surroundings, and camouflage makes this even more difficult.

In the air, it is easier to recognise aircraft seen from below. From above, aircraft blend with the terrain, particularly when they are camouflaged, or have their outlines broken up by reflected light.

Contrails

At high altitude condensation of the water vapour in the exhaust gas of an aero-engine produces a "contrail", a telltale stream of white vapour across the sky. On a clear day it is often possible to recognise the aircraft at the head of the trail, but usually binoculars are essential. When there is patchy cloud the point of entry of the contrail should be noted to find the direction of exit. Large multi-engined aircraft make several trails which usually blend into one. With a lot of experience it is possible to differentiate between certain types, but great care is needed.

Sound

Sound is very often the first indication that an aircraft or helicopter is approaching. Weather effects and the varied abilities of human ears can however make sound very misleading. It may appear to come from completely the wrong quarter, causing the observer to miss the approaching aircraft altogether. With fast aircraft, the subject may be well ahead of its noise. Sound is nevertheless important and certain basic facts can be gleaned from it. It is usually possible to differentiate between a piston engine and a jet; a turboprop is distinctive, while the beat of a helicopter rotor sounds different from the noise of a fixed-wing aircraft.

It is important to both watch *and* listen in order to associate sound with a particular type. A great deal of practice is needed before making snap judgements on sound alone, and even then there is a higher chance of error.

Teaching aircraft recognition, whether in the services or a club, is an exacting task calling for method, efficiency and, above all, background knowledge of the subject. The ace spotter who can recognise anything does not necessarily make a good instructor, as he may be too far removed from the novice's problems.

An instructor must be able to make the subject live and to translate flat pictures and silhouettes into 3D images which will remain imprinted on the pupil's mind; hence the need for background knowledge. The tools of the instructor's trade are silhouettes, black-and-white or colour photographs and slides, filmstrips, the slide projector, the episcope and the overhead projector. Sometimes a film can provide excellent material, though a particular view cannot be shown again as quickly as with the other devices. A blackboard on which instructor and students can put quick sketches is extremely useful.

Models are also good tools, both to make and look at. Putting a plastic kit together will leave a lasting impression of the subject's shape and characteristics. Models may also be used in conjunction with a "shadowgraph". The "flash trainer" is also an effective aid, though not always easy to obtain. The essence of the flash trainer is a shutter which flashes the image onto the screen for a brief period. With a little ingenuity it is possible to adapt an old camera shutter for use with either an episcope or a slide projector.

In approaching recognition training, it is essential to plan ahead and not swamp the pupils with an excess of information. An initial test will decide the standard of the class, while discussion will reveal the level of understanding of terms and nomenclature. A large sketch of the basic elements of fixed-wing aircraft and helicopters is a must for absolute beginners.

As mentioned earlier, contrasting types should be illustrated first to give the pupil some "feel"; thereafter types should be taught in groups. The make-up of the groups will depend on the priorities and interests of the class: whether they are servicemen or civilians, for instance.

A model of a Hawk assembled from a plastic kit.

Each aircraft should be the subject of a lesson on its own, with a mixture of silhouettes and photographs or slides. When instruction has been given in a dozen types, there should be a full revision session and a test. As the pupils become more proficient, so the tests should be varied and made more difficult.

The instructor must ensure that he does not overload the class, which will cause confusion, and also that he does not bore them. Boredom has been the enemy of good recognition training since aircraft were first used in war.

As time goes on, it will become apparent that certain types are more difficult to recognise, largely because they can be confused in outline with others of similar shape. Every effort should be made to show pictures and silhouettes of these difficult aircraft at frequent intervals until the points of difference are clearly understood. Care should however be taken to see that the pupils do not get into the bad habit of recognising the photograph rather than the aircraft itself.

The instructor can use a variety of methods to hold the students' interest. If an aviation incident, military or civil, has been headlined in the newspapers or shown on television recently, a short illustrated talk on the type or types involved should be given while the subject is fresh in the pupils' minds.

If possible, the classroom walls should be decorated with aircraft illustrations, preferably large ones, which can be changed or added to at intervals. If this is not possible, sections of hardboard covered with suitable pictures and captions should be taken along to the meetings. One such board can be used for an "aircraft of the week" to which the class can give special attention.

"Sillographs", which form good training and test material, can be made very simply by inking in photographs with a black felt pen or a brush and black ink or paint. The proficiency test at the end of this book is presented in sillograph form. Cartoons are also of assistance, as the exaggeration stresses key points of outline. To achieve greater variety, photographs from journals can be cut into pieces showing a fin, nose, engine nacelle or part of a wing, for example.

A scrapbook can be kept handy and added to by both instructor and class. Prizes can be given for success in recognition tests. Finally, properly organised visits to airfields and attendance at air displays will make recognition training come alive.

A plastic model of the A300 Airbus – an excellent recognition tool.

A typical modern combat aircraft: McDonnell Douglas/British Aerospace Harrier GR Mk 5

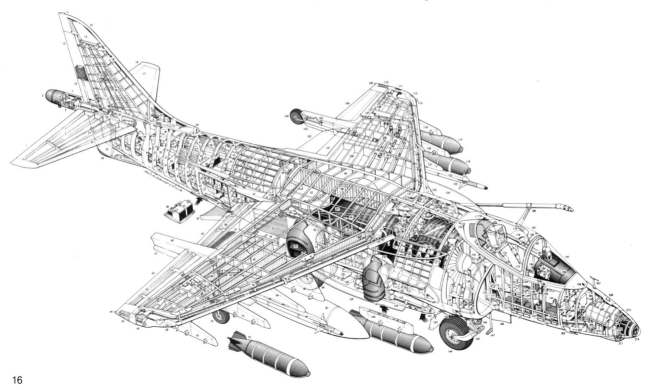

1 Starboard all-moving tailplane
2 Tailplane composite construction
3 Tail radome
4 Military equipment
5 Tail pitch control air valve
6 Yaw control air valves
7 Tail 'bullet' fairing
8 Reaction control system air ducting
9 Trim tab actuator
10 Rudder trim tab
11 Rudder composite construction
12 Rudder
13 Antenna
14 Fin tip aerial fairing
15 Upper broad band communications antenna
16 Port tailplane
17 Graphite epoxy tailplane skin
18 Port side temperature probe
19 MAD compensator
20 Formation lighting strip
21 Fin construction
22 Fin attachment joint
23 Tailplane pivot sealing plate
24 Aerials
25 Ventral fin
26 Tail bumper
27 Lower broad band communications antenna
28 Tailplane hydraulic jack
29 Heat exchanger air exhaust
30 Aft fuselage frames
31 Rudder hydraulic actuator
32 Avionics equipment air conditioning plant
33 Avionics equipment racks
34 Heat exchanger ram air intake
35 Electrical system circuit breaker panels, port and starboard
36 Avionic equipment
37 Chaff and flare dispensers
38 Dispenser electronic control units
39 Ventral airbrake
40 Airbrake hydraulic jack
41 Formation lighting strip
42 Avionics bay access door, port and starboard
43 Avionics equipment racks
44 Fuselage frame and stringer construction
45 Rear fuselage fuel tank
46 Main undercarriage wheel bay
47 Wing root fillet
48 Wing spar/fuselage attachment joint
49 Water filler cap
50 Engine fire extinguisher bottle
51 Anti-collision light
52 Water tank
53 Flap hydraulic actuator
54 Flap hinge fitting
55 Nimonic fuselage heat shield

56 Main undercarriage bay doors (closed after cycling of mainwheels)
57 Flap vane composite construction
58 Flap composite construction
59 Starboard slotted flap, lowered
60 Outrigger wheel fairing
61 Outrigger leg doors
62 Starboard aileron
63 Aileron composite construction
64 Fuel jettison
65 Formation lighting panel
66 Roll control air valve
67 Wing tip fairing
68 Starboard navigation light
69 Radar warning aerial
70 Outboard pylon
71 Pylon attachment joint
72 Graphite epoxy composite wing construction
73 Aileron hydraulic actuator
74 Starbord outrigger wheel
75 BL755 600-lb (272-kg) cluster bomb (CBU)
76 Intermediate pylon
77 Reaction control air ducting
78 Aileron control rod
79 Aileron hydraulic retraction jack
80 Outrigger leg strut
81 Leg pivot fixing
82 Multi-spar wing construction
83 Leading-edge wing fence
84 Outrigger pylon
85 Missile launch rail
86 AIM-9L Sidewinder air-to-air missile
87 External fuel tank, 300 US gal (1,135l)
88 Inboard pylon
89 Aft retracting twin mainwheels
90 Inboard pylon attachment joint
91 Rear (hot stream) swivelling exhaust nozzle
92 Position of pressure refuelling connection on port side
93 Rear nozzle bearing
94 Centre fuselage flank fuel tank
95 Hydraulic reservoir
96 Nozzle bearing cooling air duct
97 Engine exhaust divider duct
98 Wing panel centre rib
99 Centre section integral fuel tank
100 Port wing integral fuel tank
101 Flap vane
102 Port slotted flap, lowered
103 Outrigger wheel fairing
104 Port outrigger wheel
105 Torque scissor links
106 Port aileron
107 Aileron hydraulic actuator
108 Aileron/air valve interconnection
109 Fuel jettison

110 Formation lighting panel
111 Port roll control air valve
112 Port navigation light
113 Radar warning aerial
114 Port wing reaction control air duct
115 Fuel pumps
116 Fuel system piping
117 Port wing leading-edge fence
118 Outboard pylon
119 BL755 cluster bombs (maximum load, seven)
120 Intermediate pylon
121 Port outrigger pylon
122 Missile launch rail
123 AIM-9L Sidewinder air-to-air missile
124 Port leading-edge root extension (LERX)
125 Inboard pylon
126 Hydraulic pumps
127 APU intake
128 Gas turbine starter/auxiliary power unit (APU)
129 Alternator cooling air exhaust
130 APU exhaust
131 Engine fuel control unit
132 Engine bay venting ram air intake
133 Rotary nozzle bearing
134 Nozzle fairing construction
135 Ammunition tank, 100 rounds
136 Cartridge case collector box
137 Ammunition feed chute
138 Fuel vent
139 Gun pack strake
140 Fuselage centreline pylon
141 Zero scarf forward (fan air) nozzle
142 Ventral gun pack (two)
143 Aden 25-mm cannon
144 Engine drain mast
145 Hydraulic system ground connectors
146 Forward fuselage flank fuel tank
147 Engine electronic control units
148 Engine accessory equipment gearbox
149 Gearbox driven alternator
150 Rolls-Royce Pegasus 11 Mk 105 vectored thrust turbofan
151 Formation lighting strips
152 Engine oil tank
153 Bleed air spill duct
154 Air conditioning intake scoops
155 Cockpit air conditioning system heat exchanger
156 Engine compressor/fan face
157 Heat exchanger discharge to intake duct
158 Nose undercarriage hydraulic retraction jack
159 Intake milk in torque
160 Engine bay venting air scoop
161 Cannon muzzle fairing
162 Lift augmentation retractable cross-dam

163 Cross-dam hydraulic jack
164 Nosewheel
165 Nosewheel forks
166 Landing/taxiing lamp
167 Retractable boarding step
168 Nosewheel doors (closed after cycling of undercarriage)
169 Nosewheel door jack
170 Boundary layer bleed air duct
171 Nose undercarriage wheel bay
172 Kick-in boarding steps
173 Cockpit rear pressure bulkhead
174 Starboard side console panel
175 Martin-Baker Type 12 ejection seat
176 Safety harness
177 Ejection seat headrest
178 Port engine air intake
179 Probe hydraulic jack
180 Retractable in-flight refuelling probe (bolt-on pack)
181 Cockpit canopy cover
182 Miniature detonating cord (MDC) canopy breaker
183 Canopy frame
184 Engine throttle and nozzle angle control levers
185 Pilot's head-up display
186 Instrument panel
187 Moving map display
188 Control column
189 Central warning system panel
190 Cockpit pressure floor
191 Underfloor control runs
192 Formation lighting strips
193 Aileron trim actuator
194 Rudder pedals
195 Cockpit section composite construction
196 Instrument panel shroud
197 One-piece wrap-around windscreen panel
198 Ram air intake (cockpit fresh air)
199 Front pressure bulkhead
200 Incidence vane
201 Air data computer
202 Pitot tube
203 Lower IFF aerial
204 Nose pitch control air valve
205 Pitch trim control actuator
206 Electrical system equipment
207 Yaw vane
208 Upper IFF aerial
209 Avionic equipment
210 ARBS heat exchanger
211 MIRLS sensors
212 Hughes Angle Rate Bombing System (ARBS)
213 Composite construction nose cone
214 ARBS glazed aperture

17

A typical airliner: Saab-Fairchild 340

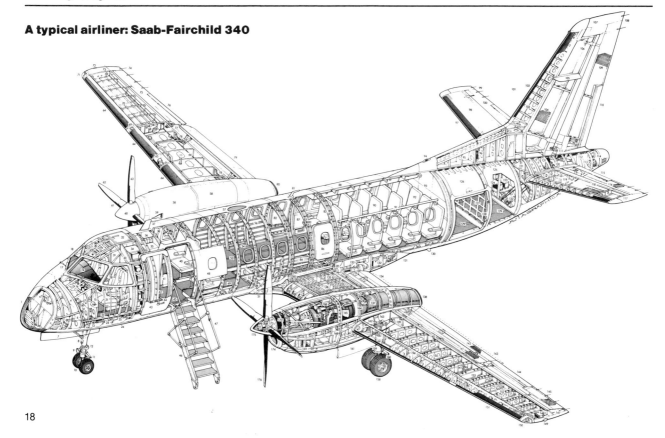

1 Radome
2 Weather radar scanner
3 Radar transmitter/receiver
4 Front pressure bulkhead
5 Nose undercarriage wheel bay
6 Hydraulic retraction jack
7 Nosewheel doors
8 Nose undercarriage leg strut
9 Taxying lamp
10 Twin nosewheels
11 Torque scissor links
12 Steering control link
13 Nosewheel leg pivot fixing
14 Rudder pedals
15 Angle of attack transmitter
16 Instrument panel
17 Windscreen wipers
18 Windscreen panels
19 Instrument panel shroud
20 Control column handwheel
21 Pilot's seat
22 Flight deck floor level
23 Underfloor control linkages
24 External hydraulic pipe duct
25 Control mechanism access panels
26 Pitot tubes
27 Safety harness
28 Centre control pedestal
29 Co-pilot's seat
30 Overhead systems switch panel
31 Starboard side toilet compartment
32 Cockpit roof escape hatch
33 Cockpit rear bulkhead
34 Radio and electronics rack
35 Galley/closet unit
36 Wardrobe
37 VHF aerial
38 Starboard side emergency exit
39 'Pull-down' window blinds
   (option)
40 Front seat row, total 34
   passengers
41 Cabin attendant's folding seat
42 Airstairs stowage
43 Entry door, open position
44 Door latch
45 Entry lobby
46 Airstairs
47 Folding handrail
48 Cabin window panel
49 Sidewall seat mountng rail

50 Cabin air vent duct
51 Landing lamp
52 Floor beam construction
53 Seat mounting rails
54 Glassfibre floor panels
55 Fuselage frame and stringer
   construction
56 Bonded fuselage skin/stringer
   panel
57 ADF aerial
58 Starboard engine cowling panels
59 NACA-type cooling air intake
60 Propeller spinner
61 Propeller blade de-icing boots
62 Dowty-Rotol four-bladed variable
   and reversible pitch, fully
   feathering propeller
63 Composite propeller blades
64 Wing leading-edge de-icing boots
65 Pressure refuelling connection
66 Starboard wing outer integral fuel
   tank, total fuel capacity 733 Imp
   gal (3,331l)
67 Fuel system piping
68 Overwing filler cap
69 Compass flux valve
70 Bonded wing skin/stringer panel
71 Starboard navigation lights
72 Strobe light
73 Glassfibre wing tip fairing
74 Static dischargers
75 Starboard aileron
76 Aileron geared tab
77 Aileron actuator
78 External flap hinges
79 Starboard single-slotted trailing
   edge flap, down position
80 Engine exhaust nozzle
81 VLF/Omega aerial (option)
82 Starboard emergency exit window
   panel
83 Wing spar attachment main
   frames
84 Wing panel centreline splice
85 Spar attachment links
86 Port emergency exit window
   panel
87 Cabin wall trim panelling
88 Fuselage skin panelling
89 Overhead hand-baggage lockers
   (option)

90 Three-abreast passenger seating
91 Overhead conditioned air
   distribution duct
92 Rear four-abreast seat row
93 Passenger cabin rear bulkhead
94 Anti-collision beacon (option)
95 Fin root fillet construction
96 HF aerial coupler (option)
97 Tailplane leading-edge de-icing
   boot
98 Starboard tailplane
99 Static dischargers
100 Starboard elevator
101 HF aerial cable (option)
102 Fin leading-edge de-icing boot
103 Leading-edge ribs
104 Aluminium honeycomb tail unit
   skin panels
105 VOR aerial
106 Fin construction
107 Rudder horn balance
108 Static dischargers
109 Honeycomb rudder construction
110 Rudder tab
111 Rudder hinge control mechanism
112 Tailcone
113 Cabin pressurisation valves
114 Rear pressure bulkhead
115 Elevator tab
116 Port elevator honeycomb
   construction
117 Elevator tip
118 Tailplane construction
119 Rear fuselage ventral access hatch
120 Elevator hinge control
121 Fin/tailplane attachment main
   frames
122 Tail control cables
123 Cockpit voice recorder
124 Air data recorder
125 Baggage compartment bulkhead
126 'Up-and-over' baggage
   compartment door
127 Baggage restraint net
128 Door guide rails
129 Baggage loading floor
130 DME aerial (option)
131 Wing trailing edge root fillet
132 Battery
133 Air conditioning plant, port and
   starboard

134 Flap inboard section
135 Wing stringers
136 Port inboard integral fuel tank
137 Heat shrouded engine exhaust
   pipe
138 Exhaust nozzle
139 Flap hydraulic jack
140 Rear spar
141 Composite flap shroud
   construction
142 Flap honeycomb construction
143 Port single-slotted trailing-edge
   flap, down position
144 Aileron geared tab
145 Static dischargers
146 Port aileron honeycomb
   construction
147 Glassfibre wing tip fairing
148 Lighting power supply
149 Strobe light
150 Port navigation light
151 Wing leading-edge de-icing boot
152 Wing rib construction
153 Fuel tank bay end rib
154 Overwing fuel filler cap
155 Port outer integral fuel tank
156 Front spar
157 Leading-edge nose ribs
158 Twin mainwheels
159 Main undercarriage leg strut
160 Torque scissor links
161 Mainwheel doors, closed after
   cycling of undercarriage leg
162 Hydraulic retraction jack
163 Main undercarriage pivot fixing
164 Engine bay fireproof bulkhead
165 Intake particle separator
166 Accessory gearbox
167 General Electric CT7-5A
   turboshaft engine
168 Engine nacelle construction
169 Ventral oil cooler
170 Gearbox mounting strut
171 Engine drive shaft
172 Propeller reduction gearbox
173 Propeller hub pitch change
   mechanism
174 Engine air intake
175 Propeller spinner
176 Port Dowty-Rotol four-bladed
   composite propeller

A typical military helicopter: Sikorsky SH-60B Seahawk

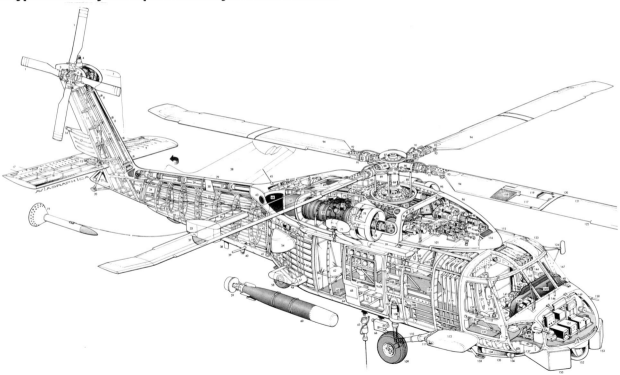

1 Graphite epoxy composite tail rotor blades
2 Lightweight cross beam rotor hub
3 Blade pitch change spider
4 Anti-collision light
5 Tail rotor final drive bevel gearbox
6 Rotor hub canted 20-deg
7 Horizontal tailplane folded position
8 Pull-out maintenance steps
9 Port tailplane
10 Tail rotor drive shaft
11 Fin pylon construction
12 Tailplane hydraulic jack
13 Cambered trailing-edge section
14 Tail navigation light
15 Tailplane hinge joint (manual folding)
16 Handgrips
17 Static dischargers
18 Starboard tailplane construction
19 Towed magnetic anomaly detector (MAD)
20 Tail bumper
21 Shock absorber strut
22 Bevel drive gearbox
23 Tail pylon latch joint
24 Tail pylon hinge frame (manual folding)
25 Transmission shaft disconnect
26 Tail rotor transmission shaft
27 Shaft bearings
28 Tail pylon folded position
29 Dorsal spine fairing
30 UHF aerial
31 Tailcone frame and stringer construction
32 Magnetic compass remote transmitters
33 MAD detector housing and reeling unit
34 Tail rotor control cables
35 HF aerial cable
36 MAD unit fixed pylon
37 Ventral data link antenna housing
38 Lower UHF/TACAN aerial
39 Fuel jettison
40 Anti-collision light

41 Tie-down shackle
42 Tailcone joint frame
43 Air system heat exchanger exhaust
44 Engine exhaust shroud
45 Emergency locator aerial
46 Engine fire suppression bottles
47 IFF aerial
48 Port side auxiliary power unit (APU)
49 Oil cooler exhaust grille
50 Starboard side air conditioning plant
51 Engine exhaust pipe
52 HF radio equipment bay
53 Sliding cabin door rail
54 Aft AN/ALQ 142 ESM aerial fairing, port and starboard
55 Tailwheel leg strut
56 Fireproof fuel tanks, port and starboard, total capacity 592 US gal (1,368l)
57 Starboard stores pylon
58 Castoring twin tailwheels
59 Torpedo parachute housing
60 Mk 46 lightweight torpedo
61 Cabin rear bulkhead
62 Passenger seat
63 Honeycomb cabin floor panelling
64 Sliding cabin door
65 Recovery Assist, Secure and Traverse (RAST) aircraft haul-down fitting
66 Ventral cargo hook, 6,000-lb (2,722-kg) capacity
67 Floor beam construction
68 Spring-loaded door segment in way of stores pylon
69 Pull-out emergency exit window panel
70 Pneumatic sonobuoy launch rack (125 sonobuoys)
71 Rescue hoist/winch
72 General Electric T700-GE-401 turboshaft engine
73 Engine accessory equipment gearbox
74 Intake particle separator air duct

75 Engine bay firewall
76 Oil cooler fan
77 Rotor brake unit
78 Engine intake ducts
79 Maintenance step
80 Engine drive shafts
81 Bevel drive gerboxes
82 Central main reduction gearbox
83 Rotor control swash plate
84 Rotor mast
85 Blade pitch control rods
86 Bi-filar vibration absorber
87 Rotor head fairing
88 Main rotor head (elastomeric, non-lubricated, bearings)
89 Blade pitch control horn
90 Lead-lag damper
91 Individual blade folding joints, electrically actuated
92 Blade spar crack detectors
93 Blade root attachment joints
94 Main rotor composite blades
95 Port engine intake
96 Control equipment sliding access cover
97 Engine driven accessory gearboxes
98 Hydraulic pump
99 Flight control servo units
100 Flight control hydro-mechanical mixer unit
101 Cabin roof panelling
102 Radar operator's seat
103 AN/APS 124 radar console
104 Tie-down shackle
105 Gearbox and engine mounting main frames
106 Maintenance steps
107 Main undercarriage leg mounting
108 Shock absorber leg strut
109 Starboard mainwheel
110 Pivoted axle beam
111 Starboard navigation light
112 Cockpit step/main axle fairing
113 Forward cabin access panel
114 Collective and cyclic pitch control rods
115 Sliding fairing guide rails

116 Cooling air grille
117 Main rotor blade glass-fibre skins
118 Honeycomb trailing-edge panel
119 Titanium tube blade spar
120 Rotor blade drooped leading-edge
121 Leading-edge anti-erosion sheathing
122 Fixed trailing-edge tab
123 Cockpit eyebrow window
124 Rear view mirrors
125 Overhead engine throttle and fuel cock control levers
126 Circuit breaker panel
127 Pilot's seat
128 Safety harness
129 Crash resistant seat mounting
130 Pull-out emergency exit window panel
131 Flight deck floor level
132 Cockpit door
133 Boarding step
134 AN/APS 124 search radar antenna
135 Ventral radome
136 Retractable landing/hovering lamp
137 Downward vision window
138 Yaw control rudder pedals
139 Cyclic pitch control column
140 Instrument panel
141 Centre instrument console
142 Stand-by compass
143 ATO/Co-pilot's seat
144 Outside air temperature gauge
145 Instrument panel shroud
146 Air data probes
147 Windscreen panels
148 Windscreen wipers
149 Hinged nose compartment access panel
150 Pitot tubes
151 Avionics equipment bay
152 Forward data link antenna
153 Forward AN/ALQ 142 ESM aerial housings

A typical general-aviation aircraft: Partenavia P68C

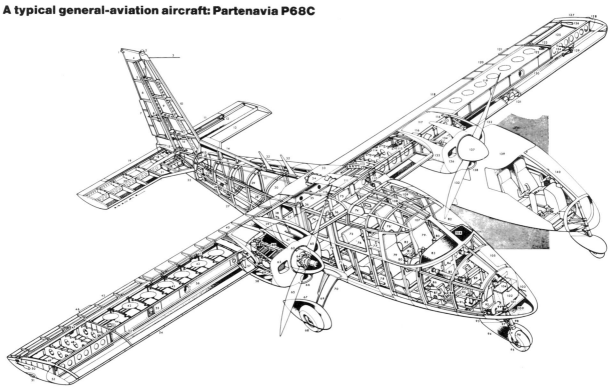

1 Tail navigation light
2 Identification light
3 Antennae
4 Rudder balance
5 Rudder upper hinge
6 Rudder structure
7 Rudder trim tab
8 Tab control linkage
9 Tailfin structure
10 Tailfin leading edge
11 Port stabilator tab
12 Tab control linkage
13 Port stabilator
14 Dorsal tailfin fillet
15 Tailfin spar/fuselage attachment points
16 Rudder control cables
17 Stabilator pivot stub
18 Stabilator tab linkage
19 Stabilator tab
20 Starboard stabilator structure
21 Leading-edge fillet
22 Fuselage frame
23 Tab control horns
24 Longeron
25 Cable pulleys
26 Tail surface control cables
27 Fuselage ventral skinning
28 Upper longeron
29 Fuselage structure
30 Fuselage frame
31 Dorsal former
32 Dorsal antennae
33 Wing centre-section/fuselage fairing
34 Heating plant (optional)
35 Cabin cross-beam
36 Fuselage frames/wing box pick-ups
37 Baggage compartment
38 Baggage loading door (starboard)
39 Starboard engine nacelle
40 Flap assembly

41 Wing box aft face
42 Cover plates
43 Starboard wing integral fuel tank (59 Imp gal/269 l capacity)
44 Filler/valve
45 Starboard aileron structure
46 Fixed tab
47 Aileron actuating hinge point
48 Wing outer structure
49 End rib
50 Aileron internal balance
51 Starboard navigation light
52 Starboard wingtip
53 Wing box forward face
54 Wing leading edge
55 Pulley attachment bracket
56 Spar sections
57 Starbord nacelle outer attachment
58 Nacelle panels
59 Exhaust pipe assembly
60 Lycoming IO-360-A1B6 four-cylinder engine
61 Nacelle fairing
62 Spinner backplate
63 Carburetter air intakes
64 Propeller hub
65 Hartzell constant-speed fully-feathering propeller
66 Engine air intake
67 Starboard mainwheel spat
68 Starboard mainwheel
69 Mainwheel leg (spring steel)
70 Leg flexible fairing
71 Leg attachment bracket
72 Fuselage main frame
73 Cabin windows
74 Three-seat rear bench
75 Wing centre-section attachment
76 Individual passenger seats (two)
77 Fuselage structure
78 Heating/ventilation duct
79 Pilots' seats
80 Control columns

81 Central console
82 Curved windscreen panels
83 Instrument panel shroud
84 Panel lower section
85 Control column assembly
86 Cable pulleys
87 Rudder pedal assembly
88 Fuselage frame
89 Control chain linkage
90 Column support cuff
91 Cable linkage
92 Forward bulkhead
93 Nosewheel spat fin
94 Nosewheel spat
95 Steerable nosewheel
96 Axle fork
97 Torque links
98 Nosewheel leg
99 Leg attachment bracket
100 Nose cone (radar optional)
101 Battery support tray
102 Battery installation
103 Pitot tube (port)
104 Windscreen de-icer (optional)
105 Control access nose panels
106 Windscreen frames
107 Overhead panel
108 Roof structure
109 Cabin entry door (port)
110 Aileron cable pulleys
111 Wing centre-section panel
112 Wing box attachments
113 Wing inboard structure
114 Ribs
115 Flap control link and pulley
116 Port engine nacelle attachments
117 Nacelle aft fairing
118 Port flap section
119 Port wing integral fuel tank (59 Imp gal/269 l capacity)
120 Port aileron
121 Fixed tab
122 Filler/valve
123 Aileron control actuating rod

124 Rod/cable transition
125 Wing outer section
126 Aileron internal balance
127 Port wingtip
128 Port navigation light
129 Aileron control linkage
130 Cable runs
131 Twin landing lights
132 Hartzell constant-speed fully-feathering propeller
133 Engine bearer support
134 Engine bearer
135 Nacelle panels
136 Engine air intake
137 Spinner
138 Carburetter air intake
139 P68C Observer variant
140 Fully-glazed nose section

GAS-TURBINE ENGINES

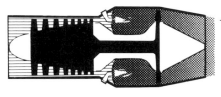

TURBOJET

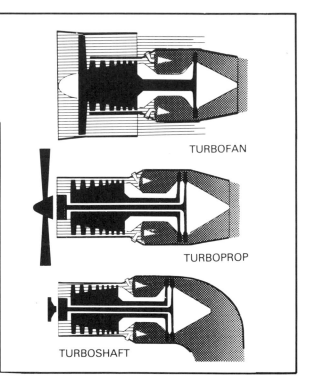

TURBOFAN

TURBOPROP

TURBOSHAFT

A basic understanding of the four major classes of gas-turbine engine is an important part of aircraft-recognition training. For instance, one of the principal differences between such broadly similar types as the C-141 Starlifter and C-5A Galaxy is the fact that the former is powered by small-diameter turbofans while the latter has high-bypass-ratio turbofans, with their distinctive outsize front fans.

Gas turbines basically consist of an air compressor at the front, combustion chambers for burning the compressed air and a turbine at the back which is driven by the hot gases. In these drawings the hot-air flow is indicated by shading. The turbojet is a reaction engine which obtains its power by thrusting backwards a large weight of air. The turbofan is also a reaction engine but it differs from the turbojet in having part of the compressed air bypassed round the hot section of the engine, finally merging with the hot-air stream at the back. The turboprop has an extra turbine which drives the propeller in front. The turboshaft engine is virtually a turboprop without a propeller, the extra turbine being coupled to a shaft to drive a helicopter rotor.

GUIDED MISSILES

A wide variety of missiles is now carried as external load on military aircraft. The missiles themselves need to be recognised in order to determine the capability of the aircraft bearing them. In addition the missiles change the outline of the aircraft. The series of side views that follows shows the weapons that can form the payload of the military aircraft in this book.
(Courtesy: *Jane's Weapons Systems*)

AIR-TO-SURFACE MISSILES

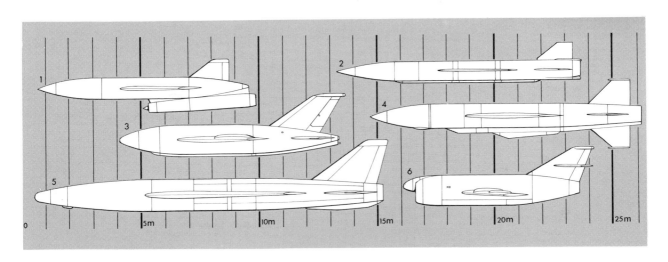

1 AS-2 Kipper   **2** AS-6 Kingfisher   **3** AS-5 Kelt   **4** AS-4 Kitchen   **5** AS-3 Kangroo   **6** AS-1 Kennel

AIR-TO-SURFACE MISSILES

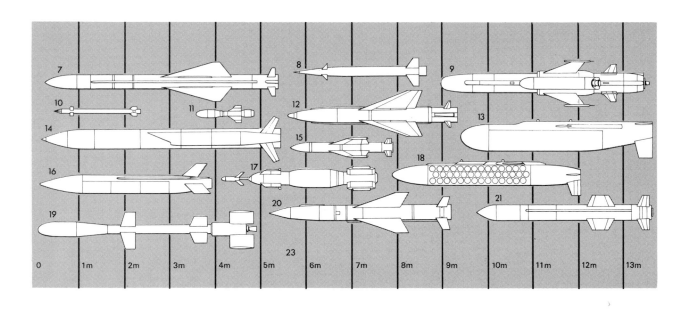

7 Exocet AM.39   **8** Martin Pescador   **9** Otomat   **10** HATCP   **11** HOT   **12** AS-30 Laser   **13** Pegase   **14** ASMP   **15** AS.15 77
16 Apache   **17** Matra LGB   **18** CWS   **19** Marte   **20** Kormoran Mk 1 & 2   **21** Gabriel Mk III

AIR-TO-SURFACE MISSILES

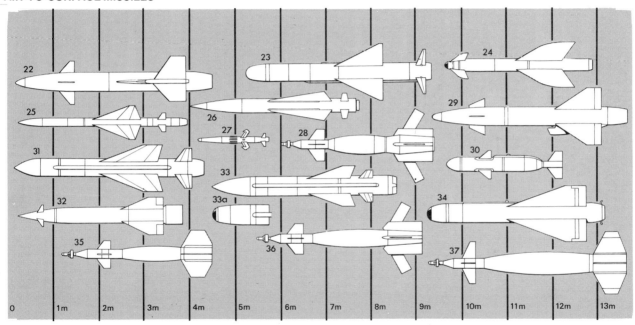

22 RB 04E **23** ASM-1 **24** Penguin Mk III **25** ALARM **26** RB 05A **27** RBS 70 **28** Paveway II (Mk 13/18) **29** RBS 15 **30** Sea Skua **31** Sea Eagle **32** AS-7 Kerry **33** Martel ARM **33**a Martel TV **34** Walleye **35** Paveway I (GBU-12) **36** Paveway II (GBU-16) **37** Paveway I (GBU-10)

AIR-TO-SURFACE MISSILES

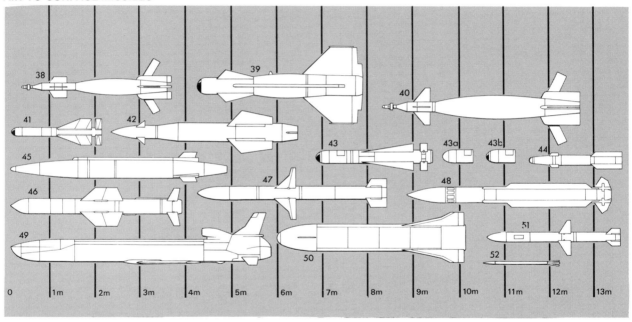

38 Paveway II (GBU-12B/B)   **39** GBU-15(V)   **40** Paveway II (GBU-10)   **41** Wasp   **42** Bullpup   **43** Maverick (AGM-65B) TV
43a Maverick laser   **43b** Maverick IR   **44** Hellfire   **45** SRAM (AGM-69A)   **46** Harpoon   **47** HARM   **48** Standard ARM
49 ALCM   **50** LAD   **51** Shrike   **52** HVM (provisional)

AIR-TO-AIR MISSILES

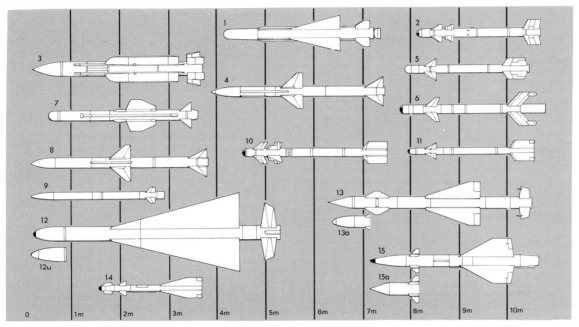

1 R 530 **2** R 550 Magic **3** Super 530 **4** Aspide **5** Shafrir **6** Python III **7** Red Top **8** Sky Flash **9** ASRAAM (provisional)
10 Kukri **11** AAM-1 **12** AA-5 Ash IR **12a** Ash Radar **13** AA-7 Apex Radar **13a** Apex IR **14** AA-8 Aphid
15 AA-3 Anab IR **15a** Anab Radar

AIR-TO-AIR MISSILES

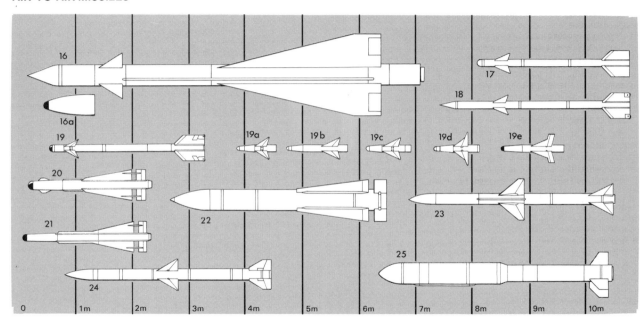

16 AA-6 Acrid Radar   **16a** Acrid IR   **17** AA-2 Atoll   **18** Advanced Atoll   **19** AIM-9B Sidewinder   **19a** AIM-9D
19b AIM-9E   **19c** AIM-9H   **19d** AIM-9L   **19e** AIM-9N/P   **20** AIM-4 Falcon   **21** AIM-4G Falcon   **22** Phoenix   **23** Sparrow III
24 AMRAAM   **25** ASAT

AIRCRAFT AND GUIDED WEAPON DESIGNATIONS

The letters and numbers used to designate aircraft can be very confusing for the student. Apart from learning shapes, he has to say exactly what they are or his visual knowledge is useless. A name is always the easiest thing to remember, but in a number of cases names are not allocated or the type will appear initially with a designation before being named later. Examples of the latter are the Panavia Tornado, which began life as the MRCA (Multi-Role Combat Aircraft), and the Lockheed L-1011, which was subsequently named TriStar.

Many nations use company design numbers and/or a name, with sub-variants simply given as mark numbers. It is necessary in many cases to know the mark numbers, as the aircraft can look very different. For instance, Britain's Nimrod AEW3 will differ significantly from the Nimrod MR2

On the civil side there are many types which are un-named and bear only design numbers, such as the Boeing 707, 727, 737 and 747, and McDonnell Douglas DC-8, DC-9, DC-10 and MD-80. Airliners also tend to acquire suffix letters or numbers to denote different variants: 747SP, 707-320C and BAe One-Eleven 500, for example.

There are four countries for which special designation systems exist: the United States, the Soviet Union, the United Kingdom and Canada.

UNITED STATES MILITARY
The US military system appears at first to be very complicated but is in fact quite logical. It is based on the use of letters and numbers.

All United States service aircraft, guided weapons etc are assigned designations which describe the machine's basic mission, its place in the sequence designed for that function, and its place in the sequence of variants of the type. The designations are broken down as follows:

Status prefix letter This is used only when required to indicate that an aerospace vehicle is not standard because of its test, modification, experimental, or prototype design. For aircraft, the symbol appears to the immediate left of the modified mission symbol or basic mission symbol. For rockets and missiles, it is to the immediate left of the launch environment symbol or mission symbol.

Modified Mission (aircraft only) This letter is used only when needed to identify modifications to the basic mission of an aircraft and appears to the immediate left of the basic mission letter. Only one modified mission symbol is used in any one designation.

Launch Environment (rockets and missiles only) This symbol identifies the launch environment or platform parameters. It appears to the immediate left of the mission symbol. Only one of these symbols is used in any one description.

Basic Mission (aircraft only) This letter identifies an aircraft's primary function or capability. It appears to the immediate left of the vehicle type letter or design number separated by a dash.

Vehicle Type (aircraft only) This letter is required only for rotary wing, vertical or short take-off/landing (VTOL/STOL) and glider aircraft and is accompanied by a basic mission or modified mission letter. It appears to the immediate left of the design number.

Mission (rockets and missiles only) This letter identifies the basic function or capability of the rocket or missile. It appears to the immediate left of the rocket- or missile-type symbol.

Vehicle Type (rockets and missiles only) This letter identifies the kind of unmanned vehicle. It appears to the immediate left of the design number separated by a dash.

Design Number This number identifies major design changes within the same mission category. Design numbers run consecutively beginning with '1' for each category. A dash separates the design number from the symbol to its immediate left.

Series This letter identifies the first production model of a particular design and later models representing major modifications that alter significantly the relationship of the vehicle to its nonexpendable system components or change its logistics support. Series symbols are consecutive beginning with 'A' and appear to the immediate right of the design number. To avoid confusion, the letters 'I' and 'O' are not used for this symbol.

Aerospace Vehicle MDS (Mission, Design, Series designators) for aircraft The following list outlines the symbols used in aircraft MDS.

Status Prefix G Permanently Grounded, J Special Test (temporary), N Special Test (permanent), X Experimental, Y Prototype, Z Planning.

Modified Mission A Attack, C Transport, D Director, E Special Electronics Installation, F Fighter, H Search and Rescue, K Tanker, L Cold Weather, M Multimission, O Observation, P Patrol, Q Drone, R Reconnaissance, S Antisubmarine, T Trainer, U Utility, W Weather.

Basic Mission A Attack, B Bomber, C Transport, E Special Electronics Installation, F Fighter, O Observation, P Patrol, R Reconnaissance, S Antisubmarine, T Trainer, U Utility, X Research.

Vehicle Type G Glider, H Helicopter, V VTOL/STOL, Z Lighter-than-air vehicle

AEROSPACE VEHICLE MDS (Mission, Design Series designators) for Guided Missiles, Rockets, and Probes The following list outlines the symbols used in guided missile, rocket, and probe MDS:

Status Prefix C Captive, D Dummy, J Special Test (temporary), M Maintenance, N Special Test (permanent), X Experimental, Y Prototype, Z Planning.

Launch Environment A Air, **B** Multiple, **C** Coffin, **F** Individual, **G** Runway, **H** Silo Stored, **L** Silo Launched, **M** Mobile, **P** Soft Pad, **R** Ship, **U** Underwater Attack.

Mission D Decoy, **E** Special Electronic Installation, **G** Surface Attack, **I** Aerial Intercept, **Q** Drone, **T** Training, **U** Underwater Attack, **W** Weather.

Type M Guided Missile/Drone, **N** Probe, **R** Rocket.

Sample aircraft mission, design, series designator

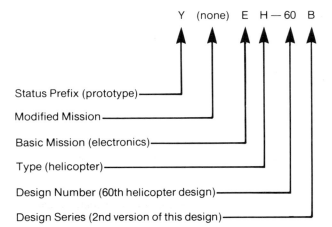

Sample missile mission, design, series designator

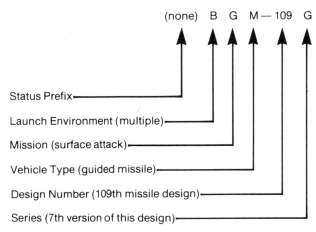

While other nations have basic type names, in the United States such descriptions are known as 'popular names' when attached to a general designation. The following is the current list of aircraft and missiles so described:

Popular name	Model Designation	Service
Academe	TC-4C	Navy
Aero Commander	U-9	Navy/Army

Popular name	Model Designation	Service	Popular name	Model Designation	Service
Albatross	HU-16E	CG	Dolphin	HH-65A	Coastguard
Apache	AH-64	Army	Dragonfly	A-37B	AF
Aquila	XMQM-105	Army	Eagle	F-15	AF
ASROC	RUR-5A	Navy	Falcon	AIM-4	AF
Atlas	GCM-16	AF	Fighting Falcon	F-16	AF
Aztec	U-11A	Navy	Firebee	BQM-34	AF/Army/Navy
Beaver	U-6	Army/Navy	Fire Bolt	AQM-81	AF
Black Hawk	UH-60A	Army	Flying Classroom	T-29	Navy
Bomarc	CQM-10B	AF	Focus I	AGM-87A	Navy
Bronco	OV-10	Navy/AF	Freedom Fighter	F-5A/B	AF
Buckeye	T-2	Navy	Galaxy	C-5A	AF
Bulldog	AGM-83A	Navy	Genie	AIR-2	AF
Bullpup	AGM-12	Navy	Greyhound	C-2	Navy
Canberra	B-57	AF	Guardian	HU-25A	Coastguard
Cardinal	MQM-61A	Army	Gulfstream II	VC-11A	Coastguard
Caribou	C-7	AF	HARM	AGM-88A	Navy/AF
Cayose	OH-6	Army	Harpoon	AGM-84A	Navy
Chaparral	MIM-72	Army	Harrier	AV-8	Navy
Chinook	CH-47	Army	Hawk	MIM-23	Army/Navy
Cobra	AH-1G	Army	Hawkeye	E-2	Navy
Cobra/TOW	AH-1Q/S	Army	Hellfire	YAGM-114A	Army
Cochise	T-42A	Army	Hercules	C-130	AF/Navy/CG
Condor	AGM-53	Navy	Honest John	MGR-1	Army
Constellation	C-121S/T	AF	Hornet	F-18	Navy
Corsair II	A-7	Navy/AF	Hound Dog	AGM-28B	AF
Crusader	F-8	Navy	Huron	C-12	AF/Army
Delta Dagger	F-102A	AF	Intruder	A-6	Navy
Delta Dart	F-106	AF	Iroquois	UH-1	Army

Popular name	Model Designation	Service	Popular name	Model Designation	Service
Jet Star	C-140	AF	Regulus	RGM-15A	Navy
Jolly Green Giant	HH-3E	AF	Sabre	QF-86H	Navy
Kiowa	OH-58	Army/Navy	Sabreliner	T-39	AF/Navy
Lance	XMGM-52	Army	Samaritan	C-131	AF
Liftmaster	C-118	AF/Navy	Sea Cobra	AH-1J	Navy
Maverick	AGM-65	AF/Navy	Sea Guard	HH-52A	CG
Mentor	T-34	AF/Navy	Sea Hawk	UH-60	Navy
Mescalero	T-41	Army/AF	Sea King	H-3	Navy/CG
Minuteman	LGM-30	AF	Sea Knight	H-46	Navy
Mohawk	OV-1	Army	Sea Ranger	TH-57A	Navy
Neptune	P-2	Navy	Sea Sparrow	RIM-7	Navy
Night Hawk	UH-60D	AF	Sea Sprite	H-2	Navy
Nightingale	C-9A/C	AF	Sea Stallion	CH-53A	Navy
Nike Hercules	MIM-14	Army	Seminole	U-8	Army
Orion	P-3	Navy	Sentry	E-3A	AF
Osage	T-55A	Army	Sergeant	MGM-29A	Army
Otter	U-1	Army	Shillelagh	MGM-51	Army
Patriot	MIM-104	Army	Shooting Star	T-33A	AF/Navy
Peacekeeper	LGM-118A	AF	Shrike	AGM-45	Navy/AF
Pelican	HH-3F	CG	Sidewinder	AIM-9	Navy/AF
Pershing	MGM-31A	Army	Skyhawk	A-4	Navy
Phantom II	F-4	Navy/AF	Skyraider	A-1	Navy
Phoenix	AIM-54A	Navy	Skytrain	C-117D	Navy
Polaris	UGM-27	Navy	Skywarrior	A-3	Navy
Provider	C-123	AF	Sparrow	AIM-7	Navy/AF
Prowler	EA-6B	Navy	SRAM	AGM-69	AF
Raven	EF-111	AF	Standard	RIM-66/67	Navy
Redeye	FIM-43	Army	Standard ARM	AGM-78	Navy/AF

Popular name	Model Designation	Service
Starfighter	F-104	AF
Starlifter	C-141	AF
Stinger	FIM-92	Army
Stratofortress	B-52	AF
Stratofreighter	KC-97L	AF
Stratojet	EB-47E	Navy
Stratolifter	C-135	AF
Stratoliner	C-137	AF
Stratotanker	KC-135	AF
Streaker	MQM-107	Army/AF
SUBROC	UUM-44A	Navy
Super Constellation	C-121C/G	AF
Super Jolly	C/HH-53B/C	AF
Super Sabre	F-100	AF
Super Stallion	CH-53E	AF
Talon	T-38	AF
Talos	RIM-8	Navy
Tarhe	CH-54	Army
Tartar	RIM-24	Navy
Terrier	RIM-2	Navy
Thunderbolt II	A-10	AF
Thunderchief	F-105	AF
Tiger II	F-5E/F	AF
Tigershark	F-20A	Northrop Foreign Sales
Titan	LGM-25C	AF
Tomahawk	BGM-109	Navy/AF
Tomcat	F-14	Navy

Popular name	Model Designation	Service
TOW	BGM-71	Army
Tracer	E-1B	Navy
Tracker	S-2	Navy
Trader	C-1A	Navy
Trident	UGM-96A	Navy
Trojan	T-28	AF/Navy
Typhon	RIM-55A	Navy
Tweet	T-37B	AF
Twin Otter	UV-18	Army/AF
U.S. Roland	XMIM-115	Army
Ute	U-21	Army
Vigilante	RA-5C	Navy
Viking	S-3A	Navy
Viper	XFGR-17A	Army
Voodoo	F-101	AF
Warning Star	EC-121K	Navy
Weapon Alpha	RUR-4A	Navy
ZAP	XAGR-14A	Navy

SOVIET UNION MILITARY AND CIVIL

In the Soviet Union there are a number of design bureaux from which all Soviet aircraft emanate. Security is such in the Soviet Union that many new designations, particularly military, are suspect and only a certain proportion can be confirmed. For this reason the North Atlantic Treaty Organisation countries have evolved a code-name system for Soviet aircraft and this has been widely adopted elsewhere.

The known current Soviet design bureaux are:

An	Antonov
Be	Beriev
Il	Ilyushin
Ka	Kamov
Mi	Mil
MiG	Mikoyan (originally with Gurevich)
Mya	Myasishchev
Su	Sukhoi
Tu	Tupolev
Yak	Yakovlev

Code names are allotted by NATO on the basis of function:

B	Bomber
C	Cargo/transport
F	Fighter/ground attack
H	Helicopter
M	Trainer, flying boat and maritime reconnaissance.

The code names, together with Soviet designations where known for current types, are as follows, including two Chinese aircraft which are developments of Soviet types:

Code name	Designation	Description
Backfire	Tu-26	Variable-geometry bomber
Badger	Tu-16	Twinjet bomber
Beagle	Il-28	Twinjet bomber
Bear	Tu-95	Turboprop bomber
Bison	M-4	Four-jet bomber
Blackjack	Tu	V-g bomber; four-jet replacement for Bear

Code name	Designation	Description
Blinder	Tu-22	Rear-jet bomber
Brewer	Yak-28	Strike/attack
Cab	Li-2	Soviet-built DC-3
Camber	Il-86	Wide-bodied jet transport
Camel	Tu-104	Twinjet transport
Careless	Tu-154	Rear trijet transport
Camp	An-8	Twin-turboprop transport
Candid	Il-76	Four-jet transport
Cash	An-28	Turboprop version of Clod
Cat	An-10	Four-turboprop transport
Charger	Tu-144	Supersonic airliner
Clank	An-30	Survey version of Coke
Classic	Il-62	Rear four-jet airliner
Cleat	Tu-114	Turboprop transport version of Bear
Cline	An-32	Overwing turboprop version of Curl
Clobber	Yak-42	Enlarged version of Codling
Clod	An-14	Light piston twin
Coach	Il-12	Piston twin
Coaler	An-72	Stol replacement for Curl
Cock	An-22	Four-turboprop heavy transport
Codling	Yak-40	Trijet light transport
Coke	An-24	Twin-turboprop transport
Colt	An-2	Biplane
Condor	An-124	Very large four-engined transport similar to US Galaxy
Cookpot	Tu-124	Smaller Camel

Code name	Designation	Description
Coot	Il-18	Four-turboprop airliner
Crate	Il-14	Developed Coach
Creek	Yak-12	Light aircraft
Crusty	Tu-134	Rear twinjet version of Cookpot
Cub	An-12	Four-turboprop transport
Cuff	Be-30	Light Stol transport
Curl	An-26	Rear-door variant of Coke
Fagot	MiG-15	First swept-wing Soviet fighter in service
Fantan-A	Q-5	Chinese development of Farmer
Farmer	MiG-19	Supersonic fighter
Fencer	Su-24	V-g bomber, same class as US F-111
Fiddler	Tu-28P	Swept-wing all-weather fighter
Finback	J-8/F-8	Chinese enlarged development of Fishbed
Firebar	Yak-28P	All-weather version of Brewer
Fishbed	MiG-21	Multi-variant delta fighter
Fishpot-B/C	Su-9/11	All-weather delta fighter; Su-11 lengthened
Fitter-A	Su-7B	Swept-wing ground attack fighter
Fitter-C/D	Su-17/20/22	V-g fighter
Flagon	Su-15	Supersonic delta fighter
Flanker	Su-27	Twin jet single-seater comparable to US F-15
Flipper	—	Experimental fighter
Flogger	MiG-23/27	V-g fighter/bomber; various versions
Forger	Yak-38	Supersonic Vtol carrier fighter

Code name	Designation	Description
Foxbat	MiG-25	Supersonic interceptor
Foxhound	—	Development of Foxbat
Freehand	—	Experimental Vtol aircraft
Fresco	MiG-17	Fighter; development of Fagot
Frogfoot	Su-25	Twin jet ground attack aircraft
Fulcrum	MiG-29	Twin jet similar to US F-14
Halo	Mi-26	Heavy helicopter
Hare	Mi-1	Light helicopter
Harke	Mi-10	Crane variant of Hook
Havoc Mi-28		New combat helicopter believed to resemble US Cheyenne
Haze	Mi-14	Naval variant of Hip
Hen	Ka-15	Light helicopter
Helix	Ka-32(?)	Development of Hormone
Hind	Mi-24	Attack helicopter
Hip	Mi-8	Military/civil helicopter
Hog	Ka-18	Development of Hen
Hokum	Ka-	New Kamov co-axial rotor combat helicopter
Hoodlum	Ka-26	General-purpose helicopter
Hook	Mi-6	Heavy military/civil helicopter
Hoplite	Mi-2	Small turbine helicopter
Hormone	Ka-25	Naval helicopter
Hound	Mi-4	Military/civil helicopter
Madge	Be-6	Flying boat
Maestro	Yak-28U	Trainer version of Firebar/Brewer
Maiden	Su-11U	Two-seater variant of Fishpot

Code name	Designation	Description
Mail	Be-12	Turboprop maritime amphibian
Mainstay	Il-	AWACS version of Candid
Magnum	Yak-30	Aerobatic jet aircraft
Mandrake	—	High-altitude reconnaissance aircraft
Mangrove	Yak-27	Reconnaissance
Mantis	Yak-32	Jet trainer
Mascot	Il-28U	Trainer variant of Beagle
Max	Yak-18	Club trainer and sporting aircraft
May	Il-38	Maritime reconnaissance version of Coot
Midget	MiG-15UTI	Trainer variant of Fagot
Mongol	MiG-21U	MiG-21 trainer
Moose	Yak-18	Trainer
Moss	Tu-126	Airborne early warning aircraft
Moujik	Su-7U	Trainer variant of Fitter-A
Mule	Po-2	Utility biplane

CANADA MILITARY

The Canadian system of military designations is similar to that of the United States. The system employs four terms, as follows:

a. **Type Designation.** This term means a two-letter prefix followed by the three-digit number assigned to each aircraft type. These three digits are the first three digits of the five or six digits that comprise the aircraft's registration or serial number. The three type designation digits commence at 100 and each aircraft type number is prefixed by 'C' for Canadian followed by the basic mission symbol (F, T, C, P or H – see subparagraph b).

b. **Basic Mission Symbol.** This term means the letter used to indicate the basic, original function of the aircraft coded as follows: F-Fighter; T-Trainer; C-Cargo/Transport; P-Patrol/Reconnaissance/Anti-Submarine Warfare; H-Helicopter.

c. **Suffix Letter.** This term means a model change or modification to the basic aircraft where such change significantly alters the aircraft's function or capability. Suffix letters, when assigned, are allotted in consecutive order commencing with the letter A. To avoid confusion, the letters I and O are not used and the letter D is reserved for dual-seat versions of single-seat aircraft. The suffix letter, when applicable, comes directly after the type designation, without space or punctuation.

d. **Popular Name.** This term means a descriptive word name (eg, Sea King, Buffalo).

Canadian designation	Canadian popular name
CF101	Voodoo
CF104	Starfighter
CF104D	Starfighter Dual
CC109	Cosmopolitan
CH113	Labrador
CH113A	Voyageur
CT114	Tutor
CC115	Buffalo
CF116	CF5
CF116D	CF5 Dual
CC117	Falcon

Canadian designation	Canadian popular name
CH118	Iroquois
CP121	Tracker
CH124A	Sea King
CC129	Dakota
CC130E	Hercules
CC130H	Hercules
CC130N	Hercules Nav Trainer
CC132	Dash-7
CT133	T-33
CT134A	Musketeer II
CH-135	Twin Huey
CH136	Kiowa
CC137	Boeing 707
CC138	Twin Otter
CH139	Jet Ranger
CP140	Aurora
CC142	Dash 8
CC142N	Dash 8 Nav trainer
CC144	Challenger
CH147	Chinook
CF188	CF18
CF188D	CF18D

UNITED KINGDOM MILITARY

The British service system of aircraft designations is the reverse of that employed in the United States in that the type name is the primary reference and role letters and mark number follow.

Role letters used by the three services are:

AEW	Airborne Early Warning
AH	Army Helicopter
AL	Army Liaison
AS	Anti-submarine
B	Bomber
B(I)	Bomber/Interdictor
B(K)	Bomber (Tanker)
B(PR)	Bomber (Photo-reconnaissance)
C	Transport
CC	Transport and Communications
D	Drone or unmanned aircraft
E	Electronic
F	Fighter
FGA	Fighter Ground Attack
FG	Fighter Ground Attack
FGR	Fighter Ground Attack Reconnaissance
FR	Fighter Reconnaissance
FRS	Fighter Reconnaissance Strike
GR	Ground Attack Reconnaissance
HAR	Helicopter, Air Rescue
HAS	Helicopter, Anti-submarine
HC	Helicopter, Cargo
HT	Helicopter, Training

HU	Helicopter, Utility
K	Tanker
MR	Maritime Reconnaissance
R	Reconnaissance
O	Observation
PR	Photographic Reconnaissance
R	Reconnaissance
S	Strike
T	Trainer
TT	Target Towing
W	Weather

Typical examples are Scout AH1 (Army Helicopter Mk 1), Harrier GR3 (Ground Attack Reconnaissance Mk 3) and Nimrod AEW3 (Airborne Early Warning Mk 3).

Aircraft and helicopter designations current in use are as follows:

Designation	Operator	Notes
Alouette		
AH2	Army	French Alouette II
Andover		
C1	RAF	Freighter
CC2	RAF	Passenger
E3	MoD (PE)	Flight checking
BAe 125		
CC1	RAF/RN	BAe 125-400
CC2	RAF	BAe 125-600
Basset		
CC1	MoD (PE)	Only three in use
Beaver		
AL1	Army	DHC-2 built in Canada

Designation	Operator	Notes
Buccaneer		
S2A	RAF	No Martel missiles
S2B	RAF	Martel-carrier
S2C	RAF	} Ex-RN aircraft
S2D	RAF	
S50	SAAF	S2 export to South Africa
Bulldog		
T1	RAF	Primary trainer
Canberra		
PR3	MoD	One only
T4	RAF & RN	B2 trainer
B6	RAF	One only
PR7	RAF	Improved PR3
B(I)8	MoD	One only
PR9	RAF	In service
D10	MoD	Unmanned target
T11	Sweden	AI trainer
D14	MoD	Version of D10
B15	RAF	B6 sold abroad
E15	RAF	Flight checking
B16	MoD	Modified B15
T17	RAF	Special B2
TT18	RAF/RN	Target-tug conversion
T19	RAF	T11 conversion
B20	RAAF	Australian-built B2
T21	RAAF	B20 trainer version
T22	RN	With Buccaneer nose radar
B52	Ethiopia	As B2
T54	India	As T4
B(I)56	Peru	As B6
PR57	India	As PR7
B(I)58	India	As B(I)8

Designation	Operator	Notes
B62	Argentina	As B2
T64	Argentina	As T4
B66	India	As B15/B16
PR67	India	PR7 conversion
T67	India	PR67 conversion
B(I)68	India	B(I)8 conversion
B72	Peru	B2 conversion
T74	Peru	T4 conversion
B(I)78	Peru	B(I)8 conversion
B82	Venezuela	B2 conversion
B(I)82	Venezuela	B2 conversion
PR83	Venezuela	PR3 conversion
T84	Venezuela	T4 conversion
B(I)88	Venezuela	B(I)8 conversion
Castor	Army	Surveillance radar
Islander		
Chinook		
HC1	RAF	US CH-47
Chipmunk		
Mks 1–9	Canada	
T10	RAF/Army	British-built trainer
Mks 21–23	Civil	
Commando	Egypt	Transport adapted from
Mk 1		Sea King
Mk 2B	Egypt/	Transport/EW
	Saudi Arabia	
Mk2A/2C	Qatar	Transport/VIP
		Transport
Devon		
C2	RAF	Service Dove
Dominie		
T1	RAF	BAe 125 military trainer

Designation	Operator	Notes
Gazelle		
AH1	Army & RM	Gazelle B
HT2	RN	Gazelle C
HT3	RAF	Gazelle D
Gnat		
T1	MoD (PE)	Trainer
Harrier		
GR3	RAF	Pegasus 103 engine
T2/2A	RAF	Two-seater
T4/4A	RAF	Two-seater
T4N	RN	Two-seter
GR5	RAF	AV-8B Harrier II
Mk 50	US Marines	AV-8A
Mk 52	British	T4, company-owned
	Aerospace	
Mk 54	US Marines	T4
Mk 55	Spanish	Known as Matador/AV-8S
	Navy	
T60	Indian Navy	Two-seater
Harvard		
T2B	MoD	Three only
Hawk		
T1	RAF	Trainer
T2	RAF	Trainer
Mk 51	Finland	Trainer
Mk 52	Kenya	Trainer/ground attack
Mk 53	Indonesia	Trainer/ground attack
Mk 60	Zimbabwe	Trainer/ground attack
Mk 61	Dubai	Trainer/ground attack
Mk 63	Abu Dhabi	Trainer/ground attack
Mk 64	Kuwait	Trainer/ground attack

Designation	Operator	Notes
Hercules		
C1	RAF	C-130K transport
W2	RAF	Meteorological conversion
C3	RAF	Stretched fuselage
Heron		
C4	RN	Light transport
Hunter		
F6	RAF	Few
F6A	RAF	F6 to FGA9 standard
T7	RAF	Two-seat trainer
T7A	MoD (PE)	T7 modified
T8	RN	T7 for Navy
T8M	RN	Sea Harrier radar trainer
FGA9	RAF	F6 with increased weapon load
GA11	RN	Naval
Mk 12	MoD (PE)	Fly-by-wire experimental
F50	RSAF	Sweden, F4
F51	RDAF	Export to Denmark
F52	Peru	Export
T53	RDAF	T7, Denmark
FGA56	India	F6 for ground attack
FGA57	Kuwait	FGA9
F58	Switzerland	F6
FGA59	Iraq	FGA9
T62	Peru	One only, F4
T66	India	T7 with modified armament
T66B	Jordan	
T66C	Lebanon	
T67	Kuwait	Two-seat version of FGA57
T69	Iraq	Two-seat version of FGA59
T70	Lebanon	T7
FGA71	Chile	FGA9

Designation	Operator	Notes
T72	Chile	T7
FGA73	Jordan	FGA9
FGA74	Singapore	FGA9
FR74A	Singapore	PR version of FGA9
T75	Singapore	T7
FGA76	Abu Dhabi	FGA9
FR76A	Abu Dhabi	PR version of FGA9
T77	Abu Dhabi	T7
FGA78	Qatar	FGA9
T79	Qatar	T7
Jaguar		
GR1	RAF	Strike
T2	RAF	Two-seat trainer
Jet Provost		
T3	RAF	Trainer
T3A	RAF	Modified avionics
T5	RAF	Pressurised
T5A	RAF	Modified avionics
T51–55	Various	Export versions
Jetstream		
T1	RAF	Twin trainer
T2	RAF/RN	Modified
T3	RN	Radar under fuselage
Lightning		
F3	RAF	Interceptor
T5	RAF	Two-seat trainer
F6	RAF	Final production version
F52	} Saudia Arabia	Interim issue of F2s, F3 export and T5 export
F53		
F55		

Designation	Operator	Notes
Lynx		
AH1	Army & RM	WG13
Mk 2	French Navy	
HAS2	RN	ASW equipment
HAS3	RN	Update
Mk 4	French Navy	
AH5	Army	
Mk 21	Brazilian Navy	
Mk 23	Argentine Navy	
Mk 25	Royal Netherlands Navy	
Mk 27	Royal Netherlands Navy	
Mk 28	State of Qatar	
Mk 80	Denmark	
Mk 81	Netherlands	
Mk 85	United Arab Emirates	
Mk 86	Norway	
Mk 88	West Germany	
Mk 89	Nigerian Navy	
Meteor		
T7	RAF/MoD	Few
NF11	MoD (PE)	One only
D16	MoD (PE)	Three only
Nimrod		
R1	RAF	Three for special EW work
MR2	RAF	Maritime reconnaissance
AEW3	RAF	Airborne early warning

Designation	Operator	Notes
Pembroke		
C1	RAF	Transport
C(PR)1	RAF	C1 photographic
C51–55	Various nations	Export C1
Phantom		
FG1	RAF	McDonnell Douglas F-4K
FGR2	RAF	McDonnell Douglas F-4M
Puma		
HC1	RAF	As French SA.330
Scout		
AH1	Army	As Wasp
Sea Devon		
C20	RN	Naval Devon
Sea Harrier		
FRS1	RN	Naval Harrier, nose radar
FRS51	Indian Navy	Nose radar
Sea Heron		
C2	RN	Transport
Sea King		
HAS1	RN	Similar to Sikorsky SH-3D
HAS2	RN	Improved HAS1
HAR3	RAF	Rescue
HAS5	RN	Updated
HC4	RN	Utility version of Commando Mk2
Mk 41	West Germany	
Mk 42/ 42A/42B	India	
Mk 43	Norway	
Mk 45	Pakistan Navy	

Designation	Operator	Notes
Mk 48	Belgium	
Mk 50	Australia	
Sea Prince		
C1	RN	Forerunner of Pembroke
T1	RN	Flying classroom
C2	RN	C1 with modified tailplane
Sea Vixen		
FAW2	MoD (PE)	Few
D3	MoD (PE)	Unmanned target version
Shackleton		
AEW2	RAF	Early-warning conversion of MR2
MR2	RAF	Two only
MR3	SAAF	Maritime reconnaissance
Sioux		
AH1	Army & RM	Bell 47G-3B-1 helicopter
Strikemaster		
Mk 80	Saudi Arabia	
Mk 81	South Yemen	
Mk 82	Muscat & Oman	
Mk 83	Kuwait	Similar to armed Jet Provost 5
Mk 84	Singapore	
Mk 87	Kenya	
Mk 88	New Zealand	
Mk 89	Ecuador	
Tornado		
GR1	RAF	Interdiction/strike version
F2	RAF	Air-defence variant
Tristar		
500	RAF	Unmodified

Designation	Operator	Notes
K1	RAF	Tanker/passenger transport
KC1	RAF	K1 with freight door
Vampire		
T33	RAAF	Trainer Vampire, Australia
T34	RAN	Navalised T11, Australia
T35	RAAF	T33 with increased range, Australia
T55	Several	Export trainer
VC10		
C1	RAF	Long-range transport
K2	RAF	Converted Standard VC10
K3	RAF	Converted Super VC10
Victor		
K2	RAF	Tanker
Wasp		
HAS1	RN	Naval Scout AH1
Wessex		
HAS1	RN	UK-built S-58
HC2	RAF	Single exhaust stub
HAS3	RN	Re-engined HAS1, has dorsal hump
HCC4	RAF	Queen's Flight
HU5	RN & RM	Commando-carrier version
Mk 31	RAN	HAS1 for Australia
Mk 52	Iraq	
Mk 53	Ghana	
Mk 54	Brunei	
Mk 60	Civil	Passenger
Whirlwind		
HAR10	RAF	Whirlwind Series 3, with Gnome engines

AIRCRAFT REGISTRATIONS

Registration markings are a useful aid to recognition if they can be seen. This is the list of national civil prefixes:

AN	Nicaragua	HA	Hungary	PK	Indonesia
AP	Pakistan	HB	Liechtenstein	PK	West Irian
A2	Botswana	HB	Switzerland	PP, PT	Brazil
A6	United Arab Emirates	HC	Ecuador	PZ	Surinam
A7	Qatar	HH	Haiti	P2	New Guinea
A9C	Bahrain	HK	Colombia	RP	Philippines
A40	Oman	HL	Korea, Republic of	RDPL	Laos, People's
B	China	HP	Panama		Democratic Republic of
CC	Chile	HR	Honduras	SE	Sweden
CCCP	Union of Soviet Socialist	HS	Thailand	SP	Poland
	Republics	HZ	Saudi Arabia	ST	Sudan
CF, C-F, C-G	Canada	H4	Solomon Islands	SU	Egypt
CN	Morocco	I	Italy	SX	Greece
CP	Bolivia	JA	Japan	S2	Bangladesh
CR	Cape Verde	JY	Jordan	S7	Seychelles, Republic
CS	Portugal	J2	Djibouti, Republic of	TC	Turkey
CU	Cuba	J6	St Lucia	TF	Iceland
CX	Uruguay	J7	Dominican Republic	TG	Guatemala
C2	Nauru	LN	Norway	TI	Costa Rica
C5	Gambia	LO, LV	Argentina	TJ	Cameroons
C6	Bahamas	LX	Luxembourg	TL	Centrafrica
C9	Mozambique	LZ	Bulgaria	TN	Congo
D	Germany (Fed. Rep.)	N	United States	TR	Gabon
DDR	Germany (Dem. Rep.)	OB	Peru	TS	Tunisia
DO	Fiji	OD	Lebanon	TT	Chad
D2	Angola	OE	Austria	TU	Ivory Coast
D6	Comores	OH	Finland	TY	Benin
EC	Spain	OK	Czechoslovakia	TZ	Mali
EI-EJ	Ireland	OO	Belgium	VH	Australia
EL	Liberia	OY	Denmark	VP-F	Falkland Islands
EP	Iran	P	Korea, Democratic		(Malvinas)
ET	Ethiopia		People's Republic of	VP-H	Belize
F	France	PH	Netherlands	VP-L	Antigua
G	United Kingdom	PJ	Netherlands Antilles	VP-V	St. Vincent

VP-W, VP-Y	Zimbabwe	5H	Tanzania, United Republic of
VQ-G	Grenada		
VR-B	Bermuda	5N	Nigeria
VR-C	Cayman Islands	5R	Madagascar
VR-H	Hong Kong	5T	Mauritania
VR-U	Brunei	5U	Niger
VT	India	5V	Togo
XA, XB, XC	Mexico	5W	Western Samoa
XT	Upper Volta	5X	Uganda
XU	Kampuchea	5Y	Kenya
XV	Vietnam, Republic of	6O	Somalia
XY, XZ	Burma	6V-6W	Senegal
YA	Afghanistan	6Y	Jamaica
YI	Iraq	7O	Yemen, People's Democratic Republic
YJ	Vanuatu		
YK	Syria	7P	Lesotho
YR	Romania	7QY	Malawi
YS	El Salvador	7T	Algeria
YU	Yugoslavia	8P	Barbados
YV	Venezuela	8Q	Maldives
ZA	Albania	8R	Guyana
ZK-ZL, ZM	New Zealand	9G	Ghana
ZP	Paraguay	9H	Malta
ZS-ZT, ZU	South Africa	9J	Zambia
3A	Monaco	9K	Kuwait
3B	Mauritius	9L	Sierra Leone
3C	Guinea Equatorial	9M	Malaysia
3D	Swaziland	9N	Nepal
3X	Guinea	9Q	Zaire, Republic of
4R	Sri Lanka	9U	Burundi
4W	Yemen Arab Republic	9V	Singapore
4X	Israel	9XR	Ruanda
5A	Libya	9Y	Trinidad and Tobago
5B	Cyprus		

BAe Hawk

F-15 Eagle

Alpha Jet

Power: 1 × Orpheus or 1 × J3 turbojet *Span:* 34ft 5in (10.5m) *Length:* 39ft 9in (12.12m)

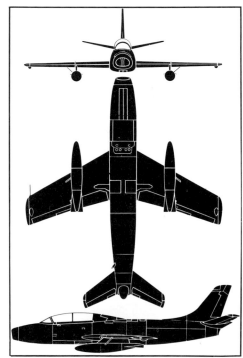

The first aircraft to be designed and built in Japan after the Second World War, the T1 Hatsutaka two-seat military trainer entered service with the Japan Air Self-Defence Force at the end of the 1950s. Bearing a superficial resemblance to the American Sabre, the T1 was initially powered by a British Orpheus engine (T1A), while later versions had the Japanese-built J3 turbojet (T1B and T1C). One machine gun is carried in the nose, and air-to-air missiles, rockets or bombs under the wings. External fuel totals 200 Imp gal (910lit) in two underwing tanks. Maximum speed of the T1A at 20,000ft (6,100m) is 575 mph (925km/hr). Some 40 T1As and 22 T1Bs were built for the Japan Air Self-Defence Force. *Country of origin:* Japan. *Picture:* T1A.

North American F-86 Sabre   *Confusion:* Fuji T1, Super Sabre, Fresco

Power: 1 × J47 turbojet   *Span:* 39ft 1in (11.91m)   *Length:* (F-86F): 37ft 6in (11.43m)

The best interceptor of its day, the F-86 outfought the MiG-15s used by the Communists in the Korean War. The type has seen service with 25 nations and 9,502 were built. Main versions are the F-86A, F-86D, F-86E, F-86F, F-86K and TF-86F. Of these, three differ in general outline, the F-86D/K having a large radome in the nose above the intake and the TF-86F having a longer fuselage with two seats in tandem. The US Navy adapted the Sabre for carrier use as the FJ-4. Sabres remain in service with several air forces, carrying a variety of air-to-air and ground-attack weapons. *Country of origin:* USA. *Silhouette: and picture:* F-86F.

Power: 1 × J57 reheated turbojet   *Span:* 38ft 9in (11.81m)   *Length:* 54ft 3in (16.54m)

First fighter with genuine supersonic level speed to enter service, the F-100 Super Sabre is still used by Turkey and Taiwan. Versions include the F-100A, C, D and F. A reconnaissance variant is designated RF-100, and the TF-100 is a two-seat trainer. An outstanding design, the Super Sabre can operate at high and low altitudes. Armament of the F-100F comprises four 20mm cannon and 6,000lb (2,720kg) of external weapons on eight wing pylons. *Country of origin:* USA. *Main silhouette:* F-100D; *lower side view:* F-100F. *Picture:* F-100F.

Fiat G.91 *Confusion:* Hunter, Etendard, G.91Y

Power: 1 × Orpheus turbojet   *Span:* 28ft 1in (8.56m)   *Length:* 33ft 9in (10.3m)

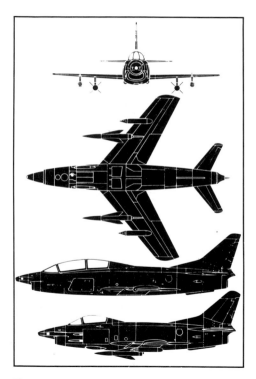

Originally a Fiat design, the G.91 won a NATO light fighter-bomber design contest in the 1950s and was adopted by the Italian and Western German air forces. Internal armament is either four machine guns or two 30mm cannon. Maximum speed is 675 mph (1,086km/hr). The two-seat advanced trainer version is the G.91T (*upper side-view silhouette*). The G.91 is also used by Portugal and Angola. *Country of origin:* Italy. *Picture:* G.91R.

Power: 2 × J85 reheated turbojets   *Span:* 29ft 6½in (9.01m)   *Length:* 38ft 3½in (11.67m)

A fighter-bomber and reconnaissance aircraft, the G.91Y was a direct development of the G.91, with twin J85 turbojets replacing the single Orpheus. After a first flight in 1966, a total of 55 G.91Ys were built for the Italian Air Force. Armament comprises two fuselage-mounted 30mm cannon and four underwing pylons for rockets, bombs or guided missiles. Maximum speed at sea level is 690 mph (1,110km/hr). Cameras are mounted in the nose. *Country of origin:* Italy.

Mikoyan-Gurevich MiG-15UTI Midget

Confusion: Sabre, Fresco, Farmer

Power: 1 × RD-45 turbojet   *Span:* 33ft (10.08m)   *Length:* 32ft 11in (10.04m)

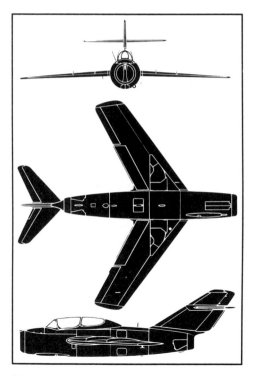

The Soviet MiG-15 swept-wing fighter, NATO code-named Fagot, caused a world sensation when it first appeared over the Korean War battlefields in 1950. Very large numbers of Fagots were built for use by many air forces. The MiG-15UTI two-seat advanced trainer, code-named Midget, was supplied throughout the Warsaw Pact and to 17 other countries. Like the Fagot, the Midget is powered by a pirated development of the Rolls-Royce Nene. The trainer carries a cannon or a machine gun in the fuselage. *Country of origin:* USSR. *Picture and main silhouette:* MiG-15UTI Midget.

Power: 1 × VK-1F reheated turbojet   *Span:* 31ft 7in (9.63m)   *Length:* 36ft 5in (11.09m)

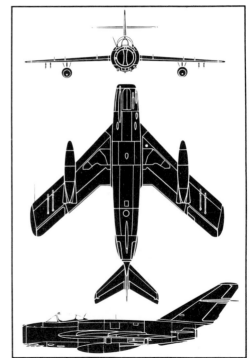

Though outwardly the MiG-17 Fresco bears a close similarity to the MiG-15 Fagot, the wing and tailplane were in fact redesigned and the rear fuselage was lengthened. Later versions (Fresco-C and D, E and F) incorporated an afterburner. Frescos are widely used in the fighter-bomber role by air forces round the world. Armament consists of underwing bombs and rocket pods plus three 23mm fuselage cannon on some variants and Alkali radar-homing missiles on others. Fresco-D, E and F carry centrebody nose radars in addition to radar gunsights in the upper engine-intake lip. *Country of origin:* USSR. *Picture and silhouette:* Fresco-F.

Mikoyan MiG-19 Farmer   *Confusion:* Fresco, Super Sabre

Power: 2 × Mikulin or 2 × Tumansky reheated turbojets   *Span:* 29ft 6in (9m)   *Length:* 42ft 11in (13.09m)

The Soviet Union's first production supersonic fighter, the MiG-19 Farmer has been widely used and remains in service in China, Cuba, Egypt, Albania, Vietnam and Pakistan. Standard variants are Farmer-B (MiG-19PF and MiG-19PM with air-to-air missiles) and Farmer-C (MiG-19SF) with Tumansky engines. Rocket projectiles and bombs can be fitted on underwing pylons for ground attack. Farmer has been built in China as the J-6 and some 2,000 are believed to be in service there. Normal gun armament is three 30mm cannon. *Country of origin:* USSR. *Silhouette:* Farmer-C. *Picture:* Farmer-B.

Power: 1 × Lyulka reheated turbojet   *Span:* 29ft 3in (8.9m)   *Length:* 57ft (17.37m)

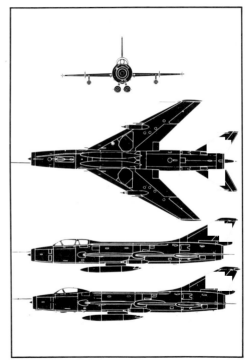

First flown in the mid-1950s, the Fitter-A fighter/ground attack aircraft is in service throughout the Warsaw Pact countries and in India and Egypt. Capable of Mach 1.6, Fitter carries two 30mm cannon, rockets and bombs. External loads are carried under both fuselage and wings. Some Fitters are equipped with rocket-assisted take-off gear to improve short-field performance. The two-seat trainer version, with pilot and pupil in tandem under an extended cockpit, is the Su-7U, code-named Moujik (upper side view). Performance figures include a maximum level speed at 36,000ft (11,000m) of 1,055 mph (1,700km/hr); service ceiling of 49,700ft (15,150m); and combat radius of 200–300 miles (320–480km). *Country of origin:* USSR.

BAe Lightning

Confusion: Fitter

Power: 2 × Avon reheated turbojets   *Span:* 34ft 10in (10.61m)   *Length:* 55ft 3in (16.84m)

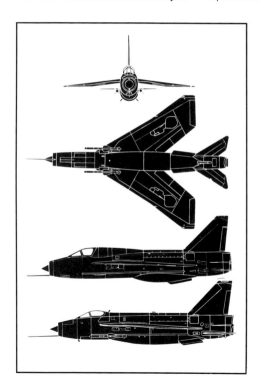

The Lightning was the RAF's first Mach 2 interceptor, entering service in its original (F1) form in 1960. In the mid-1960s the more powerful F3 entered service. A broader, square-tipped vertical tail distinguishes the F3 from earlier models. This was closely followed by the F6, the mainstay of the RAF interceptor force until the Phantom entered service. Two squadrons of Lightnings remain with the RAF until 1986/88 when they will be replaced by Tornado F.2s. The Lightning remains in service in Saudi Arabia.*Country of origin:* UK. *Main silhouette:* F6; *upper side view:* T5. *Picture:* Lightning F6.

Power: 2 × WP-6 reheated turbojets   *Span:* 31ft 10in (9.7m)   *Length overall:* 54ft 10in (16.72m)

In large scale service with the Chinese Air Force, the Fantan-A is a twin jet attack aircraft derived from the MiG-19 Farmer. Compared with the Farmer, the Fantan has flank air intakes instead of a single nose intake. Maximum level speed is 740mph (1,190km/hr) and low level combat radius is 248 miles (400km). There are eight external store points, of which two pairs in tandem are situated under the fuselage. Maximum bomb load is 4,410lb (2,000kg) and two 23mm cannon are mounted in the wing roots. *Country of origin:* China.

McDonnell Douglas F-4 Phantom II

Confusion: Buccaneer, Fishbed, Jaguar

Power: 2 × J79 reheated turbojets   *Span:* 38ft 5in (11.76m)   *Length:* 62ft 11in (18.6m)

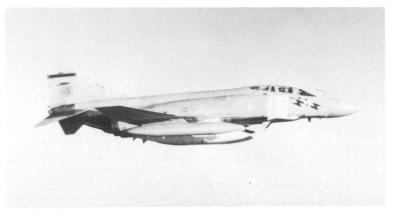

Finally phased out of production in 1979, the Phantom is probably the most numerous aircraft in Western air force inventories (over 5,000 built). Designed as an attack fighter for the US Navy, it was soon adopted by the USAF, serving in the interceptor, close support, reconnaissance (RF-4) and ECM roles. A licence-built version (F-4EJ) is in service in Japan, and Spey-engined models in the UK (F-4K/M), while certain early models in the US have been converted into pilotless target aircraft (QF-4B). A wide variety of stores can be carried, including Gatling guns, Sparrow and Sidewinder air-to-air missiles, bombs, rockets, and ECM and recce pods. Various up-date programmes for the F-4 were in progress at the time of writing. *Country of origin:* USA. *Silhouette:* F-4F. *Picture:* F-4M.

Power: 2 × Adour reheated turbofans   *Span:* 27ft 10in (8.49m)   *Length:* 50ft 11in (15.52m)

The result of a collaborative agreement signed by the British and French governments in 1965, the Jaguar strike fighter/trainer is in large-scale service with the RAF and the Armée de l'Air. Twenty-two have been sold to Oman, 18 to Nigeria, 12 to Ecuador and 40 to India plus licence manufacture rights. Single and two-seat versions have been built. Export versions known as Jaguar International, have uprated engines and provision for the carriage of overwing air-to-air missiles in addition to twin 30mm cannon and underwing bombs, rockets and drop tanks. RAF designations for Jaguar are GR1 and T2. *Country of origin:* UK/France. *Silhouette and picture:* GR1.

Mitsubishi T-2/F-1   *Confusion:* Jaguar, Phantom, Forger

Power: 2 × Adour reheated turbofans   *Span:* 25ft 10in (7.8m)   *Length:* 58ft 7in (17.85m)

Bearing a marked resemblance to the SEPECAT Jaguar, which preceded it by some two years, the T-2 was selected for development as a two-seat supersonic trainer for the Japan Air Self-Defence Force in 1967. Ninety-two T-2 advanced and T-2A combat trainers have been ordered, plus 77 of a single-seat, close-support fighter variant designated F-1. F-1 carries bombs, rockets, a 20mm cannon and air-to-air missiles and has a nose radome. Powered by licence-built Rolls-Royce Adour engines similar in output to those fitted in the basic Jaguar, the T-2 is marginally faster and lighter than its European counterpart. *Country of origin:* Japan. *Silhouette:* F-1. *Picture:* T-2.

Dassault-Breguet Mirage F.1

Power: 1 × Atar reheated turbojet   *Span:* 27ft 7in (8.4m)   *Length:* 49ft 2in (15m)

The swept-wing Mach 2 F.1 is a single-seat multi-purpose fighter/attack aircraft, over 690 examples of which have been ordered for 11 countries. The F.1A and F.1E perform the ground attack role, the F.1B and F.1D are two-seat trainers, the F.1C is an interceptor and the F.1CR is for reconnaissance. The F.1C of the Armée de l'Air is equipped for air-to-air refuelling. A variety of air-to-air and air-to-ground missiles and other weapon loads can be carried in addition to two 30mm cannon. First flown in December 1966. *Country of origin:* France. *Silhouette and picture:* F.1A.

 **Yakovlev Yak-38 Forger** *Confusion:* Harrier, Etendard, T-2/F-1

Power: 1 × turbojet + 2 × liftjets   *Span:* 24ft 7in (7.50m)   *Length:* 52ft 6in (16m)

First seen aboard the aircraft carrier *Kiev* in 1976, the naval Yak-38 Forger is the first Soviet Vtol aircraft to enter service. It is intended for use in the interceptor/attack/reconnaissance roles and in its present form is just supersonic in straight-and-level flight. The powerplant layout is unusual, consisting of a single main turbojet exhausting through vectoring nozzles at the rear plus two lift engines mounted just behind the cockpit. The outer wing sections fold upwards for movement on the deck lift and hangar stowage. Armament, carried on inner wing pylons, includes guns, bombs, rockets and air-to-air missiles. A two-seat tandem trainer version is known as Forger-B. *Country of origin:* USSR. *Silhouette and picture:* Forger-A.

Power: 1 × Pegasus vectored-thrust turbofan   *Span:* 25ft 3in (7.70m)   *Length:* (GR3): 45ft 8in (13.91m)

Of all the fixed-wing, vertical take-off aircraft to be conceived in the West in the late 1950s/early 1960s, the Harrier, derived from the P.1127, which first flew in 1960, is the only one to gain operational status. It is in large-scale service as a strike reconnaissance fighter with the RAF (GR3) and the US Marine Corps (AV-8A), serving as a close support and tactical reconnaissance aircraft. The Spanish Navy also operates a small number (designated Matador). Both the RAF and USMC have adopted a two-seat trainer version of the aircraft with elongated fuselage (RAF T2/USMC TAV-8A). Harrier carries two 30mm Aden guns, bombs, rockets and Sidewinder air-to-air missiles. RAF Harriers have been modified with a longer nose housing a laser rangefinder. *Country of origin:* UK. *Main silhouette and picture:* GR3; *upper side view:* T2.

BAe Sea Harrier

Confusion: Harrier/AV-8A, Etendard, Forger

Power: 1 × Pegasus vectored-thrust turbofan   *Span:* 25ft 3in (7.7m)   *Length:* 47ft 7in (14.5m)

Derived from the basic Harrier close-support aircraft, the Sea Harrier FRS1 has been modified for maritime operations, 57 having been ordered by the Royal Navy for operation from *Invincible*-class light aircraft carriers. Principal visible differences between Sea Harrier and its land-based counterpart are a redesigned, raised cockpit and the replacement of the laser nose with a pointed radome housing the Blue Fox radar. Armament includes 30mm Aden guns, bombs, rockets, and AIM-9L air-to-air missiles. The turbojet-powered Sea Eagle air-to-surface missile is also fitted. The Sea Harrier is also in service with the Indian Navy. *Country of origin:* UK. *Silhouette and picture:* Sea Harrier FRS1.

McDonnell Douglas AV-8B/BAe Harrier GR5

Power: 1 × Pegasus vectored-thrust turbofan   *Span:* 30ft 4in (9.24m)   *Length:* 46ft 4in (14.12m)

With raised cockpit, composite-material wing with leading-edge root extensions, fuselage underside strakes and six wing weapons/fuel pylons, the AV-8B Harrier II is a second-generation V/Stol aircraft based on the Harrier formula. Jointly produced by McDonnell Douglas and BAe, the AV-8B is expected to run to 328 examples for the US Marines plus 60GR5s for the RAF. Compared with the existing AV-8A/Harrier GR3, the AV-8B/GR5 will have radius of action raised to 692 miles (1,114km) and, for shorter sorties, a maximum external store load of 9,200lb (4,173kg). Weapons include two 30mm cannon or a 25mm Gatling gun, bombs, cluster bombs and Maverick and Sidewinder missiles. In-service dates are 1985 for the US Marines and 1986 for the RAF. Spain has ordered 12 AV-8Bs. *Country of origin:* USA/UK. *Silhouette and picture:* AV-8B.

Dassault-Breguet/Dornier Alpha Jet

Confusion: Hunter, Hawk, Harrier

Power: 2 × Larzac turbofans   *Span:* 29ft 11in (9.11m)   *Length:* 40ft 3in (12.29m)

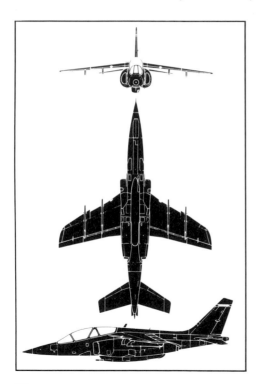

A joint venture by France and Germany, the Alpha Jet is a two-seater to be used for advanced training/light attack by the French and as the 'Close Support version' by the West Germans. First flown in 1973, the Alpha Jet has been ordered by France, West Germany and 10 other countries. Alpha Jet can carry a 30mm or 27mm gun pod under the fuselage, while the Close Support version has four wing pylons suitable for the carriage of a variety of weapons. A variant with improved systems and weapon load is known as Alpha Jet NGEA. *Country of origin:* France/West Germany. *Silhouette:* Advanced Trainer/light attack version. *Picture:* Close Support version.

Power: 2 × Viper turbojets   *Span:* 24ft 7in (7.5m)   *Length:* 42ft 8in (13m)

Flown for the first time in 1974, this ground-attack fighter is a joint development by the Yugoslav and Romanian industries. The overall programme is known as "Jurom", while the type is designated Orao 1 and 2 in Yugoslavia and IAR-93 A and B in Romania, the B version having afterburners fitted. Western suppliers provide a number of key systems. Some 400 examples of the subsonic Orao, which has a maximum weapon load of approximately 4,500lb (2,000kg), are expected to be produced for the Yugoslav and Romanian air forces. Each country has also flown single prototypes of a two-seat dual-control operational trainer, and this version is now in production. *Countries of origin:* Yugoslavia and Romania.

Aeritalia/Aermacchi/EMBRAER AM-X *Confusion:* Jurom

Power: 1 × Spey turbofan   *Span:* 29ft 1in (8.87m)   *Length:* 44ft 6in (13.57m)

A joint Italian-Brazilian development, the AM-X is a single-seat tactical fighter-bomber which will equip the air forces of both countries, 187 for Italy and 79 for Brazil. AM-X first flew in May 1984 and deliveries are expected to begin late in 1986. Brazilian aircraft will have two 30mm cannon while those in Italy will have a single multi-barrel 20mm gun. Other armament will include various types of bombs, rocket projectiles and air-to-surface and air-to-air missiles. AM-X will have an attack radius of 320 miles (520km). *Countries of origin:* Italy and Brazil.

Power: 1 × J57 reheated turbojet   *Span:* 35ft 8in (10.87m)   *Length:* 54ft 6in (16.61m)

A supersonic carrierborne fighter and reconnaissance aircraft, the Crusader first entered service in 1957 and remains in small numbers with the French Navy and the Philippines. Four 20mm cannon are mounted in the fuselage, and there are four positions for air-to-air missiles, air-to-surface missiles or bombs. Two underwing weapon/fuel tank pylons can also be fitted. The wing has variable incidence for low-speed flight. Versions in use are the F-8H, K, J and L interceptors and the RF-8G reconnaissance aircraft. Performance figures include a maximum level speed of 1,200 mph (1,930km/hr) at 36,000ft (11,000m); service ceiling of 38,400ft (11,700m); and combat radius of 440 miles (708km). *Country of origin:* USA. *Silhouette and picture:* F-8E(FN).

 **Vought A-7 Corsair II** *Confusion:* Crusader

Power: 1 × TF41 turbofan   *Span:* 38ft 8in (11.79m)   *Length:* 46ft 1in (14.05m)

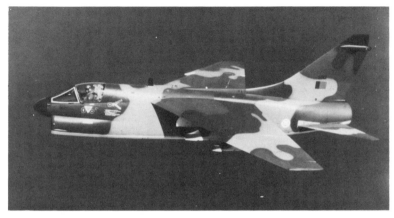

Capable of carrying a massive weapon load, the single-seat subsonic Corsair II is a standard attack aircraft in both the USAF and USN. Initially powered by American engines, the A-7 was later fitted with the Allison licence-built version of the Rolls-Royce Spey. The USAF version is the A-7D (two seat A7-K), the USN version the A-7E and the two-seat trainer is designated TA-7C. TA-7C modified for fleet operations support group is EA-7L. The type has been exported to Greece and Portugal, the latter being known as A-7P/TA-7P. Up to 15,000lb (6,804kg) of bombs, rockets, air-to-surface and air-to-air missiles and gun pods can be carried. A 20mm cannon is mounted in the fuselage. *Country of origin:* USA. *Silhouette:* A-7E. *Picture:* A-7P.

Power: 1 × **Atar turbojet**   *Span:* **31ft 6in (9.6m)**   *Length:* **47ft 3in (14.4m)**

Originally introduced aboard French aircraft carriers in 1962, the Etendard IVM was a single-seat strike fighter. Ninety Etendards were built, of which 21 were designated IVP and equipped with cameras in the nose and gun bay. All the IVPs are fitted with flight-refuelling probes. The IVP remains in squadron service with the Aeronavale, while the IVM has been replaced by the Super Etendard. *Country of origin:* **France.**

Dassault-Breguet Super Etendard   *Confusion:* Etendard, Hunter, G.91Y

Power: 1 × Atar turbojet   *Span:* 31ft 6in (9.60m)   *Length:* 46ft 11½in (14.31m)

The successor to the Etendard IVM, the Super Etendard is a transonic single-seat strike fighter designed for operation from French aircraft carriers. The engine has increased thrust, a modern navigation/attack system is fitted and an Agave radar is housed in the nose. The wing has also been modified. Production deliveries began in 1978. A total of 71 have been been acquired by the French Navy, plus 14 for the Argentinian Navy and 5 leased by Iraq. As on the IVM, the gun armament consists of twin 30mm cannon. A variety of weapons, including Exocet anti-ship missiles, can be carried on four underwing and one fuselage pylon. *Country of origin:* France.

Tupolev Tu-28P Fiddler

Power: 2 × Lyulka reheated turbojets   *Span:* 65ft (19.8m)   *Length:* 90ft (27.43m)

A long-range interceptor of massive size, the Tu-28P, code-named Fiddler, carries two crew, a large radar and up to four air-to-air missiles. As on many Soviet types, the main undercarriage retracts into blisters on the wing trailing edge. Although production is believed to have ceased in the late 1960s, Fiddler remains in Soviet Air Force service in specialist roles. Maximum speed is Mach 1.75 and range 3,100 miles (4,989km). *Country of origin:* USSR

Grumman A-6 Intruder/Prowler   *Confusion:* Hunter

Power: 2 × J52 turbojets   *Span:* 53ft (16.15m)   *Length:* (A-6E): 54ft 7in (16.64m), (EA-6B): 59ft 5in (18.11m)

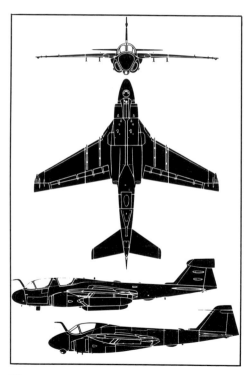

A highly versatile carrierborne aircraft, the Intruder was designed in the late 1950s as a two-seat, low-level, long-range attack bomber for the US Navy, being broadly equivalent to the Royal Navy's contemporary Buccaneer. In addition to its all-weather bombing rôle (A6A/B/E), the Intruder evolved during the Vietnam War as a tanker (KA-6D) and electronic warfare aircraft, the EA-6A/B Prowler (upper side view). The last-mentioned differ from other models in having a large electronics pod mounted on the fin, while the EA-6B has accommodation for two additional EW operators in an extended nose. *Country of origin:* USA. *Main silhouette:* A-6E; *upper side view and picture:* EA-6B.

Power: 1 × JT15D turbofan   *Span:* 27ft 8in (8.43m)   *Length:* 30ft 6in (9.31m)

A low-cost lightweight jet basic trainer, the S.211 has been developed as a private venture in Italy. The crew are seated in tandem and the four underwing hardpoints can carry bombs or rocket projectiles for weapon training. Maximum speed of the S.211 is 449 mph (723km/hr) while maximum cruising range, with external tanks, is 1,673 miles (2,693km). The prototype S.211 flew in April 1981 and deliveries to customers began in 1984. *Country of origin:* Italy.

BAe Hawk

Confusion: Hunter, Etendard, Alpha Jet, S.211

Power: 1 × Adour turbofan *Span:* 30ft 10in (9.40m) *Length* (over probe): 39ft 2in (11.96m)

First flown in 1974, the Hawk T1 was ordered by the RAF as its standard advanced trainer and entered service in 1976. The standard version carries a 30mm Aden gun pack and two wing pylons for 1,000lb (450kg) bombs. Ninety RAF Hawks will carry two Sidewinder missiles each for interception duties over the UK. Export orders have been placed by seven nations and the type is to be used as a trainer by the US Navy as the T-45. A single seat attack/intercept version is now being built as a private venture by British Aerospace, designated Hawk 200. *Country of origin:* UK.

Power: 1 × Viper turbojet   *Span:* 32ft 5in (9.88m)   *Length overall:* 38ft 11in (11.86m)

Designed to replace the Galeb and T-33 as the Yugoslav Air Force basic/advanced trainer, the two-seat Super Galeb (Seagull) first flew in July 1978. Powered by an up-rated Viper engine, the Super Galeb can carry a 23mm cannon in a removable ventral pod and has four underwing stores points for rockets, bombs, fuel tanks etc. The aircraft is in production to meet major Yugoslav orders. Maximum speed is 565 mph (910km/hr) and combat radius in the light attack roll, at low level, is 186 miles (300km). *Country of origin:* Yugoslavia.

Hindustan Aeronautics Ajeet (Gnat)   *Confusion:* Hunter, Hawk

Power: 1 × Orpheus turbojet   *Span:* 22ft 2in   *Length* (Ajeet): 29ft 9in (9.06m)

Designed originally by the Folland company as an ultra-lightweight interceptor, the Gnat Mk 1 was adopted in that role by India and Finland and as a two-seat trainer by the RAF. Two hundred Gnat Mk 1 fighters were built at Bangalore by Hindustan Aeronautics. Eighty Ajeet ground-attack fighters, with more power and systems improvements, have been built. The Ajeet has also been constructed in two-seat trainer form. Ajeet carries two 30mm cannon plus underwing bombs or rockets. Performance figures for the Gnat/Ajeet include maximum speeds of 695 mph (1,118km/hr) at 20,000ft (6,100m) and 647 mph (1,040km/hr) at 36,000ft (11,000m); ceiling of 50,000ft (15,250m); and combat radius of 500 miles (805km). RAF Gnats were replaced by the Hawk. *Countries of origin:* India/UK. *Main silhouette:* Ajeet; *lower side view:* Ajeet trainer. *Picture:* Ajeet.

Power: 1 × Avon turbojet   *Span:* 33ft 8in (10.26m)   *Length:* 45ft 10in (13.98m)

Undoubtedly the most successful and most numerous of post-war British fighter designs, with around 2,000 produced, the Hunter has been largely phased out of service by Western air forces, except in Switzerland and the UK. Many remain in service in the Middle and Far East, Africa, India and South America, however. The RAF still uses Hunters in a variety of roles, including advanced training with the two-seat T7. Hunters carry two internally mounted 30mm guns plus underwing rockets, bombs and fuel tanks. *Country of origin:* UK. *Main silhouette:* FGA9; *upper side view:* T7. *Picture:* FGA9.

BAe Buccaneer

Confusion: Jaguar, Phantom, Harrier, Saab 105

Power: 2 × Spey turbojets   *Span:* 44ft (13.4m)   *Length:* 63ft 5in (19.33m)

Originally built as a Royal Navy low-level, two-seat carrierborne strike/attack aircraft, the Buccaneer was later adopted by the RAF as a land-based type for the same purpose. First production aircraft (S1) had the Gyron Junior engine, but subsequent variants (S2) were powered by the Rolls-Royce Spey. The RAF is now the sole UK Buccaneer operator and the type will remain in service, in the maritime role, following the introduction of Tornado. The South African Air Force has one squadron. Armament is carried internally and on four wing pylons. Bullpup, Sea Eagle or Martel missiles can be carried. Buccaneer performance is characterised by outstanding stability at low level and high speed. *Country of origin:* UK. *Silhouette and picture:* S2.

Power: 2 × Aubisque or 2 × J85 turbojets   *Span:* 31ft 2in (9.5m)   *Length:* 34ft 5in (10.5m)

Produced in the 1960s as a standard basic trainer for the Royal Swedish Air Force, the two-seat 105 is unusual in having a shoulder wing and T-tail. Four versions have been built: the Sk60A for training, Sk60B for weapons training/light attack, Sk60C for reconnaissance (all with Turboméca Aubisque engines), and the 105XT exported to Austria with General Electric J85 engines. The Sk60C (upper side view) has a longer nose than other variants. One hundred and fifty 105s are in service. *Country of origin:* Sweden. *Main silhouette and picture:* Sk60A.

McDonnell Douglas F-15 Eagle   *Confusion:* Tomcat, Foxbat, Fulcrum, Flanker

Power: 2 × F100 reheated turbojets   *Span:* 42ft 9in (13.04m)   *Length:* 63ft 9in (19.44m)

A sophisticated single-seat, all-weather air-superiority fighter, the F-15 Eagle has a performance in excess of Mach 2 at altitude. In addition to a rotary cannon in the fuselage, the F-15 can carry four Sparrow and four Sidewinder air-to-air missiles. Operating in the USA and Europe with the USAF, the F-15 has also been sold to Israel, Japan and Saudi Arabia. First production aircraft flew in 1974. Current production single-seaters are F-15C and F-15D. A dual role two seater (air intercept and ground attack) is the F-15E of which 392 are scheduled to be built. The tandem two-seat version is designated F-15B. *Country of origin:* USA. *Silhouette and picture:* F-15.

Mikoyan MiG-25 Foxbat

Power: 2 × Tumansky reheated turbojets   *Span:* 41ft (12.5m)   *Length:* 70ft (21.33m)

A very-high-performance, high-altitude interceptor, the Foxbat is capable of speeds of between Mach 2.5 and 3.0. Because of its very high speed and 80,000ft (24,400m) operational ceiling Foxbat presents a problem to any air-defence system. Foxbat-A is an interceptor with a large nose radar and four underwing air-to-air missiles. Foxbat-B and -D are reconnaissance variants. Foxbat-C (MiG-25U) is a two-seat trainer and Foxbat-E is a development of the -A with new radar and up-rated engines. *Country of origin:* USSR. *Main silhouette:* Foxbat-A; *lower side view:* Foxbat-C. *Picture:* Foxbat-E.

Mikoyan MiG-31 Foxhound-A

Confusion: Tomcat, Eagle, Foxbat

Power: 2 × Tumansky turbojets   *Span:* 45ft 11in (14m)   *Length:* 76ft 3in (23.2m)

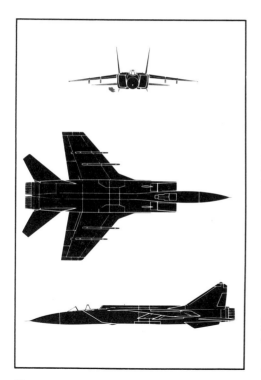

A two-seat development of the Foxbat, the Foxhound has a new radar, modified fuselage and revised wing shape. Having a full look down/shoot down capability, the type is believed to have entered service in 1982 and over 50 are now operational. Soviet sources claim that Foxhound is capable of intercepting cruise missiles at low altitude. Four AA-9 semi-active radar homing air-air missiles are carried under the fuselage. *Country of origin:* USSR. *Silhouette provisional. Picture:* Foxhound-A.

Power: 2 × reheated turbojets   *Span:* 33ft 7in (10.25)   *Length (overall):* 50ft 10in (15.5m)

Similar in size to the F-16, the MiG-29 Fulcrum is a single-seat twin-engine fighter first deployed in the Soviet Union in 1984. It has a look-down, shoot-down radar/weapon system designed to deal with low flying strike/attack aircraft. With a top speed of 1,450 mph (2,335km/hr), the Fulcrum has a radius of action 497 miles (800km) and carries six air-air missiles. Drawings etc are provisional. *Country of origin:* USSR.

Sukhoi Su-27 Flanker

Confusion: Fulcrum, F-15, Hornet, Foxbat

Power: 2 × reheated turbojets   *Span:* 47ft 7in (14.5m)   *Length:* 69ft (21m)

Approximating to the American F-15, the Flanker is a supersonic all-weather counterair fighter of the same new generation as the MiG-29 Fulcrum. Like the Fulcrum, the Flanker has twin fins and it can carry up to eight air-air missiles. Maximum speed is estimated at 1,550 mph (2,500km/hr) and combat radius 715 miles (1,150km). Flanker is mainly intended to combat low flying aircraft and cruise missiles. It is likely to be operational this year. Drawings etc are provisional. *Country of origin:* USSR.

BAe Victor 2

Tupolev Tu-16 Badger

BAe Nimrod AEW3

Confusion: Nimrod MR2

Power: 4 × Spey turbofans   *Span:* 111ft 10in (35m)   *Length:* 135ft 9in (41.37m)

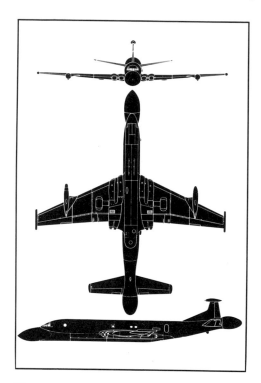

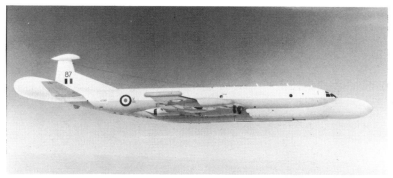

Airborne early warning is achieved by putting a high-power surveillance radar into an aircraft, making it mobile and able to "see" over long distances. It is vital to look down on low-level bombers, which cannot be detected early enough by ground installations. The RAF aircraft for this role is the Nimrod AEW3, modified from the maritime reconnaissance Nimrod. Main point of difference is the fitting of large bulbous radomes in nose and tail, the former being particularly prominent. Eleven MR Nimrods are scheduled to be converted to AEW standard. Ordered in March 1977 in preference to the Boeing E-3A Sentry (see Jet, swept wing, underwing engines), the Nimrod AEW3 will replace the RAF's Shackleton AEW2s. There have been delays with the Nimrod AEW3 and the date when a squadron would become operational is not known at the time of writing. The Nimrod force will be integrated with the new UK ground-based air-defence system. *Country of origin:* UK.

Power: 4 × Spey turbofans   *Span:* 114ft 10in (35m)   *Length:* 126ft 9in (38.63m)

Developed from the basic Comet airframe, the Nimrod MR2 is the RAF's standard long-range maritime reconnaissance aircraft. Capable of up to 12hr endurance and a maximum speed of 575 mph (926km/hr), the Nimrod is one of the most advanced anti-submarine aircraft in the West. Three Nimrod R1s are used for electronic surveillance. The R1 has a cut-off fuselage tail extension and small inset fins on the tailplane. Armament of the maritime reconnaissance variants includes bombs, mines, depth charges and torpedoes in the weapons bay. *Country of origin:* UK. *Silhouette and picture:* MR2.

BAe Victor

Confusion: Badger, Bison

Power: 4 × Conway turbofans   *Span:* 120ft (36.58m)   *Length:* 114ft 11in (35m)

One of the three V-bombers which formed the British nuclear deterrent force of the 1950s and 1960s, the Victor was unusual in having a crescent-shaped wing leading edge and high-set tailplane. The B1 had Sapphire engines while the B2 has Rolls-Royce Conways. The Victors in RAF service are all K2 tankers. Three aircraft can be refuelled simultaneously through hoses trailed from the belly and pods under the wings. The Victor is scheduled, later, to be replaced by VC10 and TriStar tankers. *Country of origin:* UK. *Silhouette and picture:* K2.

Power: 2 × Mikulin turbojets   *Span:* 108ft (32.93m)   *Length:* 114ft 2in (34.8m)

First put into service in the mid-1950s as a bomber, the 596 mph (960km/hr) Tu-16 Badger remains in use with Soviet maritime squadrons. Used for overwater surveillance and electronic intelligence-gathering, the Badger-D has a long nose radome and three underfuselage blisters. Badger-E and -F have glazed noses, the -E mounting only two blisters and having a belly camera, and -F having an electronic equipment pod under each wing. Badgers -C and -D carry Kingfisher air-to-surface missiles under the wings or a Kipper missile under the fuselage. Badgers -H and -J are used for ECM work. Badger-K is an electronic reconnaissance variant. Badgers use air-to-air refuelling and some act as tankers. There are twin tail guns. Maximum range with the maximum bomb load of 19,800lb (9,000kg) is 3,000 miles (4,800km), increasing to 3,975 miles (6,400km) with 6,600lb (3,000kg) at 480 mph (770km/hr). *Country of origin:* USSR. *Silhouette:* **Badger-C.** *Picture:* **Badger-D.**

Myasishchev M-4 Bison   *Confusion:* Badger

Power: 4 × Soloviev turbofans   *Span:* 170ft (51.82m)   *Length:* 162ft (49.38m)

Originally designed as the rival to the Boeing B-52 strategic bomber, the M-4, code-named Bison, first flew in 1953 and entered service with the Soviet Air Force in 1955. Initial versions were powered by four Mikulin turbojets but later machines were fitted with Soloviev turbofans. As ballistic missiles took over the task of nuclear delivery, the Bison was converted to the B and C standards for the long-range maritime reconnaissance role. There are three positions for twin 23mm cannon and a probe for in-flight refuelling is fitted. A number of radar and electronic warfare sets are carried, and a special feature is the bicycle undercarriage with two sets of mainwheels under the fuselage and outrigger wheels at the wingtips. Maximum speed is 625 mph (1,060km/hr) and endurance is about 15hr. *Country of origin:* USSR. *Silhouette:* Bison-A. *Picture:* Bison-B.

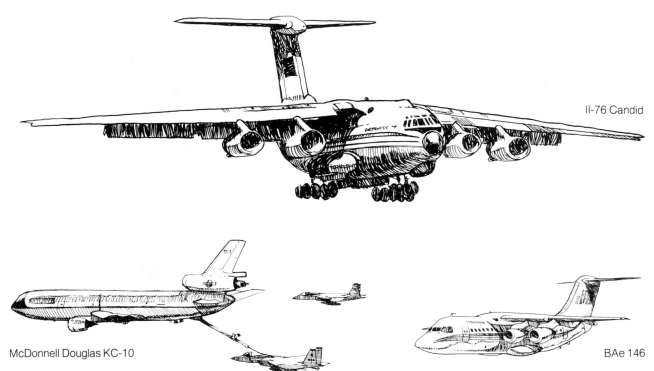

Il-76 Candid

McDonnell Douglas KC-10

BAe 146

Lockheed S-3A Viking

Confusion: Skywarrior, C-1A

Power: 2 × TF34 turbofans   *Span:* 68ft 8in (20.93m)   *Length:* 53ft 4in (16.26m)

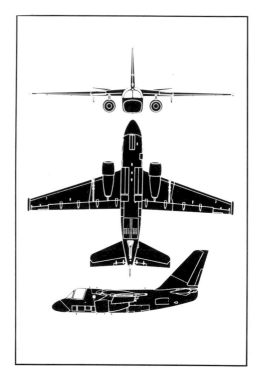

A highly sophisticated carrierborne anti-submarine aircraft, the S-3A Viking has podded turbofans and top speed of 507 mph (816km/hr). The fuselage weapons bay carries torpedoes, depth charges or mines, while weapons or fuel tanks can be carried on wing pylons. Four crew members are carried. A carrier on-board delivery (COD) version is designated US-3A and an inflight refuelling type, the KS-3A. The prototype of the US-3A, produced by modifying a development S-3A, first flew in 1976 and underwent sea trials aboard the USS *Kitty Hawk* in 1978. All 160 S-3As are to be modified as S-3Bs with new radar, improved electronic systems and Harpoon anti-ship missiles. *Country of origin:* USA. *Silhouette:* S-3A. *Picture:* KS-3A.

Power: 2 × JT8D turbofans   *Span:* 100ft 4in (30.6m)   *Length:* 95ft 2in (29m)

A medium-range tactical transport, the C-1A equips the Japan Air Self-Defence Force. Up to 60 troops or vehicles/freight, loaded via the rear doors and ramp, can be carried. Twenty-four C-1As were delivered, in addition to two prototypes and two pre-production models. Maximum speed is 489 mph (787km/hr), and range with full payload 865 miles (1,295km). At reduced payload (4,850lb, 2,200kg) and with maximum fuel, range increases to 2,084 miles (3,353km). One C-1, designated C-1 Kai, has been fitted with larger flat radomes in nose and tail for ECM purposes. *Country of origin:* Japan.

Yakovlev Yak-28P Firebar

Confusion: Flashlight, Brewer

Power: 2 × Tumansky reheated turbojets   *Span:* 41ft (12.5m)   *Length:* 72ft (21.95m)

Developed from the Flashlight/Mangrove series, the Yak-28P Firebar is an all-weather interceptor with low-supersonic performance. Firebar has a long, pointed nose radome, two seats in tandem and two or four underwing air-to-air missiles. The Firebar first flew in 1960, was built in large numbers and remains in standard service with the Eastern Bloc. Like the rest of the family, the Firebar has a bicycle undercarriage with outrigger wheels near the wingtips. At high altitude the Firebar has a radius of action of 550 miles (885km). *Country of origin:* USSR.

Yakovlev Yak-28 Brewer

Power: 2 × Tumansky reheated turbojets   *Span:* 41ft (12.05m)   *Length:* 70ft (21.34m)

A redesigned and higher-powered successor to the Flashlight, the Brewer has a glazed nose similar to that of an interim reconnaissance variant, the Yak-27R Mangrove, which differs little externally. Brewer is a multi-purpose tactical bomber (Brewer-A, -B and -C), reconnaissance (-D) and electronic countermeasures (-E) aircraft. A key task of Brewers now in Soviet service is electronic warfare, for which a variety of sensors are housed in fuselage blisters. The trainer version is the Yak-28U, code-named Maestro, which has an additional cockpit forward of the main position and no glazing on the nose. *Country of origin:* USSR. *Silhouette and picture:* Brewer-D.

Douglas A-3 Skywarrior   *Confusion:* Viking, C-1A

Power: 2 × J57 turbojets   *Span:* 72ft 6in (22.10m)   *Length:* 76ft 4in (23.27m)

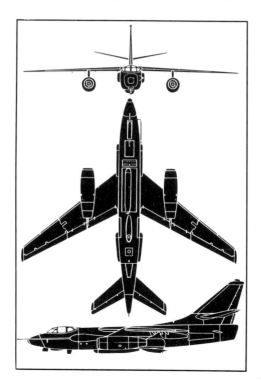

Introduced in the 1950s and originally used as a standard US Navy bomber, the Skywarrior now performs the electronic countermeasures and tanker roles. The ECM version, with a variety of fuselage bulges housing special equipment, is known as the EKA-3B. The airborne tanker is designated KA-3B. The original armament of two 20mm cannon in the tail has been deleted from the present versions, which are conversions of earlier bomber/reconnaissance aircraft. In late 1984 there were some 50 Skywarriors still in service. *Country of origin:* USA. *Silhouette and picture:* EKA-3B.

Power: 2 × JT8D turbofans   *Span:* 93ft (28.35m)   *Length:* 100ft (30.48m)

A very successful short/medium-haul transport, this type first entered service with Lufthansa in 1967 as the 115-seat 737-100. Seating was subsequently increased to 130 in the 737-200, a variant which has sold in large numbers round the world. At the time of writing, 1,224 737s had been sold, to 128 airlines. Nineteen 737s designated T-43A were delivered to the USAF as navigation trainers. The 737-200 can fly 2,370 miles (3,815km) with maximum payload. Maximum cruising speed is 576 mph (927km/hr). *Country of origin:* USA. *Silhouette and picture:* 737-200.

Boeing 737-300

Confusion: 737, A300, A310, 757, 767

Power: 2 × CFM56 turbofans   *Span:* 94ft 7in (28.91m)   *Length:* 109ft 7in (33.40m)

A major contender in the new generation of quiet short-haul jets, the 737-300 differs from the -200 in wing and tailplane span, fuselage length, fin outline and engine nacelle shape. In all-tourist configuration the aircraft seats 140 passengers and has a still-air range of 1,925 miles (3,098km). By September 1984 the order book for 737-300s stood at 165 with 79 on option. *Country of origin:* USA.

Power: 2 × CF6 or 2 × JT9D turbofans   *Span:* 147ft 1in (44.84m)   *Length:* 175ft 11in (53.62m)

First flown in 1972, the 330-seat wide-body A300 is built by a European consortium of companies: Aérospatiale, Deutsche Airbus, British Aerospace, Casa and Fokker. The B2 and B4 are basic versions, the latter having more fuel and leading-edge flaps. The A300 is intended for medium-range routes and can fly 2,530 miles (4,074km) with full payload and reserves. Maximum cruising speed is 578 mph (930km/hr). By September 1984, the order book for A300s stood at 246. *Countries of origin:* France/Germany/Netherlands/Spain/UK, plus other associated countries. *Silhouette:* A300B2. *Picture:* A300B4.

Airbus Industrie A310

Confusion: A300, 757, 767, TriStar, DC-10

Power: 2 × CF6 or JT9D turbofans   *Span:* 144ft (43.9m)   *Length:* 153ft (46.6m)

A combination of a shortened-fuselage A300 and a new advanced-technology wing produced the Airbus A310, a direct rival to the Boeing 767. Like the 767, the A310 is offered with two different powerplants. By September 1984 121 A310s had been ordered. First flown in April 1982, the type went into service in April 1983, with Lufthansa and Swissair the first two users. With maximum payload the A310 can fly 2,540 miles (4,090km) at a speed of 514 mph (828km/hr). A310-200 is the basic version, while A310-300, with longer range, is scheduled to fly towards the end of 1985. *Countries of origin:* France/Germany/Netherlands/Spain/UK, plus other associated countries.

Power: 2 × JT9D or CF6 turbofans   *Span:* 156ft 4in (47.65m)   *Length:* 159ft 2in (48.5m)

First flown in September 1981, the Boeing 767 is a medium-haul wide-body airliner seating a maximum of 255 passengers. The 767 and the Airbus A310 are direct competitors and they closely resemble each other in external shape. First delivery of the 767 was made in August 1982. By autumn 1984 firm orders totalled 188. Like its sister aircraft the 757, the 767 is offered with a choice of powerplants. Companies in Italy and Japan are building elements of the 767. With its full payload the 767 has a range of 2,554 miles (4,110km) and cruising speed is 528 mph (850km/hr). *Country of origin:* USA. *Picture:* 767-200ER.

Boeing 757 *Confusion:* A300, A310, 767

Power: 2 × RB.211 or 2 × PW2037 turbofans   *Span:* 124ft 6in (37.95m)   *Length:* 155ft 3in (47.32m)

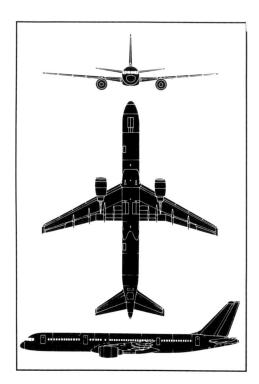

Reversing the trend towards wide-body twin-aisle transports, the slim-body twin-fan single-aisle Boeing 757 airliner first flew in February 1982, with deliveries to airlines beginning ten months later. Firm orders for the short/medium-haul 757 total 139, with some airlines selecting Rolls-Royce and others Pratt & Whitney powerplants. In mixed-class international layout the 757 seats 204 passengers, cruises at 528 mph (850km/hr) and has a maximum range of over 2,476 miles (3,984km). The 757 and the wide-body 767 form a new family of Boeing airliners which will be used in large numbers round the world. *Country of origin:* USA. *Picture:* 757-200.

Power: 3 × RB.211 turbofans   *Span:* 155ft 4in (47.35m)   *Length* (except -500): 177ft 8in (54.17m)

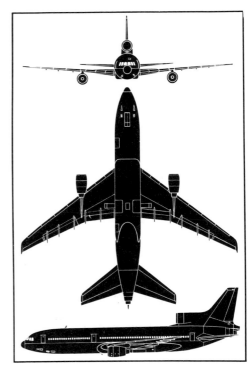

Produced to meet the same wide-body requirement as the McDonnell Douglas DC-10, the Lockheed TriStar was the first aircraft to be equipped with the Rolls-Royce RB.211 big-fan engine. The various versions are the 1011-1, 1011-100, 1011-200, 1011-250 and the 1011-500; the last-named has a 13ft 6in (4.11m) reduction in fuselage length. Capacity varies up to 400 passengers in all-economy. Cruising speed is Mach 0.84 and maximum range, achieved by the -500, is 6,100 miles (9,815km). Lockheed closed the TriStar line in August 1983 with the 250th production aircraft. *Country of origin:* USA. *Silhouette:* L-1011-500. *Picture:* L-1011-1.

McDonnell Douglas DC-10 *Confusion:* TriStar, A300, A310, 767

Power: 3 × CF6 or 3 × JT9D turbofans   *Span* (30/40): 165ft 4in (50.41m)   *Length* (30/40): 182ft (55.5m)

Over 350 DC-10 wide-body airliners have been sold to 53 operators. The Series 10 was the initial version, followed by the Series 30 and 40, both with 10ft (3.05m) more wingspan. The Series 10 and 30 have CF6 engines and the Series 40 the JT9D. Convertible cargo versions are in service and the USAF has ordered the type for use as an airborne tanker/cargo aircraft designated KC-10. Like the TriStar, which it resembles, the DC-10 first flew in 1970. Maximum seating is for 380 and maximum range is 7,197 miles (11,580km). *Country of origin:* USA. *Silhouette:* DC-10-30. *Picture:* KC-10A.

Power: 4 × JT3D turbofans   *Span:* 142ft 5in (43.41m)   *Length:* 150ft 6in (45.87m)

Along with the Boeing 707 and the Comet, the DC-8 pioneered the airline jet age, and 294 of the Series 10-50 were built. First flown in 1958, the DC-8 went into service in 1959, some fitted with Rolls-Royce Conway engines. The Series 50 can carry up to 173 passengers for 5,720 miles (9,205km). Known as the Jet Trader, a freight and freight/passenger version was introduced into airline service in 1962. *Country of origin:* USA. *Silhouette:* DC-8-50. *Picture:* DC-8-53.

McDonnell Douglas DC-8 Super 60/Super 70 *Confusion: 707*

Power: 4 × JT3D turbofans   *Span* (Super 63): 148ft 5in (45.23m)   *Length* (Super 63): 187ft 5in (57.12m)

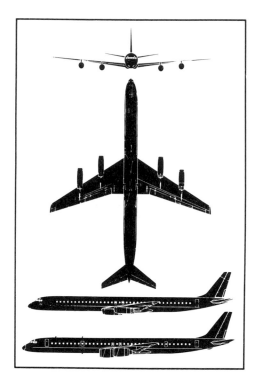

The process of "stretching" jet transports is nowhere more evident than in the DC-8, the ultimate variant of which, the Series 63, has grown by more than 30ft (9.14m) compared with earlier versions. The Super 62, with more wingspan than the Series 50, is the shortest version of this range. The Super 61 has the Series 50 wing and a 20ft (6.08m) fuselage extension, while the Super 63 has the longest fuselage and the bigger wing. The Super 63 can carry up to 259 passengers. In all, 262 Super Sixties were built. Re-engined with CFM56 advanced turbofans, the 61, 62 and 63 became the Super 71, 72 and 73 respectively. Some seventy of the Super 70 series are now in service. *Country of origin:* USA. *Silhouette:* Super 63; *lower side view:* Super 73. *Picture:* Super 70.

Power: 4 × JT3D or 4 × Conway turbofans   *Span:* 145ft 9in (44.2m)   *Length:* 152ft 11in (46.61m)

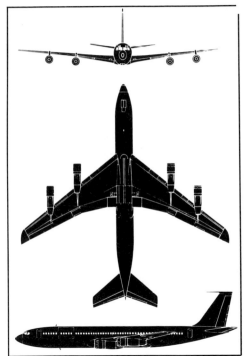

The most successful of the first generation of medium/long-range jet airliners, the 707 first flew in prototype form in 1954. Initial versions seated up to 181 passengers , while the smaller 720 seated 153. Later versions such as the -320 and -420 carry up to 195 passengers and there are variants for cargo and mixed passenger/cargo. The 707 has a maximum cruising speed of 605 mph (973km/hr) and can fly 6,240 miles (10,040km) with maximum fuel. Boeing offers conversions of the 707 as a mixed tanker/transport with hose-drogue or boom refuelling equipment. 982 707/720s have been produced. *Country of origin:* USA. *Silhouette:* 707-320. *Picture:* 707-320C.

Boeing KC-135 *Confusion:* 707, DC-8

Power: 4 × J-57 turbojets, or JT3D or CFM56 turbofans   *Span:* 130ft 10in (39.88m)   *Length:* 136ft 3in (41.53m)

First flown in 1956, the KC-135A is an air-air refuelling tanker version of the 707 airliner. Altogether 732 KC-135As with J57 engines were built. To extend the life of the type, JT3D turbofans are being fitted to some aircraft, while 300 others, plus eleven French Air Force machines, are being re-equipped with General Electric/SNECMA CFM56 turbofans with much more bulbous nacelles. This version is known as the KC-135R. *Country of origin:* USA. *Silhouette:* KC-135R. *Picture:* KC-135 with JT-3D.

Power: 4 × TF33 turbofans *Span:* 145ft 9in (44.42m) *Length:* 152ft 11in (46.61m)

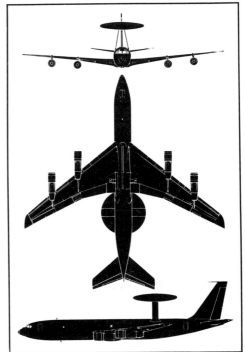

A radar station in the sky, the E-3A Sentry is also known as AWACS (Airborne Warning and Control System). The aircraft is basically a 707 transport fitted with a very large circular radome above the fuselage and a complete air-defence operations centre in the cabin. The 17-man crew track numerous hostile targets and direct fighters onto them. The Sentry has been produced for the US Air Force, NATO and Saudi Arabia. The first development aircraft, flown in 1972, was known as the EC-137. The first E-3A was delivered to the USAF's Tinker Air Force Base in 1977 and the type is fully operational in the USA and Europe. *Country of origin:* USA. *Silhouette and picture:* E-3A.

Ilyushin Il-86 Camber

Confusion: 707, 747, DC-8

Power: 4 × Kuznetsov turbofans   *Span:* 157ft 8in (48.06m)   *Length:* 195ft 4in (59.54m)

The Soviet Union's first wide-bodied jet, the Il-86, Nato code-named Camber, was first reported in 1972, subsequently underwent extensive redesign, and finally flew in December 1976. Seating up to 350 passengers, the Il-86 is intended for use over sectors of 1,460 miles (2,350km) at a speed of around 560 mph (900–950km/hr). The Il-86 entered service with Aeroflot in 1980. A longer-range version is under development believed to be designated Il-96. This is expected to have new, more economical, high by-pass ratio turbofan engines. *Country of origin:* USSR.

Power: 4 × JT9D, CF6 or RB.211 turbofans *Span:* 195ft 8in (59.64m) *Length:* 231ft 4in (70.51m)

The largest airliner in the world, the Boeing 747 was the first of the wide-bodied "jumbo jets". It can seat up to 490 passengers in economy class and cruise at 589 mph (948km/hr) over sectors of up to 7,080 miles (11,395km). Initial version was the -100, followed by the -200 with more fuel. Passenger/cargo and all-cargo 747s are known as the -200C and -200F respectively. A short-range variant is designated 747SR. The short-fuselage 747SP (Special Performance) carries 360 passengers for up to 9,570 miles (15,400km). Latest version is the 747-300 (formerly 747EUD), with the upper front fuselage extended aft to accommodate 37 more passengers. At the time of writing the 747 order book stood at 637. *Country of origin:* USA. *Main silhouette:* 747-200B; *lower side view:* 747-300. *Picture:* 747-300.

Boeing B-52 Stratofortress   *Confusion: 747*

Power: 8 × J57 turbojets or 8 × TF33 turbofans   *Span:* 185ft (56.42m)   *Length:* 157ft 7in (48.03m)

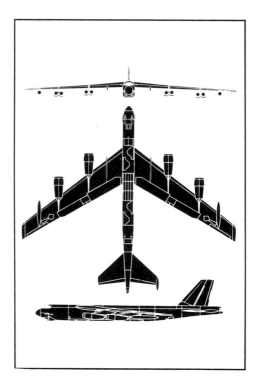

In service since 1957, the B-52 still forms the backbone of the USAF's Strategic Air Command with nearly 300 available. The force is being progressively modified to carry the Boeing AGM-86B air-launched cruise missiles. Main versions in service are the B-52G and B-52H, the former with J57 and the latter with TF33 engines. With a crew of six and full weapon load, the B-52 can carry 60,000lb (27,215kg) of internal weapons, plus missiles or other equipment on wing pylons. Outboard external fuel tanks can be fitted. The aircraft carries a wide variety of ECM systems. A multi-barrel radar-controlled 20mm Gatling gun is carried in the tail. *Country of origin:* USA. *Silhouette and picture:* B-52H.

Power: **4 × TF33 turbofans**   *Span:* **160ft (48.74m)**   *Length:* **168ft 4in**

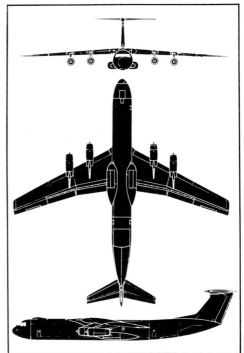

The USAF's first pure-jet strategic freighter, the Starlifter entered service in 1964. Altogether 285 Starlifters were built and they are in use in many parts of the world with Military Airlift Command. Up to 59,800lb of cargo, or vehicles, equipment, guns and missiles can be carried. Range with maximum payload of 89,096lb (44,450kg) is 2,650 miles (4,264km). The Starlifter is loaded through rear under-fuselage doors. All Starlifters in the USAF have now been rebuilt to C-141B standard, with longer fuselage. *Country of origin:* USA. *Silhouette and picture:* C-141B.

117

Ilyushin Il-76 Candid *Confusion:* Starlifter, Galaxy, 747, BAe 146

Power: 4 × D-30 turbofans   *Span:* 165ft 8in (50.5m)   *Length:* 152ft 10in (46.59m)

The Soviet answer to the Lockheed Starlifter, the Il-76 first flew in 1971. A massive strategic transport, the Candid is designed to operate from short, rough airfields. Maximum payload is 88,185lb (40,000kg) and cruising speed 528 mph (850km/hr). Tanks, guns and a variety of other vehicles and equipment can be loaded through rear doors. The Il-76 is in use with both the Soviet Air Force and Aeroflot, and has been exported. There are two versions, Candid -A and -B. An Airborne Warning and Control System (AWACS) version, with a large top-fuselage mounted radome, is NATO code-named Mainstay. *Country of origin:* USSR.

Power: 4 × TF39 turbofans *Span:* 222ft 8in (67.88m) *Length:* 247ft 10in (75.54m)

The world's second largest transport, the Galaxy can carry up to 345 troops on two decks, or 265,000lb (120,200kg) of freight for 2,950 miles (4,745km). First flown in 1968, the Galaxy went into service as the C-5A in 1970. The 77 aircraft in service form four squadrons in Military Airlift Command. Cruising at 537 mph (864km/hr), the Galaxy has a maximum-fuel range of 6,500 miles (10,460km). All Galaxies are being retrofitted with a new, stronger wing. The USAF has requested funds for 50 C-5Bs, an up-dated version which is externally similar. At the time of writing five C-5Bs had been ordered. *Country of origin:* USA.

 **BAe 146** *Confusion:* Starlifter, Candid

Power: 4 × ALF502 turbofans   *Span:* 86ft 5in (26.34m)   *Length* (Series 100): 85ft 10in (26.16m)

Unusual as a civil transport, combining four jets, high wing and T-tail, the BAe 146 is a short-field, short-haul feederliner first flown in September 1981. Two versions are in production: the Series 100 with 71/93 seats, and the Series 200 with length increased to 93ft 8in (28.55m) and seating 82/109. Mixed passenger/freight versions are on offer. The Series 200 cruises at 436 mph (702km/hr) over ranges of up to 1,704 miles (2,743km). The order book so far covers 36 firm plus 45 options. A stretched 120 seat version, the 146-300, is under development and is scheduled to fly in 1987. Two Series 100s have been ordered for the Queen's Flight. *Country of origin:* UK. *Main silhouette:* 146 Series 200; *side view:* 146 Series 100. *Picture:* Series 200.

Power: 4 × Kuznetsov turboprops   *Span:* 159ft (48.5m)   *Length:* 155ft 10in (47.5m)

Originally employed by the Soviet Air Force as a long-range strategic bomber (Bear-A and B), the Bear is now used for maritime and electronic warfare work by the Soviet Navy. The 530 mph (805km/hr) Bear is very unusual in having swept wings combined with turboprop engines driving contra-rotating propellers. Bear-C has a nose radome and rear-fuselage radomes, Bear-E has a smaller nose radome and under-fuselage cameras, and Bear-F has larger wing trailing-edge fairings. Standard armament is two 23mm cannon in the tail. Performance figures for Bear-A include a maximum level speed at 41,000ft (12,500m) of about 500 mph (805km/hr) and maximum range of 7,800 miles (12,555km). A new version of the aircraft, Bear-H, is now in production and will probably carry AS-15 cruise missiles. *Country of origin:* USSR. *Main silhouette:* **Bear-B**; *middle side view:* **Bear-C**; *lower side view and picture:* **Bear-D**.

Tupolev Tu-126 Moss   *Confusion:* Bear, Sentry

Power: 4 × Kuznetsov turboprops   *Span:* 168ft (51.2m)   *Length:* 188ft (57.3m)

Adapted from the Tu-114 Cleat airliner (which has the wings and tail of Bear), the Moss is an airborne early warning and control aircraft in the same operational class as the Sentry and Nimrod AEW. The Moss carries a massive radar scanner of 37.5ft (11.4m) diameter above the rear fuselage. The cabin operations room houses radar operators and control staff. The aircraft is equipped for in-flight refuelling. Moss is designed to work with advanced interceptors. Having located incoming low-level strike aircraft, Moss would pass their height and speed to fighters armed with "snap-down" missiles capable of being fired from a height of 20,000ft (6,100m) or more. It could also warn Soviet strike aircraft if they were about to come under attack. About 10 Tu-126s are in service with the Soviet Air Force. *Country of origin:* USSR.

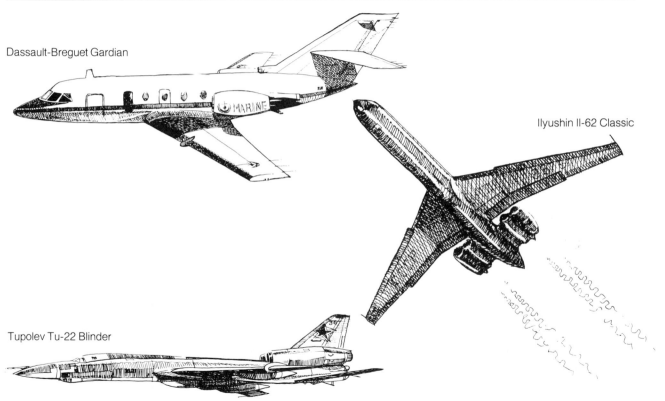

Dassault-Breguet Gardian

Ilyushin Il-62 Classic

Tupolev Tu-22 Blinder

Gulfstream Aerospace Gulfstream II/III/IV

Confusion: One-Eleven, Fellowship, Falcon

Power: 2 × Spey turbofans *Span:* 68ft 10in (20.98m) *Length:* 79ft 11in (24.36m)

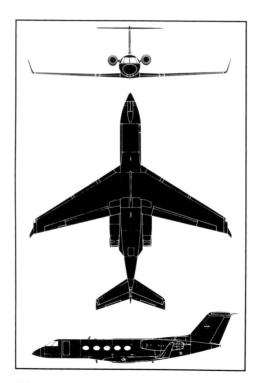

The Gulfstream II is one of the largest purpose-built executive transports, offering luxury accommodation for 19 passengers. The aircraft cruises at 495 mph (976km/hr) and range with maximum fuel is an impressive 4,275 miles (6,880km). The Gulfstream II first flew in 1966. Wingtip tanks can be fitted. More than 40 Gulfstream IIs are being converted to II-Bs, incorporating Gulfstream III wings. The first Gulfstream III with lengthened fuselage and Whitcomb winglets, first flew on December 2, 1979. The re-engineered, advanced Gulfstream IV, with Rolls-Royce Tay turbofans, is due to go into service at the end of 1986. This version has modified nacelles and one extra window per side. *Country of origin:* USA. *Silhouette:* Gulfstream III. *Picture:* Gulfstream II.

Power: 2 × TFE731 turbofans *Span:* 53ft 3in (16.3m) *Length:* 55ft 6in (16.9m)

The Citation III bears little resemblance to its straight-wing predecessors, described in the next section. With a high-aspect-ratio swept wing and T-tail, the Citation III is an executive transport seating six to thirteen passengers. Cruising speed is 436 mph (746km/hr) and range with six passengers is 2,858 miles (4,600km). The prototype Citation III first flew in May 1979 and production deliveries began in spring 1983. By early June 1984 41 Citations were in service. *Country of origin:* USA.

Aérospatiale Caravelle *Confusion:* One-Eleven, DC-9

Power: 2 × Avon or 2 × JT8D turbojets   *Span* (Caravelle 12): 112ft 6in (34.30m)   *Length:* 118ft 10in (36.24m)

Designed originally by Sud-Est, the Caravelle was the first pure-jet short-haul airliner to go into service. Caravelles I, IA, III, VI-N and VI-R had Rolls-Royce Avon engines while the Series 10R, 11R, Super B and 12 have the Pratt & Whitney JT8D. Early versions accommodated 64–80 passengers, while the Super B and Series 12 carry 104 and 139 respectively. Maximum cruising speed of the Caravelle 12 is 512 mph (825km/hr) and range is 2,150 miles (3,465km). The Caravelle is still in general use and a total of 279 were built, excluding prototypes. *Country of origin:* France. *Main silhouette:* Caravelle 11R; *top and bottom side views:* Caravelle 6R and 12 respectively. *Picture:* Caravelle 10B.

Power: 2 × Spey turbofans *Span* (Series 500): 93ft 6in (28.5m) *Length:* 107ft (32.61m)

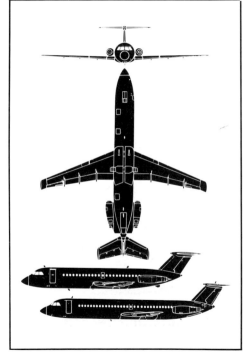

A successful short-haul transport, the One-Eleven first flew in 1963, remains in production, under licence, in Romania as the Rombac 1-11. Some 227 One-Elevens have been ordered and the type has been developed through the Series 200, 300, 400, 475 and 500. The short-fuselage versions carry up to 89 passengers, while the long-fuselage Series 500 can accommodate up to 119. Maximum cruising speed is 541 mph (871km/hr), and range up to 1,865 miles (3,000km). The Series 475 is intended for operations from very short airfields. *Country of origin:* UK. *Main silhouette:* Series 500; *upper side view:* 400. *Picture:* 500.

Fokker F28 Fellowship

Confusion: One-Eleven, Gulfstream II, Trident, Crusty

Power: 2 × Spey turbofans   *Span* (Mk 6000): 82ft 3in (25.07m)   *Length* (Mk 6000): 87ft 9in (26.76m)

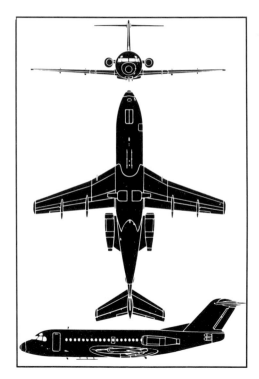

The Fellowship twin-engined short-haul transport first flew in 1967 and has sold steadily, with 217 ordered by April 1984 The different versions are: Mk 1000, short fuselage, up to 65 seats; Mk 2000, longer fuselage, 79 seats; Mk 3000, like 4000 but with short fuselage, 65 passengers; Mk 4000, long fuselage, 85 passengers; Mk 5000, wings of Mk 6000 with 65-seat cabin; Mk 6000, long-span wings and long fuselage with up to 85 seats. Fellowships have also been sold for cargo and VIP use. A distinctive feature of the F28 is the large twin-shell airbrake in the tail. Cruising speed is 416 mph (670km/hr). *Country of origin:* Netherlands. *Silhouette and picture:* Mk 4000.

Power: 2 × Tay turbofans   *Span:* 92ft 1½in (28.08m)   *Length:* 115ft 10in (35.31m)

Scheduled to fly in March 1986, the 100/110-seat Fokker 100 is a completely new design which will be a rival to the BAe 146. Short Brothers are responsible for wing development and MBB for large parts of the fuselage and tail. Swissair has ordered eight aircraft, together with six options. The type is to go into service in 1987. *Country of origin:* Holland. *Picture:* Model.

McDonnell Douglas DC-9

Confusion: Crusty, One-Eleven, Gulfstream II, Fellowship

Power: 2 × JT8D turbofans *Span* (Series 40): 93ft 5in (28.47m) *Length* (Series 40): 125ft 7in (38.28m)

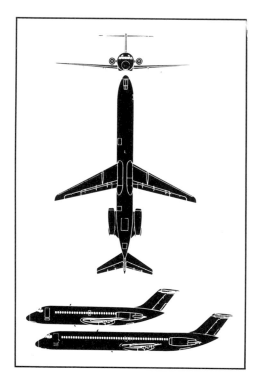

First flown in 1965, the DC-9 was steadily developed and stretched to meet a demand for more seats. Initially, as the DC-9 Series 10, the aircraft carried up to 90 passengers; the long-fuselage Series 30 then appeared, with extended wings and capacity for up to 119. Extended wings and short fuselage resulted in the Series 20, while further fuselage stretches produced the Series 40 (125 passengers) and Series 50 (139 passengers). Military variants are designated C-9A Nightingale and VC-9C by the USAF and C-9B Skytrain II by the USN. Around 1,000 DC-9s were ordered. The Series 40 cruises at 510 mph (821km/hr) and has a range of up to 1,070 miles (1,723km). *Country of origin:* USA. *Main silhouette:* DC-9-50; *upper side view:* DC-9-10. *Picture:* DC-9-30.

Power: 2 × JT8D turbofans   *Span:* 107ft 10in (32.85m)   *Length:* 147ft 10in (45.08m)

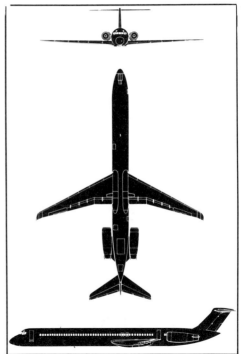

Formerly known as the DC-9 Super 80, the MD-80 is probably the ultimate in stretching. It is 43ft 5in (13.26m) longer than the original DC-9 Series 10, while passenger capacity has gone up from 90 to 172. Wing area is 28 per cent greater than that of the DC-9 Series 50 and tailplane area is enlarged. Three versions of the MD-80 family are in production, MD-81, MD-82 and MD-83, differing primarily in engines, weights and ranges. The MD-83 can carry 155 passengers more than 2,900 miles (4,670km) with a cruising speed of Mach 0.76. The type first flew in 1979 and by end June 1984 the company had received 453 orders and options for the MD-80 series. *Country of origin:* USA.

Tupolev Tu-22 Blinder

Confusion: Fiddler

Power: 2 × reheated turbojets   *Span:* 91ft (27.74m)   *Length:* 133ft (40.5m)

A most unusual military design, the Blinder bomber has two large turbojets mounted above the rear fuselage, a sharply swept wing, and main undercarriage housed in wing fairings. First flown around 1960, the Blinder is capable of Mach 1.5 at altitude. In basic form, as Blinder-A, the type was used as a reconnaissance bomber, while the B carried a Kitchen missile under the fuselage. The maritime reconnaissance Blinder-C is also equipped with a variety of electronic intelligence equipment. A trainer version, Blinder-D, has an additional raised cockpit. A flight refuelling probe is carried in the nose. *Country of origin:* USSR. *Silhouette:* Blinder-C. *Picture:* Blinder-B.

Power: 2 × Soloviev turbofans   *Span* (Tu-134): 95ft 2in (29m)   *Length:* 112ft 8in (34.35m)

Designed as a successor to the Tu-124 Cookpot, the Tu-134, NATO code-named Crusty, followed the contemporary Western trend of rear-mounted turbofans and T-tails. The Tu-124-type main undercarriage, housed in wing fairings, was retained. First flown in 1962, the 72-seat type went into service with Aeroflot in 1967. A stretched version, the 80-seat Tu-134A, entered service in 1970. Some Tu-134As have the glazed nose replaced with a streamlined radome. The Tu-134 has a maximum cruising speed of 540 mph (870km/hr) and a range of 1,490 miles (2,400km). Internal modification schemes are available which convert aircraft to B, B-1 and B-3 standard. Over 200 Tu-134/134As have been built and a number are in use with Warsaw Pact airlines. *Country of origin:* USSR. *Silhouette and picture:* Tu-134A.

Tupolev Tu-154 Careless

Confusion: Trident, 727, DC-9, One-Eleven

Power: 3 × Kuznetsov turbofans   *Span:* 123ft 2in (37.55m)   *Length:* 157ft 2in (47.9m)

The Tu-154, code-named Careless, was designed as the Soviet counterpart to the Boeing 727 and the Trident, but with the added ability to operate from short, rough runways. The trijet, T-tail Careless retains the characteristic Tupolev main undercarriage housed in wing fairings. First flown in 1968, the Careless entered service with Aeroflot in 1972 and has been exported to other Eastern European countries and to Egypt. The latest version is the Tu-154B-2 with improved avionics and seating for 154–180 passengers. Over 350 Tu-154s have been produced. Cruising speed is 560 mph (900km/hr). *Country of origin:* USSR.

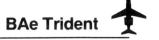
Power: 3 × Spey turbofans   *Span* (2E/3B): 98ft (29.87m)   *Length* (3B): 131ft 2in (39.98m)

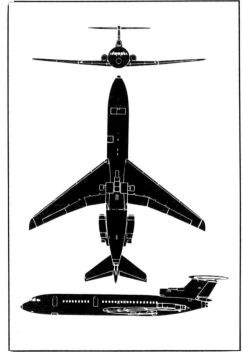

The Trident was built for the then British European Airways in the early 1960s. The original 1 and 1E versions were followed by the 2E with more range, and the 3B with a longer fuselage. The 3B carries up to 180 passengers compared with 132 on the 2E. The Trident, of which a total of 117 were sold, pioneered the use of Autoland for all-weather operations. China bought a large fleet of Trident 2Es and 3Bs. The Trident can cruise at up to 600 mph (965km/hr), and the 2E has a range of 2,464 miles (3,965km). *Country of origin:* UK. *Silhouette:* 2E. *Picture:* 3B.

Boeing 727 *Confusion:* Trident, Careless, DC-9, One-Eleven

Power: 3 × JT8D turbofans   *Span* (-200): 108ft (32.92m)   *Length* (-200): 153ft 2in (46.69m)

The most widely sold of all Western jet airliners, 1,831 Boeing 727s were built before the type went out of production in August 1984. The only rear-engined aircraft in the Boeing family, the 727 first flew in 1963. The 727-100 seats up to 131 passengers and can be converted to carry cargo. The stretched -200, seating up to 189 passengers, became available in the mid-1960s. This was followed by the Advanced 727-200 with greater all-up weight and more fuel and range. The -200 has range of 2,645 miles (4,260km) and an economical cruising speed of 570 mph (917km/hr). *Country of origin:* USA. *Main silhouette:* -200; *upper side view:* -100. *Picture:* -200.

Power: 4 × Conway turbofans   *Span:* 146ft 2in (44.55m)   *Length* (Super VC10): 171ft 8in (52.32m)

The VC10 was designed to meet a British Overseas Airways Corporation requirement for a long-range airliner with good hot-and-high airfield performance. The type has proved very robust and reliable in service. The VC10 first flew in 1962, followed by the larger, longer-fuselage Super VC10 in 1964. The Super VC10 has a maximum range of 7,128 miles (11,470km) and cruises at 550 mph (886km/hr). The VC10 is used by the RAF as a standard passenger/freight transport and a batch has been converted as three-point in-flight refuelling tankers with more to follow. As a tanker, the VC10 is known as the VC10K Mk 2 and the Super VC10 as the VC10K Mk 3. A total of 54 VC10/Super VC10s were built. *Country of origin:* UK. *Main silhouette:* K Mark 2; *upper side view:* VC10. *Picture:* VC10 C1.

Ilyushin Il-62 Classic

Confusion: VC10/Super VC10

Power: 4 × Kuznetsov or 4 × Soloviev turbofans   *Span:* 141ft 9in (43.2m)   *Length:* 174ft 3in (53.12m)

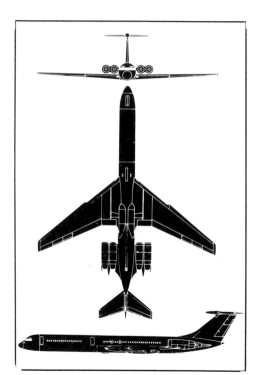

The Soviet Union's first commercial four-engined long-range jet transport, the Il-62, code-named Classic, first flew in 1963 and went into service with Aeroflot in 1967. Classic and the VC10 are the only rear-engined four-jet airliners to be built. Classic normally seats 186 passengers. The basic aircraft is powered by Kuznetsov engines, while the Il-62M, introduced in 1974, has Soloviev turbofans. The Il-62M has more power, more fuel and better payload range figures. The aircraft cruises at up to 560 mph (900km/hr) and in Il-62M form has a maximum range of 6,400 miles (10,300km). A high-density variant, the Il-62M-MK, can seat up to 195 passengers. Range with maximum payload 50,700lb (23,000kg) and reserves is 4,960 miles (8,000km). *Country of origin:* USSR. *Silhouette and picture:* Il-62M.

Power: 3 × Lotarev turbofans   *Span:* 114ft 6in (34.90m)   *Length:* 119ft 4in (36.38m)

Following on from the straight-wing Yak-40 Codling, the Yakovlev bureau designed the larger swept-wing Yak-42, code-named Clobber, which first flew in 1975 and went into service with Aeroflot in 1980. The Clobber is replacing the Tu-134 Crusty and it is expected that up to 2,000 of the type may ultimately be built. The cabin seats up to 120 passengers and the range of the aircraft is 1,243 miles (2,000km), cruising at 466 mph (750km/hr). Clobber is being offered for export in straight passenger form and as a combined passenger/cargo aircraft. A stretched 140 seat version has been built. *Country of origin:* USSR.

BAe 125 *Confusion:* Falcon, Corvette

Power: 2 × Viper turbojets or 2 × TFE731 turbofans   *Span:* 47ft (14.33m)   *Length* (Series 700): 50ft 8in (15.46m)

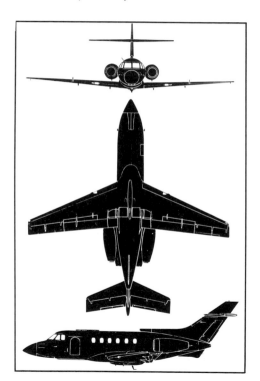

Some 573 BAe 125 twinjet business aircraft had been sold worldwide before the Series 800, detailed overleaf, was introduced. Main versions were the Series 400, 600 and 700. The 600 has a longer fuselage than earlier variants and seats up to 14 passengers. All 125s up to and including the Series 600 are powered by Rolls-Royce Viper engines. Thereafter, the company introduced the Series 700, with Garrett AiResearch turbofans and a longer, more pointed nose. The 125-700 cruises at 464 mph (747km/hr) and has a range of 2,683 miles (4,318km). The Viper-powered 125s used in the RAF are called the Dominie T1 as trainers and CC1 and CC2 as communications aircraft. *Country of origin:* UK. *Silhouette:* Series 700. *Picture:* Dominic TI.

Power: 2 × TFE 731 turbofans   *Span:* 51ft 4in (15.66m)   *Length:* 51ft 2in (15.6m)

Successor to the 600 and 700 Series 125s, the Series 800 has a redesigned wing, changed fin shape, curved windscreen and the prominent rear underkeel of the earlier versions is deleted. Range, with maximum payload, has been increased to 3,305 miles (5,318km). By June 1985, 32 Series 800s had been sold. *Country of origin:* UK.

Sabreliner

Confusion: BAe 125, Falcon, Corvette

Power: 2 × JT12A turbojets or 2 × CF700 or TFE731 turbofans   *Span* (Series 65): 50ft 5in (15.37m)   *Length* (Series 65): 46ft 11in (14.30m)

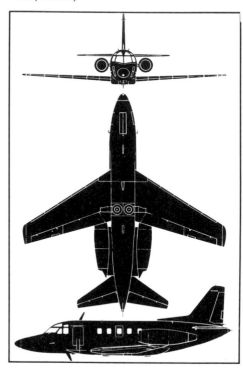

Originally supplied in quantity to the USAF and US Navy as the T-39 and CT-39, the Rockwell Sabreliner was developed into the Series 40 and 60 executive transports. The former carries nine passengers and the latter ten in a lengthened fuselage, both powered by JT12A engines. The 75A is powered by CF700 turbofans and has various refinements, including a wider-span tailplane. Over 600 Sabreliners have been delivered including the Sabreliner 65, with TFE731 engines and a redesigned wing. Eight passengers can be carried. In 1983 the Sabreliner Corp. took over the Sabreliner Division of Rockwell International to provide support for aircraft in service and to provide modifications. *Country of origin:* USA. *Silhouette:* Series 75A. *Picture:* Series 65.

Power: 2 × JT15D turbofans   *Span:* 43ft 5in (13.23m)   *Length:* 48ft 4in (14.73m)

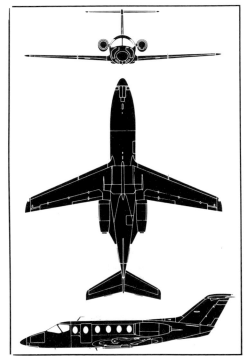

Made in component form in Japan, the Diamond twin-engined executive aircraft is assembled and flown at Mitsubishi Aircraft Internatinal Inc at San Angelo, Texas. First flown in August 1978, the Diamond 1 began to be delivered in January 1982. The aircraft seats 6–8 passengers, cruises at 466 mph (750km/hr) and has a maximum range of 1,484 miles (2,389km). From aircraft number 66, production switched to the Diamond 1A with higher rated engines and improved performance. *Country of origin:* Japan/USA. *Picture:* Diamond 1A.

Dassault-Breguet Mystère-Falcon 10/100

Confusion: Falcon 20, BAe 125, Corvette

Power: 2 × TFE731 turbofans   *Span:* 42ft 11in (13.08m)   *Length:* 45ft 5in (13.85m)

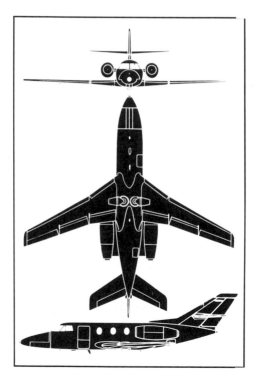

Essentially a scaled-down version of the Mystère-Falcon 20, the Mystère-Falcon 10 executive aircraft first flew in December 1970 and deliveries began in 1973. The 10 was replaced on this production line by the 100 with increased take-off weight and a fourth cabin wndow on the starboard side. The French Navy uses seven 10s as Mystère-Falcon 10 MER for fighter intercept training. Several hundred of the two types have been ordered. Typical weight of the 100 with four passengers, two pilots, and maximum fuel, is 18,255lb (8,280kg). Fast cruise is 492kts (912km/hr) and range 1,880nm (3,480km). *Country of origin:* France. *Silhouette:* Mystère-Falcon 10. *Picture:* Mystère Falcon 100.

Dassault-Breguet Mystère-Falcon 20/200

Power: 2 × CF700 turbofans or 2 × ATF3-6 turbofans   *Span:* 53ft 6in (16.30m)   *Length:* 56ft 3in (17.15m)

Dassault and Aérospatiale combined to build the successful Mystère 20/Falcon 20 8/10-seat executive aircraft. First flown in 1963, the aircraft is also used as an air force transport, freighter and trainer. Several hundred have been built and the type is in use in many places round the world. Main versions are the 20F and 200, the latter having Garrett AiResearch ATF3-6 engines in place of GE CF700s. The Mystère-Falcon 200 maritime surveillance aircraft is known in the French Navy as the Gardian and in the US Coast Guard as the HU-25A Guardian. This variant has large side windows for observation. Latest version, for a variety of military purposes, is the Gardian 200. *Country of origin:* France. *Silhouette:* 20F. *Scrap side section:* 200. *Picture:* HU-25A.

Dassault-Breguet Falcon 50

Confusion: Clobber, Falcon 10, Falcon 20

Power: 3 × TFE731 turbofans   *Span:* 61ft 10in (18.86m)   *Length:* 60ft 8in (18.5m)

Seeking more range for executive and other duties, Dassault designed a three-engined development of the Falcon series with new wings but retaining the front and centre-fuselage sections of the Falcon 200. The resulting Falcon 50 seats 8–9 passengers and has a large fuselage fuel tank. Initial deliveries were made in 1979, following a first flight in 1976. Maximum cruising speed is 540 mph (870km/hr) and range with four passengers is 3,450 miles (5,560km). The order book totals over 130. *Country of origin:* France.

Dassault-Breguet Mystère-Falcon 900

Power: 3 × TFE-731 turbofans   *Span:* 63ft 5in (19.33m)   *Length:* 30ft (119m)

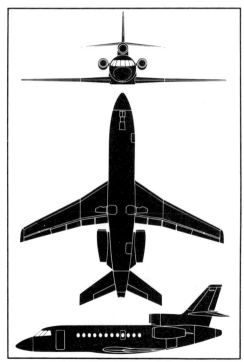

First flown in September 1984, the Mystère-Falcon 900 is an intercontinental tri-jet executive transport seating 19 passengers. Similar in layout to the Mystère-Falcon 50, the 900 has increased dimensions and a larger fuselage. Range, cruising at Mach 0.75, with maximum fuel and eight passengers, is 4,370m (7,035km). Production Mystère-Falcon 900s will commence delivery in mid-1986. *Country of origin:* France.

147

Aérospatiale SN 601 Corvette *Confusion:* BAe 125, Learjet, Falcon 10, Falcon 20

Power: 2 × JT15D turbofans   *Span:* 42ft 2in (12.87m)   *Length:* 45ft 4in (13.83m)

Produced only in small numbers, the Corvette is a 6/14-passenger executive/air taxi/freighter aircraft first flown as the SN 600 in the summer of 1970. Maximum cruising speed is 472 mph (760km/hr) and range 967 miles (1,555km). Fuel tanks are fitted to the wingtips. A crew of two is carried. Production was terminated after completion of the 40th example. Performance figures include an economical cruising speed of 352 mph (566km/hr) at 39,000ft (11,900m); maximum rate of climb at sea level of 2,700ft/min (823m/min); and service ceiling of 41,000ft (12,500m). *Country of origin:* France.

Confusion: BAe 125, Falcon 10, Falcon 20, Corvette, Challenger **Lockheed JetStar**

Power: 4 × JT12 or 4 × TFE731 turbofans   *Span:* 54ft 5in (16.16m)   *Length:* 60ft 5in (18.42m)

Derived from the original twin-Orpheus JetStar I, the JetStar II is powered by four TFE731 turbofans. The JetStar II seats up to ten and cruises at 508 mph (817km/hr). Differences from earlier versions include a new engine nacelle shape, shortened long-range tanks on the wings, and the addition of a small air intake in the base of the fin. Production is complete. *Country of origin:* USA. *Silhouette and picture:* JetStar II.

149

Canadair Challenger

Confusion: BAe 125, Falcon 10, Falcon 20, Corvette

Power: 2 × ALF502 or 2 × CF34 turbofans   *Span:* 61ft 10in (18.83m)   *Length:* 68ft 5in (20.82m)

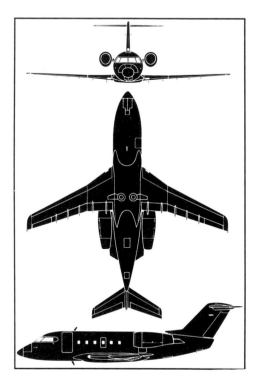

Designed for use as an executive jet, commuter airliner and express cargo aircraft, the Canadair CL-600 Challenger (later re-designated Challenger 600) first flew in August 1978. It has a roomy cabin seating up to 28 passengers and has a cruising speed of 463 mph (745km/hr). A later version is the CL-601. The next version is the Challenger 601 with GE CF34 engines. More recently a winglet modification programme was introduced for the Challenger 600/601. By early 1984 some 107 Challengers had been ordered. *Country of origin:* Canada. *Silhouette:* Challenger 600. *Picture:* Challenger 601.

Power: 2 × CJ610 turbojets   *Span:* **47ft 6in (14.49m)**   *Length:* **54ft 6in (16.61m)**

Remarkable in having forward-swept wings, the HFB 320 Hansa business jet and light transport first flew in 1964. In executive form the Hansa carries 7/9 passengers and two crew, while up to 12 passengers can be accommodated in a high-density layout. Fifty Hansas were built, including eight for the German Air Force. Production of the type is complete. The Hansa cruises at 513 mph (825km/hr) and has a range of 1,472 miles (2,370km). Maximum payload of the passenger version is 3,913lb (1,775kg). Maximum rate of climb at sea level and an all-up weight of 16,530lb (7,500kg) is 4,250ft/min (1,295m/min). *Country of origin:* West Germany.

Jet, straight wing, rear engines

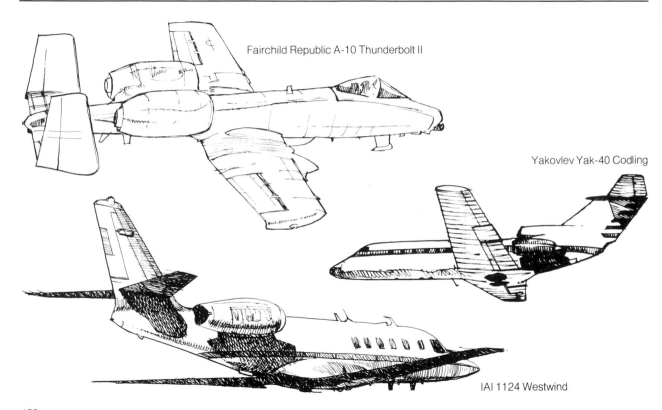

Fairchild Republic A-10 Thunderbolt II

Yakovlev Yak-40 Codling

IAI 1124 Westwind

Power: 2 × JT15D turbofans *Span* (Citation I): 47ft 1in (14.35m) *Length* (Citation II): 47ft 2in (14.39m)

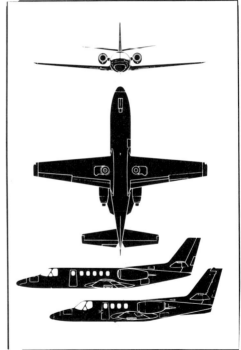

Initially known as the Fanjet 500, the Cessna Citation seven/eight-seat twin-turbofan executive transport first flew in 1969. The original production version, the Citation 500, was superseded by the Citation I with longer-span wings and uprated turbofans. The Citation II has increased span, a longer fuselage and accommodation for up to 10 passengers. Citation II cruises at 420 mph (675km/hr) and has a range of 1,986 miles (3,167km). Over 480 Citations have been built. *Country of origin:* USA. *Main silhouette:* Citation 500; *upper side view:* Citation II. *Picture:* Citation I.

153

Cessna Citation S/11

Confusion: Citation 1/11

Power: 2 × JT15D turbofans   *Span:* 52ft 2in (15.9m)   *Length:* 47ft 2in (14.39m)

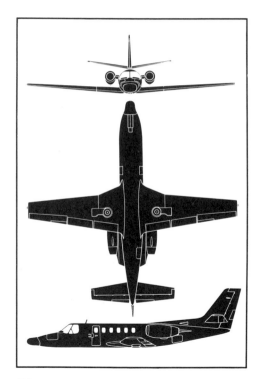

The Citation 11 was replaced on the production line in 1984 by the S/11 version having a revised wing with extended inboard leading edges and modified engine cowlings. The full production S/11 flew in February 1984. Cruising speed is 463 mph (746km/hr). The US Navy has ordered 15 Citation S/11s as trainers under the designation T-47A; these have shorter, 46ft 6in (14.18m) span wings. *Country of origin:* USA.

Power: 2 × Viper turbojets   *Span:* 37ft 6in (11.43m)   *Length:* 42ft 2in (12.85m)

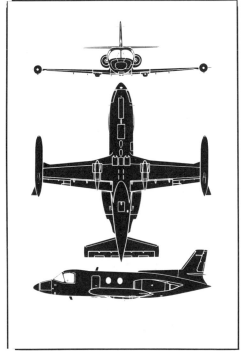

A light jet utility/executive aircraft, the PD-808 was first flown in 1964 and ordered by the Italian Defence Ministry. A maximum of ten passengers can be seated in the cabin, cruising speed is 449 mph (722km/hr) and range is 1,270 miles (2,045km). The Italian Air Force uses the PD-808 as a transport, VIP aircraft, navigation trainer and ECM aircraft. All versions carry one or two flight crew; the VIP transport carries six passengers and the electronic countermeasures version is operated by two pilots and three equipment specialists. The designation PD recalls the two companies which launched the project, Piaggio and Douglas. *Country of origin:* Italy.

Gates Learjet 23/24/25

Confusion: Learjet 35/36

Power: 2 × CJ610 turbojets   *Span:* 35ft 7in (10.84m)   *Length* (25D): 47ft 7in (14.5m)

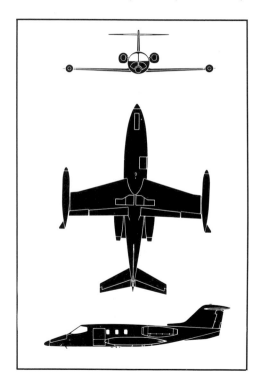

Flown for the first time in 1963, the Gates Learjet series of executive transports has been steadily developed and built in large numbers. With six seats and two crew, the Learjet 24 cruises at 481 mph (774km/hr). The tailplane/fin bullet of earlier versions was deleted from the Model 24. The Learjet 25 is 4ft 2in (1.27m) longer and seats two extra passengers. The latest version is the 25D. A belly camera installation has been fitted to some aircraft. *Country of origin:* USA. *Silhouette:* Learjet 24D. *Picture:* Learjet 24.

Power: 2 × TFE731 turbofans   *Span:* 39ft 6in (12m)   *Length:* 48ft 8in (14.82m)

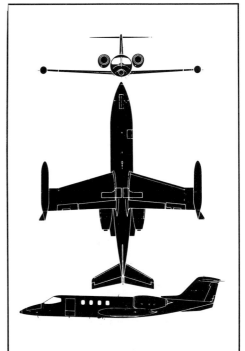

A new series of enlarged Learjet executive aircraft was introduced in 1973. Both wingspan and length have been increased, there are five starboard windows instead of four, and the engine nacelles are more bulbous. The wingtips have short rectangular extensions on which the fuel tanks are mounted. Like the Learjet 25, the 35/36 seats eight passengers. Currently in production are the 35A and six-seat, longer-range 36A. A variety of military and paramilitary versions are offered and 80 aircraft are in service with the USAF, designated C-21A. *Country of origin:* USA. *Silhouette:* Learjet 35. *Picture:* Learjet 35A (with towed target underneath).

Gates Learjet 28/55

Confusion: Learjet 35/36, Citation

Power: 2 × TFE731 turbofans   *Span* (55): 43ft 9in (13.35m)   *Length* (55): 47ft 8in (14.53m)

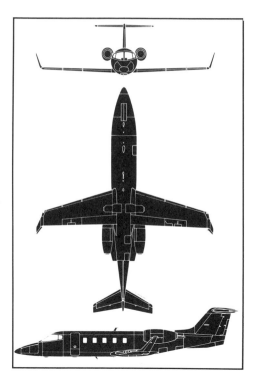

The Gates Learjet 28 Longhorn, an improved version of the Learjet 25, has a redesigned wing with vertical winglets at the tips. The 29 Longhorn is externally similar but with increased fuel capacity. Gates Learjet has now married a new wide-body ten-passenger fuselage to the wing of the 28/29 to produce the 55 Longhorn. The first 55 Longhorn flew in April 1979 and the first production aircraft in August 1980. Deliveries began in April 1981 and by June 1984, 100 had been delivered. The 55 has an economical cruising speed of 462 mph (763km/hr) and a maximum range with four passengers of 2,665 miles (4,290km). Extended range versions are the 55ER and LR. *Country of origin:* USA. *Silhouette:* 55 Longhorn. *Picture:* 28 Longhorn.

Power: 2 × TFE731 turbofans　*Span:* 44ft 9½in (13.65m)　*Length:* 52ft 3in (15.93m)

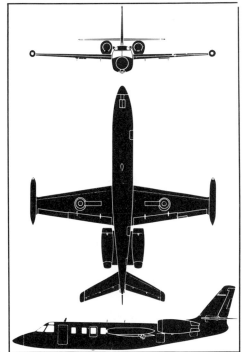

Originally powered by two CJ610 turbojets and known as the IAI 1123, the current production Westwind executive aircraft (1124) has two Garrett-AiResearch turbofans. Produced by Israel Aircraft Industries, the Westwind carries two pilots and up to ten passengers. Economical cruising speed is 460 mph (741km/hr), and with seven passengers range is over 2,785 miles (4,490km). A naval tactical support and coastguard version is available, designated 1124 Sea Scan. A longer-range development is the Westwind II with improved wing and winglets on the tip tanks. Over 195 Westwinds of all types have been sold. *Country of origin:* Israel. *Silhouette:* IAI 1124. *Picture:* Westwind II.

Yakovlev Yak-40 Codling

Confusion: Citation

Power: 3 × Ivchenko turbofans   *Span:* 82ft (25m)   *Length:* 66ft 9in (20.36m)

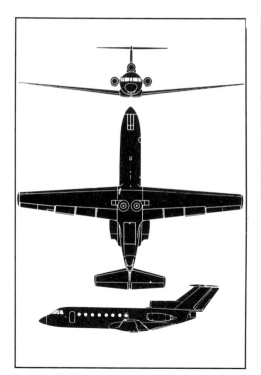

Around 900 examples of the Yak-40, code-named Codling, have been built and the type is the most widely used aircraft on Soviet internal short-haul services. First flown in 1966, Codling went into service with Aeroflot in 1968 and since then many have been exported. Seating up to 32 passengers, Codling cruises at 292 mph (470km/hr) and has a maximum range of 1,240 miles (2,000km). A cargo version with a large door on the port side has been built. Most of the 900+ Yak-40s built so far are in service with Aeroflot, some as air ambulances. Examples have been delivered to Italy, and others are in service in Afghanistan, Bulgaria, Czechoslovakia, France, West Germany, Poland and Yugoslavia. Military users include the Soviet and Polish air forces. *Country of origin:* USSR.

Fairchild Republic T-46A

Power: 2 × Garrett turbofans   *Span:* 38ft 8in (11.78m)   *Length:* 29ft 6in (8.99m)

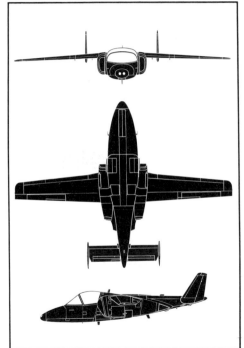

In July 1982, Fairchild Republic was selected by the US Air Force to build its next generation trainer, the T-46A, to replace the 30 year old Cessna T-37. Scheduled to make its first flight in spring 1985, the T-46A has side-by-side seating and the unusual feature of twin fins and rudders. It is expected that some 700 T-46As will be built for the USAF, while a multi-mission version, with four underwing pylons, is being offered as the AT-46A. The T-46A has a take-off weight of 6,817lb (3,092kg) and a maximum speed of 440 mph (708km/hr). *Country of origin:* USA. *Silhouette:* T-46A. *Picture:* AT-46A (mock-up).

Fairchild Republic A-10 Thunderbolt II   *Confusion:* Citation

Power: 2 × TF34 turbofans   *Span:* 57ft 6in (17.53m)   *Length:* 53ft 4in (16.26m)

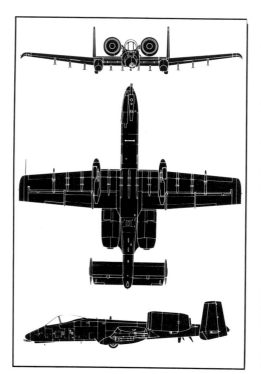

An entirely new type of battlefield close-support aircraft, the single-seat A-10A Thunderbolt II is heavily armoured and carries massive armament for ground attack. With a combat speed of 443 mph (712km/hr) and a radius of action of 620 miles (1,000km), the Thunderbolt can carry 12,000lb (5,450kg) of weapons externally. In addition to bombs, rockets and guided missiles, the Thunderbolt II has a seven-barrel 30mm gun mounted in the nose. A total of 825 Thunderbolts are being built and the type is in service in the USA and Europe. A combat-readiness trainer version is designated A-10B. *Country of origin:* USA. *Silhouette and picture:* A-10A.

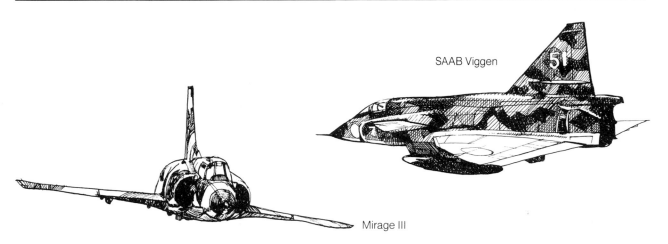

SAAB Viggen

Mirage III

Sukhoi Su-15 Flagon

General Dynamics/Convair F-106 Delta Dart

Confusion: Mirage III, Kfir, Mirage 2000, Draken

Power: 2 × J75 reheated turbojets   *Span:* 38ft 3in (11.67m)   *Length:* 70ft 9in (21.55m)

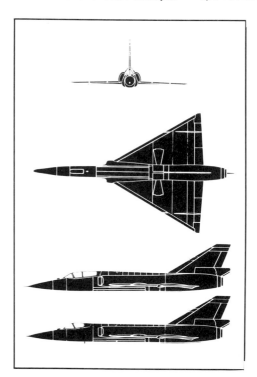

The F-106A Delta Dart was developed from the earlier F-102 delta-wing fighter. First flown in 1956, the Delta Dart had a very impressive performance for its day, with a maximum speed of over Mach 2 and a combat radius of 600 miles (966km). The Delta Dart continues in US service and frequent updating of the nav-attack system and weapons has kept it up to standard. Armament consists of one internal multi-barrel 20mm Gatling gun and external Genie and Falcon air-to-air missiles. Auxiliary fuel tanks can be carried under the wings. *Country of origin:* USA. *Silhouette:* F-106A; The two-seat version of the Delta Dart (upper side view) is designated F-106B. *Picture:* F-106A.

Power: 1 × Atar reheated turbojet   *Span:* 27ft (8.22m)   *Length* (IIIE): 49ft 3in (15.03m)

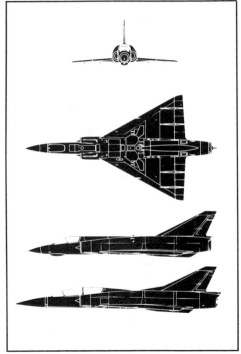

One of the most successful single-seat fighter/ground-attack aircraft produced in Europe, the Mirage III has been sold to many countries. First flown in 1956, it has been built in several versions: IIIC interceptor, IIIE ground attack, IIIB and IIID two-seat trainers and IIIR reconnaissance aircraft. Basic armament consists of two 30mm cannon in the fuselage. Bombs, rockets, guided missiles and long-range tanks can be carried on centreline and underwing pylons. The aircraft is capable of Mach 2.2 and radius of action for ground attack is 745 miles (1,200km). *Country of origin:* France. *Main silhouette:* Mirage IIIE; *lower side view:* Mirage IIID. *Picture:* Mirage IIIS.

Dassault-Breguet Mirage 5/50

Confusion: Mirage III, Mirage 2000, Kfir

Power: 1 × Atar 9C turbojet   *Span:* 27ft (8.22m)   *Length:* 51ft (15.55m)

The ground-attack version of the Mirage III is designated Mirage 5. Over 1,400 III/5s have been ordered. The Mirage 5 has simplified avionics and a longer nose than the Mirage III. The prototype was first flown in May 1967. Armament combinations include cannon, bombs and missiles. Maximum speed of the Mirage 5 is 1,460 mph (2,350km/hr) at 40,000ft (12,000m). Service ceiling is 55,775ft (17,000m). Mirage 5 designations indicate the customer country: 5SDE (*Arabie SaouDitE*—Saudi Arabia) and 5AD (Abu Dhabi), for example. The two-seat trainer has the letter "D" after the country designation. A new development is the Mirage 50 with up-rated Atar 9K50 engine and new electronics systems. The latest variant on offer is the Mirage 3NG with canard surfaces just aft of the intakes, advanced radar and fly-by-wire controls. *Country of origin:* France. *Silhouette:* Mirage 5. *Picture:* Mirage 50.

Power: 1 × M53 reheated turbofan   *Span:* 29ft 6in (9m)   *Length:* 50ft 3in (15.33m)

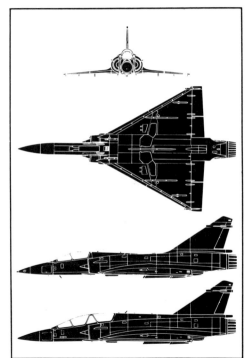

Although bearing a superficial resemblance to the Mirage III/5, the Mirage 2000 is a completely new aircraft which provides the French Air Force with a very advanced Mach 2+ interception capability. The controls are electrically signalled ("fly-by-wire"), with computer control. In its primary role the single-seat Mirage 2000 will carry Super Matra 530 and R550 Magic air-to-air missiles and external fuel tanks. A variety of weapons can be carried for ground attack, including rocket projectiles, bombs and laser-guided weapons. A two seat "Penetration" version known as Mirage 2000N, with a stand-off nuclear missile, has also been ordered by the FAF. *Country of origin:* France. *Main silhouette:* Mirage 2000; *lower side view:* Mirage 2000N. *Picture:* Mirage 2000.

Dassault-Breguet Mirage IVA/IVP

Confusion: Mirage III/5, Mirage 2000, Kfir

Power: 2 × Atar reheated turbojets   *Span:* 38ft 10in (11.85m)   *Length:* 77ft (23.5m)

The Mirage IVA was designed in the 1950s as France's nuclear deterrent bomber. Its shape owes much to the Mirage III but it is much larger. Seating two in tandem, the Mirage IVA first flew in 1959 and 62 had been completed when production ended in March 1968. In late 1984 there were 43 Mirage IVAs still in use. Of these, 18 are to be retained after 1986, modified as the Mirage IVP. The IVP will carry the ASMP tactical nuclear stand-off missile in place of the free-fall nuclear bomb currently recessed in the fuselage underside. *Country of origin:* France. *Silhouette and picture:* Mirage IVA.

Power: 1 × J79 reheated turbojet   *Span:* 27ft (8.22m)   *Length:* 53ft 8in (16.35m)

An extensively redesigned Mirage 5 built in Israel and powered by a General Electric J79 engine, the Kfir first went into service with the Israeli Air Force in 1975 as the Kfir-CI. A modified version, the C2, has additional small winglets, or canards, just behind the air intakes and an extended wing leading edge. A dual-role interceptor and ground-attack aircraft, the Kfir has two fuselage-mounted 30mm cannon and seven hard points for air-to-air and air-to-ground missiles, bombs or drop tanks. The Kfir has a top speed of over 1,450 mph (2,335km/hr). A two-seat trainer derivative is designated Kfir-TC2. Latest production version is the Kfir-C7 with improved performance. *Country of origin:* Israel. *Main silhouette:* Kfir-C2; *lower side view:* Kfir-TC2. *Picture:* Kfir-C2.

Saab Viggen

Confusion: Kfir

Power: 1 × RM8A reheated turbofan   *Span:* 34ft 9in (10.6m)   *Length* (including probe): 53ft 6in (16.3m)

A high-performance Mach 2 multi-role aircraft, the Saab Viggen entered service with the Swedish Air Force in 1971. The Viggen is unusual in having a double-delta layout with the tailplane forward of the wing. The various versions are as follows: AJ37 all-weather attack; JA37 interceptor; SF37 reconnaissance; SH37 maritime reconnaissance; and SK37 two-seat operational trainer with raised rear cockpit. A wide variety of weapons can be carried on three underfuselage and four underwing pylons. The Viggen can operate from unprepared strips and roads. *Country of origin:* Sweden. *Silhouette:* JA37. *Picture:* AJ37.

Aérospatiale/BAe Concorde

Power: 4 × Olympus 593 reheated turbojets   *Span:* 83ft 10in (25.56m)   *Length:* 202ft 4in (61.66m)

The world's only fully operational supersonic airliner, the Anglo-French Concorde can carry 128 passengers at a speed of Mach 2 for 3,915 miles (6,300km). It first went into service with British Airways and Air France in 1976. Eighteen Concordes were built, of which 14 entered service. The external layout is unusual: the engines are boxed under the wing in two pairs, while the wing is ogive-shaped in planform and steeply cambered at the leading edge. Concorde's service ceiling is 60,000ft (18,300m), higher than that of any other airliner in service. Concorde commercial services were inaugurated on January 21, 1976, when the fifth and sixth production aircraft (Air France F-BVFA and British Airways G-BOAA) flew Paris-Dakar-Rio de Janeiro and London-Bahrain respectively. *Countries of origin:* France/UK.

Saab Draken

Confusion: F-106

Power: 1 × RM6 reheated turbojet   *Span:* 30ft 10in (9.4m)   *Length:* 50ft 4in (15.4m)

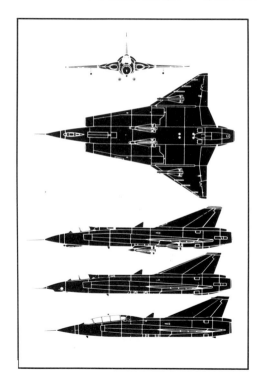

With its unusual double-delta wing and Mach 2 performance, the Saab Draken fighter first flew in 1955. It remained in production until 1976 and is in service with Sweden, Denmark and Finland. Apart from its high performance, the Draken can operate from small airfields. Various versions have been produced, including the J35A, B, D and F, plus the SK35C two-seat trainer and S35E reconnaissance aircraft. *Country of origin:* Sweden. *Main silhouette:* J35F; *middle side view:* S35E; *bottom side view:* SK35C. *Picture:* J35F.

Confusion: F-16

McDonnell Douglas A-4 Skyhawk

Power: 1 × J65 or J52 turbojet   *Span:* 27ft 6in (8.38m)   *Length:* 40ft 3in (12.27m)

Designed as a carrierborne attack aircraft, the A-4 Skyhawk was nicknamed the "Bantam Bomber". Although small, it can carry a very heavy weapon load (in later versions over 9,000lb) plus two cannon. Variants have gone from A-4A through to -4S. The two-seat trainer is designated TA-4. All versions from the F model onwards carry a dorsal hump containing avionics equipment, while the -4M was the first sub-type to be known as Skyhawk II. The Skyhawk has a top speed of 670 mph (1,078km/hr) and a range of 920 miles (1,480km). Over 3,000 were built and production has been completed. *Country of origin:* USA. *Main silhouette:* A-4M; *middle side view:* A-4E; *bottom side view:* TA-4F. *Picture:* A-4M.

General Dynamics F-16 Fighting Falcon   *Confusion:* Skyhawk

Power: 1 × F100 reheated turbojet   *Span:* 31ft (9.45m)   *Length:* 47ft 8in (14.52m)

Highly manoeuvrable and capable of speeds in excess of Mach 2, the F-16 fighter is being built in the USA and in NATO countries and is in service with many air forces. Over 1,250 F-16s have been built. A particular feature is the "shark's mouth" intake. A multi-barrel 20mm cannon is mounted in the fuselage, together with weapons or tanks on four underwing pylons and air-to-air missiles on the wingtips. The production single-seater is known as the F-16A while the tandem two-seat trainer is designated F-16B. A larger tailplane was fitted from late 1981, and the F-16C and D with up-dated systems are in production. *Country of origin:* USA. *Silhouette and picture:* F-16A.

Power: 2 × AL-21F reheated turbojets   *Span* (Flagon-A): 30ft (9.15m)   *Length* (including probe): 68ft (20.25m)

A Mach 2.5 twin-engined all-weather fighter, the Su-15, code-named Flagon, is used in large numbers by the Soviet Air Force. In its early form, Flagon-A, the aircraft had the same wing shape as the Fishpot. The latest variants, Flagon-D, E and F, have wing leading edges with distinctive compound sweep. The Flagon has a massive nose-mounted radome and large air-to-air missiles are carried on the outboard sections of the wing. Like Fishpot, Flagon can carry twin auxiliary tanks under the fuselage. The two-seat version is known as Flagon-C. Flagon-F is distinguished from the D and E by its ogival, not conical, radome. Flagon can carry a belly gun pack. *Country of origin:* USSR. *Main silhouette:* Flagon-F; *lower side view:* Flagon-C. *Picture:* Flagon-F.

Sukhoi Su-9/Su-11 Fishpot   *Confusion:* Flagon, Fishbed

Power: 1 × AL-7F reheated turbojet   *Span:* 27ft 8in (8.43m)   *Length* (including probe): 56ft (17m)

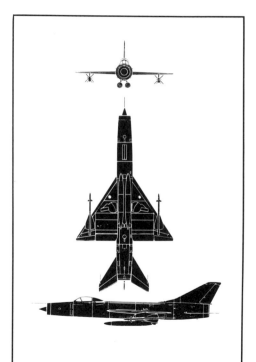

The Soviet Air Force's first all-weather fighter, Fishpot went into service in 1959 as the Su-9 Fishpot-B with a small radome in the air intake. In the second half of the 1960s an improved version (Su-11 Fishpot-C) reached the squadrons; this has a bigger intake with a larger central radome. Twin auxiliary fuel tanks can be carried under the fuselage and air-to-air missiles under the wings. The tandem two-seat trainer version is known as Maiden. *Country of origin:* USSR. *Silhouette:* Fishpot-C. *Picture:* Fishpot-B.

Power: 1 × R-13 reheated turbojet   *Span:* 23ft 5in (7.15m)   *Length* (including probe): 51ft 8in (15.76m)

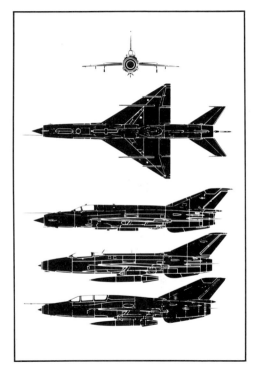

The MiG-21 Fishbed fighter is one of the world's most widely used combat aircraft, serving with 28 air forces. Fishbed has been produced in a variety of versions, including the original with a small nose radome (Fishbed-C), all-weather variant with enlarged nose radome (Fishbed-D), main production standard with wider-chord fin (Fishbed-F), deeper dorsal fairing (Fishbed-J), reconnaissance version with pod (Fishbed-H), and latest variants with enlarged dorsal fairing (Fishbed-K, L and N). The two-seater trainer is known as Mongol. Fishbed can fly at over Mach 2 and carries a gun and guided missiles. *Country of origin:* USSR. *Main silhouette:* Fishbed-J; *middle side view:* Fishbed-C; *lowest side view:* Mongol. *Picture:* Fishbed-J.

Lockheed SR-71 *Confusion:* —

Power: 2 × JT11D reheated turbojets   *Span:* 55ft 7in (16.95m)   *Length:* 107ft 5in (32.74m)

The layout of the SR-71A high-altitude strategic reconnaissance aircraft is unique, with the engines mounted on the delta wing and twin canted fins on the engine nacelles. Carrying a crew of two in tandem, the aircraft can fly at up to Mach 3 and has an operational ceiling of over 80,000 (24,384m). A variety of cameras and electronic sensors are carried. Trainer versions are designated SR-71B and -71C. First aircraft in the series was the Falcon missile-armed YF-12A interceptor, which was cancelled when it was decided not to go ahead with the American advanced bomber-defence programme. Three YF-12As and about 30 SR-17s were built. *Country of origin:* USA. *Silhouette:* SR-71A. *Picture:* SR-71B.

Tu-22M/Tu-26 Backfire

Tornado F2

MiG-23 Flogger

Panavia Tornado IDS

Confusion: Tornado ADV, Flogger, F-111, Fencer

Power: 2 × RB.199 reheated turbofans   *Span* (wings fully spread): 45ft 7in (13.9m)   *Length:* 54ft 9in (16.7m)

In full scale service, the two-seat Tornado IDS (Interdictor Strike) forms the offensive backbone of the RAF, the West German Air Force and Navy and the Italian Air Force. Total production of the IDS version is scheduled to reach 644, and in the RAF the type is designated Tornado GR1. Capable of twice the speed of sound at altitude, the IDS can fly at up to 920 mph (1,480km/hr) at low level. *Country of origin:* Germany/Italy/UK.

Power: 2 × RB.199 reheated turbofans   *Span* (wings fully spread): 45ft 7in (13.9m)   *Length:* 59ft 3in (18.06m)

Developed by British Aerospace for the RAF, the Tornado ADV (Air Defence Variant) will become the RAF's standard all-weather fighter in the second half of the 1980s. With a longer fuselage and a new airborne interception radar, the Tornado ADV carries a single 27mm cannon and four Sky Flash air-to-air missiles under the fuselage. Two Sidewinder missiles and long-range fuel tanks can be carried under the wings. A Mach 2 aircraft with long endurance, the Tornado ADV is known in the RAF as the F2, and 165 are to be built. Like the Tornado IDS, the ADV is equipped for in-flight refuelling. *Country of origin:* Germany/Italy/UK.

Grumman F-14 Tomcat   *Confusion:* F-111, Fencer, Tornado

Power: 2 × TF30 or F110 reheated turbofans   *Span* (**wings fully spread**): 64ft 1in (19.55m)   *Length:* 62ft (18.9m)

The United States Navy's counterpart to the USAF F-15, the two-seat F-14A Tomcat is an all-weather carrierborne interceptor. With its powerful fire-control system, Tomcat can engage several targets simultaneously with Phoenix, Sparrow or Sidewinder air-to-air missiles. Tomcat is unusual in having twin fins and variable-geometry wings. Performance includes speeds of just over Mach 1 at sea level and Mach 2+ at high altitude. A new version of the Tomcat with General Electric F110 engines is designated F-14D. *Country of origin:* USA.

Power: 2 × TF30 reheated turbofans   *Span* (wings fully spread): 63ft (19.2m)   *Length:* 73ft 6in (22.4m)

This all-weather two-seat strike/attack aircraft, used by the USAF in Europe and America, carries heavy underwing armament and is capable of over Mach 2 at altitude. Versions are the F-111A (141 built), F-111E (94 built), F-111F (82 built) and FB-111A (77 built). All versions have generally similar outlines. Principal performance figures include maximum speeds of 1,650 mph (2,655km/hr) at 49,000ft (15,000m) and 915 mph (1,472km/hr) at sea level; ceiling of 60,000ft (18,300m); and maximum weapon loads of 24 × 1,000lb or 50 × 750lb bombs. *Country of origin:* USA. *Main silhouette:* FB-111A; *upper side view:* F-111E. *Picture:* EF-111A.

Mikoyan MiG-23S Flogger-B/E/G

Confusion: Flogger-D, Tornado, Fencer, F-111

Power: 1 × Tumansky reheated turbofan   *Span* (wings fully spread): 46ft 9in (14.25m)   *Length:* 55ft 1in (16.8m)

A standard Soviet interceptor, this Mach 2+ type is in widespread use in Eastern Europe and has been exported to the Middle East, Far East, Africa and Cuba. It carries cannon and missile armament. A two-seat variant is known as the Flogger-C, and Flogger-G is an improved interceptor. The Flogger-E export variant is generally similar to the Soviet Air Force version but is equipped to a lower standard. It is fitted with a smaller radar (NATO code-named Blue Jay) in a shorter nose radome, and lacks the undernose laser rangefinder and Doppler navigation equipment of Flogger-B. *Country of origin:* USSR. *Silhouette and picture:* Flogger-B.

Mikoyan MiG-27 Flogger-D

Power: 1 × Tumansky reheated turbofan   *Span* (wings fully spread): 46ft 9in (14.25m)   *Length:* 54ft (16.46m)

A tactical strike development of Flogger-B, the Flogger-D is one of the major types facing the West in Europe. It differs from Flogger-B in having fixed air intakes and tailpipe nozzle, and a laser rangefinder nose. There are five external racks for missiles and bombs. Compared with the MiG-23 Flogger-B, the MiG-27 has a completely redesigned forward fuselage. The ogival radome is replaced with a sharply tapered nose. A Gatling-type gun replaces the interceptor's twin-barrelled weapon. Flogger-F is an export version of the MiG-23 with outline as for MiG-27 Flogger-D, while Flogger-H is similar but with the addition of avionics pods forward of the nosewheel doors. MiG-27 Flogger-J has a lipped top to the nose and a nose under-blister- Some -Js have wing root extensions. *Country of origin:* USSR. *Silhouette and picture:* Flogger-D.

185

 **Sukhoi Su-17 Fitter-C** *Confusion:* Fitter-A, Fitter-B

Power: 1 × Lyulka or 1 × Tumansky reheated turbojet   *Span* (wings fully spread): 45ft (13.7m)   *Length:* 61ft 6in (18.75m)

The single-seat Fitter-C tactical strike fighter is unusual in being a variable-geometry development of a fixed-wing aircraft. Compared with Fitter-A, the outer wings pivot, the engine is more powerful, and armament and fuel have been increased. Export versions are designated Su-20 and Su-22. Certain other Fitters, such as the -J, have a changed fin and bulged rear fuselage associated with the fitting of a Tumansky engine. Operators include the Warsaw Pact countries and Peru. *Country of origin:* USSR. *Silhouette:* Fitter-C. *Picture:* Fitter-J

Power: 2 × Tumansky reheated turbofans   *Span* (wings fully spread): 56ft 6in (17.25m)   *Length:* 69ft 6in (20m)

One of the most advanced types in the Soviet inventory, the Sukhoi Su-24, code-named Fencer, is a low-level supersonic attack aircraft in the same class as is the American F-111. Some 500 two-seat Fencers are in service, with production continuing at a high rate. Armament comprises two 30mm cannon in the lower fuselage and nuclear/conventional bombs, rocket projectiles, or missiles on eight wing and fuselage pylons. With wings fully swept to 70°, maximum speed at altitude is in excess of Mach 2. Three versions -A, -B and -C have been identified, with minor external variations. *Country of origin:* USSR. *Silhouette:* Fencer-C.

Rockwell International B-1B   *Confusion:* Backfire

Power: 4 × F101 reheated turbofans   *Span* (wings fully spread): 136ft 8in (41.66m)   *Length:* 146ft 8in (44.7m)

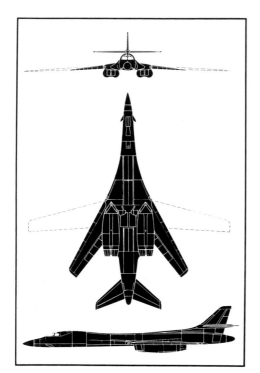

First flown in 1974, the B-1 supersonic long-range bomber was to have been the subject of large orders for the US Air Force. These were cancelled by the Carter administration and only four prototypes were completed. President Reagan revived the project and a new programme for 100 B-1Bs was announced in 1981. Externally similar to the B-1, the B-1B carries a crew of four and is armed with Air Launched Cruise Missiles (ALCMs) and Short Range Attack Missiles (SRAMs). The B-1B can operate low down at supersonic speeds or can achieve speeds of up to Mach 2 at altitude. Maximum range is 6,100 miles (9,820km). *Country of origin:* USA.

Tupolev Tu-22M/Tu-26 Backfire

Power: 2 × Kuznetsov reheated turbofans   *Span* (wings fully spread): 115ft (35m)   *Length:* 138ft (42m)

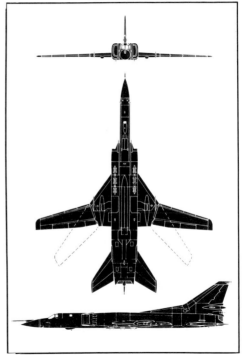

The Soviet strategic bomber force will consist largely of Backfires by the mid-1980s. Carrying either nuclear or conventional weapons, Backfire can fly for 3,400 miles (5,470km) and is capable of supersonic speeds at all altitudes. Three versions exist: the preliminary Backfire-A, the definitive B, and Backfire-C with wedge type intakes. Production of Backfire is running at a rate of about 30 a year, and over 260 are in service. A new swing-wing bomber, 25 per cent larger than Backfire, is under development. It is NATO-code-named Blackjack. *Country of origin:* USSR. *Silhouette and picture:* Backfire-B.

Jet, straight wing, fuselage/wing engine(s)

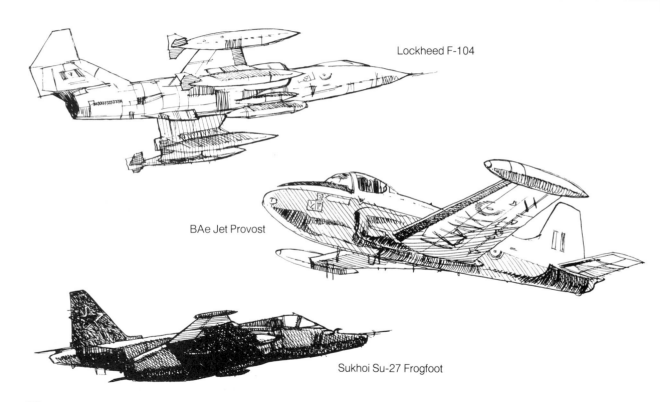

Lockheed F-104

BAe Jet Provost

Sukhoi Su-27 Frogfoot

Power: 1 × J85 turbojet   *Span:* 38ft 6in (11.13m)   *Length:* 32ft (9.75m)

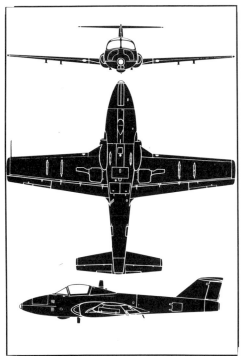

Originally developed as a private venture, the Canadair CL-41 Tutor side-by-side two-seat trainer was adopted by the Royal Canadian Air Force. Production was completed in 1966 after 190 had been built. Twenty CL-41Gs with fuselage pylons were built for Malaysia, in which service the type is known as the Tebuan. Basic armament comprises bombs, rockets and gun pods on wing hardpoints. Maximum speed is 480 mph (774km/hr). *Country of origin:* Canada. *Silhouette and picture:* CL-41G.

Morane-Saulnier MS.760 Paris   *Confusion:* Delfin, Tutor

Power: 2 × Marboré turbojets   *Span:* 33ft 3in (10.15m)   *Length:* 33ft (10.05m)

A four-seat high-speed civil and military communications aircraft, the MS.760 Paris first flew in July 1954. Some 165 Paris Mks I and II were built. The Paris II has higher-powered engines and more fuel capacity. A prototype of the Paris III, with six seats and extended wingtips, was built. The Paris I has a maximum speed of 405 mph (650km/hr) and a range of 930 miles (1,500km). For weapon training the Paris II can carry 7.5mm machine guns and guns and bombs or rockets. The Paris remains in service in France and Argentina. *Country of origin:* France. *Silhouette and picture:* Paris I.

Power: 1 × M-701 turbojet   *Span:* 33ft 9in (10.29m)   *Length:* 35ft 5½in (10.81m)

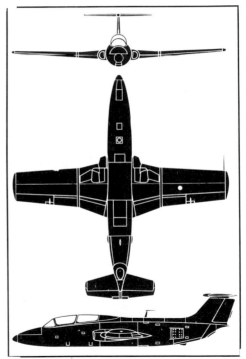

Designed as a Communist-bloc basic trainer, the L-29 Delfin, NATO code-named Maya, first entered service in 1963. The air forces of Czechoslovakia, the Soviet Union, East Germany, Bulgaria, Romania and Hungary use the Delfin, and other countries outside the Warsaw Pact have been supplied with the type. Two underwing pods can carry bombs, rockets, drop tanks or 7.62mm guns. An aerobatic version of the Delfin with a single seat is designated the L-29A Akrobat. *Country of origin:* Czechoslovakia. *Silhouette and picture:* L-29.

RFB Fantrainer
Confusion: Delfin, CL-41

Power: 1 × Allison 250 turboshaft   *Span:* 31ft 10in (9.7m)   *Length:* 30ft 3in (9.25m)

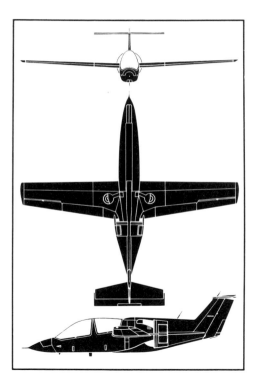

Although not strictly a 'jet', the Fantrainer looks exactly like one in the air, albeit without a rear jetpipe. A unique two-seat basic trainer, the Fantrainer has a turboshaft engine driving a ducted fan in the fuselage just aft of the wings. First flown in 1978, the aircraft is now on offer in two forms, the model 400 with a 420hp engine and the 600 with a 650hp unit. The Royal Thai Air Force has ordered 47 Fantrainers and two are being leased to Lufthansa. Take-off weight of the model 400 is 3,968lb (1,799.7kg) and maximum speed 230 mph (370km/hr). *Country of origin:* West Germany. *Picture:* Fantrainer model 600.

Power: 2 × J85 turbojets   *Span:* 33ft 9in (10.3m)   *Length:* 29ft 3in (8.93m)

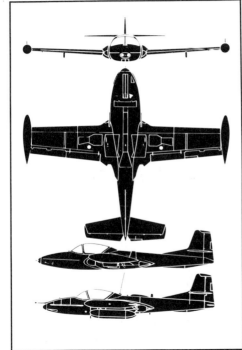

The standard USAF basic trainer (T-37B), the Dragonfly originally flew with Continental T69 engines. Many Dragonflies are in service with a number of air forces as trainers, with underwing pylons (T-37C) and with a Minigun in the fuselage and four weapon stations on the wings (A-37). A large number of Dragonflies have been built. Maximum speed is 507 mph (816km/hr) and range with weapon load is 460 miles (740km). *Country of origin:* USA. *Main silhouette:* T-37A; *lower side view:* A-37C. *Picture:* A-37B.

Lockheed T-33A Shooting Star   *Confusion:* Galeb

Power: 1 × J33 or 1 × Nene turbojet   *Span:* 38ft 10½in (11.85m)   *Length:* 37ft 9in (11.48m)

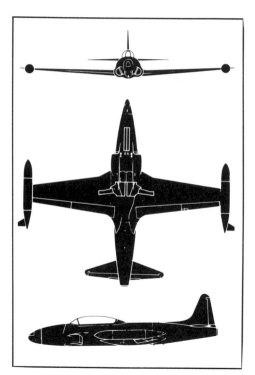

Trainer version of the US Air Force's first operational jet fighter, the T-33A (originally TF-80C) first flew as far back as 1948. A total of 6,600 T-33s were built and the type is still in service in some numbers. Some Shooting Stars were built with noses modified for reconnaissance. Several air forces still operate T-33s, some of them licence-built. Maximum speed is 600 mph (960km/hr) and endurance 3.12hr. *Country of origin:* USA

Power: 1 × SO-1 turbojet *Span:* 59ft 8in (18.18m) *Length:* 41ft 9in (12.74m)

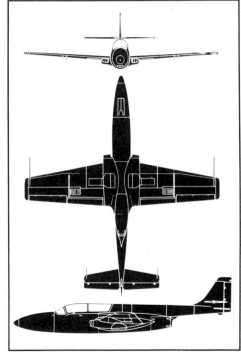

The Polish Air Force took delivery of its first TS-11 Iskra tandem two-seat aerobatic trainer in 1963. The layout is unusual, with the engine exhausting under the fuselage and the tail assembly being carried by a long boom. Forward-firing machine guns are housed in the fuselage, and weapons can be carried on four underwing pylons. Several hundred Iskras have been built. Main performance figures include a maximum level speed at 16,400ft (5,000m) of 447 mph (720km/hr); maximum rate of climb at sea level of 2,913ft/min (888m/min); service ceiling of 36,000ft (11,000m); and range with maximum fuel of 907 miles (1,460km). The Iskra is operated by Poland and India. *Country of origin:* Poland.

SOKO G-2 Galeb/Jastreb   *Confusion:* Iskra, Delfin

Power: 1 × Viper turbojet   *Span:* 34ft 4in (10.47m)   *Length:* 33ft 11in (10.34m)

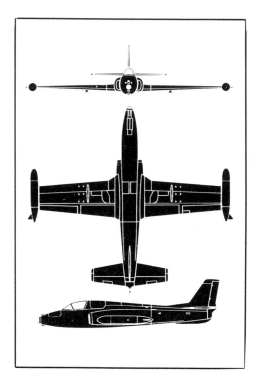

The first Yugoslav jet to enter production, the G-2 Galeb was first flown in 1961 and is now the standard Yugoslav Air Force basic trainer. Also in service is the TJ-1 Jastreb single-seat ground-attack version. This is equipped with three nose machine guns and eight underwing pylons for weapons, compared with the Galeb's two machine guns and smaller weapon load. Maximum speed is 470 mph (756km/hr) and maximum endurance 2hr 30min. *Country of origin:* Yugoslavia. *Silhouette and picture:* Jastreb.

Power: 1 × Viper turbojet   *Span:* 35ft 11in (10.7m)   *Length:* 34ft 9in (10.6m)

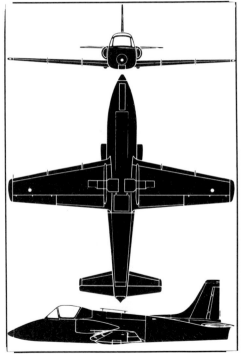

Designed to replace the Vampire trainers licence-built in India, the HJT-16 Kiran basic trainer was first flown in 1964. The aircraft bears a superficial resemblance to the Jet Provost/Strikemaster but is in fact totally of Indian design. The crew of two are seated side-by-side. A weapon-carrying variant is the Mk IA. A development of the Kiran I is the Orpheus-powered Mk II, intended for counter-insurgency work and weapons training. Two fuselage machine guns and four underwing pylons are fitted. Maximum speed of the Kiran I is 432 mph (659km/hr). *Country of origin:* India. *Silhouette:* Kiran I. *Picture:* Kiran II.

BAe Strikemaster   *Confusion:* Kiran, MB.326

Power: 1 × Viper turbojet   *Span:* 35ft 4in (10.77m)   *Length:* 33ft 8in (10.27m)

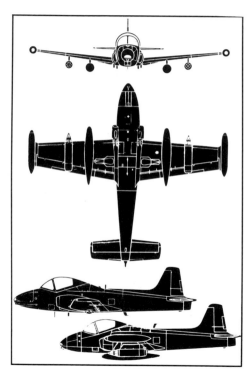

A two-seat basic trainer/light strike aircraft, the Strikemaster was developed from the Jet Provost, which was the RAF's first jet trainer. The Strikemaster has improved performance, more power and increased weapon load compared with the Jet Provost. The Jet Provost first flew in 1954 and the Strikemaster in 1967. The Strikemaster has a top speed of 472 mph (760km/hr) and a weapon load of 3,000lb (1,360kg) plus two fuselage-mounted machine guns. The Strikemaster has been widely exported. *Country of origin:* UK. *Main silhouette:* Strikemaster; *upper side view:* Jet Provost. *Picture:* Strikemaster.

Power: 1 × Viper turbojet   *Span:* 35ft 7in (10.85m)   *Length:* 34ft 11in (10.64m)

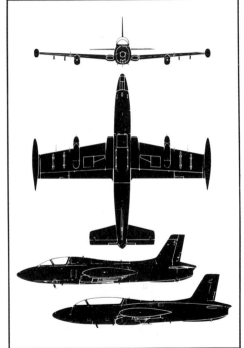

The MB.326 is a highly successful two-seat basic/advanced trainer and single-seat trainer/light attack aircraft (326K). Several hundred 326s of various versions have been built, and licence production has been undertaken in Australia and South Africa; in the latter country the type is called the Impala. Up to 4,000lb (1,815kg) of armament can be carried on underwing pylons, including rockets, bombs, AS.12 missiles and gun pods. A reconnaissance pack can be fitted. Maximum speed is 426 mph (686km/hr). *Country of origin:* Italy. *Main silhouette:* MB.326; *upper side view:* MB.326K. *Picture:* MB.326K.

Aermacchi MB.339A

Confusion: Hawk, MB.326

Power: 1 × Viper turbojet   *Span:* 35ft 8in (10.86m)   *Length:* 36ft (10.97m)

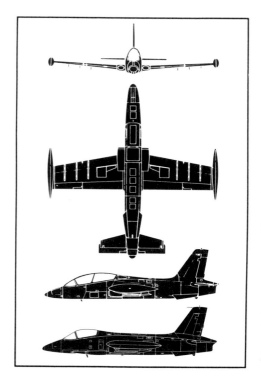

Based on and bearing a close resemblance to its predecessor, the MB.326, the two-seat MB.339A basic/advanced trainer has a redesigned forward fuselage. Auxiliary fuel tanks are carried at the wingtips and there are six underwing hardpoints for up to 4,000lb (1,815kg) of bombs and rocket projectiles. Cameras or an armament pod can be carried under the forward fuselage. The prototype was flown in 1976 and the type has been produced for several air forces and navies. A single-seat tactical support variant is known as the MB.339K Veltro 2. Maximum speed is 558 mph (898km/hr). *Country of origin:* Italy. *Main silhouette:* MB.339A; *lower side view:* MB.339K Veltro 2. *Picture:* MB.339A.

Power: 1 × TFE731 turbofan   *Span:* 34ft 9in (10.6m)   *Length:* 40ft 11in (12.5m)

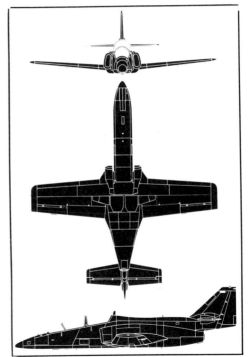

A two-seat basic/advanced jet trainer and light ground-attack aircraft, the C-101EB Aviojet went into service with the Spanish Air Force in 1980. In its armed export version the C-101BB can carry two machine guns or a cannon under the fuselage and there are six wing positions for external stores such as bombs, rockets, guided missiles or ECM pods. In pure light attack form the aircraft is designated C-101CC. Maximum speed is 482 mph (775km/hr) and range 1,865 miles (3,000km). *Country of origin:* Spain.

AIDC AT-3 *Confusion:* Aviojet

Power: 2 × TFE 731 turbofans   *Span:* 34ft 4in (10.46m)   *Length* overall: 42ft 4in (12.9m)

A two-seat basic and advanced trainer attack aircraft built by Aero Industry Development Center in Taiwan, the AT-3 first flew in September 1980. Over 50 production AT-3s have been ordered for the Chinese Nationalist Air Force. The AT-3 has a maximum speed of 558 mph (898km/hr) and an endurance of 3hr 12min. A weapons bay is situated under the rear cockpit, which can accommodate various stores including machine gun packs. There is one external stores station under the fuselage and two under each wing. *Country of origin:* Taiwan.

Power: 1 × TFE 731 turbofan *Span:* 31ft 9in (9.69m) *Length:* 35ft 10in (10.93m)

Sixty-four IA 63 two-seat tandem basic/advanced jet trainers have been ordered for the Argentine Air Force to replace the MS 760 Paris III. First flown in October 1984, the IA 63 is expected in operational service in 1986. The West German firm of Dornier provided major technical assistance in the development phase and the IA 63 bears a close resemblance to a straight-wing Dassault-Breguet/Dornier Alpha Jet. Top speed of the IA 63 at sea level is 460 mph (740km/hr), maximum rate of climb 5,315ft (1,620m/min) and service ceiling 42,325ft (12,900m). *Country of origin:* Argentina.

 **Aero L-39 Albatross** *Confusion:* Galeb, Delfin

Power: 1 × Walter Titan turbofan   *Span:* 29ft 11in (9.11m)   *Length:* 39ft 9in (12.11m)

Successor to the L-29 Delfin, the tandem two-seat Albatross advanced trainer has engine intakes repositioned in the upper fuselage sides behind the cockpit. A single-seat light ground-attack/reconnaissance version, the L-39ZA, has four underwing pylons and a 23mm cannon in a pod mounted on the belly below the cockpit. The L-39V is the basic Albatross equipped with a target-towing winch for anti-aircraft artillery practice. The Albatross has a top speed of 379 mph (610km/hr). Deliveries began in 1973 and production (including exports) has already totalled over 1,500 units. The L-39 was selected as the standard jet trainer of all the Warsaw Pact countries with the exception of Poland, and first entered service with the Czechoslovak Air Force in the spring of 1974. *Country of origin:* Czechoslovakia. *Silhouette and picture:* L-39.

Power: 2 × J85 reheated turbojets   *Span:* 25ft 3in (7.7m)   *Length:* 46ft 4½in (14.13m)

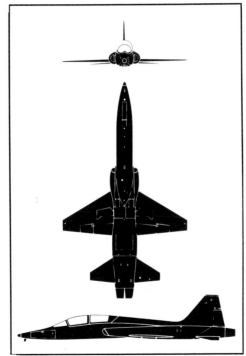

Very similar in outline to the Northrop F-5, the two-seat T-38A Talon was in fact a separate development with a different structure. The Talon was the first supersonic advanced trainer to be put into production, entering service with the USAF in 1961. A total of 1,187 Talons were built before production finished in 1972. The Talon has a maximum range of 1,093 miles (1,759km). *Country of origin:* USA.

Northrop F-5 *Confusion:* Talon, Starfighter, Hornet, Tigershark

Power: 2 × J85 reheated turbojets   *Span:* 26ft 8in (8.13m)   *Length:* 48ft 2in (14.68m)

The most successful lightweight jet combat aircraft ever built, the Northrop F-5 flew for the first time in 1959. It is used for interception, ground attack and reconnaissance. The F-5A is a single-seater with four wing pylons and two 20mm nose guns, the RF-5A is the reconnaissance variant and F-5B is a two-seater trainer. The F-5E Tiger II air-superiority fighter has increased power, improved nav-attack system and a modified wing with leading-edge root extensions. Tiger II has a maximum speed of 1,076 mph (1,732km/hr) and a range of 1,974 miles (3,175km). The reconnaissance version of Tiger II is designated RF-5E Tiger Eye (with extended nose) and the two-seat version F-5F. *Country of origin:* USA. *Main silhouette:* F-5A; *first upper view:* F-5B; *second upper view:* F-5E; *top side view:* RF-5E. *Picture:* CF-5A.

Northrop F-20 Tigershark

Power: 1 × **F404-GE** reheated turbofan   *Span* (over missiles): **28ft (8.53m)**   *Length:* **46ft 6in (14.19m)**

Latest in Northrop's series of lightweight fighters is the F-20 Tigershark (previously known as F-5G), evolved from the Tiger II. In place of the two turbojets of earlier variants the F-20 has a single turbofan. Performance, including acceleration and top speed, is much improved. The F-20 prototype, with systems similar to those of the F-5E, flew in August 1982. The second aircraft, which flew in August 1983, had digital avionics and an enlarged canopy. First orders for the type were awaited when this volume went to press. *Country of origin:* USA.

Lockheed F-104 Starfighter   *Confusion:* F-5, Hornet, Tigershark

Power: 1 × J79 reheated turbojet   *Span:* 21ft 11in (6.68m)   *Length:* 54ft 9in (16.69m)

A single-seat all-weather tactical strike and reconnaissance fighter, the Lockheed F-104 Starfighter first flew in 1954 and has since been built in very large numbers. Unlike its swept-wing contemporaries, the Starfighter was designed with a very thin, straight wing. Air-to-air missiles or auxiliary fuel tanks can be carried on the wingtips, while a variety of missiles, bombs or fuel tanks can be accommodated on four underwing pylons. Standard fuselage-mounted armament is a 20mm rotary cannon. Top speed at altitude is 1,320 mph (2,124km/hr) or Mach 2. Main service variant is the multi-role F-104G. The F-104S, licence-built in Italy, carries two Sparrow medium-range air-to-air missiles. The tandem two-seat trainer version, shown in the upper side view, is designated TF-104G. *Country of origin:* USA. *Main silhouette:* F-104S. *Picture:* F-104G.

McDonnell Douglas/Northrop F/A-18A Hornet

Power: 2 × F404 reheated turbofans   *Span:* 37ft 6in (11.43m)   *Length:* 56ft (17.07m)

Based on a Northrop private-venture design, the F-18 Hornet is a single-seat carrierborne air-superiority fighter with Mach 1.8 performance and high manoeuvrability. McDonnell Douglas is the prime contractor for the Navy and Marine Corps versions F/A-18A fighter, A-18 attack aircraft and TF/A-18A two-seat trainer, while Northrop is a co-producer. In fighter form the Hornet carries a six-barrel 20mm cannon plus air-to-air missiles and other stores on nine wing positions, including the wingtips. The Canadian version is known as CF-18 and that for Spain, EF-18. The first Hornet unit became operational in 1983. *Country of origin:* USA. *Silhouette and picture:* F/A-18A.

Sukhoi Su-25 Frogfoot *Confusion:* Citation, Magister

Power: 2 × turbofans *Span:* 50ft 10in (15.5m) *Length:* 47ft 6in (14.5m)

The Soviet counterpart to the American A-10 Thunderbolt, the Su-25 Frogfoot is a large shoulder-wing, single-seat, twin-engined ground attack aircraft. It has been in action in Afghanistan for more than two years. The type is also in service with the Czech Air Force. Top speed is about 546 mph (880km/hr), radius of action 345 miles (556km) and up to 400kg of bombs can be carried on eight underwing pylons. A single cannon is carried under the fuselage. *Country of origin:* USSR.

Aérospatiale Magister

Power: 2 × Marboré turbojets   *Span:* 37ft 5in (11.4m)   *Length:* 33ft (10.06m)

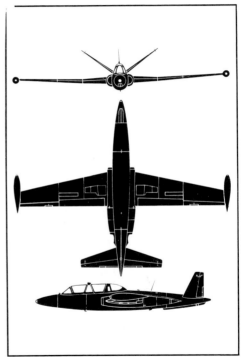

Nearly 1,000 CM.170 Magister two-seat basic trainers were built before production ceased. First flown in 1951, the Magister has a distinctive layout, with high-aspect-ratio wings and V-tail. The CM.170-2 is known as the Super Magister. Top speed is 403 mph (700km/hr) and endurance 2hr 40min. Two machine guns are mounted in the nose, and rockets, bombs or missiles can be carried under the wings. The Magister has been used as a light ground attack aircraft, serving with the Israeli Air Force in the Middle East. A navalised version known as the Zephyr was produced for shipboard carrier familiarisation duties by the French Navy. *Country of origin:* France. *Silhouette and picture:* Magister.

Lear Fan Model 2100 *Confusion: —*

Power: 2 × PT6B turboshafts   *Span:* 39ft 4in (12m)   *Length:* 40ft 7in (12.4m)

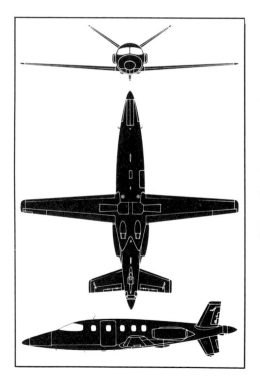

Radical in both design and construction, the Lear Fan 2100 is a six-passenger V-tail aircraft primarily made of composite materials and powered by two turboshaft engines linked to drive a single propeller at the rear. It has been included in this section as, in the air, it looks exactly like a small rear-engined jet aircraft. Originating in Reno in the USA, the 2100 was also scheduled to be built in Northern Ireland. The 2100 has a maximum speed of 425 mph (684km/hr) and a range of 1,752 miles (3,200km). First flight of the prototype was in January 1981 At the time of writing the project had been stopped and was in need of funds. *Country of origin:* USA.

Power: 2 × J60 or J85 turbojets   *Span:* 38ft 11in (11.62m)   *Length:* 38ft 3in (11.67m)

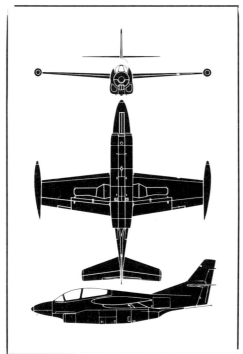

A shipborne basic trainer/attack aircraft, the T-2 Buckeye first flew, as the T2J-1 (T-2A) with one J34 engine, in 1958. The T-2B has two J60 engines and the T-2C and D two J85s. The wing was based on that of the early FJ-1 Fury fighter. Armament is carried on underwing stations. Maximum speed is 522 mph (840km/hr) and range 1,047 miles (1,685km). Buckeyes were exported to two countries: Venezuela (24 examples) and Greece (40). *Country of origin:* USA. *Silhouette and picture:* T-2C.

Ilyushin Il-28 Beagle   *Confusion:* Canberra

Power: 2 × VK-1 turbojets   *Span:* 70ft 5in (21.45m)   *Length:* 57ft 11in (17.65m)

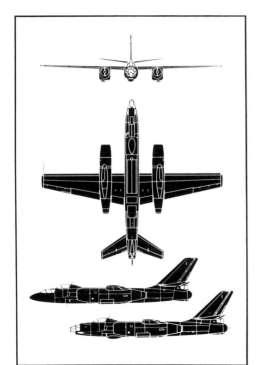

Although it is over 30 years since the Il-28 bomber, code-named Beagle, entered service, it is still in use with various air forces in Africa, Asia and South-east Asia and in small numbers in Eastern Europe. The trainer version, the Il-28U, has a second, lower cockpit and is code-named Mascot. In bomber form the Beagle carries 2,205lb (1,000kg) of bombs internally and two 23mm cannon in the tail. Maximum speed is 559 mph (900km/hr) and maximum range 1,355 miles (2,180km). A Chinese-built version is known as the Harbin H-5. *Country of origin:* USSR. *Main silhouette:* Il-28; *upper side view:* Il-28U. *Picture:* H-5.

Power: 2 × Avon turbojets   *Span:* 63ft 11in (19.5m)   *Length:* 65ft 6in (19.96m)

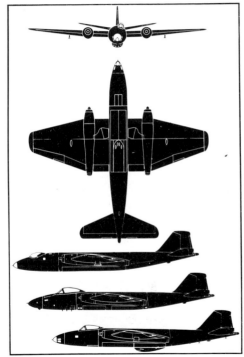

Still in widespread use 30 years after its first flight, the very successful Canberra, originally by English Electric, is used for tactical bombing, reconnaissance, training, electronic warfare and target towing. Production totalled 1,461, including examples licence-built in the USA (as the B-57) and Australia. The internal bomb bay is supplemented by two underwing pylons and, in some versions, four 20mm cannon in a ventral pack. Later versions have a raised offset cockpit. Maximum speed is 580 mph (930km/hr) and range 3,790 miles (6,100km). UK-operated variants include the T.4, PR.7, E.15, T.17, T.18 and T.19 Canberras can be seen with various nose radars, used for ECM training and target towing. *Country of origin:* UK. *Main silhouette:* B(I).8; *top side view:* B.6; *middle side view:* PR.9. *Picture:* B.58.

General Dynamics B-57 Canberra *Confusion:* Canberra, Beagle

Power: 2 × J65 turbojets or 2 × TF33 turbofans *Span* (RB-57F): 122ft 5in (37.32m) *Length:* 69ft (21.03m)

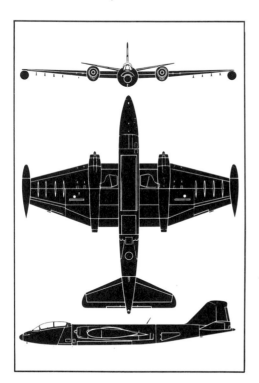

Some 500 Canberras were licence-built in the United States, serving as light bombers (B-57A), reconnaissance bombers (RB-57A), intruders (B-57B and C), electronic warfare trainers (EB-57B), reconnaissance aircraft (RB-57D), night interdictors (B-57G) and target tugs (B-57E). A later development is the RB-57F strategic reconnaissance aircraft, with a much larger wing, nose radome, auxiliary underwing jets, turbofan engines and a large square-cut fin. At least a dozen RB-57Fs were converted from B-57Bs. Ceiling of this variant is 75,000ft (22,875m) and range is in excess of 4,000 miles (6,435km). The WB-57F was modified for weather reconnaissance. *Country of origin:* USA. *Silhouette and picture:* B-57B.

Power: 1 × J57 or 1 × J75 turbojet   *Span:* 80ft (24.38m)   *Length:* 49ft 7in (15.11m)

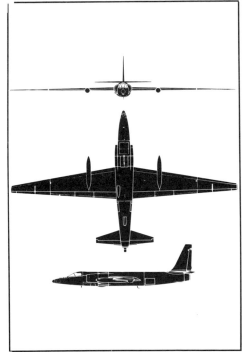

A high-altitude special-purpose reconnaissance aircraft, the single-engined U-2 came to the world's attention in 1960 when one was shot down over the Soviet Union. A very-high-aspect-ratio wing gives the U-2 a service ceiling of about 80,000ft (24,384m); cruising speed is 460 mph (740km/hr) and endurance over eight hours. Variants include the U-2A, B, C, D and R. The D has two seats. Special sensing equipment and cameras are carried and there are two large integral wing pods. The production line was reopened to turn out 12 much modified U-2s (U-2R) and 35 aircraft with improved sensors and designated TR-1A and B. One example was supplied to NASA as the ER-2. *Country of origin:* USA. *Silhouette:* U-2. *Picture:* TR-1A.

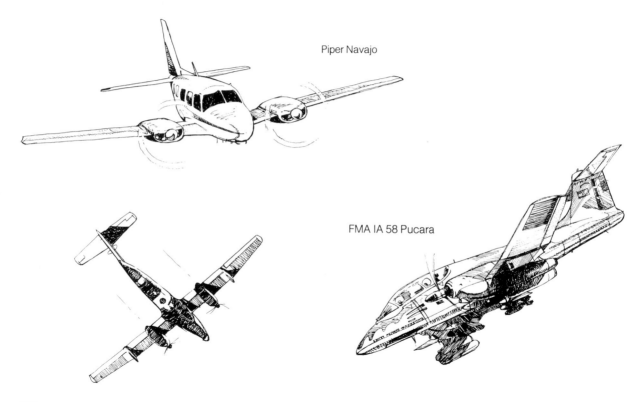

Piper Navajo

FMA IA 58 Pucara

Power: 2 × Gipsy Queen piston engines   *Span:* 57ft (17.40m)   *Length:* 39ft 3in (11.96m)

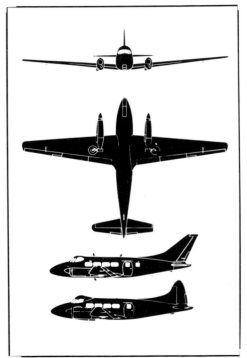

A total of 534 Dove 8/11-seat light transports were built over nearly 20 years. Series numbers were allotted largely to signify power increases in the Gipsy Queen engines. The military version of the Dove, the Devon, remains in service in a number of countries. The Royal Navy uses the name Sea Devon. Economical cruising speed is 187 mph (310km/hr) and range 880 miles (1,415km). A small number of Doves were re-engined by Riley and fitted with a swept fin and rudder. *Country of origin:* UK. *Main silhouette:* Dove; *upper side view:* Riley Dove. *Picture:* Dove.

Saunders ST-27 *Confusion:* Dove, Metro/Merlin IV

Power: 2 × PT6A turboprops *Span:* 71ft 6in (21.79m) *Length:* 59ft (17.98m)

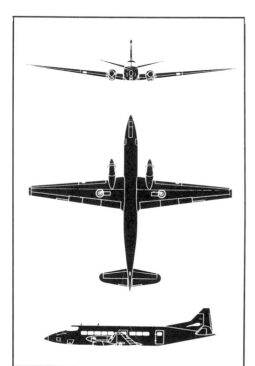

A much modified version of the British four-engined Heron light transport, the Saunders ST-27 is a 23-passenger commuter transport. With two turboprops instead of four piston engines, the S-27 has a maximum cruising speed of 230 mph (370km/hr) and a range with maximum payload of 115 miles (185km). Alternative interior layouts allows the carriage of mixed passengers and cargo or, with the rear bulkhead removed, all cargo. Usable volume of the all-passenger and passenger/cargo versions is 723ft^3 (20.47m^3), compared with the 828ft^3 (23.45m^3) of the all-cargo arrangement. Only a small number had been produced before financial support for the project dried up. *Country of origin:* Canada.

Power: 2 × TPE331 turboprops   *Span:* 57ft (17.37m)   *Length:* 59ft 4in (18.09m)

Developed from the Merlin, the Metro is a 20-passenger commuter airliner with a range of 500 miles (804km). The Metro II has deeper windows than the Metro, and both versions are characterised by long noses. An executive transport version of the Metro II is designated Merlin IVA and has seating for 12/15 passengers. The Metro III and IIIA have a new, longer-span wing, while the IIIA also has PT6A engines. The III has a range of 714 miles (1,149km). Introduced in 1981, the Metro IIIC incorporates the wing introduced on the Metro III, as well as the latter's streamlined nacelles and new main landing gear doors. The all cargo version of the Metro III is known as the Expediter while the Fairchild IVC (formerly Merlin IVC) is a corporate version. *Country of origin:* USA. *Silhouette:* Metro IIIA. *Picture:* Merlin IVA.

223

FMA IA 50 Guarani

Confusion: Metro/Merlin IV

Power: 2 × Bastan turboprops   *Span:* 64ft 3in (19.59m)   *Length:* 50ft 2½in (15.3m)

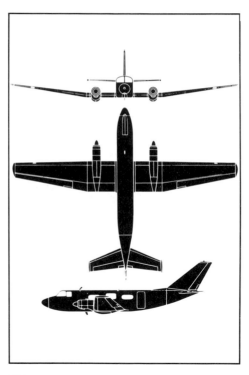

Developed from the Huanquero, the IA 50 Guarani seats up to 15 passengers or can be used for navigation training or air ambulance work. Compared with the Huanquero, the Guarani has a swept single fin. Both types can carry tip tanks. Cruising speed is 280 mph (450km/hr) and range 1,240 miles (1,995km). First flown as the Guarani I, embodying 20 per cent of the structural components of the Huanquero, this type was developed into the Guarani II, the defintive standard. The Guarani II features more powerful engines, de-icing equipment, a single swept fin and rudder in place of the Guarani I's twin-fin arrangement, and a shorter rear fuselage to save weight. The type was phased out of production in 1973. *Country of origin:* Argentina. *Silhouette and picture* Guarani II.

Power: 2 × R-2800 piston engines *Span:* 105ft 4in (32.12m) *Length:* 79ft 2in (24.14m)

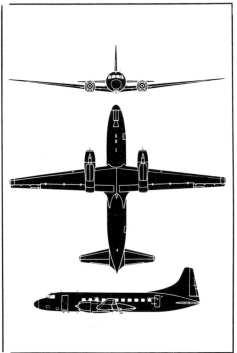

Originally built as the 40-seat Convair 240, the Metropolitan was developed into a number of variants. The 340 had a lengthened fuselage seating 44 passengers, while the 440 ultimately had accommodation for up to 52. Versions were also produced for the US Air Force and US Navy for air ambulance work, transport, crew training and ECM training. Altogether 1,081 240/340/440s were completed. The 440 cruises at 289 mph (465km/hr) for 1,300 miles (2,092km). *Country of origin:* USA. *Silhouette:* CV-340. *Picture:* CV-440.

Convair 540/580/600/640

Confusion: Convair 440, Guarani, 4-0-4, Crate

Power: 2 × Allison 501 or 2 × Dart turboprops   *Span:* 105ft 4in (32.12m)   *Length:* 79ft 2in (24.14m)

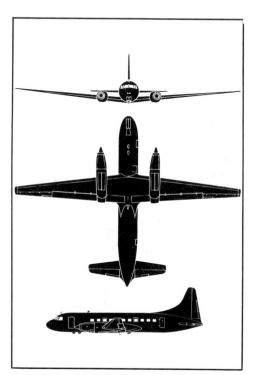

The Convair 340 and 440 both proved capable of conversion to turboprop power. Pacific Automotive converted more than 115 to Allison 501 turboprops (CV-580), while kits were produced for refitting 340/440s with Rolls-Royce Darts to produce the CV-600/640. The 640 with Darts can carry 56 passengers for 1,230 miles (1,975km) at a speed of 300 mph (482km/hr). Original operators included Caribair, Hawaiian Airlines and Pacific Western. *Country of origin:* USA. *Silhouette and picture:* CV-640.

Power: 2 × R2800 piston engines   *Span:* 93ft 3in (28.44m)   *Length:* 74ft 7in (22.75m)

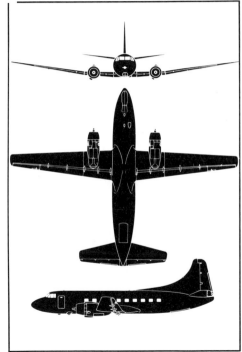

Developed from the Martin 2-0-2, which first flew in 1946, the 4-0-4 pressurised twin-engined transport entered service in 1951. The type was a rival to the Convair 340/440, which it resembles in outline. Over one hundred 4-0-4s were built and a number remain in use in the USA and South America. Forty passengers are carried, cruising speed is 280 mph (448km/hr) and range is 1,080 miles (1,730km). Other performance figures include a maximum speed of 312 mph (500km/hr) at 14,500ft (4,420m); initial rate of climb of 1,905ft/min; service ceiling of 29,000ft (8,845m); and a maximum range of 2,600 miles (4,160km). *Country of origin:* USA.

Ilyushin Il-14 Crate

Confusion: DC-3, Commando, Convair 340/640, 4-0-4

Power: 2 × Ash-82 piston engines   *Span:* 104ft (31.69m)   *Length:* 73ft 2in (22.3m)

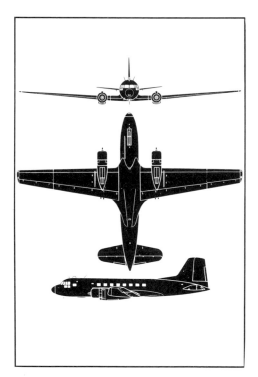

Some 3,600 Il-14 Crate transports were built for both civil and military use. The civil version seats 18/26 passengers, while the military Crate has portside double freight doors. A stretched version, the Il-14M, carries 24/28 passengers. A line in Czechoslovakia produced a 32-passenger variant, the Avia 14-32, the freighter 14T and the photographic survey 14FG. In 1960 the Czechs produced a pressurised 42-passenger Crate with circular windows known as 14-42. The -14M has a cruising speed of 193 mph (310km/hr) and a range of 810 miles (1,304km). The Crate is still in service in the Eastern Bloc and has been widely exported. *Country of origin:* USSR. *Silhouette and picture:* Il-14M.

Power: 2 × Hercules piston engines   *Span:* 91ft 2½in (27.8m)   *Length:* 68ft 5in (20.85m)

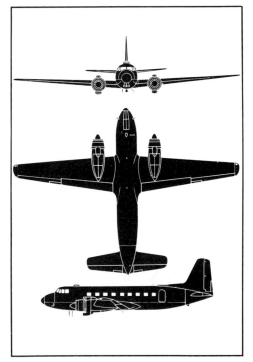

Used by the Spanish Air Force as a troop transport, freighter, crew trainer and air ambulance, the CASA 207 Azor first flew in 1955. Up to 36 passengers can be carried over 1,150 miles (1,850km) at a cruising speed of 266 mph (428km/hr). Other performance figures include a maximum speed of 285 mph (458km/hr) at 6,100ft (1,860m), and a service ceiling of 28,200ft (8,600m). Designed originally for commercial use as a DC-3 replacement, the Azor failed to attract civil interest and was built solely for the Spanish Air Force. Only 20 Azors were produced. The Azor succeeded a smaller transport, the 14-passenger CASA 202 Halcon. *Country of origin:* Spain.

Douglas DC-3/Dakota *Confusion:* Crate, Commando, Azor

Power: 2 × R-1830 piston engines   *Span:* 95ft (28.96m)   *Length:* 64ft 5in (19.63m)

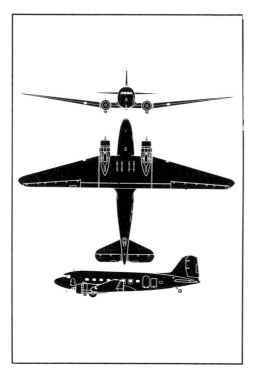

Probably the most famous of all airliners, the DC-3/Dakota first flew in 1935 and nearly 13,000 were built, including some 2,000 in Russia and Japan. Some 700 DC-3/Dakotas are still in use and there have been many variants, including turboprop developments. The basic DC-3 seats up to 36 passengers and cruises at 194 mph (312km/hr) for 1,510 miles (2,430km). *Country of origin:* USA. *Silhouette and picture:* DC-3.

Power: 2 × R-2800 piston engines   *Span:* 108ft (32.92m)   *Length:* 76ft 4in (23.26m)

Like the ubiquitous DC-3/Dakota, the Curtiss Commando twin radial-engined transport has remained in service continuously since the Second World War. The type is in civil and military use, carrying either passengers or freight. Passenger versions can carry up to 62 passengers for 1,170 miles (1,880km) at a cruising speed of 187 mph (301km/hr). A total of 3,180 Commandos were built, of which a number are still operating, particularly in the Caribbean and South America. *Country of origin:* USA.

231

 **Dassault-Breguet Atlantic** *Confusion:* Commando, Crate, Neptune

Power: 2 × Tyne turboprops   *Span:* 119ft 1in (36.3m)   *Length:* 104ft 2in (31.75m)

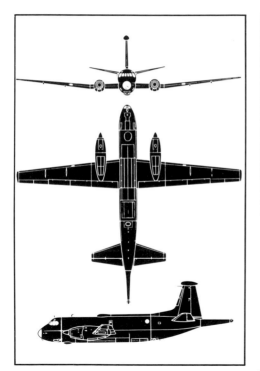

A multi-national European product, the Atlantic long-range maritime patrol aircraft is in service in France, West Germany, Italy, the Netherlands and Pakistan. First flown in 1961, the Atlantic has a 12-man crew and can cruise at 195 mph (320km/hr) for 18hr. The weapon load of acoustic torpedoes, depth charges or mines is carried internally. An updated version is the Atlantique 2, (ATL2), previously known as the Atlantic NG (*Nouvelle Génération*), with improved systems and structure, and capable of carrying Exocet missiles in the weapons bay. The French Navy has a requirement for 42 Atlantique ATL2s. *Country of origin:* France. *Silhouette:* Atlantic Mk 1. *Picture:* Atlantic NG.

Power: 2 × T64 turboprops plus 2 × J3 turbojets   *Span:* 97ft 8½in (29.78m)   *Length:* 95ft 11in (29.23m)

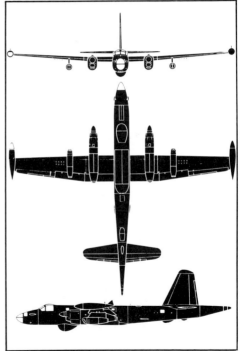

Originally designed and built by Lockheed in America, the P-2 Neptune maritime patrol and anti-submarine aircraft was subsequently manufactured under licence in Japan. After completing a number of P-2H Neptunes, Kawasaki developed a longer, higher-powered and longer-range version, the P-2J. Carrying 12 crew, the P-2J cruises at 230 mph (370km/hr) and has a range of 2,765 miles (4,450km). Up to 8,000lb (3,630kg) of weapons can be carried in the internal bomb bay, while rocket projectiles may be fitted under the wings. Details of the P-2J's operational equipment remain classified but this is known to be comparable in standard to that carried by the P-3 Orion and to include APS-80J search radar, exhaust-gas detector, and magnetic anomaly detector (MAD) in the tail boom. A total of four P-2Js have been converted to UP-2J target tugs. *Country of origin:* **Japan/USA.** *Silhouette and picture:* P-2J.

Grumman OV-1 Mohawk

Confusion: —

Power: 2 × T53 turboprops   *Span:* 48ft (14.63m)   *Length:* 41ft (12.50m)

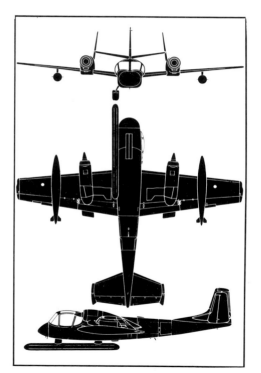

Developed as a US Army battlefield surveillance aircraft, the OV-1 Mohawk carries a wide range of cameras and electronic sensors, and can operate from small, rough sites. OV-1A has cameras, OV-1B sideways-looking radar (SLAR), OV-1C cameras and infra-red sensors, and OV-1D cameras and sideways-looking radar or infra-red. The SLAR is mounted in a long, rectangular under-fuselage pod which extends well forward of the nose. Large auxiliary fuel tanks are carried under the wings. The crew of two are seated side by side and maximum speed is 305 mph (491km/hr). *Country of origin:* USA. *Silhouette and picture:* OV-1B.

Power: 2 × M332 piston engines   *Span:* 40ft 2½in (12.25m)   *Length:* 25ft 6in (7.77m)

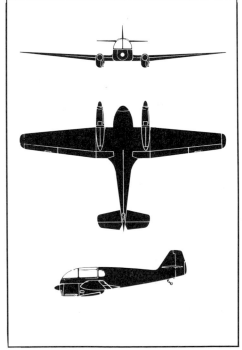

The original Aero 4/5-seat light twin was flown in 1947. It was followed by the Super Aero 45 and later by the 145 with uprated engines. The 45/145 remained in production until 1961, by which time some 700 had been built, of which over 600 had been exported. A particular recognition point is the streamlined, unstepped nose. The 145 cruises at 155 mph (250km/hr) for up to 1,055 miles (1,700km). Other performance figures include a maximum speed of 175 mph (280km/hr); initial climb rate of 985ft/min (400m/min); and service ceiling of 19,360ft (5,900m). Empty weight is 2,116lb (960kg) and normal loaded 3,306lb (750kg). *Country of origin:* Czechoslovakia. *Silhouette and picture:* Aero 145.

Beechcraft Baron

Confusion: Aero 145, Navajo, Apache

Power: 2 × Continental piston engines   *Span:* 37ft 10in (11.53m)   *Length:* 29ft 10in (9.09m)

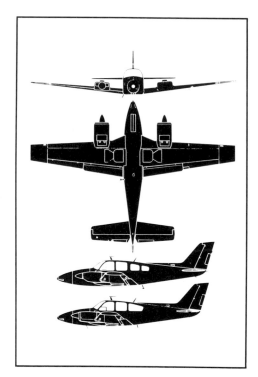

The B55 Baron four-passenger light transport was developed from the D95 Travel Air, which was itself a scaled-down Twin Bonanza. First flown in 1960, the Baron has been steadily updated over the years and has appeared under a variety of designations: A55, B55, C55, D55, E55, Turbo Baron and Baron 58/58TC. A pressurised variant is called the Baron 58P; over 300 examples have been delivered. Maximum cruising speed is 230 mph (370km/hr) and range 1,212 miles (1,950km). *Country of origin:* USA. *Main silhouette:* D55; *upper side view:* Baron 58. *Picture:* Baron 58.

Power: 2 × Lycoming piston engines   *Span:* 40ft 8in (12.4m)   *Length* (-31C): 32ft 7½in (9.94m)

There have been several variants of the PA-31 Navajo since it was first introduced in 1964. Seating 6/8, the Navajo is used as an executive aircraft and a commuter airliner. When fitted with turbo-supercharged engines the type is called the Turbo-Navajo. The PA-31P, produced in 1970, has a pressurised cabin with fewer windows, and a longer fuselage. The PA-31C can fly 1,226 miles (1,973km) at a cruising speed of 238 mph (383km/hr). *Country of origin:* USA. *Main silhouette:* PA-31; *upper side view:* PA-31P. *Picture:* PA-31.

Piper PA-23 Apache   *Confusion:* Baron, Navajo

Power: 2 × Lycoming piston engines   *Span:* 37ft 2in (11.33m)   *Length:* 27ft 7in (8.41m)

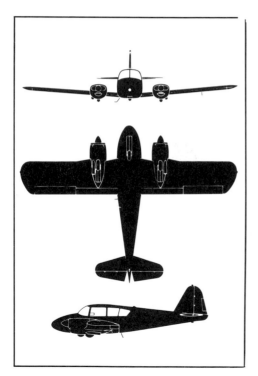

Originally known as the Twin-Stinson, the Piper PA-23-160 Apache first flew in 1952. In this form it had a curved fin, rudder and tailplane. Ten years later it was followed on the line by the PA-23-235 with a more bulbous cabin, a larger, square-cut fin and rudder, and square-cut tailplane. The Apache is similar to the Aztec but has 4/5 seats, a shorter nose and lower-powered engines. The 235 cruises at 191 mph (307km/hr) for up to 980 miles (1,900km). *Country of origin:* USA. *Silhouette:* PA-23-160. *Picture:* Apache 235.

Power: 2 × Lycoming piston engines   *Span:* 37ft 2½in (11.34m)   *Length:* 31ft 3in (9.52m)

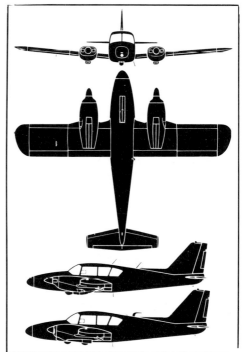

Originally built as the five-seat Aztec A in 1959, the Piper PA-23 evolved into the six-seat, longer-nosed Aztec B in 1962. The Aztec C, introduced in 1970, had redesigned engine nacelles and a longer nose, and Aztec D was externally similar. The latest version is the Aztec F. Aztecs of various marks are fitted with turbo-superchargers. As is the case with many American light aircraft, new designations often denote updated equipment and fittings rather than any change in outline. The Aztec F cruises at 210 mph (338km/hr) for 830 miles (1,335km). *Country of origin:* USA. *Main silhouette:* Aztec D; *lower side view:* Aztec B. *Picture:* Turbo Aztec F.

Gulfstream Aerospace GA-7 Cougar

Confusion: Cessna 310

Power: 2 × Lycoming piston engines   *Span:* 36ft 10½in (11.23m)   *Length:* 29ft 10in (9.1m)

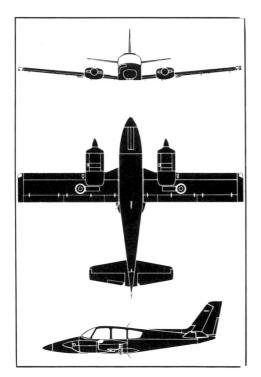

Originally a Grumman product, the GA-7 Cougar is intended for business and training use and can seat 4/6 people. First flown in 1974, the Cougar was significantly re-engineered before the production prototype flew in 1977. Gulfstream Aerospace's first entry into the lightweight twin-engined market, the Cougar was intended mainly for business use and for private pilots who already have instrument-flying experience. It can also be used as an economical twin-engined trainer. The production prototype flew for the first time on January 14, 1977, and delivery of production aircraft began in February 1978. Production has now ceased. The Cougar has a maximum range of 1,265 miles (2,035km) and cruises at 190 mph (305km/hr). *Country of origin:* USA.

Power: 2 × Continental piston engines   *Span:* 36ft 11in (11.25m)   *Length:* 31ft 11½in (9.74m)

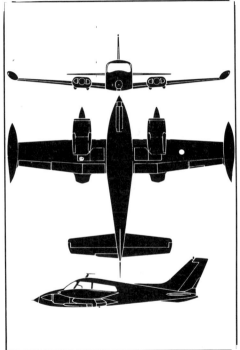

First flown in 1953, the Cessna 310 four-seat twin had a straight fin in its original form. In addition to hundreds of civil sales, the type was adopted by the USAF as the U-3A. With engine improvements incorporated, the 310 was marketed as the Riley 65 Rocket and Turbo Rocket. In 1960 the Cessna Model 310 appeared with a swept fin and more windows. Over 5,000 310s have been built and a large number of variants are flying, including some with turbo-supercharged engines and a further USAF version, the U-3B. Another development is the 320C Skyknight, seating up to seven. Cruising speed is 166 mph (267km/hr) and range is up to 709 miles (1,141km). *Country of origin:* USA. *Silhouette and picture:* Cessna 310.

Piper PA-30/PA-39 Twin Comanche *Confusion:* Seneca

Power: 2 × Lycoming piston engines   *Span:* 36ft 9½in (11.22m)   *Length:* 25ft 2in (7.67m)

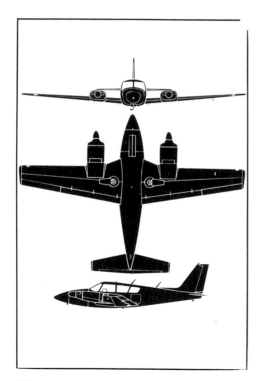

Developed as a twin version of the PA-24 Comanche single-engined light aircraft, the Twin Comanche first flew in 1961 and has been built in large numbers. A four/six-seater, it cruises at 198mph (319km/hr) and has a range of 830 miles (1,335km). There are many variants, differing mainly in engine power, propellers and internal layout. Some are fitted with wingtip fuel tanks. From 1971 the PA-30 was succeeded by the externally similar PA-39. Refinements introduced with the later Twin Comanche variants include turbo-supercharging, first applied to the Turbo Twin Comanche B and C, and counter-rotating propellers (to eliminate torque effects) on the Twin Comanche C/R. *Country of origin:* USA. *Silhouette:* PA-39. *Picture:* PA-30C.

Power: 2 × Continental piston engines   *Span:* 38ft 11in (11.85m)   *Length:* 28ft 7½in (8.73m)

The PA-34 Seneca six-passenger light transport and trainer was introduced in 1971. It has twin turbo-supercharged Continental engines, cruises at 177 mph (285km/hr) and has a range of 1,016 miles (1,635km). Poland holds a licence to build the Seneca II and distribute it in Eastern Europe. These aircraft are powered by PZL-Franklin engines and designated PZL-112 M-20 Mewa (Gull). Latest version of the PA-34 has detail modifications and is called the Seneca III. *Country of origin:* USA. *Silhouette:* Seneca II. *Picture:* Seneca III.

Cessna 340A   *Confusion:* Duke, Aerostar

Power: 2 × Continental piston engines   *Span:* 38ft 1in (11.6m)   *Length:* 34ft 4in (10.46m)

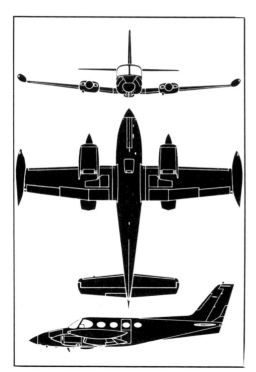

Developed from the Cessna 310, the Model 340A is a four-passenger pressurised business aircraft. The layout is similar to that of the 310 but the fuselage cross-section is different and the windows are circular. The 340 in effect replaced the 320C Skyknight. As with other similar types in the Cessna range, the powerplants are Continental flat-four piston engines, which have a distinctive rectangular appearance in the head-on view. Range of the 340A is 1,580 miles (2,543km) at an economical cruising speed of 206 mph (332km/hr). Later 340A variants feature a number of improvements, including better forward view as a result of structural changes, and a new strobe lighting system. *Country of origin:* USA.

Power: 2 × Lycoming piston engines   *Span:* 36ft 8in (11.18m)   *Length:* 34ft 10in (10.61m)

The first of the Aerostar series of light transport aircraft flew in 1967 as the Model 600. The 601P has more wingspan and a pressurised fuselage. A six-seater, the Aerostar 601 is one of a small number of types with a straight wing and swept tail surfaces. The 601B cruises at 270 mph (434km/hr) and has a range of 1,435 miles (2,309km). Around 1,000 Aerostars of all types have been sold. The latest version is the 700P with higher powered engines. Introduced in 1981, the Aerostar 602P is generally similar to the 601P. *Country of origin:* USA. *Silhouette:* 601P. *Picture:* 602P.

Cessna T303 Crusader

Confusion: Duke, Chancellor

Power: 2 × Continental piston engines   *Span:* 38ft 10in (11.48m)   *Length:* 30ft 5in (9.27m)

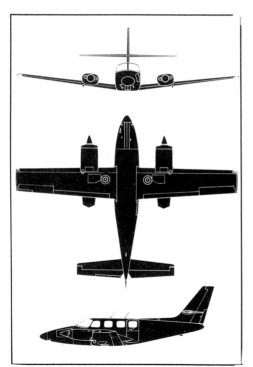

First flown in 1978 as the four-seat Model 303, the Crusader is now designated T303. With six seats and turbo-supercharged engines, the Crusader is the first completely new twin-engined type to be put into production by Cessna for a decade. Deliveries began in September 1981 and more than 230 had been delivered by summer 1984. Cruising speed is 207 mph (333km/hr) and maximum range 1,156 miles (1,861km). *Country of origin:* USA.

Power: 2 × Lycoming piston engines   *Span:* 39ft 3in (11.96m)   *Length:* 33ft 10in (10.31m)

A pressurised, turbo-supercharged light transport, the Beech B60 Duke seats 4/6 passengers, cruises at 268 mph (431km/hr) and has a range of 1,163 miles (1,872km). A total of 596 Dukes were built in two versions, the A60 and B60 before production ceased. The B60, powered by Lycoming TIO-541-E1C4 engines, entered production in 1974. *Country of origin:* USA. *Silhouette and picture:* B60.

Beechcraft Queen Air/Seminole *Confusion:* King Air

Power: 2 × Lycoming piston engines   *Span:* 50ft 3in (15.32m)   *Length:* 35ft 6in (10.82m)

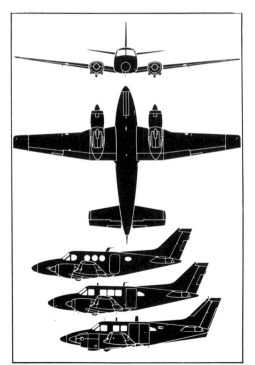

Like the rest of the Beech range, the Queen Air has been built in very large numbers for both civil and military use. A four/nine-passenger twin, the Queen Air has been produced as the 65/A65, U-8F (US Army), Model 70/80/A80/B80 and U-21A, B, C, E and G (US Army). The U-8F, characterised by a straight fin, is called the Seminole. The Queen Air is in service both as an executive aircraft and a feederliner. The B80 seats 11 passengers and is called the Queen Airliner. It has a maximum cruising speed of 224 mph (360km/hr) and a range of 1,550 miles (2,494km). *Country of origin:* USA. *Main silhouette:* B80; *top side view:* B88; *bottom side view:* U-21. *Picture:* B80.

Power: 2 × PT6A turboprops   *Span* (100): 45ft 10½in (13.98m)   *Length:* 39ft 8½in (12.1m)

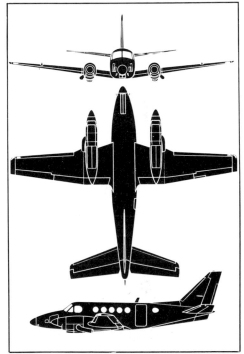

Based on the 65-80 Queen Air but with a redesigned pressurised fuselage, the King Air is a 16-seat twin-turboprop business aircraft. Models include the 90/A90/B90/C90/E90/100/B100 and T-44 advanced trainer for the USAF. Latest version is the C90A. Over 1,000 King Air 90s have been built and the type is in use in many countries. Maximum cruising speed is 285 mph (460km/hr) and range 1,507 miles (2,425km). *Country of origin:* USA. *Silhouette:* B100. *Picture:* E90.

Beechcraft B99 Airliner

Confusion: King Air, Queen Air

Power: 2 × PT6A turboprops   *Span:* 45ft 10½in (14m)   *Length:* 44ft 7in (13.58m)

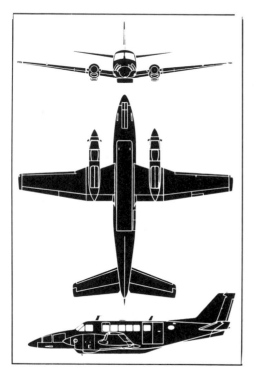

The B99 Airliner is a twin-turboprop unpressurised 17-seat feederliner/air taxi. It first flew in 1966 and deliveries began in 1968. Similar in outline to other Beech twins of similar size, the B99 has a particularly long nose. A main cargo door allows the aircraft to be used for all-cargo or passenger/cargo operations. Maximum cruising speed is 282 mph (454km/hr) and range 531 miles (853km). Offering increased power and systems refinements, the C99, now on the production line, is known as the C99 Airliner. Deliveries began in 1981. *Country of origin:* USA.

Cessna 441 Conquest

Power: 2 × TPE331 turboprops   *Span:* 49ft 4in (15.04m)   *Length:* 39ft (11.89m)

Designed to fill a slot between piston-engined and turbofan business aircraft, the Cessna 441 Conquest seats eight/ten passengers in a pressurised cabin. It has a high-aspect-ratio wing, while the general layout is similar to that of other Beech twins. Range is 1,291 miles (2,077km) and maximum cruising speed 319 mph (513km). The prototype Conquest flew in 1975 and over 200 have been delivered. *Country of origin:* USA.

Piper PA-31-350 Chieftain *Confusion:* Conquest, Titan

Power: 2 × Lycoming piston engines   *Span:* 40ft 8in (12.4m)   *Length:* 34ft 8½in (10.55m)

The PA-31-350 Chieftain has a longer fuselage than the Navajo and is a 6/10-seat executive/commuter/cargo aircraft. Cargo can be carried both in the cabin and in the nose. The Lycoming engines have turbo-superchargers. Cruising speed is 251 mph (404km/hr) and range 1,019 miles (1,640km). By 1 January 1984, 1,800 Chieftains had been sold. *Country of origin:* USA.

Power: 2 × Continental piston engines   *Span:* 46ft 4in (14.12m)   *Length:* 39ft 6in (12.04m)

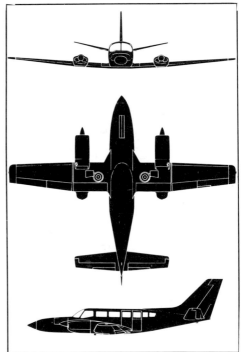

Intended to provide greater payload/range performance than the Cessna 402, the Cessna Titan was originally known as the 404. The cabin is convertible to cargo, feederliner and executive configurations and double doors can be fitted for loading large cargo. The all-passenger Titan is called the Ambassador, while the utility passenger/cargo version is known as the Courier. There are no significant external differences between the two variants. Maximum cruising speed is 229 mph (369km/hr) and range 1,598 miles (2,572km). Several hundred Titans have been delivered. *Country of origin:* USA.

Cessna 421 Golden Eagle   *Confusion:* Cessna 401

Power: 2 × Continental piston engines   *Span:* 41ft 1in (12.53m)   *Length:* 36ft 4½in (11.09m)

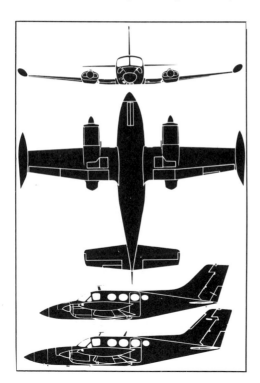

This series of pressurised business aircraft began in 1967 with the Model 421, which was developed into the 421B Golden Eagle and the 421B Executive Commuter. In 1975 came the 421C Golden Eagle, which had a new outer wing without the distinctive wingtip fuel tanks. The 421C Executive Commuter seats up to 11 as a feederliner and has a maximum cruising speed of 279 mph (450km/hr) and a range of 1,440 miles (2,317km/hr). Latest versions are Golden Eagle, Golden Eagle II and Golden Eagle III. *Country of origin:* USA. *Main silhouette:* Model 421A; *lower side view:* Model 421B. *Picture:* Model 421C.

Power: 2 × **PT6A turboprops** *Span:* **44ft 1in (13.45m)** *Length:* **35ft 10in (10.9m)**

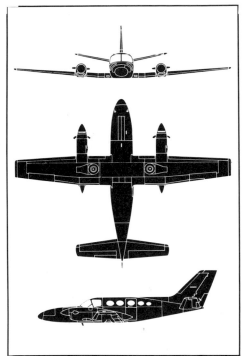

A turboprop six/eight-seat pressurised business executive transport, the Conquest I (originally known as Corsair) is based on the airframe of the 421 Golden Eagle. Design began on November 1, 1977, and construction of a prototype was initiated three months later on January 30, 1978. This flew for the first time on September 12, 1978, and construction of a pre-production aircraft was started during 1979. By April 1984, 182 of the earlier Corsairs and the Conquest I had been delivered. At a cruising speed of 242 mph (389km/hr) the Corsair has a range of 1,895 miles (3,050km). A total of 1,100lb (499kg) of baggage and up to six passengers can be carried. *Country of origin:* USA.

 **Cessna 401/402** *Confusion:* Cheyenne

Power: 2 × Continental piston engines   Span: 39ft 10in (12.15m)   Length: 36ft 1in (11m)

The Cessna 401 and 402 have basically similar airframes, the series having the names Utililiner and Businessliner for the six/eight-seat feeder and nine-seat executive versions. Several variants with differing cockpit, cabin and equipment standards have been built. Production of the 401 finished in 1972 and thereafter the 402 was standard. The 402 Businessliner has a maximum range of 1,639 miles (2,637km) and a maximum cruising speed of 218 mph (351km/hr). Wingtip tanks are fitted as standard. *Country of origin:* USA. *Silhouette:* Model 401B. *Picture:* Model 402.

Piper PA-31T Cheyenne II/PA-31T2 Cheyenne II XL

Power: 2 × PT6A turboprops   *Span:* 42ft 8in (13.01m)   *Length:* 34ft 8in (10.57m)

The first turboprop-powered Piper aircraft, the PA-31T Cheyenne II light transport first flew in 1969. The airframe is similar to that of the pressurised Navajo. Seating is provided for eight including the pilot. Large wingtip fuel tanks are fitted. Economical cruising speed is 244 mph (393km/hr) and range is 1,702 miles (2,739km). A lower-powered version is known as the Cheyenne I, while the Cheyenne II XL has a 2ft fuselage stretch. 524 Cheyenne IIs were built and by January 1984, 69 Cheyenne II XLs had been sold. *Country of origin:* USA. *Silhouette:* Cheyenne II. *Picture:* Cheyenne II XL.

Cessna 414A Chancellor

Confusion: Conquest, Titan

Power: 2 × Teledyne Continental piston engines   *Span:* 44ft 1in (13.4m)   *Length:* 36ft 4in (11.09m)

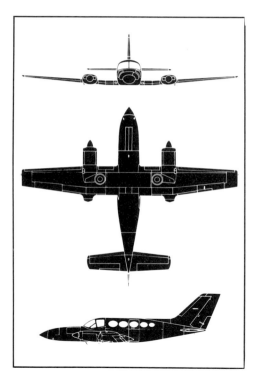

Cessna introduced the pressurised twin-engined Model 414 on December 10 1969, as a 'step-up' aircraft for owners of Cessna or other light unpressurised twins. It combined the basic fuselage and tail unit of the Model 421 with the wing of the Model 402 and had 310hp turbocharged engines. Successor to the 414, the 414A Chancellor is a utility transport seating up to six passengers in a pressurised cabin. Major changes from the Model 414 included a new 'wet' wing of increased span, and extended nose and baggage area. First introduced in 1978, the Chancellor has been built in I, II and III versions with differing equipment. Maximum speed is 275 mph (443km/hr) and range at 166 mph (267km/hr) is 1,490 miles (2,340km). Over 1,000 414/414A aircraft have been built. *Country of origin:* USA.

Power: 2 × TPE331 turboprops   *Span:* 46ft 3in (14.1m)   *Length:* 42ft 2in (12.85m)

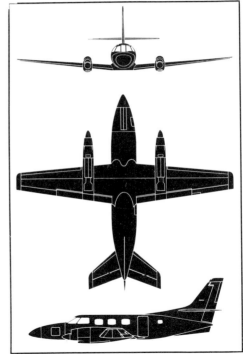

Produced in large numbers, the Swearingen Merlin series of executive transports has been steadily developed since its introduction in 1966. The original version was an eight-seater with two PT6 engines (IIA). Re-engined with TPE331s, this became the Merlin IIB. Merlin IIIA is an 8/11 passenger stretched version with four large side windows. The IIIB is powered by uprated TPE331s. The Merlin IIIC, was introduced in 1981 and was superceded in 1984, by the 8-10 passenger Fairchild 300 – similar to the IIIC but with winglets. *Country of origin:* USA. *Silhouette:* Merlin IIIC. *Picture:* Merlin IIIB.

Piper T-1040

Confusion: Chieftain, Cheyenne

Power: 2 × PT6A turboprops   *Span:* 41ft 1in (12.5m)   *Length:* 36ft 8in (11.18m)

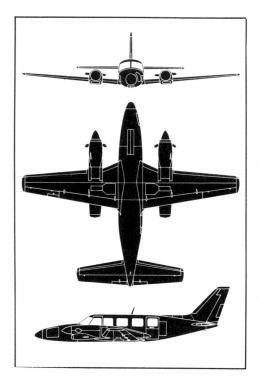

A commuter airliner, the nine-passenger T-1040 combines the wings, nose and tail of the Cheyenne with the fuselage of the Chieftain and is powered by two 500 shp turboprops. The prototype T-1040 (T = transportation) first flew in July 1981 but only a small number has so far been built. The aircraft is a product of the recently created Airline Division of Piper, which hopes to sell 100 – 150 units per year. With full payload the T-1040 has a range of 450 nautical miles (724km), flying at a cruising speed of 238kt (441km/hr). *Country of origin:* USA.

Power: 2 × TPE331 turboprops   *Span:* 52ft (15.85m)   *Length:* 47ft 1in (14.37m)

In its original form the Jetstream was developed by Handley Page and then Scottish Aviation. Thirty Astazou-powered Jetstreams 1 and 2 are still in civil service, while T1s and T2s are used by the RAF and the Royal Navy. British Aerospace Scottish Division (formerly Scottish Aviation) has now produced a much modified version called Jetstream 31, powered by two Garrett turboprops and aimed at the commuter and light business markets. A flight development aircraft flew in March 1980 and the first production aircraft was rolled out in January 1982. Four Jetstreams, as T Mk 3 have been ordered for the Royal Navy. Jetstream 31 can carry eight passengers for 1,025 miles (1,649km) and has a maximum cruising speed of 303 mph (488km/hr). Over 67 Jetstreams have been sold. In executive shuttle layout the 31 carries 12 passengers. *Country of origin:* UK.

Gulfstream Aerospace Gulfstream I/I-C

Confusion: Jetstream 31, BAe 748, YS-11A

Power: 2 × Dart turboprops   *Span:* 78ft 6in (23.92m)   *Length:* 63ft 9in (19.43m)

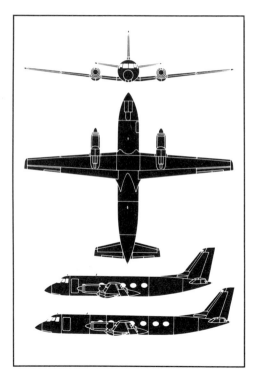

A long-range twin-engined business aircraft, the Grumman Gulfstream I seats up to 24 passengers. The layout is similar to that of the BAe 748, particularly in the engine/undercarriage nacelle arrangement. Maximum cruising speed is 348 mph (560km/hr) and range with maximum fuel is 2,540 miles (4,088km). Military versions include the TC-4C for the US Navy and the VC-4A for the US Coast Guard. Over 200 Gulfstream Is have been built. The 37-passenger Gulfstream I-C commuter airliner, has a 10ft 8in (3.25m) fuselage extension. *Country of origin:* USA. *Main silhouette:* Gulfstream I; *lower side view:* Gulfstream I-C. *Picture:* Gulfstream I.

Power: 2 × Dart turboprops   *Span:* 98ft 6in (30.02m)   *Length:* 67ft (20.42m)

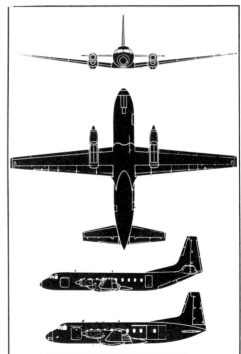

First flown in 1960, the 748 is still in production and over 370 examples have been sold so far. Seating up to 58 passengers and with a maximum cruising speed of 278 mph (448km/hr), the 748 has been sold to many civil and military operators around the world. India has built a large number of 748s under licence. The Andover C1 cargo version has an upswept rear fuselage with loading doors, while some variants have a large aft side-loading door. The military 748 is the Coastguarder for maritime patrol. Latest civil version is the Super 748, with later mark Dart engines and internal refinements. *Country of origin:* UK. *Main silhouette:* 748 Military Transport; *upper side view:* Andover C1. *Picture:* Coastguarder.

NAMC YS-11A

Confusion: Gulfstream I, BAe 748, Saab-Fairchild 340

Power: 2 × Dart turboprops   *Span:* 105ft (32m)   *Length:* 86ft 3½in (26.3m)

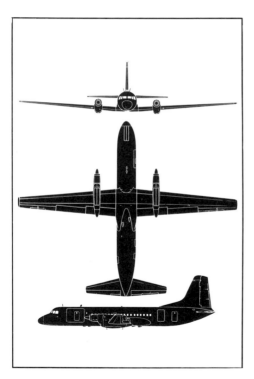

The YS-11A short-medium-range airliner went into service in 1965 and a total of 174 were built, including 22 for the Japan Maritime and Air Self-Defence Forces. The variants are designated -100, -200, -300, -400, -500 and -600. Up to 60 passengers can be carried at 290 mph (466km/hr) for 680 miles (1,090km). A big freight door can be fitted on the forward port side. The YS-11A is particularly large for a twin-engined machine. The type has been exported and some are in service in the United States. *Country of origin:* Japan. *Silhouette:* YS-11A-300. *Picture:* JMSDF YS-11A.

Power: 2 × CT7 turboprops   *Span:* 70ft 4in (21.44m)   *Length:* 64ft 8in (19.72m)

The first jointly designed and developed US-European transport aircraft, the Saab-Fairchild 340 is a 34-seater intended for economical operation over short-haul, low-density routes. First flown in January 1983, the 340 entered service in June 1984. Over 100 orders and options for the type have been placed. Fairchild is building wings, tail and engine nacelles, while Saab makes the fuselage and undertakes final assembly. The 340 cruises at 290 mph (467km/hr) and has a range of 1,115 miles (1,795km) with maximum payload. *Country of origin:* Sweden/USA.

EMBRAER EMB-110 Bandeirante

Confusion: Jetstream 31, Merlin II/III

Power: 2 × PT6A turboprops   *Span:* 50ft 3in (15.32m)   *Length:* 49ft 9in (15.08m)

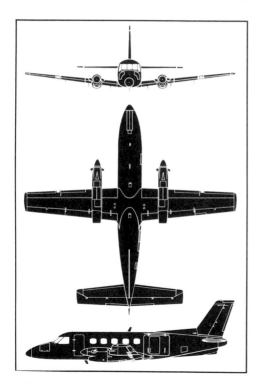

A very successful commuter transport, the EMB-110 Bandeirante seats 21 passengers (in 110P2 form), cruises at 224 mph (360km/hr) and has a range of 1,191 miles (1,916km). First deliveries went to the Brazilian Air Force in 1973. There are twelve versions of the Bandeirante, including the 110P1 (quick-change passenger transport), B1 (aerial photography), S1 (geophysical survey), K1 (military transport with longer fuselage), 110A (navigation/landing aid calibration), 110E (eight-seat executive transport) and 111 (radar-equipped maritime patrol aircraft). Over 400 Bandeirantes are now in service. *Country of origin:* Brazil. *Silhouette:* EMB-110K1. *Picture:* EMB-111.

Power: 2 × Lycoming piston engines   *Span:* 38ft 6½in (11.75m)   *Length:* 27ft 7in (8.41m)

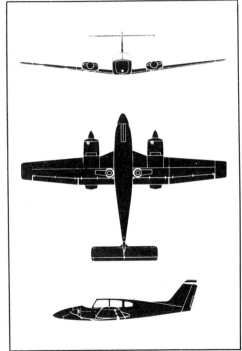

Bearing a close resemblance to the Beechcraft Duchess 76, the T-tail PA-44 Seminole is one of a new generation of American light aircraft intended for training and light transport duties. First flight was in 1976 and deliveries began in the spring of 1978. Although similar in appearance to other Piper aircraft, the Seminole is in fact a new design. Turbo Seminole is the name given to the turbo-supercharged version. Range is 960 miles (1,546km) and cruising speed 178 mph (286km/hr) *Country of origin:* USA. *Silhouette:* Seminole. *Picture:* Turbo Seminole.

Beechcraft Duchess 76

Confusion: Seminole

Power: 2 × Lycoming piston engines   *Span:* 38ft (11.59m)   *Length:* 29ft (8.84m)

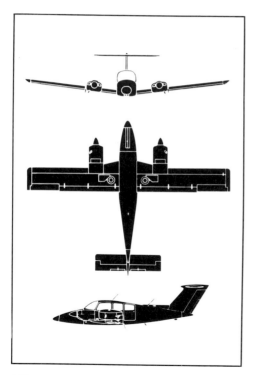

Embodying some parts from the single-engined Beechcraft Sierra, the Duchess 76 is a four-seat T-tail cabin monoplane designed for transport and training. The accent is on low cost and ease of production, and an unusual feature is the fitting of pilot doors on both sides of the aircraft. The Duchess first flew in production form in 1977. Several hundred have been delivered. Maximum cruising speed is 185 mph (298km/hr) and range is over 800 miles (1,290km). *Country of origin:* USA.

Power: 2 × PT6A or 2 × TPE 331 turboprops   *Span:* 47ft 8in (14.6m)   *Length:* 38ft (11.58m)

The PA-42 Cheyenne III first appeared in 1979 and differed from the rest of the Cheyenne family in having greater wingspan, longer fuselage, more windows, uprated engines and a prominent T-tail. A higher-powered version, the Cheyenne IIIA went into production in January 1984. Eight passengers are carried and cruising speed is 360 mph (580km/hr). A further variant, the Cheyenne 400LS flew in February 1983, powered by Garrett TPE 331 engines. *Country of origin:* USA. *Silhouette:* **Cheyenne 400LS**. *Picture:* Cheyenne III.

269

Beechcraft Super King Air 200 *Confusion:* Cheyenne III, Xingu

Power: 2 × PT6A turboprops   *Span:* 54ft 6in (16.61m)   *Length:* 43ft 9in (13.34m)

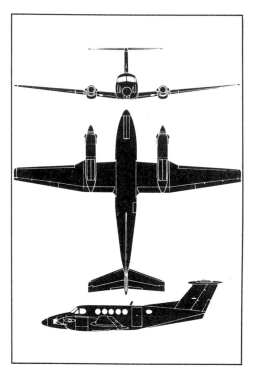

The Super King Air 200 represents a major departure in Beech twin design, with a wing of much higher aspect ratio and a T-tail. The prototype flew in 1972 and deliveries continue. In addition to civil applications as a feederliner/executive aircraft, the type has been ordered by the USAF, US Navy and US Army as the C-12A/C/D, UC-12B, RU-21J, RC-12D. A geographic survey version is the Model 200T, and a further variant is known as the Maritime Patrol B200T. The Super King Air 200 cruises at 313 mph (503km/hr) and has a range of 2,172 miles (3,495km). *Country of origin:* USA. *Silhouette and picture:* Super King Air 200.

Power: 2 × PW115 turboprops   *Span:* 64ft 11in (19.78m)   *Length:* 65ft 7in (20m)

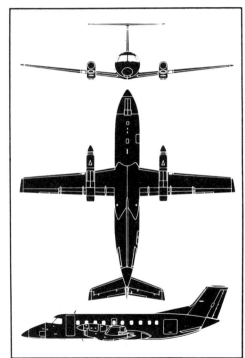

First flown in July 1983, the EMB-120 Brasilia is a twin turboprop passenger and cargo aircraft. Seating 30, the Brasilia has a cruising speed of 303 mph (487km/h) and a range of 691 miles (1,112km). Options were held on 118 Brasilias in mid-1984 and deliveries were due to commence in mid-1985. Military versions, including one for ASW, are projected. *Country of origin:* Brazil.

EMBRAER EMB-121 Xingu

Confusion: Super King Air 200, Pucara, Brasilia

Power: 2 × PT6A turboprops   *Span:* 46ft 1in (14.05m)   *Length:* 40ft 2in (12.25m)

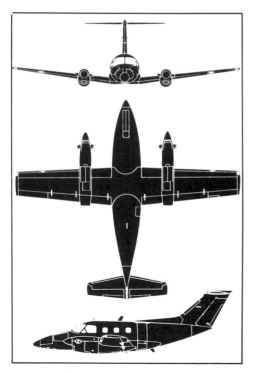

A pressurised 5/6-passenger business aircraft, the EMB-121 Xingu first flew in 1976 and deliveries began in 1977. In addition to civilian sales, the Xingu has been bought by the Brazilian Air Force. Maximum cruising speed is 304 mph (489km/hr) and range is 1,343 miles (2,160km). The uprated Xingu II flew in 1981, and is now in production. By spring 1984, 110 Xingus had been built. *Country of origin:* Brazil. *Silhouette and picture:* Xingu I.

Power: 2 × Astazou turboprops   *Span:* 47ft 7in (14.5m)   *Length:* 46ft 9in (14.25m)

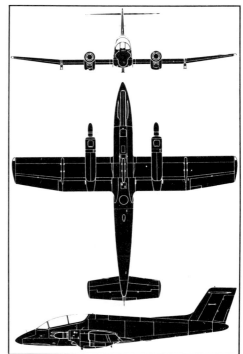

The IA 58 Pucara counter-insurgency (Coin) aircraft, first flew in 1969. Highly manoeuvrable, the Pucara is capable of using very short rough fields. The Pucara was widely used in the Falklands conflict in 1982. Two 20mm cannon and four machine guns are fitted in the fuselage and 3,307lb (1,500kg) of bombs, rockets or missiles are carried on one underfuselage and two underwing pylons. The Pucara is in service with the Argentinian Air Force. Maximum speed is 310 mph (500km/hr) and range is 1,890 miles (3,042km). The IA 58B Brava version has two 30mm cannon instead of the 20mm weapons fitted to the initial version, and a redesigned fuselage. A prototype has flown with Garrett TPE 331 engines and is known as the IA 66. *Country of origin:* Argentina.

Beech 18 *Confusion:* Huanquero

Power: 2 × R-985 piston engines   *Span:* 49ft 8in (15.14m)   *Length:* 32ft 2½in (10.7m)

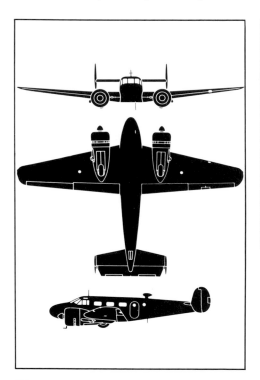

The original Beech 18 entered production in 1937 and several thousand had been completed by the end of the Second World War. Civil manufacture recommenced after the war and development led to the E18, G18 and H18 Super models, of which over 750 were built. Compared with early marks, the later 18s have extended rectangular wingtips, various nose lengths and changed window shapes. The H18 Super 18 carries nine passengers for 1,530 miles (2,460km). Long-nose turboprop conversions of the Beech 18 by Hamilton Aviation are called the Westwind III and Westwind II STD. *Country of origin:* USA. *Silhouette:* Beech 18. *Picture:* H18 Super 18.

Power: 2 × M337 piston engines   *Span:* 40ft 4½in (12.31m)   *Length:* 28ft 3in (8.61m)

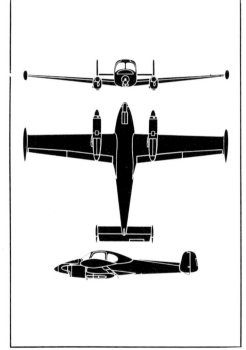

The successor to the Aero 145, the L-200 Morava is a four/five-seat light business aircraft first flown in 1957. Over 400 have been built and many have been exported within Eastern Europe. The three versions—the L-200, L-200A and L-200D—are all similar in external appearance. The Morava can be converted to carry two stretchers. Cruising speed is 159 mph (256km/hr) and range 1,063 miles (1,710km). *Country of origin:* Czechoslovakia. *Silhouette and picture:* L-200.

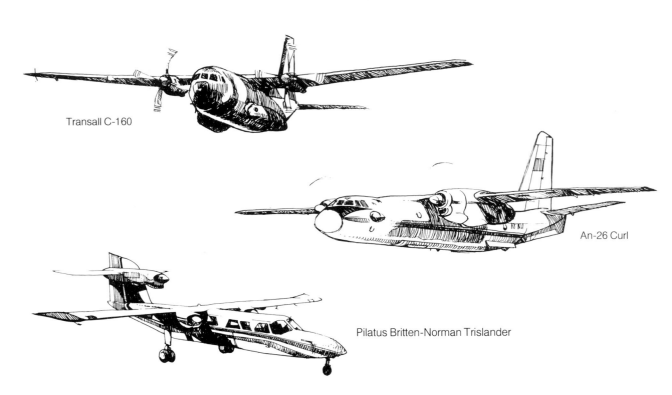

Transall C-160

An-26 Curl

Pilatus Britten-Norman Trislander

Power: 2 × Lycoming piston engines or 2 × TPE 331 turboprops   *Span:* 46ft 7in (14.2m)   *Length:* 43ft (13.1m)

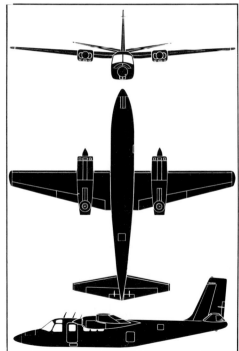

Beginning in 1948 with the Aero Commander, the Commander range is very extensive and many hundreds have been produced. From the 520 six-seater the design progressed to the Grand Commander with a longer fuselage and accommodation for nine passengers. Also in the series are the Shrike Commander four-seater, the shorter-wing, pressurised, eight-seat Hawk Commander, and a Garrett AiResearch turboprop version of the Hawk, the Commander Jetprop 840. Other versions are the Jetprop 900, 980 and 1000. The 840 has a range with maximum payload of 1,233 miles (1,985km) at 285 mph (460km/hr). *Country of origin:* USA. *Silhouette:* Aero Commander. *Picture:* Commander Jetprop 980.

Mitsubishi MU-2 *Confusion:* Turbolet

Power: 2 × TPE331 turboprops   *Span:* 39ft 2in (11.94m)   *Length:* 39ft 5in (12.02m)

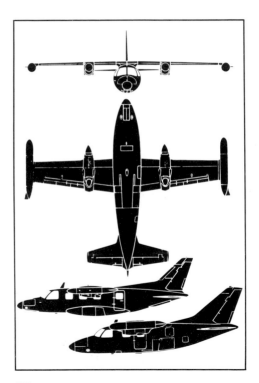

A utility transport first flown in 1963, the MU-2 seats up to 11 passengers. Various versions, from the MU-2A to P, vary in power, weights and performance. The MU-2E is used by the Japan Air Self-Defence Force for rescue work. Wingtip tanks are standard. MU-2s are now assembled in the United States at a plant in Texas. The MU-2N has a cruising speed of 300 mph (480km/hr) and a range of 1,450 miles (2,330km). The MU-2N is called the Marquise and the MU-2P the Solitaire. By March 1984 MU-2 orders totalled 745. *Country of origin:* Japan/USA. *Main silhouette:* MU-2B; *upper side view:* MU-2J. *Picture:* MU-2J.

Power: 2 × M601 or 2 × PT6A turboprops   *Span:* 57ft 4in (17.48m)   *Length:* 44ft 8in (13.61m)

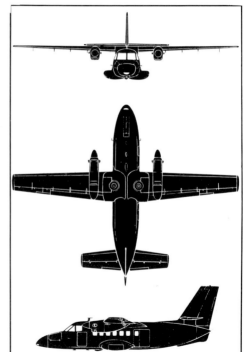

A light passenger/freight transport, the L-410 Turbolet first flew in 1969. Cruising at 236 mph (380km/hr) for up to 124 miles (200km), the Turbolet carries 17/19 passengers. The first production version, the L-410A, is powered by American PT6A engines, while the L-410M has two Czech M601A turboprops. A survey/photographic version, the L-410AF, has a large glazed nose on which is mounted a non-retractable nosewheel. Current production model is the L-410UVP, with increased span, larger fin and tailplane dihedral. *Country of origin:* Czechoslovakia. *Silhouette:* L-410A. *Picture:* L-410UVP.

Piaggio P.166 *Confusion:* MU-2

Power: 2 × Lycoming piston engines or 2 × Lycoming turboprops   *Span:* 48ft 2½in (14.69m)   *Length:* 39ft 3in (11.9m)

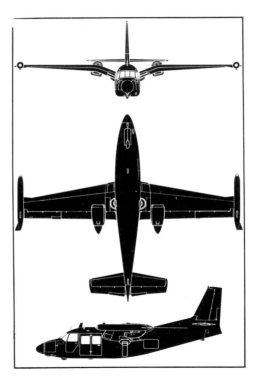

Produced in large numbers, the P.166 with two pusher engines was first flown in 1957. This light transport, seating up to nine passengers, has been built in both military and civil forms. Current versions are the P.166-DL2 with piston engines and P.166-DL3 with turboprops; the latter first flew in 1976. Wingtip tanks are fitted as standard. A maritime surveillance version is known as the P.166-DL3-MAR. Economical cruising speed of the -DL3 is 186 mph (300km/hr) and range with maximum payload 460 miles (741km). *Country of origin:* Italy. *Silhouette:* P.166-DL3. *Picture:* P.166M.

Power: 2 × TPE331 turboprops   *Span:* 55ft 7in (16.97m)   *Length* (-200): 54ft 3in (16.55m)

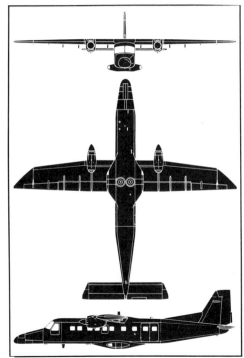

The Dornier Do 228 commuter transport is a combination of a new-technology wing with the modified fuselage of the Do 128 and a retractable undercarriage. The basic Do 228-100 has a length of 49ft 4in (15.03m) and seats 15 passengers, while the -200 is longer and seats 19. Both versions are fitted with Garrett AiResearch turboprops. The 228-100 went into service in Norway in the summer of 1982, following first flights by the -100 and -200 in 1981. The 228 is being licence-built in India. There are two maritime patrol versions A and B on offer. Economical cruising speed is 206 mph (332km/hr) and range (Do228-200) is 715 miles (1,150km). *Country of origin:* West Germany. *Silhouette:* -200. *Picture:* -100.

Aérospatiale N 262/Frégate

Confusion: Turbolet, Pembroke

Power: 2 × Bastan turboprops   *Span:* 71ft 10in (21.9m)   *Length:* 63ft 3in (19.28m)

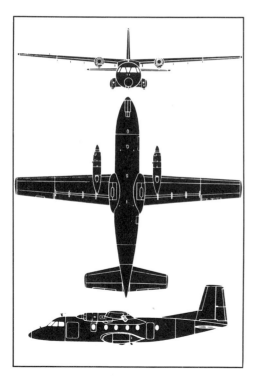

Descended from an earlier unpressurised transport, the Nord N 260 Super Broussard, the pressurised N 262/Frégate short-range airliner is used by civil and military operators. First flown in 1962, the 262 has been produced in four series: A, B, C and D. Only four Bs were built and the standard basic production version was the 262A. A few Series C with more powerful engines were built; military counterpart of the C is the Series D for the French Air Force. The 262C cruises at 247 mph (397km/hr) over a range of 1,490 miles (2,400km) with 26 passengers. *Country of origin:* France. *Silhouette and picture:* Series C.

282

Power: 2 × Leonides piston engines   *Span:* 64ft 6in (19.6m)   *Length:* 46ft (14m)

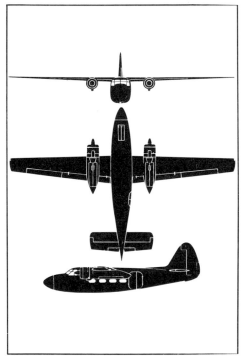

Still in service with the RAF as a six/ten-seat communications and light transport, the Pembroke C1 first flew in 1952. Derived from the civil Prince transport, the Pembroke was supplied to a number of air forces. Some Pembrokes were used for photographic purposes. Double freight doors are fitted on the port side. Cruising speed is 155 mph (255km/hr) and range 1,150 miles (1,850km). The RAF's Pembroke C1s were fitted with new wing main spars during the early 1970s to prolong their service lives. The Royal Swedish Air Force operates two ten-passenger Pembroke 52s. *Country of origin:* UK. *Silhouette and Picture:* C1.

Grumman S-2/C-1 Tracker/Trader

Confusion: Pembroke, Herald

Power: 2 × R-1820 piston engines   *Span* (S-2D to -2G): 72ft 7in (22.13m)   *Length:* 43ft 6in (13.26m)

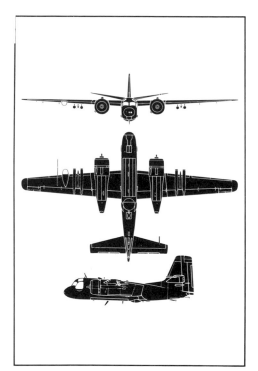

Used on land or aboard aircraft carriers, the Grumman S-2 Tracker is an anti-submarine aircraft. A carrier on-board delivery version, the C-1 Trader, can seat nine passengers. The Tracker first flew in 1953 and carries homing torpedoes, depth bombs and depth charges internally and torpedoes, rockets or bombs under the wings. Various versions were built, from the S-2A to the -2G, and over 1,000 of the type were produced. With a normal crew of four, the Tracker has a maximum speed of 265 mph (426km/hr) and nine hours' endurance. Non-US Tracker operators include Canada, Argentina, Turkey, Peru, Brazil, South Korea and the Japan Maritime Self-Defence Force. *Country of origin:* USA. *Silhouette:* S-2D. *Picture:* S-2A.

Power: 2 × **Dart turboprops**   *Span:* **95ft 2in (29m)**   *Length* (Mk 500): **82ft 2½in (25.06m)**

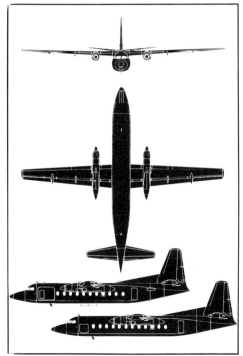

Orders for the F27 Friendship short/medium-haul airliner have totalled over 755 since it first flew in 1955, and the type remains in production. The Friendship was built under licence in the USA as the FH-227. Variants are the Mks 100, 200, 300, 400/600 and the long-fuselage, 52-passenger 500. The Mk 500 also has a large side freight door. Friendships are in use as military transports. Military versions include F27 Maritime, Maritime Enforcer, Sentinel and a proposed AEW variant called Kingbird. The Mk 500 has a cruising speed of 298 mph (480km/hr) and a range of 1,082 miles (1,741km). *Country of origin:* Netherlands. *Main silhouette:* Mk 500; *upper side view:* FH-227. *Picture:* F.27 Maritime Enforcer.

285

Antonov An-24/An-26 Coke/Curl *Confusion:* Friendship, Clank, Cline

Power: 2 × Ivchenko turboprops   *Span:* 95ft 9½in (29.2m)   *Length:* 77ft 2½in (23.53m)

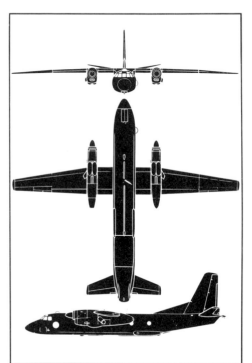

Over 1,000 Antonov An-24 transports, code-named Coke, have been built since the type first flew in 1960. Initially fitted with 44 seats, the aircraft was developed to accommodate 50 passengers as the -24V. A subsequent variant was fitted with higher-powered engines and modified wing. An under-fuselage rear door is fitted to the -24T, while the -24RT and -24RV each have an auxiliary turbojet in the starboard nacelle. The An-26 Curl is a development with an upswept rear fuselage and enlarged rear loading ramp. The basic An-24V Series II has a range of 1,490 miles (2,400km) and a cruising speed of 280 mph (450km/hr). *Country of origin:* USSR. *Silhouette and picture:* An-26.

Antonov An-30 Clank

Power: 2 × Ivchenko turboprops   *Span:* 95ft 9½in (29.2m)   *Length:* 79ft 7in (24.26m)

Designed for aerial survey, the An-30, code-named Clank, is a direct development of the An-24 Coke. It is fitted with a longer glazed nose and a raised flight deck. Cameras are mounted in the fuselage, which has its own darkroom, and a computer controls the flight profile. The An-30 has fewer windows than the passenger versions of the An-24. An auxiliary turbojet is mounted in the starboard nacelle. This is used for engine starting, and for take-off, climb and cruise power in the event of main engine failure. The An-30's primary role is aerial photography for map-making, for which it is equipped with large survey cameras mounted above four apertures in the cabin floor. The openings are covered by doors which can be opened under remote control from the crew photographer's station. *Country of origin:* USSR.

Antonov An-32 Cline

Confusion: Coke/Curl, Clank, Friendship

Power: 2 × Ivchenko turboprops   *Span:* 95ft 9½in (29.2m)   *Length:* 78ft 1in (23.8m)

A major increase in power is the main feature of the An-32 Cline, which is a direct development of the An-24 Coke. Main differences are bigger engine nacelles mounted over the wings and a greatly enlarged ventral fin. Higher power gives the Cline better airfield performance, particularly at high altitudes and temperatures. Payloads include 39 passengers, 30 parachutists or 24 stretchers. A rear loading door is fitted. Range is 1,367 miles (2,200km). Operating from airfields 12,125-14,750ft (4,000-4,500m) above sea level, the An-32 can carry 6,600lb (3,000kg) of freight for 680 miles (1,100km). *Country of origin:* USSR.

DHC DHC-4A Caribou

Power: 2 × R-2000 piston engines   *Span:* 95ft 7in (29.15m)   *Length:* 72ft 7in (22.13m)

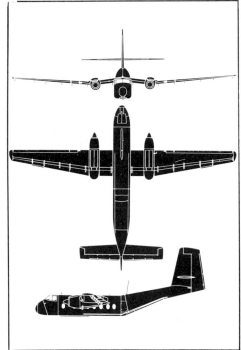

A short take-off and landing (Stol) utility transport, the DHC-4A Caribou first flew in 1958. The civil variant accommodates 30 passengers, while in military service 32 troops, three tons (3,050kg) of freight, two jeeps or stretchers can be carried. Under the upswept rear fuselage there is a large single loading door. In Canadian Forces service the Caribou is known as the CC-108. The US Army ordered 159 CV-2 Caribous. These aircraft were later taken over by the USAF, which designated them C-7A. Range is 1,307 miles (2,103km) and cruising speed 182 mph (293km/hr). *Country of origin:* Canada.

DHC DHC-5 Buffalo/Transporter *Confusion:* Caribou

Power: 2 × CT64 turboprops   *Span:* 96ft (29.26m)   *Length:* 79ft (24.08m)

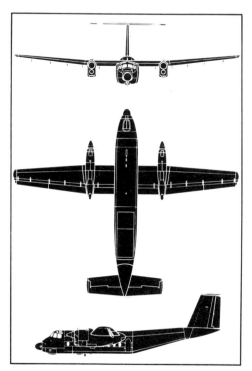

Originally called the DHC-5 Caribou II, the Stol turboprop development of the Caribou was renamed Buffalo. A military transport, the Buffalo carries 41 troops, jeeps, stretchers or freight loaded through an underfuselage rear door. The Caribou first flew in 1964. In USAF service it is known as the C-8A, and as the CC-115 with the Canadian Forces. Specially equipped Buffalos are used for maritime patrol. Range is 691 miles (1,112km) at a maximum cruising speed of 261 mph (420km/hr). The 44-seat civil passenger/cargo version of the DHC-5D Buffalo is the DHC-5E Transporter. *Country of origin:* Canada.

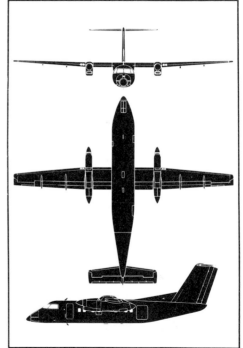

Power: 2 × PW120 turboprops   *Span:* 84ft 11in (25.89m)   *Length:* 73ft (22.25m)

A 30/40-seat short-haul transport, the de Havilland Canada Dash 8 first flew in June 1983. There are two basic versions, the Commuter and the Corporate, the latter carrying 17 passengers over longer ranges. The Corporate has a maximum cruising speed of 311 mph (500km/h) and can fly four 185km stages without refuelling. By September 1984 102 orders and options had been placed for the Dash 8. *Country of origin:* Canada.

Fairchild C-123 Provider *Confusion:* G.222, Transall

Power: 2 × R-8000 piston engines and 2 × J44 turbojets   *Span:* 110ft (33.53m)   *Length:* 76ft 3in (23.93m)

A tactical assault transport, the C-123 Provider can carry up to 60 equipped troops, stretchers or cargo. It was first flown in 1949 and production totalled 307. Originally produced as C-123Bs, 183 Providers were later converted to C-123K standard with underwing auxiliary jets. A further 10 were fitted with wingtip jets as the C-123H. Equipped with spraying gear for mosquito control, the Provider becomes the UC-123B. Underwing fuel tanks are standard, while some Providers have nose radomes. C-123s were supplied to air forces in the Far East and South America. *Country of origin:* USA. *Silhouette:* C-123K. *Picture:* C-123H.

Power: 2 × T64 turboprops   *Span:* 94ft 2in (28.7m)   *Length:* 74ft 5½in (22.7m)

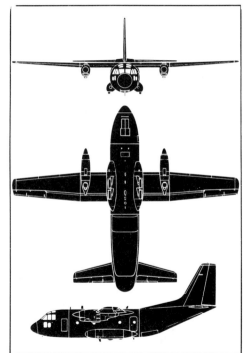

A general-purpose pressurised military transport, the G.222 is in production for the Italian Air Force and export customers. Capable of operating from rough strips, the 222 can carry 44 equipped troops, 36 stretchers or freight loaded through a large underside rear door. The prototype 222 first flew in 1970 and the type can also be used for firefighting (G.222SAA), radio/radar calibration (G.222RM), maritime surveillance and electronic warfare (G.222VS). With Rolls-Royce Tyne turboprops the type is known as the G.222T. Range of the G.222 is 435 miles (700km) and continuous cruising speed is 224 mph (360km/hr). Over 80 222s have been ordered. *Country of origin:* Italy. *Silhouette:* G.222. *Picture:* G.222T.

Transporter Allianz C-160 Transall

Confusion: G.222, Provider, Aviocar

Power: 2 × Tyne turboprops   *Span:* 131ft 3in (40m)   *Length:* 106ft 3½in (32.4m)

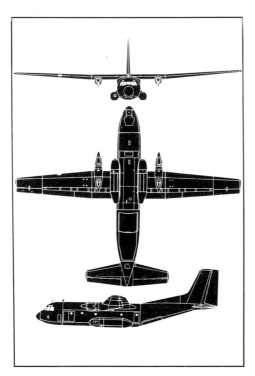

A joint Franco-German development, the C-160 Transall is a general-purpose military transport. It can carry up to 93 troops, freight or vehicles. A total of 179 were produced before production ceased in 1972. The line has since been reopened and production resumed with the Transall 'Second Series'. The aircraft of the new batch have updated electronics, increased maximum take-off weight, and a reinforced wing embodying an optional fuel tank. Surveillance, electronic warfare and airborne command versions are on offer. As well as France and Germany, South Africa and Turkey also use the Transall. The aircraft can operate from semi-prepared surfaces. Cruising speed is 306 mph (492km/hr) and range 730 miles (1,175km). *Country of origin:* France/Germany.

Airtech CN-235

Power: 2 × CT7 turboprops   *Span:* 84ft 8in (25.81m)   *Length:* 70ft 1in (21.35m)

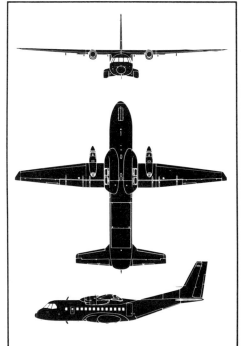

A joint venture by CASA of Spain and PT Nurtanio of Indonesia, the Airtech CN-235 is a twin turboprop commuter transport which first flew in November 1983. Seating up to 44 passengers, the CN-235 can fly four 115 mile (185km) stage lengths on short haul routes before needing to refuel. Maximum cruising speed is 280 mph (452km/h). Production lines have been set up in both countries and, by March 1984, 110 CN-235s had been ordered. *Countries of origin:* Spain and Indonesia

Aérospatiale/Aeritalia ATR 42 *Confusion:* Transall, Buffalo

Power: 2 × PW 120 turboprops   *Span:* 80ft 7in (24.57m)   *Length:* 74ft 5in (22.67m)

Jointly produced by Aérospatiale in France and Aeritalia in Italy, the ATR 42 commuter aircraft made its first flight in August 1984. Seating 40/50 passengers, the ATR 42 cruises at 250 knots (463km/hr) over ranges up to 1,094 miles (1,760km). By end August 1984 orders had been received for 69 ATR 42s. Projected versions include troop transport and maritime search. *Countries of origin:* France/Italy.

Power: **2 × TPE331 turboprops**   *Span:* **62ft 4in (19m)**   *Length:* **49ft 9in (15.16m)**

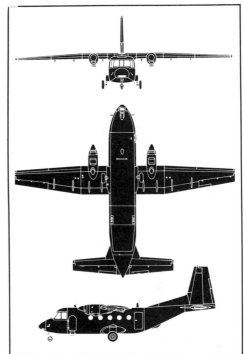

Used for both military and civil purposes, the Aviocar is a Stol utility transport, trainer and survey aircraft. More than 345 have been sold, and there are production centres in Spain and Indonesia. The C-212-5 Series 100, the first production version, has now been superseded on the line by the Series 200 with more powerful engines and greater weight. In civil transport form the Aviocar seats up to 26 passengers, cruises at 216 mph (347km/hr) and has a range of 230 miles (370km) with full payload. An anti-submarine and maritime patrol version with a nose radome, has been developed. *Country of origin:* Spain. *Silhouette:* Series 200. *Picture:* Series 100.

Pilatus Britten-Norman Islander/Defender *Confusion:* Trislander, P.68 Victor

Power: 2 × Lycoming piston engines   *Span:* **49ft (14.94m)**   *Length* (long nose): **39ft 5in (12.02m)**

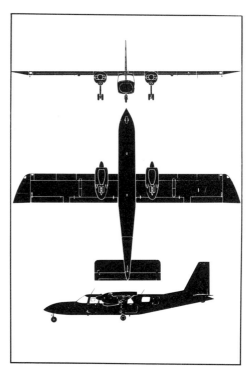

First flown in 1965, the 10-passenger BN-2 Islander light transport has sold all over the world and over 1,000 have been ordered. Licence production is going on in Romania and the Philippines. Compared with earlier versions, the BN-2A-85 Islander has a longer nose and an extra rear cabin window on each side. Military variants with underwing stores are the Defender and the Maritime Defender. Range at a cruising speed of 160 mph (257km/hr) is 870 miles (1,400km). Latest version is the BN-2-T Turbine Islander, powered by two Allison turboprops. A surveillance version with a large circular nose radar is also on offer. *Country of origin:* UK.*Silhouette:* BN-2A-85. *Picture:* BN-2-T.

Power: 3 × Lycoming piston engines   *Span:* 53ft (16.15m)   *Length* (Mk III-2): 43ft 9in (13.33m)

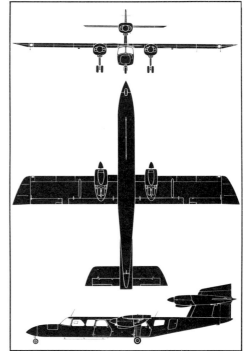

The BN-2A Trislander is derived from the twin-engined Islander and has 75 per cent of its components in common. Essential difference is the fitting of a third engine in the redesigned fin. Some Trislanders have been produced with a short nose, while the Mk III-2 has a long nose . Trislanders were produced in Belgium for a time. The aircraft carries 16/17 passengers, cruises at 175 mph (282km/hr) and has a range with maximum payload of 160 miles (257km). Over 80 Trislanders have been delivered and the licence for the type is held by International Aviation Corp, where the name has been changed to Tri-Commutair. *Country of origin:* UK. *Silhouette and picture:* Mk III-2.

Partenavia P.68 Victor

Confusion: Islander, Twin Otter

Power: 2 × Lycoming piston engines or 2 × Allison 250 turboprops   *Span:* 39ft 4½in (12m)   *Length:* 30ft 8in (9.35m)

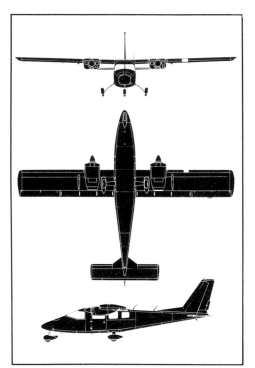

A streamlined light transport, the original P.68 was first put into production in 1964. A variety of versions have emerged, including the six-passenger P.68B, the P.68R with retractable undercarriage, P.68C, currently in production, and P.68TC with turbosupercharged engines. An Italian/German development, the P.68 Observer, has a transparent nose and is designed for police and observation duties. Cruising speed of the P.68B is 184 mph (296km/hr) and range 1,029 miles (1,656km). Aeritalia is now developing a turboprop, retractable-undercarriage version designated AP.68B. *Country of origin:* Italy. *Silhouette:* P.68C. *Picture:* P.68C.

Power: 2 × Lycoming piston engines   *Span:* 45ft 3½in (13.8m)   *Length:* 29ft 6in (9m)

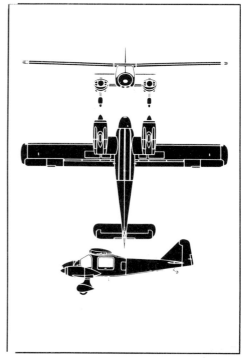

A twin-engined version of the Do 27, the Do 28 seven-passenger light transport retains the basic wings and fuselage of the single-engined type. Some 120 Do 28s were built, including military aircraft and six floatplanes. First flight was in 1959. The nose was redesigned, the tailplane enlarged and wingspan increased to produce the Do 28B1. The B2 has supercharged engines. Maximum cruising speed of the B1 is 170 mph (274km/hr) and range 768 miles (1,235km). *Country of origin:* West Germany. *Silhouette:* Do 28B1. *Picture:* Do 28B2.

Dornier Do 28D/Do 128 Skyservant   *Confusion:* Do 28B

Power: 2 × Lycoming piston engines or 2 × PT6A turboprops   *Span:* 51ft (15.55m)   *Length:* 37ft 5in (11.41m)

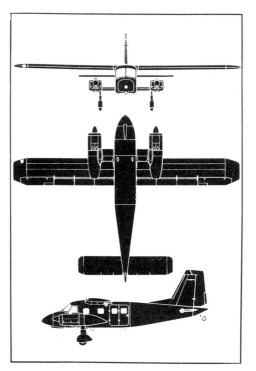

Retaining the same layout as the Do 28 but virtually a complete redesign, the Do 28D Skyservant first flew in 1966. A Stol utility transport, the Skyservant seats up to 14 passengers or can carry freight. Six air forces have bought Skyservants, the largest operator being the Luftwaffe with 101. Now on the line is the the turboprop-powered Do 128-6 with PT6A engines, following the end of Do 128-2 Skyservant production. *Country of origin:* West Germany. *Silhouette:* Do 28D2. *Picture:* Do 128-6.

Power: 2 × Allison turboprops   *Span:* 54ft (16.46m)   *Length:* 47ft 1in (14.35m)

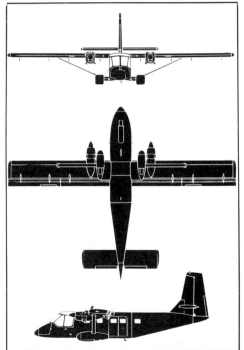

A twin-turboprop high-wing utility transport and feederliner, the GAF Nomad first flew in 1971. The prototype was known as the N2, while the initial production variant was the 17-passenger N22B. Patrol and surveillance versions of the N22B are known as the Search Master B and L. For general-purpose military work the N22B is known as the Missionmaster. Latest version of the Nomad is the N24 with increased fuselage length and seating for 19 passengers. The N24 Nomad has a range of 985 miles (1,585km) and a cruising speed of 167 mph (269km/hr). A total of over 160 Nomads has been sold. *Country of origin:* Australia. *Silhouette:* N22B. *Picture:* N24A.

DHC DHC-6 Twin Otter

Confusion: Nomad, Clod, Cash

Power: 2 × PT6 turboprops   *Span:* 65ft (19.81m)   *Length:* 51ft 9in (15.77m)

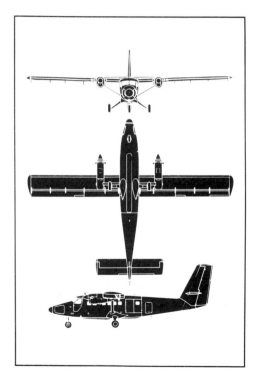

A general-purpose civil and military transport, the DHC-6 Twin Otter can operate from short, rough fields and accommodate up to 20 passengers or freight. First flown in 1965, the Twin Otter has been built in three forms, the 100, 200 and 300 series. Service designations are CC-138 (Canadian Forces) and UV-18A (US Army). Maximum cruising speed is 210 mph (337km/hr), at which the range is 1,103 miles (1,775km). The floatplane version has a short nose and small additional fins above and below the tailplane. A Twin Otter Series 300 supplied to China for survey work has a nose probe and wingtip pods. *Country of origin:* Canada. *Silhouette:* Series 200. *Picture:* Series 300.

Power: 2 × Ivchenko piston engines   *Span:* 72ft 2in (21.99m)   *Length:* 37ft 6in (11.44m)

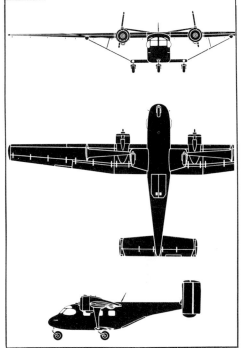

A rough-field Stol utility transport, the An-14, code-named Clod, was produced in quantity, mainly for Aeroflot. With a one-man crew, the Clod has seating for seven passengers. The prototype flew in 1958 but production was delayed for a major redesign to the present standard, with a high-aspect-ratio wing and large endplate fins. In the Soviet Union the Clod is known as the Pchelka ("Little Bee"). Clamshell rear doors simplify freight loading. Cruising speed is 112 mph (180km/hr). *Country of origin:* USSR.

PZL Mielec (Antonov) An-28 Cash

Confusion: Clod, Skyvan, Shorts 330, 360

Power: 2 × Glushenko turboprops   *Span:* 72ft 4in (22.06m)   *Length:* 43ft (13.1m)

Originally developed by the Antonov Bureau in the Soviet Union as a turboprop version of the An-14 Clod, the An-28 Cash is now produced in Poland. The Cash has a high aspect-ratio braced wing, sponson-mounted undercarriage and rear under-fuselage doors. It is intended for a variety of roles including flying training, carriage of passengers (17), mail and freight, fire-fighting, geological survey and agricultural work. Initial deliveries from the Polish line began early in 1984. The An-28 cruises at 209 mph (337km/h) over ranges up to 348 miles (350km). *Countries of origin:* USSR/Poland.

Power: 2 × TPE331 turboprops   *Span:* 64ft 11in (19.79m)   *Length:* 40ft 1in (12.21m)

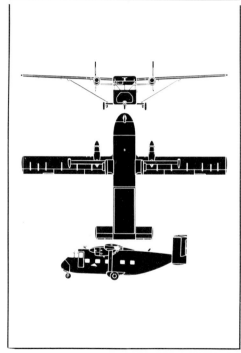

A rugged Stol general-purpose transport, the Skyvan originally flew in 1963 with piston engines. It was then fitted with French Astazou turboprops and finally with Garrett AiResearch turboprops. Some 150 Skyvans have been built for military, paramilitary and civil use. The Skyliner feederliner can carry up to 19 passengers, while freighter versions can lift 4,600lb (2,085kg) of cargo or vehicles. Freight is loaded through an underside rear door. Skyvan Series 3 has a range of 694 miles (1,115km) and a maximum cruising speed of 195 mph (314km/hr). *Country of origin:* UK. *Silhouette and picture:* Series 3.

Shorts 330/Sherpa/C-23A   *Confusion:* Skyvan, Shorts 360, Cash, Skyservant

Power: 2 × PT6A turboprops   *Span:* 74ft 8in (22.76m)   *Length:* 58ft (17.69m)

A 30-seat feederliner and utility transport, the Shorts 330 is similar in basic configuration to the smaller Skyvan. The fuselage is rectangular in cross-section and the wing has a high aspect ratio. Unlike the Skyvan, the 330 has a retractable undercarriage. Over 115 Sherpas have been ordered, including the standard 330-200 passenger version, the 330-UTT military utility transport and the Sherpa freighter with rear door, 18 of which have been ordered by the USAF as the C-23A. Cruising speed of the 330-200 is 184 mph (296km/hr) and range with maximum fuel, 1,053 miles (1,695km). *Country of origin:* UK. *Silhouette:* 330. *Picture:* C-23A Sherpa.

Power: 2 × PT6A turboprops   *Span:* 74ft 8in (22.75m)   *Length:* 70ft 6in (21.49m)

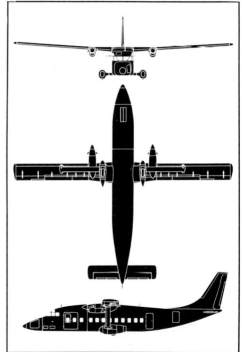

Retaining the high-aspect-ratio wing of the Shorts 330, the new 360 differs from the former in having a 3ft extension in the forward fuselage and a redesigned rear fuselage with a single swept fin. Flown for the first time in 1981, the 360 is now in production at Belfast alongside the 330. A short-range commuter transport, the 360 carries 36 passengers and cruises at 243 mph (391km/hr), and has a maximum range of 655 miles (1,054km). Deliveries began in the last quarter of 1982 and over 100 have been ordered. *Country of origin:* UK.

Grumman E-2 Hawkeye

Confusion: —

Power: 2 × T56 turboprops   *Span:* 80ft 7in (24.56m)   *Length:* 57ft 7in (17.55m)

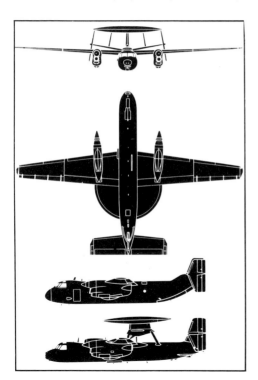

The first US Navy turboprop-powered type to enter service, the E-2 Hawkeye is a carrierborne early-warning aircraft. Virtually an airborne radar station, the Hawkeye carries a massive oval radome mounted above the fuselage and houses complex electronic gear operated by a five-man crew. The differences between the various Hawkeye versions (E-2A, B and C) lie in the radar and internal equipment. The transport version of Hawkeye is the C-2A Greyhound, which can accommodate 39 passengers, stretchers or cargo. The aircraft has a range of 1,650 miles (2,660km). *Country of origin:* USA. *Main silhouette:* E-2C; *upper side view:* C-2A. *Picture:* E-2C.

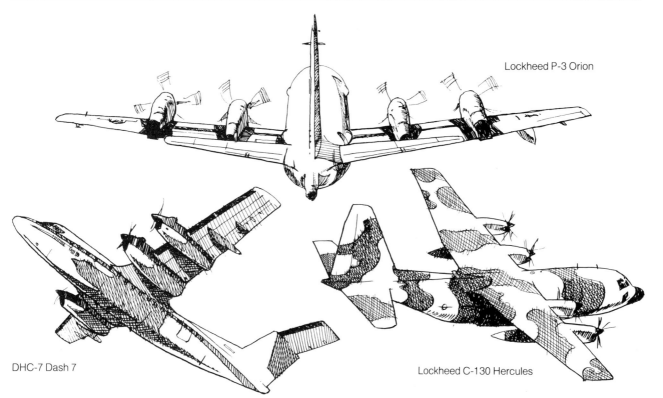

Lockheed P-3 Orion

DHC-7 Dash 7

Lockheed C-130 Hercules

de Havilland Heron

Confusion: Viscount

Power: 4 × Gipsy Queen piston engines   *Span:* 71ft 6in (21.8m)   *Length:* 48ft 6in (14.8m)

A scaled-up, four-engined Dove, the Heron first flew in 1950 and altogether 150 were built. As a short-range light transport the Heron seats 14/17, cruises at 225 mph (362km/hr) and has a range of 1,180 miles (1,900km). Herons are used as executive aircraft and for military purposes. Re-engined conversions, include the Shin Meiwa DH 114TAW, the Saunders ST-27 and the Riley Turbo Skyliner. Powered by four 290 hp Lycoming engines with Rajay turbo-superchargers, the Turbo Skyliner has a maximum level speed at 12,000ft (3,660mph) of 285 mph (495km/hr); cruising speed at 75 per cent power of 225 mph (362km/hr); service ceiling of 20,000ft (6,100m); and a two-engines-out service ceiling of 15,000ft (4,570m). A total of 18 Riley Turbo Skyliners were converted from Heron Series 2X, 2A and 2DA aircraft. *Country of origin:* UK. *Silhouette:* Heron. *Picture:* Riley Turbo Skyliner.

Power: 4 × Dart turboprops   *Span* (700): 93ft 8½in (28.56m)   *Length* (700): 81ft 10in (25.04m)

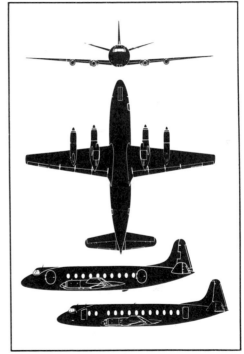

The world's first turboprop transport to go into service, the Viscount short-range airliner first flew in 1948 and 441 were built. The first production version was the Series 700 with up to 59 passengers. This was followed by the stretched 800 series with seating for up to 65 passengers. The Viscount remains in service in many countries. Several 700s and 800 were built or converted for executive use. Scottish Aviation designed a convertible passenger/cargo interior for Series 800 Viscounts. Nine pallets can be loaded and maximum cargo weight is 14,900lb (6,759kg). The 700 cruises at 312 mph (502km/hr) and has a range of 1,750 miles (2,815km). *Country of origin:* UK. *Main silhouette:* Viscount Series 800; *upper side view:* Viscount Series 700. *Picture:* Viscount Series 700.

Vickers Vanguard/Merchantman

Confusion: Viscount, Coot

Power: 4 × Tyne turboprops   *Span:* 118ft 7in (36.15m)   *Length:* 122ft 10½in (37.45m)

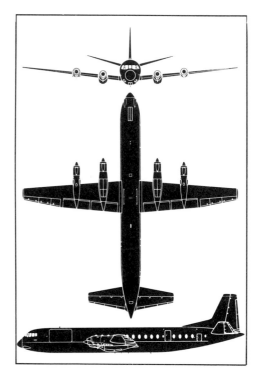

Designed to a British European Airways specification, the Type 951 Vanguard first flew in 1959. It was expected to be a major successor to the Viscount, but the advent of pure-jet aircraft like the Caravelle precluded large-scale production. Altogether 43 Vanguards were built, of which nine were converted into Merchantman freighters. As a passenger-carrying aircraft the Vanguard seats up to 139 passengers, has a maximum cruising speed of 425 mph (684km/hr) and a range of 1,830 miles (2,945km). *Country of origin:* UK. *Silhouette and picture:* Vanguard.

Ilyushin Il-18/Il-20 Coot

Power: 4 × Ivchenko turboprops   *Span:* 122ft 8½in (37.4m)   *Length:* 117ft 9in (35.9m)

Over 700 Il-18 Coot medium-range airliners were built and the type was exported to a number of countries. It first came into service in 1959 and was known in Russia as the Moskva. Several versions were produced, including the Il-18V with 89/100 passengers and the Il-18D with 122 passengers. The Il-18D cruises at 388 mph (625km/hr) over ranges of up to 4,040 miles (6,500km). A military development is the electronic surveillance Il-20 Coot-A, with forward fuselage side bulges, a large underfuselage pannier and dorsal aerial fairings. The pannier, measuring 33ft 7½in (10.25m) long by 3ft 9in (1.15m) deep, is believed to house sideways-looking radar. *Country of origin:* USSR. *Silhouette:* Il-18. *Picture:* Il-20 Coot-A.

Ilyushin Il-38 May

Confusion: Coot, Orion, Electra

Power: 4 × Ivchenko turboprops   *Span:* 122ft 9in (37.4m)   *Length:* 131ft (39.92m)

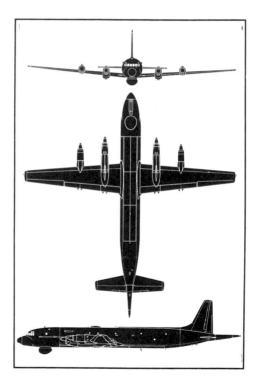

Like the American Orion, the Il-38, code-named May, is a civil airliner developed for maritime reconnaissance and anti-submarine warfare. The May marries the wings and tail assembly of Coot to a new fuselage with a bulbous radome under the forward section and a magnetic anomaly detector (MAD) fairing extending from the tail. May has a cruising speed of 370 mph (595km/hr) and a range of 4,500 miles (7,240km). Armament includes homing torpedoes and depth charges. About 60 Il-38s are in Soviet service and the type has been exported to India. *Country of origin:* USSR.

Power: 4 × Allison 501 turboprops *Span:* 99ft (30.18m) *Length:* 104ft 6½in (31.81m)

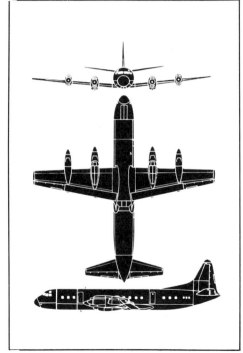

A medium-range four-turboprop airliner, the Lockheed Electra first flew in 1957. Early in its career the Electra suffered two disastrous crashes, the result of metal fatigue. A number of modifications were required by the airworthiness authorities, including strengthening of the wing and engine nacelle structure, and the provision of thicker wing skins. Two versions of the Electra were built: the L-188A and the longer-range L-188C. A total of 168 Electras were completed. The Orion maritime reconnaissance aircraft was evolved from the Electra. The L-188C seats 98 passengers, cruises at 405 mph (652km/hr) and has a range of 2,770 miles (4,458km). *Country of origin:* USA. *Silhouette:* L-188C. *Picture:* L-188A.

Lockheed P-3 Orion   *Confusion:* Electra, May, Coot

Power: 4 × T.56 turboprops   *Span:* 99ft 8in (30.37m)   *Length:* 116ft 10in (35.61m)

A development of the civil Lockheed Electra, the P-3 Orion long-range anti-submarine aircraft first flew in 1958. Carrying a crew of ten, the Orion is equipped with sophisticated search equipment, including the distinctive tail-mounted magnetic anomaly detector (MAD) probe. Armament includes torpedoes and depth charges. A number of versions of the Orion have been built, the latest being the CP-140 for Canada and the avionics have been continuously up-dated. Over 580 Orions have been delivered. The P-3C Orion has a four-engine loiter endurance of 12.3hr and patrol speed is 237 mph (381km/hr). *Country of origin:* USA. *Silhouette and picture:* P-3C.

Confusion: DC-6, DC-7   **Douglas DC-4/C-54 Skymaster**

Power: 4 × R-2000 piston engines   *Span:* 117ft 6in (35.8m)   *Length:* 93ft 11in (28.6m)

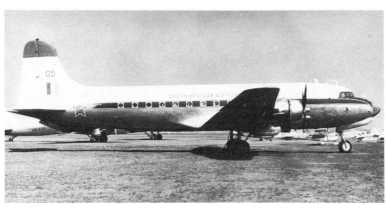

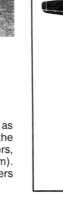

First flown as long ago as 1938, the DC-4 was widely used in military as well as civil forms. The Air Force variant was known as the C-54 Skymaster and the naval version as the R-5D. As an airliner the DC-4 seats 44 passengers, cruises at 227 mph (363km/hr) and has a range of 1,500 miles (2,480km). Military versions have a large freight door on the port side. Many Skymasters later found their way onto the civil market. *Country of origin:* USA.

Douglas DC-6   *Confusion:* DC-4, DC-7

Power: 4 × R-2800 piston engines   *Span:* 117ft 6in (13.58m)   *Length:* 100ft 7in (30.66m)

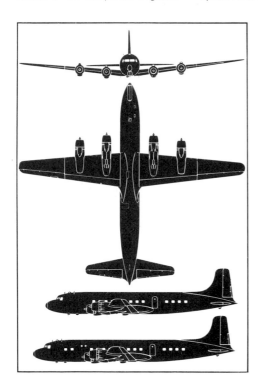

A stretched, pressurised version of the DC-4, the DC-6 first flew in 1946 and 176 were built. Some air forces also acquired DC-6s. The DC-6A was a freighter with a new fuselage, while the DC-6B was a 54-passenger airliner version of the DC-6A. The military DC-6A was designated C-118A. Cruising speed of the DC-6 is 313 mph (501km/hr) and range 3,820 miles (6,112km). The C-118 Liftmaster, still widely used by air forces around the world, can carry 76 fully equipped troops, 60 stretchers or 27,000lb of cargo. Large freight loading doors are fitted fore and aft of the wing. With a maximum level speed at 18,100ft (5,520m) of 360 mph (579km/hr), the C-118 has a normal range of 3,860 miles (6,212km). A total of 167 Liftmasters were built. *Country of origin:* USA. *Main silhouette:* DC-6B; *upper side view:* DC-6. *Picture:* C-118.

Power: 4 × R-3350 piston engines   *Span* (-7C): 127ft 6in (38.86m)   *Length:* 112ft 3in (34.21m)

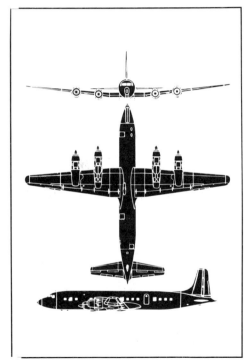

A stretch of the DC-6B fuselage produced the DC-7, seating up to 95 coach-class passengers. A change to Wright turbo-compound engines raised weight and improved performance. More fuel was provided on the -7B, which had intercontinental range. The last of the DC-4/DC-7 line was the -7C with increased wingspan and a longer fuselage. Some 120 DC-7Cs were built and a number were converted to DC-7CF freighters. The DC-7C cruises at 310 mph (499km/hr) for up to 4,100 miles (6,595km). Maximum payload is 21,500lb (9,750kg) and service ceiling 21,700ft (6,615m). Production of the DC-7 series ran to 120 DC-7s, 96 DC-7Bs and 120 DC-7Cs; these totals include some aircraft converted to DC-7F freighters. *Country of origin:* USA. *Silhouette and picture:* DC-7C.

Canadair CL-44   *Confusion:* Britannia, DC-7C

Power: 4 × Tyne turboprops   *Span:* 142ft 3½in (43.38m)   *Length:* 15ft 10in (46.28m)

The Cl-44 is a lengthened and re-engined version of the Britannia. In its initial form, as the CC-106 Yukon, the aircraft first flew in 1959 and went into service with the Royal Canadian Air Force. The type then evolved into the civil CL-44D, the world's first swing-tail long-range transport. The whole rear fuselage hinges to allow freight to be loaded. A total of 40 CL-44s were built. Cruising speed is 380 mph (612km/hr) and range 5,260 miles (8,460km). Maximum payload is 64,372lb (29,200kg) of cargo, or 45,685lb (20,800kg) in passenger configuration. Up to 214 passengers can be accommodated by the short-haul version, and 189 by the transatlantic variant. Convertible passenger/cargo variants have also been built. *Country of origin:* Canada. *Silhouette and picture:* CL-44.

Power: 4 × Griffon piston engines   *Span:* 119ft 10in (36.52m)   *Length:* 87ft 4in (26.62m)

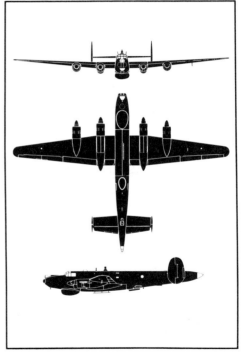

Originally produced for maritime reconnaissance, the Shackleton was converted for airborne early warning as the AEW2. Fitted with a large radome under the forward fuselage, the AEW2 carries a crew of 12 and can remain on station for up to 15hr. The type is due to be superseded in due course in the RAF by the Nimrod AEW3. *Country of origin:* UK. *Silhouette and picture:* AEW2.

Boeing KC-97 Stratofreighter *Confusion:* Guppy

Power: 4 × R-4360 piston engines
       + 2 × J47 turbojets   *Span:* 141ft 3in (43.05m)   *Length:* 117ft 5in (35.79m)

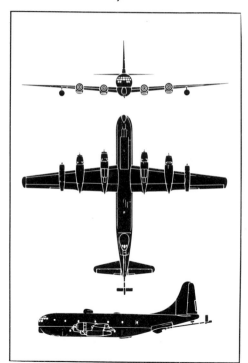

Combining the wings, tail and landing gear of the Boeing B-29/B-50 Superfortress with a large double-bubble fuselage, the KC-97 Stratofreighter was produced in very large numbers. The airliner version is called the Stratocruiser. The type is used as a convertible tanker transport and has a large aerial refuelling boom under the rear fuselage. Various versions were built, including the KC-97E, F, G, K and L. Earlier marks did not have underwing auxiliary turbojets but could be fitted with auxiliary fuel tanks in the same positions. As a tanker the KC-97L can carry 10.825gal (49.210lit) of fuel, and up to 96 troops as a transport. Cruising speed is 301 mph (485km/hr). *Country of origin:* USA. *Silhouette and picture:* KC-97L.

Power: 4 × R4360 piston engines or 4 × Allison 501 turboprops   *Span:* 156ft 3in (47.62m)   *Length:* 143ft 10in (43.84m)

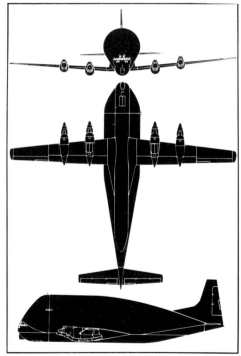

Retaining the wings and engines of the Boeing Stratocruiser airliner, the Aero Spacelines Guppy has a vast fuselage originally designed to accommodate space launcher stages. Subsequently the type has been used to airlift other specialised freight, including wings for the Airbus A300. In 1980 Airbus Industrie acquired production rights to the design, and is currently having two further examples built. Range with maximum payload is 505 miles (813km) and maximum cruising speed is 288 mph (463km/hr). The normal flight crew is four. Variants are known as Pregnant Guppy, Super Guppy and Mini-Guppy. *Country of origin:* USA. *Silhouette and picture:* Guppy.

Lockheed C-130 Hercules

Confusion: Belfast, Cub

Power: 4 × T56 turboprops   *Span:* 132ft 7in (40.41m)   *Length:* 97ft 9in (29.78m)

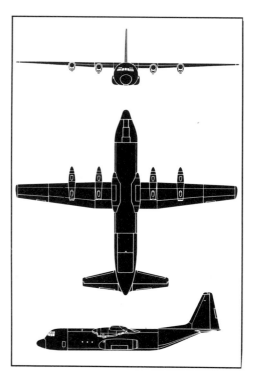

One of the most successful military transports built in the West, the C-130 Hercules first flew in 1954 and has been in production since 1955. Over 1,730 have been built for operators in 55 nations. There are many versions, including the C-130D for Arctic work, WC-130B and -130E for weather reconnaissance, AC-130E gunship, KC-130F Marine Corps tanker, C-130F for the US Navy, -130H and -130N for rescue, -130P for helicopter refuelling, EC-130Q for Navy communications and C-130K for the RAF. Twin underbody strakes are being fitted to many Hercules and 30 RAF K-130s have a 15ft (4.57m) fuselage-extension, designated Hercules C Mk 3. A civil version is designated L-100. The C-130H, which carries 92 troops or freight, cruises at 340 mph (547km/hr) and has a range with maximum payload of 2,450 miles (3,943km). *Country of origin:* USA. *Silhouette:* L-100. *Picture:* C-130K.

Antonov An-12 Cub

Power: 4 × Ivchenko turboprops   *Span:* 124ft 8in (38m)   *Length:* 121ft 4½in (37m)

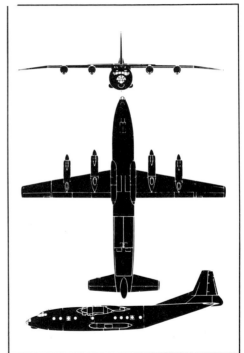

Produced in very large numbers, the An-12, code-named Cub, is used in both military and civil forms. The Cub has a crew of five and can carry 100 paratroops, vehicles, guns or missiles, loaded through the large rear ramp. Cubs serving with the Soviet and other air forces have a twin 23mm gun turret in the tail. This is replaced by a fairing on the civil version, which is known as the An-12V. Electronic intelligence and electronic countermeasures versions are coded Cub-B and Cub-C respectively. The Cub cruises at 342 mph (550km/hr) and has a range of 2,110 miles (3,400km). *Country of origin:* USSR. *Silhouette:* An-12V; *Picture:* Cub-A.

DHC Dash 7 *Confusion:* Hercules

Power: 4 × PT6 turboprops   *Span:* 93ft (28.35m)   *Length:* 80ft 8in (24.58m)

Capable of very short take-offs and landings, the DHC-7 Dash 7 seats 50 passengers or carries a mixture of passengers and freight. First flown in 1975, over 95 Dash 7s are in service. The Dash 7 operates over short routes and, in addition to its good airfield performance, is very quiet in operation. Cruising speed is 235 mph (379km/hr) and range is 696 miles (1,120km). A maritime reconnaissance version with belly radome is known as the DHC-7R. This variant differs principally from the airliner in having increased fuel tankage, providing 10–12hr of endurance at normal patrol speeds; two observer's stations with bubble windows; nose-mounted Texas Instruments search radar; and equipment for maritime surveillance. An all-cargo version is designated Series 101. *Country of origin:* Canada. *Silhouette and picture:* Dash 7.

Power: 4 × Kuznetsov turboprops   *Span:* 211ft 3½in (64.4m)   *Length:* 189ft 8in (57.8m)

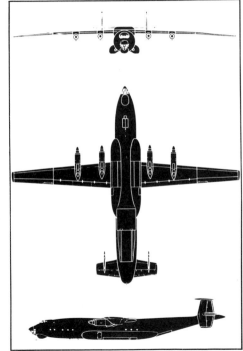

The second largest transport in the world (after the C-5A Galaxy), the Antonov An-22 Antheus, code-named Cock, is a heavy freighter for military and civil use. A crew of five/six, 28/29 passengers and a wide variety of vehicle, gun, missile and freight loads can be carried. The first Cock flew in 1965 and the type went into service with the Soviet Air Force in 1967. Some 55 of the type remain in service. An unusual feature is the fitting of two radomes in the nose. The four turboprop engines drive large contra-rotating propellers. Cock has a range of 6,800 miles (10,950km) and cruises at 422 mph (679km/hr). The An-22 has set a number of world records, including no fewer than 14 payload-to-height marks on one occasion in 1967, when 100,000kg (220,500lb) of metal blocks were carried to a height of 25,748ft (7,848m). *Country of origin:* USSR.

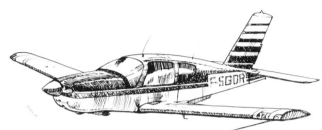

SOCATA TB 20 Trinidad

SIAI-Marchetti SF.260C

Beech Bonanza V35

Power: 1 × Avia piston engine   *Span:* 32ft 5in (9.88m)   *Length:* 26ft 2in (7.98m)

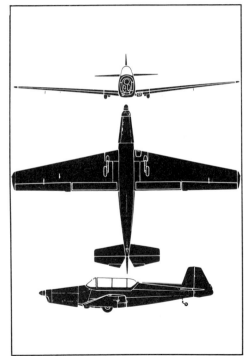

The Zlin Trener, Trener-master and Akrobat series has been in production in Czechoslovakia since 1947; more than 1,400 aircraft have been built. First of the series to feature a retractable undercarriage was the Z 326 of 1957. The single-seat competition aircraft were designated Akrobats and scored a number of successes in international aerobatics contests. Various engines have been used but all models have the distinctive swept wing leading edge and large, angular rudder. Last of the series is the Z 726, which first flew in 1973. Generally similar to the Z 526F, it has a slightly shorter wing and metal-covered rudder and elevators. Production ended in 1977 after 32 had been built. Maximum cruising speed of the 526F is 130 mph (210km/hr). *Country of origin:* Czechoslovakia. *Silhouette:* Zlin 526. *Picture:* Zlin 526A Akrobat.

CZAAL L-40 Meta-Sokol

Confusion: Zlin 526

Power: 1 × Walter Minor piston engine   *Span:* 33ft (10.06m)   *Length:* 24ft 9in (7.54m)

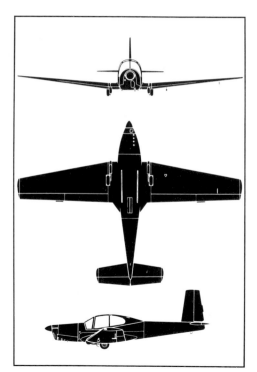

Over 200 L-40 Meta-Sokols were built between 1954 and 1961, most of which were exported. A number remain in service in Europe, and three L-40s are registered in Britain. On the ground the type's most easily identified feature is its unique reverse tricycle undercarriage. The main wheels are half-concealed when retracted. Also distinctive is the tall, almost parallel fin and rudder. Cruising speed is 137 mph (220km/hr), maximum range 688 miles (1,107km), maximum rate of climb at sea level is 630ft/min (192m/min), and service ceiling 14,765ft (4,500m). *Country of origin:* Czechoslovakia.

Power: 1 × Lycoming piston engine   *Span:* 34ft 9in (10.6m)   *Length:* 26ft 4in (8.03m)

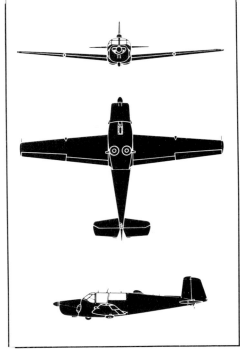

First flown in 1945, the Saab-91 Safir was built in four main versions: the Saab-91A, powered by a 145hp de Havilland Gipsy Major 10; the Saab-91B, powered by a 190hp Lycoming; the Saab-91C, widely used for private and light commercial work and as an air force trainer; and the Saab-91D, generally similar to the -91C, but powered by a 180hp Lycoming driving a constant-speed propeller. Most military -91s have been withdrawn, although a small number are reported to be in service in Ethiopia. Others remain in private use in Europe. Maximum speed at sea level is 165 mph (266km/hr). *Country of origin:* Sweden. *Silhouette and picture:* Saab-91D.

 **Neiva N621 Universal** *Confusion:* Pilatus P-3

Power: 1 × Lycoming piston engine   *Span:* 36ft 1in (11m)   *Length:* 28ft 2½in (8.6m)

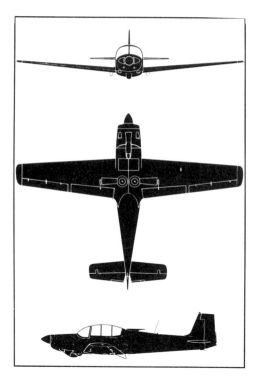

Designed as a replacement for Brazilian Air Force Fokker S-11/S-12s and North American T-6 Texans, the Neiva flew for the first time in 1966. The Brazilian Air Force designation for this tricycle-undercarriage 2/3 seater is the T-25. About 160 T-25s were delivered to the Brazilian Air Force, together with 30 of an armed version known as the AT-25. Two underwing hard-points are provided for 7.62mm machine gun pods. Some 10 T-25s were delivered to Chile. Maximum cruising speed is 177 mph (285km/hr). *Country of origin:* Brazil.

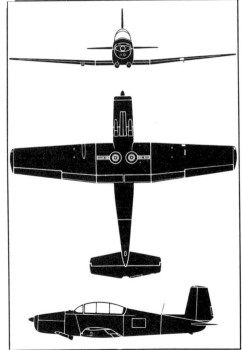

Power: 1 × Lycoming piston engine *Span:* 34ft 1in (10.4m) *Length:* 28ft 8in (8.75m)

The Pilatus P-3 is an all-metal tandem two-seat trainer built primarily for the Swiss Air Force; another six aircraft went to Brazil. First flight was in 1953, with the first of 18 pre-production aircraft following the next year. Powered by a 260 hp Lycoming, the P-3 has a cruising speed of about 155 mph (249km/hr). Suitable for primary and advanced training, including aerobatics, night flying and instrument flying, the P-3 can be equipped for weapon training with one 7.9mm machine gun in an underwing pod, four practice bombs or two air-to-ground rockets. The P-3 will be superseded in Swiss Air Force service by the PC-7. *Country of origin:* Switzerland.

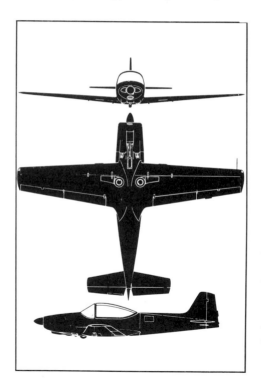

Laverda Super Falco F8L

Confusion: Rangemaster

Power: 1 × Lycoming piston engine   *Span:* 26ft 3in (8m)   *Length:* 21ft 4in (6.5m)

The Falco first flew in 1955, powered by a 90hp Continental. Since then four production versions have been built: F8L Series I, an initial production batch of ten built by Aviamilano in 1956 and powered by 135hp Lycomings; F8L Series II, also built by Aviamilano, with a 150hp Lycoming; F8L America, built by Aeromere for the US market; Super Falco Series IV, generally similar to the F8L America but powered by a 160hp Lycoming and built by Laverda (the former Aeromere company). An extremely clean design, the Super Falco seats two side-by-side and is fully aerobatic. Maximum cruising speed is 180 mph (290km/hr), and maximum sea-level climb rate 984ft/min (300m/min). *Country of origin:* Italy. *Silhouette and picture:* Super Falco.

Power: 1 × Continental piston engine   *Span:* 34ft 9in (10.59m)   *Length:* 27ft 6in (8.38m)

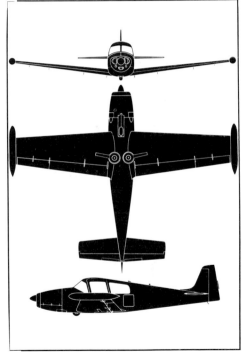

The five-seat Navion Rangemaster is a much modified development of the original Navion, produced first by North American Aviation and later, between 1948 and 1950, by Ryan, which acquired the rights in 1947. The Rangemaster retains the original Navion wing and undercarriage but is otherwise completely re-engineered. First flight was in 1960, with production commencing the next year. Fitted with wingtip fuel tanks, the type has excellent range and cruises at more than 185 mph (298km/hr) on its 260hp Continental. A large number of Navions of all types are still active, particularly in the US. *Country of origin:* USA.

EMBRAER EMB-312 (T-27) Tucano

Confusion: PC-7, Mentor, Epsilon

Power: 1 × PT6A turboprop or 1 × TPE 331-12 turboprop   *Span:* **36ft 6in (11.14m)**   *Length:* **32ft 4in (9.86m)**

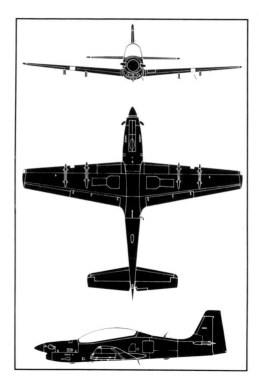

First flown in August 1980, the two-seat T-27 Tucano is in service with the Brazilian Air Force, which has ordered 118 and has options on 50 more. The Tucano is designed for pilot training, but is also suitable for counter-insurgency work. Egypt has ordered 120 Tucanos, and has options on 60 more. Most of the Egyptian order will be licence-built. The RAF has ordered 130 of a developed version built entirely in Northern Ireland by Shorts. Shorts-built aircraft will be powered by a Garrett TPE 331-12 engine and are identified by exhausts set below the fuselage. *Country of origin:* Brazil.

Aérospatiale TB 30 Epsilon

Power: 1 × Lycoming piston engine   *Span:* 26ft (7.92m)   *Length:* 24ft 10in (7.59m)

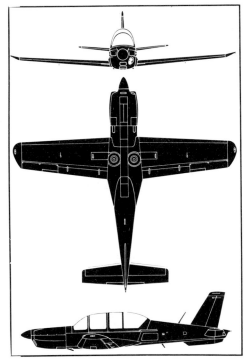

The TB 30 Epsilon is the French Air Force's standard primary trainer. It entered service in 1983 and 150 are scheduled for production. An armed version is offered for export, fitted with four underwing hardpoints to carry a variety of stores, including two 7.62mm machine gun pods. Maximum speed of the Epsilon trainer is 236mph (380km/hr) and endurance 3.75hr. Pilots trained on the Epsilon will progress to the Alpha Jet. *Country of origin:* France.

ICA IAR-825TP Triumf

Confusion: Tucano, PC-7, Epsilon

Power: 1 × PT6A turboprop   *Span:* 33ft 9½in (10.3m)   *Length:* 29ft 2½in (8.9m)

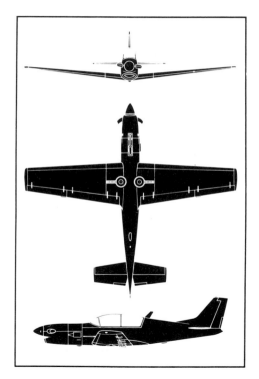

First flown on 12 June 1982, the IAR-825 has been designed as a multi-role trainer for the Romanian Air Force. Based on the piston-engined IAR-823, 60 of which were delivered to the Romanian Air Force, the -825 features a new fuselage and tail unit. In much the same class as the Brazilian Tucano, the IAR-825 is powered by a Canadian Pratt & Whitney PT6A turboprop of 680hp. *Country of origin:* **Romania**.

Pilatus PC-7 Turbo-Trainer

Power: 1 × PT6 turboprop   *Span:* 34ft 1½in (10.4m)   *Length:* 32ft (9.75m)

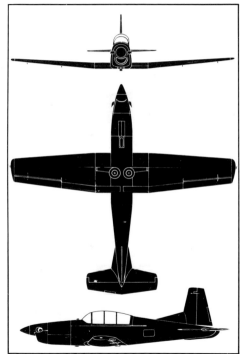

The PC-7 Turbo-Trainer is designed for basic, intermediate and aerobatic training. Over 340 have been ordered by 12 nations. Principal users are Bolivia, Iraq, Malaysia, Mexico and Switzerland, which ordered 40. All PC-7s are fitted with six underwing hardpoints as standard and up to 2,300lb (1,000kg) of stores can be carried. At least two PC-7s have been civilian registered. Powered by a 550hp Pratt & Whitney turboprop, the PC-7 has a cruising speed of more than 186 mph (300km/hr). *Country of origin:* Switzerland.

 **Beechcraft T-34 Mentor/T-34C** *Confusion:* PC-7, KM-2B, Tucano, Epsilon

Power: 1 × Lycoming piston engine
      or 1 × P & W turboprop (T-34C)
    Span (T-34): 32ft 10in (10m)   *Length* (T-34): 25ft 11in (7.9m)

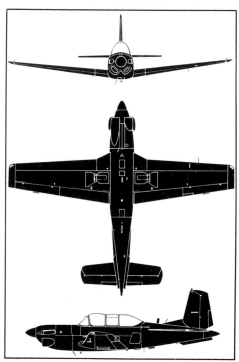

Derived from the Bonanza 33 series, more than 450 piston-engined T-34As were built for the USAF and a further 423 T-34Bs for the US Navy. The T-34C, which first flew in 1973, is extensively revised, and is powered by a 715shp Pratt & Whitney turboprop. The US Navy ordered 334 T-34Cs. Six civil versions are in service in Algeria and 89 armed T-34C-1s have been exported. *Country of origin:* USA. *Silhouette and picture:* T-34C.

Power: 1 × Lycoming piston engine *Span:* 32ft 10in (10m) *Length:* 26ft 4in (8.04m)

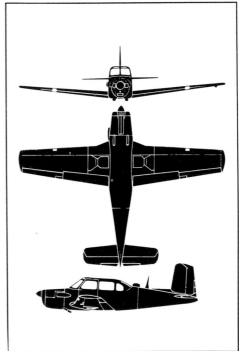

The KM-2B is a modification of the original KM-2 development of the Beechcraft Mentor, combining the airframe and powerplant of the KM-2 with the two-seat tandem cockpit of the T-34A Mentor. The KM-2B first flew in 1974 and was selected by the Japan Air Self-Defence Force (JASDF) to replace its T-34As in the primary training role the following year. The JASDF ordered 50 examples of the type, designating them T-3. The first of these made its first flight on January 17, 1978, and 44 had been delivered to the JASDF by February 1981. Powered by a 340hp Lycoming flat-six engine, the KM-2B has a cruising speed of about 158 mph (254km/hr), maximum level speed of 228 mph (367km/hr), maximum rate of climb of 1,520ft/min (463m/min) and service ceiling of 26,800ft (8,170m). *Country of origin:* Japan. *Silhouette:* KM-2. *Picture:* KM-2B.

343

SIAI-Marchetti S.205/S.208 *Confusion:* Ranger

Power: 1 × Lycoming piston engine   *Span:* 35ft 7½in (10.86m)   *Length:* 26ft 3in (8m)

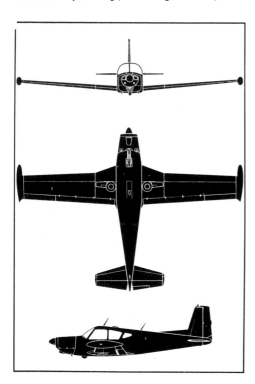

The S.205 four-seat all-metal light aircraft first flew in 1965. The type was designed from the outset to take a variety of engines, from 180 to 300hp, and there is also a version with fixed undercarriage. A new version, the S.205AC powered by a 200hp Lycoming, has been ordered by the Italian Aero Club. The first of 140 were delivered in 1977. The S.208, a five-seater based on S.205 components, flew for the first time in May 1967. In addition to an order for 40 from the Italian Air Force (S.208M), the S.208 has also been delivered to customers in Europe and Africa. A version designated S.208AG has been developed for general duties and features a fixed undercarriage. Maximum cruising speed is 187 mph (300km/hr). *Country of origin:* Italy. *Silhouette:* S.208. *Picture:* S.208M.

Power: 1 × Lycoming piston engine   *Span:* 35ft (10.67m)   *Length:* 23ft 2in (7.06m)

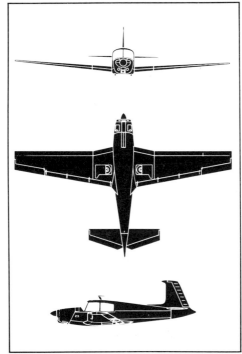

The four-seat all-metal Mooney Ranger is one of several Mooney light aircraft featuring the distinctive fin and rudder with its unswept leading edge. Originally known as the Mark 21, the Ranger first flew in 1961, although the earlier M-20 had flown in 1953. Other models in the series are the Executive, with a 200hp Lycoming, and the Mooney 201 (M20J), which first flew in 1976. The Mark 22 (originally known as the Mustang) is a five-seat pressurised version which first flew in 1964. Powered by a 310hp Lycoming turbosupercharged engine, it has the basic wing of the Ranger but is rather longer than the earlier version. *Country of origin:* USA. *Silhouette:* Ranger. *Picture:* Mooney 201.

Gardan/Socata GY-80 Horizon *Confusion:* Ranger, Picchio

Power: 1 × Lycoming piston engine   *Span:* 31ft 10in (9.70m)   *Length:* 21ft 9½in (6.64m)

Designed by Yves Gardan, this four-seat all-metal light aircraft was put into series production by Sud Aviation from 1963. Four versions with engines of different power were originally offered. By mid-1968 more than 260 Horizons had been delivered to customers, mainly in Europe. Design and construction are conventional and the tricycle undercarriage retracts rearwards, with the wheels half concealed. Powered by a 160hp Lycoming, the Horizon has a cruising speed of about 145 mph (233km/hr). Other performance figures include a sea-level rate of climb of 660ft/min (201m/min), service ceiling of 13,450ft (4,100m), and range with 44 Imp gal (200lit) fuel of 590 miles (950km). *Country of origin:* France.

Power: 1 × Continental piston engine   *Span:* 34ft 2in (10.41m)   *Length:* 26ft 4in (8.02m)

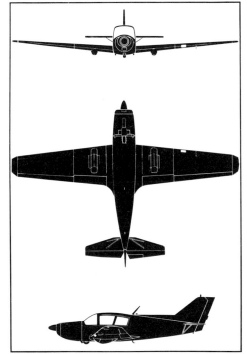

The Viking series of light aircraft consists of three models developed from the earlier Bellanca 260C and Standard Viking 300: the Model 17-30A Super Viking 300A, powered by a 300hp Continental; Model 17-31A Super Viking 300A, identical to the Model 17-30A with the exception of engine and propeller; and the Model 17-31ATC Turbo Viking 300A, which has two Rajay turbochargers added to its 300hp Lycoming. Total production of all models of Viking had reached more than 1,500 by the beginning of 1978. Production ceased in 1980. Accommodation is provided for four persons and top speed of all models is more than 222 mph (357km/hr). *Country of origin:* USA. *Silhouette:* Viking 300. *Picture:* Super Viking.

General Avia F15F/F15E Picchio *Confusion:* Viking

Power: 1 × Lycoming piston engine   *Span:* 32ft 6in (9.9m)   *Length:* 25ft 5in (7.75m)

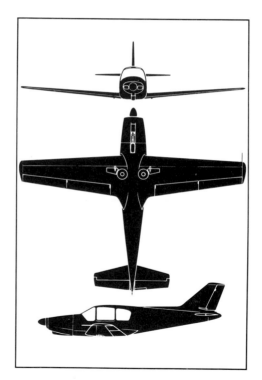

The F15F four-seat light aircraft is a derivative of the Procaer F15E Picchio. First flight was in October 1977 and a pre-production batch was under construction during 1978. The F15E Picchio is slightly shorter than the F15F and features a conventional enclosed cabin compared with the new aircraft's fully glazed sliding canopy. The first F15 Picchio flew in 1959 and successive models built since then have featured a number of detail design changes including the addition of wingtip fuel tanks. Most important change was the switch to all-metal construction with the F15E, which first flew in 1968. Cruising speed of the F15F is 174 mph (280km/hr). *Country of origin:* Italy. *Silhouette:* F15E. *Picture:* F15F.

Power: 1 × Continental piston engine   *Span:* 33ft 6in (10.21m)   *Length:* 26ft 8in (8.13m) (F33): 27ft 6in (8.38m) (A36)

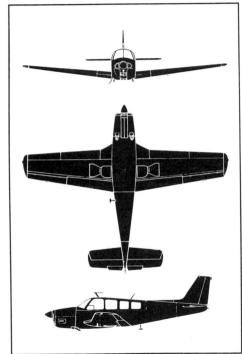

The Bonanza Model F33 is a four/five-seat executive aircraft, similar to the Bonanza Model V35 but featuring a conventional tail unit with swept fin and rudder. Originally known as the Debonair, it first flew in September 1959. An aerobatic version was built and is in service as a trainer in several air forces. Other Model F33s are used as trainers by US and European airlines. Production of the Model 33 had reached more than 2,400 by early 1984. The Bonanza Model A36 is a six-seat utility version and, like the Model 33, is powered by a 300hp Continental. Slightly longer than the Model 33, it is distinguished by an additional cabin window on each side of the rear fuselage. Production had reached more than 2,540 by early 1984. The Bonanza 36 has a maximum cruising speed of 212 mph (340km/hr). *Country of origin:* USA. *Silhouette:* A36. *Picture:* A36TC.

Beechcraft Bonanza Model V35B

Confusion: Bonanza 33/36

Power: 1 × Continental piston engine   *Span:* 33ft 6in (10.21m)   *Length:* 26ft 5in (8.05m)

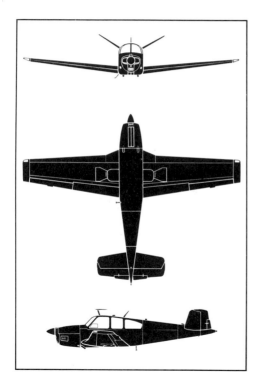

This four/five-seat V-tail light aircraft first flew in December 1945 and production had reached almost 10,000 by 1984. Current production version is the V35B. Powered by a 285hp Continental driving a two-blade constant-speed propeller, the V35B has a cruising speed of about 200 mph (322km/hr). Externally the V35 Bonanza has changed ittle over the years and is immediately identifiable by the distinctive arrangement of the tail. Internal refinements continue to mirror changing tastes and advances in avionic equipment. *Country of origin:* USA. *Silhouette and picture:* V35B.

Piper PA-28R-200 Arrow

Power: 1 × Lycoming piston engine   *Span:* 32ft 2½in (9.82mm)   *Length:* 24ft 7in (7.5m)

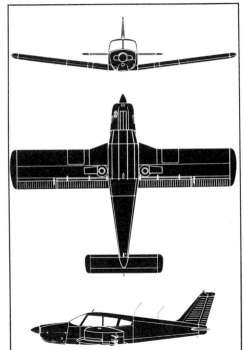

The Cherokee Arrow II is generally similar in appearance to the Cherokee Archer II but has a retractable undercarriage, more powerful engine and the untapered wings of the PA-28-180 Archer. First flown in 1975, it was superseded in 1977 by the PA-28R-201 Arrow III, which has the new longer-span tapered wings. Third in the Arrow series is the Turbo Arrow III, which is identical to the Arrow III but has a 200hp turbocharged Continenal engine driving a two-blade constant-speed propeller. The Turbo Arrow III is a few inches longer than the standard aircraft and has a remodelled cowling with a larger airscoop and more pointed spinner. The Arrow IV (see page 359) has a T-tail. *Country of origin:* USA. *Silhouette and picture:* Arrow II.

Robin HR 100 *Confusion:* Arrow

Power: 1 × Lycoming piston engine   *Span:* 29ft 9½in (9.08m)   *Length:* 24ft 11in (7.59m)

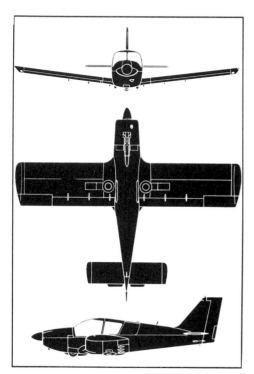

There are three basic models in the HR 100 series of French light aircraft. The fixed-undercarriage four-seat HR 100/210 Safari II is a development of the original all-metal production HR 100/200, of which 31 were built. It first flew in 1971 and remained in production until 1976, some 78 having been built. The retractable-undercarriage four/five-seat HR 100/285 Tiara first flew in 1972 and featured a new vertical tail and wing structure. Powerplant was a 285hp Lycoming driving a three-blade constant-speed propeller. The HR 100/250TR is similar to the Tiara but has a lower-powered engine. Third of the basic models is the six-seat HR 100/4+2, which first flew in May 1975. It is one foot longer than the Tiara and features an additional set of cabin windows. Powerplant is a 320hp Lycoming driving a three-blade propeller. Maximum cruising speed is 168 mph (270km/hr). *Country of origin:* France. *Silhouette:* HR 100 Tiara. *Picture:* HR 100/280.

Power: 1 × Lycoming piston engine   *Span:* 35ft 7in (10.85m)   *Length:* 25ft (7.63m)

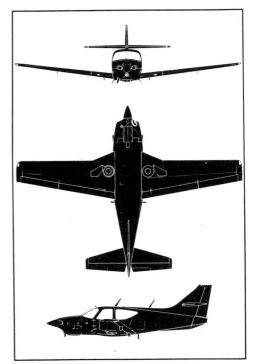

These attractive four-seat light aircraft are all basically similar, the differences lying in equipment and powerplants. The Commander 112 first flew in December 1970, with production aircraft being delivered from 1972. Successive models were improved in exterior and interior detail but retained the same exterior shape. The Commander 114 was introduced in 1976 and differs from the Model 112 principally in having a 260hp engine rather than the 112's 210hp unit. All aircraft have the characteristic mid-set tailplane and sharply tapered rear cabin windows. Cruising speed is 175 mph (281km/hr). Other performance figures include a maximum rate of climb at sea level of 1,000ft/min (305m/min), and a range with maximum fuel, no reserves, of 1,130 miles (1,818km). *Country of origin:* USA. *Silhouette:* Commander 112. *Picture:* Commander 114.

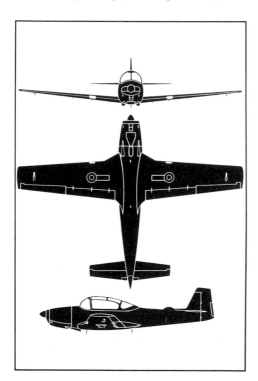

Piaggio P.149 *Confusion:* Guepard

Power: 1 × Lycoming piston engine   *Span:* 36ft 6in (11.12m)   *Length:* 28ft 9½in (8.8m)

The P.149, developed from the P.148, is a four/five-seat all-metal light aircraft. First flown in 1953, the type was built in quantity as a liaison and training aircraft for the Federal German Air Force and was subsequently built under licence by Focke-Wulf in Germany. Some East African countries have small numbers of ex-German P.149Ds. Powered by a 270hp Lycoming driving a three-blade constant-speed propeller, the P.149D cruises at 165 mph (266km/hr). Other performance figures include a maximum level speed at sea level of 192 mph (309km/hr); maximum rate of climb at sea level of 980ft/min (300m/min); service ceiling of 19,850ft (6,050m); and range (including allowance for starting, warm-up, take-off and climb, plus 30min reserves) of 680 miles (1,095km). *Country of origin:* Italy. *Silhouette and picture:* P.149D.

Wassmer WA-40/Super IV/CE.43 Guepard

Power: 1 × Lycoming piston engine   *Span:* 32ft 9½in (10m)   *Length:* 26ft 6½in (8.09m)

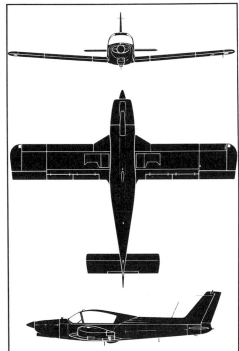

Several versions of the Wassmer WA-40 four/five-seat cabin light aircraft have been built since the first flew in 1959. Later aircraft introduced a swept fin and rudder (WA-40A) and improved engine cowling. The Super IV/21 is externally similar to the Super IV but is powered by a 250hp Lycoming driving a constant-speed propeller. The Cerva CE.43 Guepard is an all-metal derivative of the Super IV/21 and first flew in 1971. Production ended in 1976 after 43 had been built. Wassmer went into liquidation in 1977 and responsibility for Wassmer and Cerva products passed to Issoire-Aviation. *Country of origin:* France. *Silhouette:* WA-40A. *Picture:* Super IV.

SIAI-Marchetti SF.260 *Confusion:* Guepard

Power: 1 × Lycoming piston engine   *Span:* 27ft 5in (8.35m)   *Length:* 23ft 3½in (7.1m)

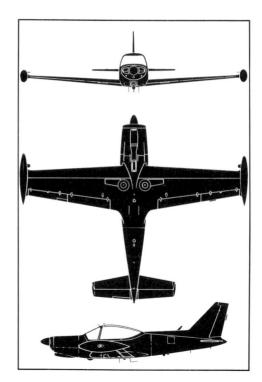

The SF.260 has been built in both civil and military versions since it first entered production in 1964. Derived from the Aviamilano F.250, it is of conventional construction and is fully aerobatic. Miitary versions are the SF.260M two/three-set trainer, first flown in 1970, and the SF.260W Warrior weapons trainer/tactical support aircraft, first flown in 1972. This versions is fitted with two or four underwing stores pylons. Both types are widely deployed throughout the world. Civil versions are the SF.260A, B and C. The SF.260A was marketed in the US as the Waco Meteor. Outwardly similar to the military versions, civil SF.260s are also widely distributed throughout the world. *Country of origin:* Italy. *Silhouette:* SF.260. *Picture:* SF.260M.

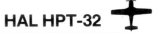

Power: 1 × Lycoming piston engine   *Span:* 31ft 2in (9.5m)   *Length:* 25ft 4in (7.7m)

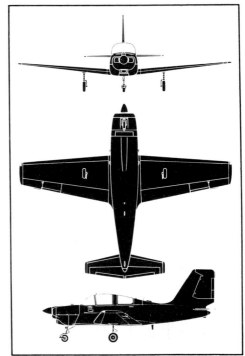

With side-by-side forward seats and an additional seat behind, the HPT-32 is to be the standard basic trainer for the Indian Air Force. Some 60 aircraft have been ordered to date. Any further orders will probably be for the HTT-34, a modified version, fitted with a 420shp Allison turboprop. Four underwing store points are provided for weapon training, and the type can also be used for observation, liaison and sports flying. Maximum speed is 135 mph (217km/hr) and endurance 4hr. *Country of origin:* India.

Beechcraft Sierra 200 *Confusion:* SkyRocket II

Power: 1 × Lycoming piston engine   *Span:* 32ft 9in (9.98m)   *Length:* 25ft 9in (7.85m)

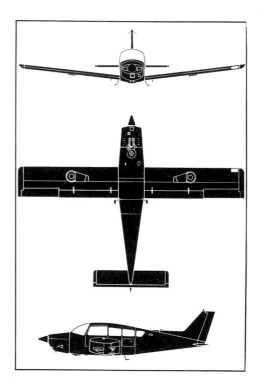

Originally known as the Musketeer Super R, this type was first introduced in 1969. In 1971 the manufacturer renamed the entire Musketeer range and the Super R became the Sierra 200. Since then several detail improvements have been made, including the fitting of a more powerful engine and general aerodynamic cleaning-up. With accommodation for four to six persons, the Sierra can be identified by its four cabin windows on each side (against three in the similar but fixed-undercarriage Sundowner 180). Powered by a 200hp Lycoming flat-four, the Sierra has a cruising speed of about 160 mph (257km/hr). *Country of origin:* USA.

Power: 1 × Continental piston engine   *Span:* 35ft (10.67m)   *Length:* 28ft 11in (8.81m)

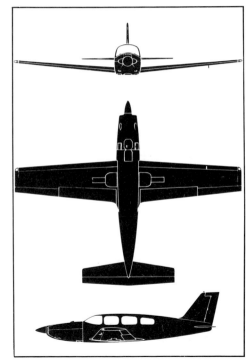

Design of this sleek six-seat executive aircraft was begun as long ago as 1956 by the late G. M. Bellanca. The choice of innovative materials for the type's construction lengthened development time, but it is claimed that the glass-fibre epoxy laminate used has a higher strength/weight ratio than aluminium and is also aerodynamically extremely smooth. The prototype first flew in March 1975 and has since set a number of speed records. By early 1978 orders for some 70 aircraft had been recorded. Cruising speed is 255 mph (410km/hr). Other performance figures include a maximum cruising speed (83 per cent power) of 331 mph (532km/hr); rate of climb at sea level of 1,900ft/min (579m/min); and a range at 15,000ft (4,570m) and 75 per cent power of over 1,215 miles (1,955km). *Country of origin:* USA.

Yakovlev Yak-18 Max/Yak-18P Moose *Confusion:* Texan

Power: 1 × Ivchenko or 1 × Vedeneev piston engine   *Span:* 34ft 9in (10.6m)   *Length:* 27ft 5in (8.35m)

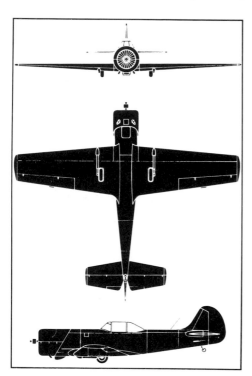

Several versions of this Russian two-seat basic trainer have been built since it first appeared in 1946. The original aircraft was a tailwheel-undercarriage type with a five-cylinder radial engine closely cowled with individual cylinder helmets. Introduced in 1957, the Yak-18A was a cleaned-up version of the Yak-18U with a tricycle undercarriage and a more powerful nine-cylinder radial engine. Widely used as a club aircraft, the Yak-18A has been exported in large numbers throughout the Communist world. A further development, the Yak-18P Moose, is a single-seater specifically designed for advanced training and competition aerobatics. A four-seat tourer development is the Yak-50, used extensively for Aeroflot training. *Country of origin:* USSR. *Silhouette and picture:* Yak-18P.

Power: 1 × R-1340 piston engine　　*Span:* 42ft (12.8m)　　*Length:* 29ft 6in (8.99m)

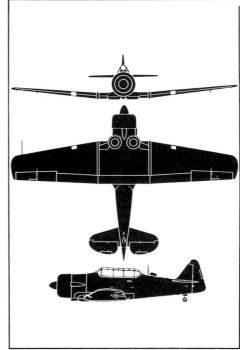

The extremely long-lived T-6 Texan was first produced before the Second World War and was widely used as an advanced trainer in that conflict, more than 10,000 being built in North America. The type was known as the Harvard in RAF service. The Texans to be seen today are virtually the same as the wartime aircraft. The type is still in wide use throughout South America and elsewhere as an air force trainer and racing aircraft. *Country of origin:* USA. *Silhouette:* T-6G. *Picture:* SNJ-3 (naval version).

 **AIDC T-CH-1** *Confusion:* Trojan

Power: 1 × T53 turboprop   *Span:* 40ft (12.19m)   *Length:* 33ft 8in (10.26m)

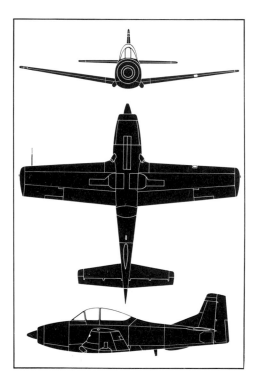

This tandem two-seat trainer was designed to fill a Nationalist Chinese Air Force requirement for an advanced trainer/ground attack aircraft. It first flew in November 1973 and entered series production in May 1976, 50 having been built before production ceased in late 1981. Powered by a licence-built 1,450hp Lycoming turboprop, the T-CH-1 cruises at more than 250 mph (402km/hr). Externally, the design owes much to the North American T-28A, particularly in the arrangement of the cockpit and tail assembly. Cruising speed is 196 mph (315km/hr). *Country of origin:* Taiwan.

Power: 1 × R-1820 piston engine   *Span:* 40ft 7½in (12.38m)   *Length:* 32ft 10in (10m)

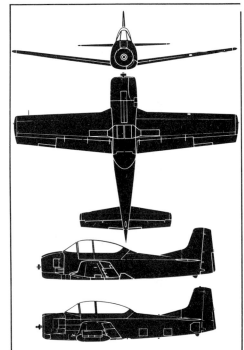

Originally designed as a replacement for the T-6 Texan, this tandem two-seat trainer first flew in September 1949. First operated by the US Air Force and US Navy, the type has since been used by a number of air forces throughout the world. The T-28A, T-28B and T-28C were all trainers, but the T-28D, slightly larger and fitted with a more powerful engine, has been widely used in the counter-insurgency role. A total of six underwing stations can accommodate a variety of armament. T-28s of all versions can still be seen in South America, South-east Asia and North Africa, as well as in the US. *Country of origin:* USA. *Main silhouette:* T-28C; *lower side view:* T-28D. *Picture:* T-28D.

Piper PA-46-310P Malibu

Confusion: Saratoga SP, Lance

Power: 1 × Continental piston engine   *Span:* 43ft (13.11m)   *Length:* 28ft 4¾in (8.66m)

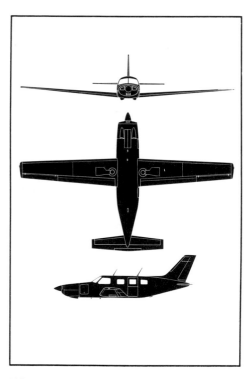

Claimed to be the world's first pressurised cabin aircraft powered by a single piston engine, the Malibu is a large six-seater able to cruise at heights up to 25,000ft (7,620m). First deliveries were made in November 1983. Powered by a 310hp turbocharged Continental, the Malibu cruises at up to 248 mph (398km/h). *Country of origin:* USA.

Power: 1 × Lycoming piston engine   *Span:* 32ft 10in (10m)   *Length:* 27ft 8½in (8.44m)

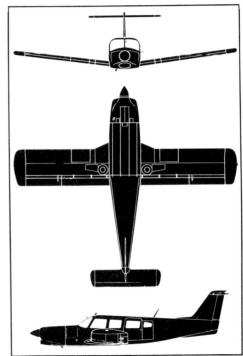

There are three main versions of the Piper Lance. The original model, first flown in August 1974, was essentially a retractable-undercarriage Cherokee Six and featured a conventional tail unit. The Lance II and Turbo Lance II both have the now fashionable T-tail arrangement, while the Turbo Lance also has the extra power of a 300hp turbocharged Lycoming engine. The T-tail is claimed to reduce drag and to increase performance. Main distinguishing point of the Turbo Lance is the large air inlet for the turbocharger located beneath the propeller spinner. *Country of origin:* USA. *Silhouette:* Turbo Lance II. *Picture:* Lance II.

Piper Arrow IV   *Confusion:* Lance

Power: 1 × Lycoming piston engine   *Span:* 35ft 5in (10.8m)   *Length:* 27ft (8.23m)

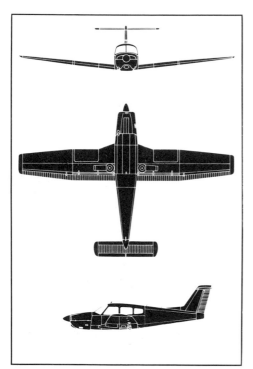

Developed from the fixed-undercarriage Archer II, the Arrow IV is a four-seat monoplane with a T-tail and retractable tricycle undercarriage. The T-tail was introduced in 1979 and two versions of the type are now available, the Arrow IV and the Turbo Arrow IV. The Arrow IV has a cruising speed of 193 mph (311km/hr) and a range of 840 miles (1,353km). *Picture:* Turbo Arrow IV. *Country of origin:* USA.

Power: 1 × Dart turboprop   *Span:* 51ft 2in (15.6m)   *Length:* 45ft 6in (13.86m)

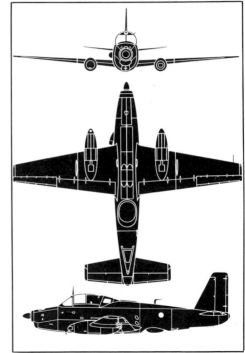

The three-seat Alizé (Tradewind) is a carrier-based anti-submarine aircraft currently in service with the navies of France and India. First flight was in 1956 and two prototypes and three pre-production aircraft preceded 75 production Alizés into *Aéronavale* service from mid-1959. Armament includes a torpedo or depth charges, AS.12 air-to-surface missiles or rockets. The Alizé has a large retractable radome underneath the rear fuselage. Noticeable also are the large landing gear/weapons nacelles on the wing leading edges. *Country of origin:* France.

Federal Aircraft Factory C-3605   *Confusion:* —

Power: 1 × T53 turboprop   *Span:* 45ft 1in (13.74m)   *Length:* 39ft 6in (12.03m)

Conversion of a number of C-3603 fighter-bombers of 1940s vintage for target towing began in 1967. Even after 25 years' service with the Swiss Air Force the type still had at least another ten years of useful airframe life remaining, and it was decided that the C-3603 could best be used as a target tug for air-to-air gunnery training. Produced under the direction of Ing Jean-Pierre Weibel, the first conversion flew in August 1968, followed by 23 production aircraft; the first aircraft entered service in 1971. The modification involved fitting an additional section to the front fuselage to accommodate the 1,100hp Lycoming turboprop, and the addition of a third, central fin. Accommodation is provided for two beneath a continuous transparent canopy. Cruising speed is about 260 mph (418km/hr). *Country of origin:* Switzerland.

Ayres Turbo-Thrush

SOCATA TB 10 Tobago

Gulfstream Aerospace T-Cat

Beech Sundowner 180/Sport 150

Confusion: Lynx, Airtrainer CT4

Power: 1 × Lycoming piston engine   *Span:* 32ft 9in (9.98m)   *Length:* 25ft 9in (7.85m)

The Beechcraft Musketeer series began with the Model 23 Musketeer, which first flew in 1961. The series has been progressively improved over the years, although the basic exterior appearance has remained largely unchanged. In 1974 Beech renamed the series as follows: the original Musketeer Super R became the rectractable-undercarriage Sierra 200; the Musketeer Custom became the Sundowner 180; and the Musketeer Sport became the Sport 150. These new designations reflect the engine power. Main external difference between the Sundowner 180 and the Sport 150 is the former's extra cabin window on each side. Cruising speeds are about 140 mph (225km/hr) for the Sundowner and 125 mph (200km/hr) for the Sport. *Country of origin:* USA. *Silhouette:* Sierra 200. *Picture:* Sundowner 180.

Power: 1 × Lycoming piston engine *Span:* 31ft 6in (9.6m) *Length:* 22ft (6.71m)

A larger development of the AA-1 series, the AA-5 first flew in 1970. This all-metal four-seat aircraft was built in four versions; the basic AA-5A with 150hp Lycoming engine; the de luxe Cheetah, externally identical to the AA-5A but with additional internal equipment; the AA-5B with 180hp Lycoming; and the de luxe Tiger, which has the same internal equipment as the Cheetah. The AA-5B series first flew in 1974. The Cheetah was known as the Traveler until 1976. Cruising speeds are 145 mph (235km/hr) for the AA-5A and 160 mph (260km/hr) for the AA-5B. *Country of origin:* USA. *Silhouette:* AA-5A. *Picture:* Cheetah.

Power: 1 × Lycoming piston engine   *Span:* 24ft 5½in (7.46m)   *Length:* 19ft 3in (5.86m)

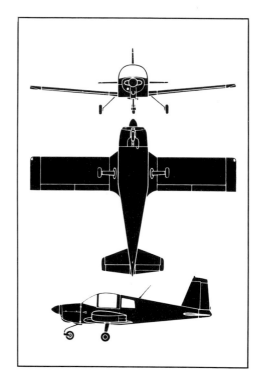

Designed originally as a trainer version of the American Aviation AA-1 Yankee, the AA-1A first flew in 1970. It was re-designated AA-1B Trainer in 1973. The AA-1C was introduced in 1977 and incorporated a number of minor design changes as well as a more powerful 115hp Lycoming engine. The T-Cat is externally identical to the AA-1C but includes a number of internal equipment changes. The Lynx is designed to be both a trainer and sports aircraft and is equipped with a de luxe interior and exterior finish, and wheel fairings. Cruising speed of the T-Cat and Lynx is about 130 mph (210km/hr). *Country of origin:* USA. *Silhouette and picture:* AA-1 Trainer.

Power: 1 × Continental piston engine   *Span:* 26ft (7.92m)   *Length:* 23ft 2in (7.06m)

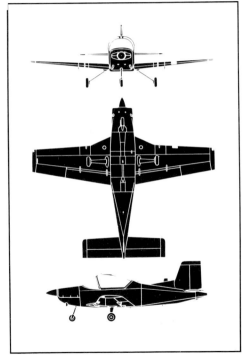

The original Victa Airtourer was a two-seat all-metal fully aerobatic light aircraft which first flew in 1959. Production aircraft were powered by a 100hp Continental engine. A four-seat development, the Aircruiser, was flown in 1967 but not produced in quantity. Aerospace of New Zealand acquired the Australian company's Airtourer and Aircruiser designs in 1971 and re-engineered the latter into a two/three-seat military trainer. Called the Airtrainer CT4, it is powered by a 210hp Continental and cruises at about 160 mph (260km/hr). A small number serve with the Royal New Zealand Air Force. *Country of origin:* New Zealand.

 **AIDC PL-1B Chiensou** *Confusion:* HR 200

Power: 1 × Lycoming piston engine   *Span:* 28ft (8.53m)   *Length:* 19ft 8in (5.99m)

The PL-1B is a Taiwan-built version of the PL-1 Laminar, an amateur-designed two-seat light aircraft. First flown in 1962, this conventional tricycle-undercarriage all-metal light aircraft was adopted for use by the Taiwanese Air Force after an example was built and flown at Taichung in 1968. The production version is designated PL-1B Chiensou; a total of 55 were built. Powered by a 150hp Lycoming piston engine, the PL-1B cruises at about 130 mph (210km/hr). Other variants of the basic Pazmany PL-1 include the PL-2, with wing dihedral increased from 3° to 5°, wider cockpit and extensively changed internal structure to simplify construction, and the Indonesian-built Lipnur LT-200. *Country of origin:* Taiwan/USA.

Power: 1 × Lycoming piston engine   *Span:* 27ft 4in (8.33m)   *Length:* 21ft 9½in (6.64m)

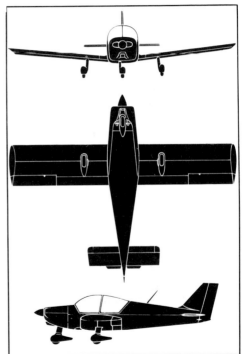

Although the all-metal two-seat HR 200 series bears an external resemblance to the HR 100/210 it is an entirely new design. Slightly smaller overall, it is intended for schools and clubs. First flight was in 1971 and there are four versions: HR 200/100S, basic version; HR 200/100 Club, similar to the HR 200/100 with 108hp Lycoming engine but with wheel fairings and Hoffmann propeller; HR 200/120B with 118hp Lycoming engine; and HR 200/160 with 160hp Lycoming engine. Main distinguishing feature is the large forward-sliding clear canopy giving almost all-round vision. Cruising speed ranges from about 120 mph (195km/hr) for the HR 200/100 to 155 mph (250km/hr) for the HR 200/160. *Country of origin:* **France**. *Silhouette and picture:* HR 200/100 Club.

Robin DR 400 *Confusion:* HR 200

Power: 1 × Lycoming piston engine   *Span:* 28ft 7¼in (8.72m)   *Length:* 22ft 10in (6.96m)

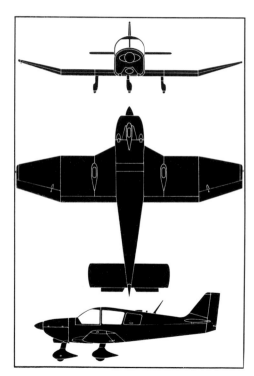

There are several aircraft in the DR 400 all-wood series of light aircraft. The DR 400/100 2+2 is a development of the earlier DR 220 2+2 and first flew in 1972. It is powered by a 100hp Lycoming engine. The DR 400/120 Petit Prince also flew for the first time in 1972 and is powered by a 118hp Lycoming engine. The DR 400/140B Major is powered by a 160hp Lycoming engine and is externally the same as the 2+2 and Petit Prince. The DR 400/600 Chevalier replaced the earlier DR 360 Major 160 and is powered by a 160hp Lycoming engine. Most powerful aircraft in the range is the DR 400/180 Regent (together with the DR 400/180R Remorqueur glider tug), which replaced the earlier DR 235 Regent and DR 380 Prince. This four/five-seater is powered by a 180hp Lycoming. *Country of origin:* France. *Silhouette and picture:* DR 400/180.

SOCATA TB 9 Tampico/TB 10 Tobago

Power: 1 × Lycoming piston engine   *Span:* 32ft (9.76m)   *Length:* 25ft (7.63m)

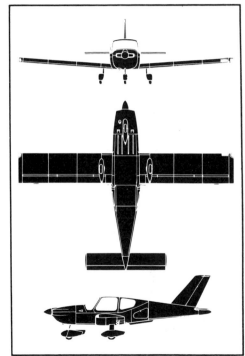

The TB 9 Tampico is a 160hp four-seater, while the TB 10 Tobago is powered by a 180hp Lycoming and is classed as a four/five seater. An aerobatic version designated TB 11 was built, but is not currently offered. The fin of the TB 9 and TB 10 is comparatively tall and is not fitted with a fillet where it joins the fuselage. A more powerful version with retractable landing gear is the TB 20 Trinidad. Sales of all versions reached 430 by 1984. *Country of origin:* France. *Silhouette and picture:* Tobago.

Piper PA-28/PA-32 Cherokee

Confusion: DR 400, Saratoga

Power: 1 × Lycoming piston engine   *Span:* 30ft (9.14m)   *Length:* 23ft 6in (7.16m)

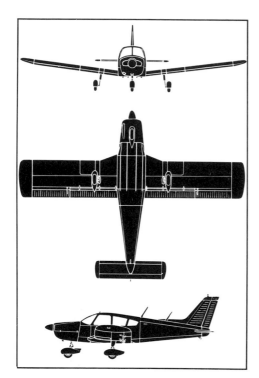

The original PA-28-140 Cherokee 140 two-seater was announced in 1964. The PA-28-180 Cherokee 180 is a four-seater powered by a 180hp Lycoming engine. Slightly longer than the 140, it has three cabin windows each side. The PA-28-235 is slightly larger than the Model 180 and is powered by a 235hp Lycoming. The introduction of the PA-28-161 Warrior in 1973 saw the first use of a new increased-span tapered wing. The 1977 versions, designated Warrior II, have the original 150hp engine replaced by a 160hp unit. The PA-28-181 Archer four-seater was introduced in 1972 and the 235hp PA-28-236 Dakota first appeared in 1978. The Cherokee Six (PA-32) has a longer fuselage and four windows per side. *Country of origin:* USA. *Silhouette:* Cherokee 180. *Picture:* Archer II.

Power: 1 × Lycoming piston engine   *Span:* 36ft 2in (11.02m)   *Length:* 27ft 8in (8.44m)

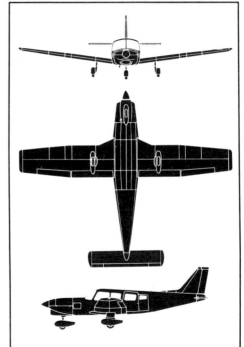

A large six/seven seater of typical Piper outline, the Saratoga was first introduced in late 1979. It is produced in four versions; a basic model with fixed or retractable landing gear, and two corresponding turbo-charged models. Turbo Saratogas can be identified by a prominent air intake below the propeller. Saratogas resemble the Cherokee Six in having four windows per side, but have longer-span wings. Cruising speed of the Saratoga is 166 mph (267km/hr). *Country of origin:* USA.

Power: 1 × Continental piston engine   *Span:* 30ft 10in (9.4m)   *Length:* 24ft 7¼in (7.5m)

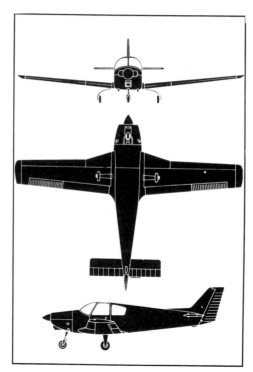

The IA 80 Piranha two-seat light training and general-purpose aircraft was developed by the former Wassmer company as the WA 80 Piranha and first flew in 1975. With a fuselage similar to that of the four-seat WA 51 Pacific, it is a particularly roomy aircraft. Of all-plastic construction, it has an extremely smooth finish. Powered by a 100hp Rolls-Royce Continental engine, the IA 80 has a cruising speed of about 120 mph (190km/hr) and a range of 435 miles (700km). Other performance figures include a never-exceed speed of 187 mph (302km/hr); maximum speed at sea level of 149 mph (240km/hr); flaps-up stalling speed of 59 mph (95km/hr) and flaps-down stalling speed of 50 mph (80km/hr). Orders for about 20 Piranhas were placed, but the company now concentrates on the manufacture of sailplanes. *Country of origin:* France.

Power: 1 × Lycoming piston engine   *Span:* 31ft 11¾in (9.75m)   *Length:* 24ft 7¼in (7.5m)

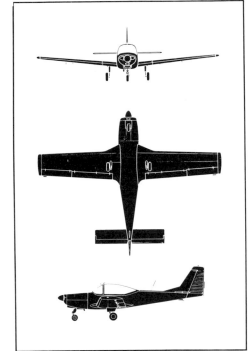

Following an agreement with the Italian company SIAI-Marchetti in 1967, FFA has developed and produced the two/three-seat AS 202 Bravo light trainer and sporting aircraft. First flown in 1969, the Bravo is currently available in two versions: AS 202/15 powered by a 150hp Lycoming engine, of which some 28 had been delivered by the beginning of 1978; and the AS 202/18A powered by a 180hp Lycoming. More than 150 Bravos had been built by 1983. FFA has also flown the prototype of a 260hp Lycoming-engined version, the AS 202/26A. Cruising speed of the AS 202/15 is about 130 mph (210km/hr) and maximum range is 553 miles (890km). *Country of origin:* Switzerland. *Silhouette and picture:* AS 202/15.

Fournier RF-6B/RFB RS 180 Sportsman   *Confusion:* Bravo

Power: 1 × Lycoming piston engine/
       1 × Continental piston engine

Span: 34ft 5½in (10.5m)

Length (RS 180): 23ft 5½in (7.15m)

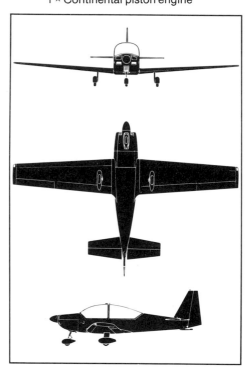

Designed by René Fournier, the four-seat RS 180 Sportsman first flew in 1973, powered by a 125hp Lycoming engine. Early production aircraft were designated RF6-180 and had the tailplane positioned on the top of the fuselage; in early 1978 the designation was changed to RS 180 and the tailplane was repositioned midway up the fin. The Fournier RF-6B, a generally similar but smaller two-seat version, first flew in 1974. Intended primarily for aerobatics and training, it has a one-piece transparent canopy and is powered by a 100hp Rolls-Royce Continental engine. Cruising speed of the RS 180 is about 145 mph (235km/hr) and that of the RF-6B about 120 mph (190km/hr). Load factors for the RF-6B are +9g and 4.5g. Production was suspended in 1981. *Country of origin:* France/West Germany. *Silhouette:* RF-6-180. *Picture:* RS-180.

Power: 1 × Lycoming piston engine   *Span:* 30ft 11in (9.42m)   *Length:* 26ft 9½in (8.17m)

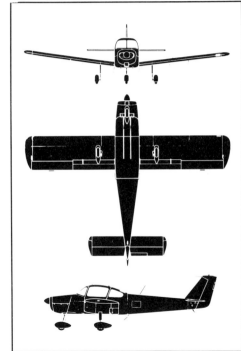

Design of this all-metal four-seat light aircraft began in 1964 and the type first flew in the following year. First production version was the FA-200-160 with a 160hp Lycoming engine. Two other versions have been built: the FA-200-180 with 180hp Lycoming engine, and the FA-200-180AO with a 180hp Lycoming and fixed-pitch propeller. Total production all versions had reached 298 by early 1982, when production ceased. *Country of origin:* Japan.

Valmet L-70 Vinka/Miltrainer

Confusion: Uirapuru, FA-200

Power: 1 × Lycoming piston engine   *Span:* 32ft 4in (9.85m)   *Length:* 24ft 7in (7.5m)

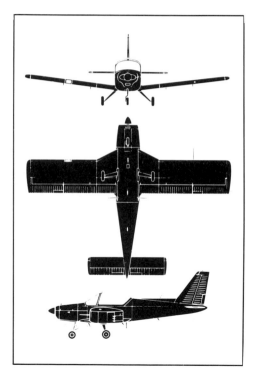

This two/four-seat training/touring light aircraft was first flown in 1975 and was produced to meet a requirement of the Finnish Air Force for a basic trainer to replace its Saab Safirs. Thirty were ordered, with deliveries to be completed by the end of 1982. Of conventional appearance and construction, the Vinka has a large one-piece rearward-sliding canopy and forward-swept wing-root leading edges. Powered by a 200hp Lycoming engine, the Vinka cruises at about 140mph (225km/hr). The Vinka is known as the Miltrainer for export purposes. *Country of origin:* Finland.

Power: 1 × Lycoming piston engine   *Span:* 27ft 11in (8.5m)   *Length:* 21ft 8in (6.6m)

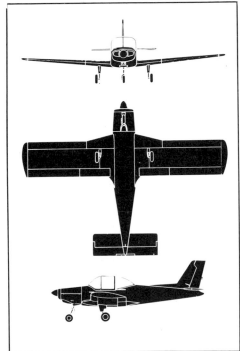

The two-seat Uirapuru first flew in 1965, powered by a 108hp Lycoming engine; it was followed by a second aircraft powered by a 150hp engine. An order for 30 A-122As was placed by the Brazilian Air Force in 1967, the aircraft being designated T-23 by the military. Powered by a 160hp Lycoming engine, the type was subsequently ordered by both Bolivia and Paraguay, while the quantity in Brazilian service was increased to 100. The civil version is designated A-122B and is similar to the A-122A but with a revised canopy. A total of 155 Uirapurus of all versions had been built by early 1977, when production ended. Cruising speed of the A-122A is about 115 mph (185km/hr), that of the A-122B about 120 mph (195km/hr). *Country of origin:* Brazil. *Silhouette and picture:* A-122A.

Zlin 42/43/142

Confusion: Pup/Bulldog

Power: 1 × Avia piston engine   *Span:* 29ft 10¾in (9.11m)   *Length:* 23ft 2½in (7.07m)

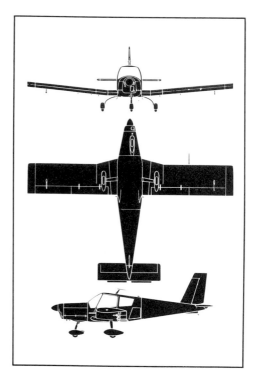

The two-seat Zlin 42, the first of a series of sporting and touring aircraft to be developed by the Moravan factory, first flew in 1967. Initial production aircraft were powered by a 180hp M137A engine and the principal operator was East Germany. Production of the Zlin 42M began in 1974. The Zlin 43, a larger, two/four-seat version of the Zlin 42, is powered by a 210hp Avia M337A. Latest version, with altered cockpit hood and more powerful engine, is the 142. *Country of origin:* Czechoslovakia. *Silhouette:* Zlin 43. *Picture:* Zlin 42M.

Power: 1 × Continental or   *Span* (Pup): 31ft (9.45m)   *Length* (Pup): 22ft 11in (6.99m)
1 × Lycoming piston engine

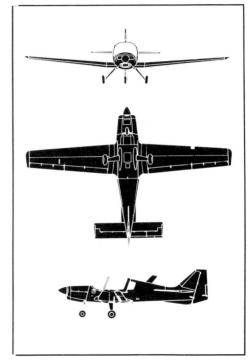

Three versions of the all-metal Pup were built. The B-121 Series 1 Pup 100, a two-seater powered by a 100hp Rolls-Royce Continental, first flew in 1967. The B.121 Series 2 Pup 150 was powered by a 150hp Lycoming engine and first flew in 1968. This version was fitted with an optional seat for a third adult or two children. Final variant was the Series 3 Pup 160, six of which were built for Iran. The Bulldog was developed in 1968 as a military trainer version and differed externally in being slightly larger and in having a fully transparent sliding canopy. It first flew in 1969 and production aircraft were fitted with a 200hp Lycoming. Customers include the RAF, Ghana, Nigeria, Jordan, Lebanon, Kenya and the Hong Kong Royal Auxiliary Air Force. Production was completed in 1982. *Country of origin:* UK. *Silhouette:* Bulldog. *Picture:* Pup 150.

Robin DR 221 Dauphin

Confusion: Bulldog/Pup

Power: 1 × Continental or 1 × Lycoming piston engine   *Span:* 28ft 7in (8.72m)   *Length:* 22ft 11½in (7m)

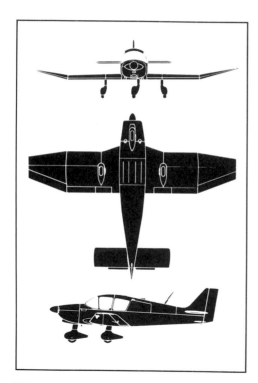

The three/four-seat DR 221 Dauphin, a development of the DR 220 2+2 range, first flew in 1967. All of the aircraft in this range have the characteristic cranked wing of Jodel-inspired light aircraft. The basic DR 220 and the strengthened DR 220A are both powered by a 100hp Rolls-Royce Continental, while the DR 220/108 is fitted with a 115hp Lycoming. The Dauphin is powered by a 115hp Lycoming and cruises at about 125 mph (205km/hr). Other performance figures include a maximum rate of climb at sea level of 650ft/min (198m/min); service ceiling of 12,800ft (3,900m); and maximum range of 565 miles (910km). More than 140 DR 220s and DR 221s were built before production switched to later Robin designs. *Country of origin:* France. *Silhouette:* DR 220. *Picture:* DR 221.

Power: 1 × Continental piston engine   *Span:* 31ft 11in (9.74m)   *Length:* 22ft 10½in (6.97m)

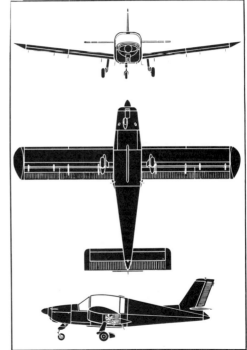

The Rallye family of light aircraft embraces several different aircraft, all originating from the Morane-Saulnier company's 90hp Rallye-Club of 1959. About 580 Rallyes were built by Morane-Saulnier. About a dozen different versions were built with engines ranging from 100hp to 235hp. Current production aircraft are the R 235 Gabier and the armed Guerrier, operated by Rwanda and Senegal. The Rallye 100 is built under licence in Poland under the name Koliber. Cruising speeds range from 105 mph (170km/hr) for the lowest-powered up to 150 mph (245km/hr) for the 235hp variants. *Country of origin:* France. *Silhouette:* Rallye 100T. *Picture:* R 235 Guerrier.

Power: 1 × Lycoming piston engine   *Span:* 42ft (12.81m)   *Length:* 31ft 10in (9.70m)

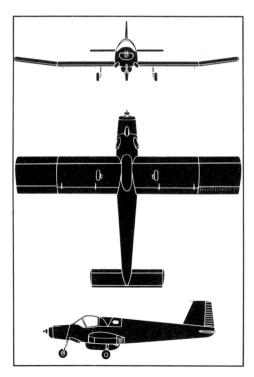

The FU-24 was initially designed by the Sargent-Fletcher company in the USA for agricultural top-dressing work in New Zealand and first flew in 1954. All manufacturing and sales rights were acquired by Air Parts in New Zealand in 1964 after 70 aircraft had been built in the US. Subsequently the type entered quantity production at Hamilton Airport, New Zealand, and more than 285 FU-24s had been completed by 1982. Customer countries include Australia, Bangladesh, Iraq, Pakistan, Thailand and Uruguay. Powered by a 400hp Lycoming, the FU-24 has an operating speed of 105–130 mph (170–210km/hr). A new version of the FU-24, the Cresco, is powered by an Avco Lycoming LTP101 turboprop and has many components in common with the standard aircraft. *Country of origin:* New Zealand. *Silhouette:* FU-24. *Picture:* Cresco.

Power: 1 × Lycoming piston engine   *Span:* 30ft (9.14m)   *Length:* 24ft (7.32m)

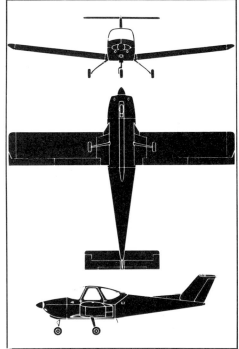

The prototype of this two-seat light trainer, designated PD 285, first flew in 1975, fitted at that time with a conventional tail. Production aircraft, designated Model 77, have the now fashionable T-tail. Some 304 Skippers had been delivered, mainly to Beech Aero Centres, by 1981, when production was temporarily suspended. The Skipper bears a marked resemblance to the Piper Tomahawk. *Country of origin:* USA.

Robin R 3000 *Confusion:* Skipper, Tomahawk

Power: 1 × Lycoming piston engine   *Span:* 32ft 2¼in (9.81m)   *Length:* 24ft 7¾in (7.51m)

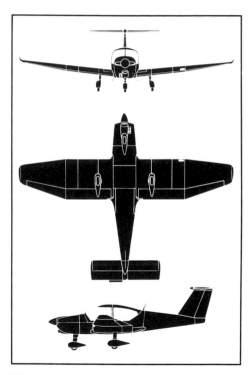

Latest in the Robin series of light aircraft, The R 3000 is available with 116hp and 140hp engines. The second prototype, flown in June 1981, introduced the distinctive upturned wingtips. Unlike the Skipper or the Tomahawk, which also have high-set tailplanes, the R 3000 is fitted with streamlined undercarriage fairings. When fitted with the 116hp Lycoming 0-235 engine, maximum cruising speed is 133 mph (215km/hr). *Country of origin:* France.

Power: 1 × Lycoming piston engine   *Span:* 34ft (10.36m)   *Length:* 23ft 2in (7.06m)

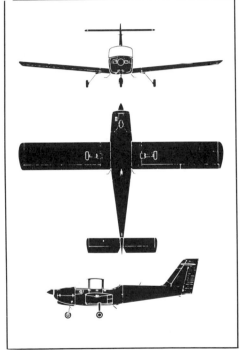

First introduced in 1978, this two-seat trainer followed the fashion of mounting the tailplane high on the fin. The cabin is also arranged for maximum all-round visibility by cutting down the rear fuselage decking. The Tomahawk bears a marked resemblance to Beechcraft's Skipper, but the Piper aircraft has a more substantial-looking vertical tail and lacks the small dorsal fin fairing of the Beechcraft. In 1981 the Tomahawk II was introduced, which incorporated internal changes. Production reached 2,497 of both versions before manufacture was temporarily suspended for 1983-1984. *Country of origin:* USA.

Nord 3202

Confusion: Chipmunk

Power: 1 × Potez piston engine   *Span:* 31ft 2in (9.5m)   *Length:* 26ft 8in (8.12m)

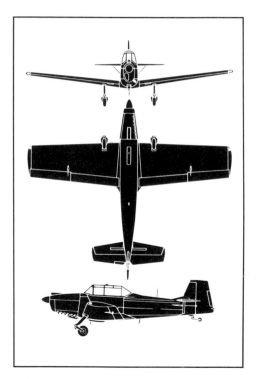

The Nord 3202 tandem two-seat primary trainer flew for the first time in 1957. Developed from the Nord 3200 and 3201, it was adopted as a replacement for the Stampe SV.4 trainers of the French Army Air Force. The first 50 of the 100 Nord 3202s built were powered by Potez 4D.32 engines. The second 50 were powered by Potez 4D.34Bs uprated from 240 to 260hp and were fitted with radio compasses. Production of the Nord 3202 ended in 1961. *Country of origin:* France.

Power: 1 × de Havilland piston engine *Span:* 34ft 4in (10.47m) *Length:* 25ft 5in (7.75m)

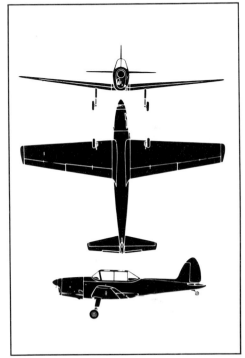

Designed by the Canadian de Havilland company, the tandem two-seat Chipmunk first flew in 1946. Some 220 were produced in Canada for both civil and military users; a further 60 were produced under licence by OGMA in Portugal. Production in the UK consisted of T.10s for the RAF and Mk 21s and 23s for civil users; Mk 22s are refurbished ex-RAF aircraft for civil use. The Mk 23 was a single-seat agricultural aircraft and the Mk 22A was a Bristol tourer version with a one-piece blown hood and wheel spats. Powered by a 145hp de Havilland Gipsy Major 10, the Chipmunk has a maximum cruising speed of about 143 mph (230km/hr). Range is 453 miles (730km). *Country of origin:* Canada. *Silhouette and picture:* T.10.

HAL HT-2 *Confusion:* Chipmunk, I-115

Power: 1 × Blackburn piston engine   *Span:* 35ft 2in (10.72m)   *Length:* 24ft 8½in (7.53m)

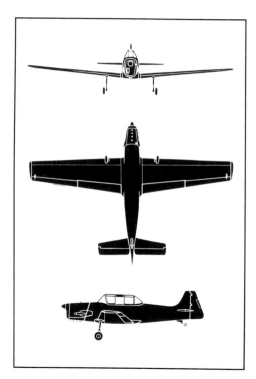

The tandem two-seat HT-2 was the first Indian powered aircraft of indigenous design and first flew in 1951. About 160 have been built, mostly for the Indian Air Force, Navy and civil users. In addition to two aircraft presented to Indonesia and Singapore, twelve were supplied to Ghana. Similar in appearance to the DHC-1 Chipmunk, though with a more angular fin and rudder, the HT-2 is powered by a 155hp Blackburn Cirrus Major III and cruises at about 115 mph (185km/hr). *Country of origin:* India.

Power: 1 × ENMA piston engine   *Span:* 31ft 3in (9.54m)   *Length:* 24ft 1in (7.35m)

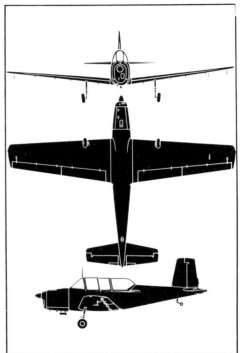

First flown in 1952, the I-115 tandem two-seat trainer was put into production as a standard type for the Spanish Air Force with the designation E.9. Designed as a replacement for the Spanish Air Force's Bücker Bü 131 biplane trainers, the I-115 entered quantity production May 1954. A total of 450 I-115s were built, and the type has the distinction of being the first aircraft of indigenous design to enter series production for the Spanish Air Force after the war. At the end of their military career most of the 115s were transferred to Spanish flying clubs, although some were retained by the Air Force for liaison and training. Of all-wood construction, the I-115 has a maximum speed of 143 mph (230km/hr), cruises at 126 mph (240km/hr) and has a ferry range of 620 miles. *Country of origin:* Spain.

Mudry CAP 10/CAP 20/CAP 21 *Confusion:* Emeraude

Power: 1 × Lycoming piston engine   *Span* (CAP 10): 26ft 5¼in (8.06m)   *Length* (CAP 10): 23ft 6in (7.16m)

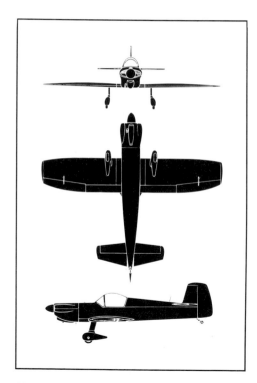

Developed from the Piel Emeraude, the two-seat all-wood CAP 10 is intended for use as a training, touring or aerobatic aircraft. First flight was in 1968, and a total of 89 had been built by mid-1978, including some 30 for the French Air Force. The CAP 20 is essentially a single-seat derivative of the CAP 10, although of almost completely new design. It has been refined considerably since it first flew in 1969, and the latest version, the CAP 20L, is suitable for competition aerobatics. Production was terminated in 1981 to make way for the CAP 21, with a new wing and undercarriage. Powered by a 200hp Lycoming engine, the CAP-20L cruises at about 165 mph (265km/hr), compared with 155 mph (250km/hr) for the 180hp CAP 10B. *Country of origin:* France. *Main silhouette:* CAP 20. *Picture:* CAP 20L.

Confusion: CAP 10, P.148   **Piel/Scintex CP 301 Emeraude**

Power: 1 × Continental piston engine   *Span:* 26ft 4½in (8.04m)   *Length:* 20ft 8in (6.3m)

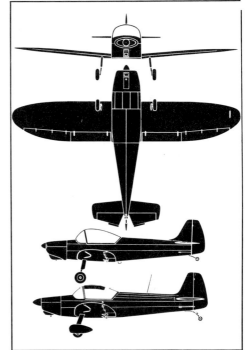

Designed by Claude Piel, the two-seat, all-wood Emeraude was first flown in 1952, with the first production aircraft flying the following year. Several versions have been built, commercially and by amateurs, powered by a variety of engines from 65 to 125hp. The Scintex Emeraude is largely similar to the Piel-built aircraft but features a one-piece blown canopy in place of the upwards-opening canopy doors of the latter. The CP 301 was built under licence in small quantities in Britain, where it was known as the Fairtravel Linnet, and in West Germany by Binder Aviatik. The Super Emeraude is a slightly larger version with higher payload and improved performance. Powered by a 90hp Continental piston engine, the CP 301 Emeraude cruises at about 125 mph (200km/hr). *Country of origin:* France. *Main silhouette:* CP 301; *lower side view:* Super Emeraude. *Picture:* Super Emeraude.

Piaggio P.148

Confusion: Emeraude

Power: 1 × Lycoming piston engine   *Span:* 36ft 6in (11.12m)   *Length:* 27ft 8½in (8.45m)

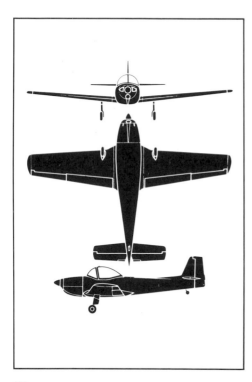

The Piaggio P.148 side-by-side two-seat primary trainer was selected for Italian Air Force training schools in 1951. A total of about 100 were ordered and the type first flew in 1951, with production deliveries commencing the following year. In 1962 a small number of ex-Italian Air Force P.148s were delivered to the Somali Air Corps as part of an Italian technical aid programme. The type is also in service in limited quantities with the Zaire Air Force; these are ex-Italian aircraft. Normally flown as a two-seater, the P.148 was certificated as a three-seater, the third position being located centrally behind the side-by-side front seats. The P.148 has many components in common with the P.149. Powered by a 190hp Lycoming engine, the P.148 cruises at about 125 mph (201km/hr). *Country of origin:* Italy.

Power: 1 × Continental piston engine   *Span:* 26ft 11½in (8.22m)   *Length:* 21ft 4in (6.5m)

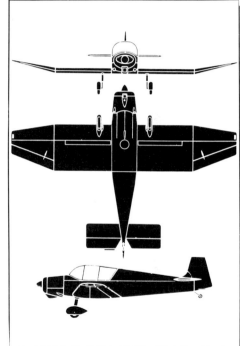

The D.11, the first two-seat light aircraft in the Jodel series, was developed from the D.9 Bébé. It first flew in 1950. The type has been built extensively by amateurs throughout Europe and North America. The D.112 is more widespread and is a refined version of the D.11. It has been built by Wassmer, SAN and Alpavia, aircraft built by the last two named companies being known as D.117s. Amateur-built examples powered by the 95hp Continental C90 are usually designated D.119. There are about 1,500 commercially built aircraft in the series. Cruising speed is approximately 120 mph (195km/hr).*Country of origin:* France. *Silhouette and picture:* D.11.

Jodel DR.1050/DR.1051 Ambassadeur/Sicile   *Confusion:* D.11/112

Power: 1 × Continental or 1 × Potez piston engine   *Span:* 28ft 7½in (8.72m)   *Length:* 20ft 10in (6.35m)

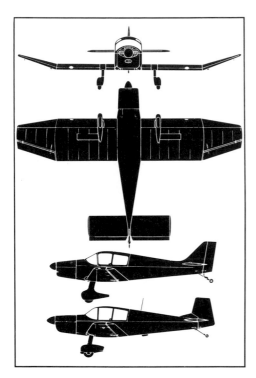

Centre Est was formed in 1957 to design and build the Jodel range of light aircraft. First in the series was the DR 100 Ambassadeur, which first flew in 1958. The first DR.1050 with a 100hp Continental was flown in 1959. A further version with a 105hp Potez engine was built in 1960 and designated DR.1051. These aircraft were also built under licence by Société Aéronautique Normande (SAN). In 1963 an improved Ambassadeur was announced, named the Sicile, with either a Continental (DR.1050) or Potez (DR.1051) engine. Last of the series were the DR.1050MM1 and DR.1051MM1 Sicile Record, with swept-back fin and rudder and one-piece elevator. Total production of the DR.100 and its derivatives amounted to more than 800 aircraft. *Country of origin:* France. *Main silhouette:* DR.1050; *upper side view:* DR.1050MM1. *Picture:* DR.1050.

Jodel D.140 Mousquetaire/Abeille/D.150 Mascaret

Power: 1 × Continental or 1 × Potez piston engine   *Span:* 33ft 8in (10.27m)   *Length:* 26ft (7.92m)

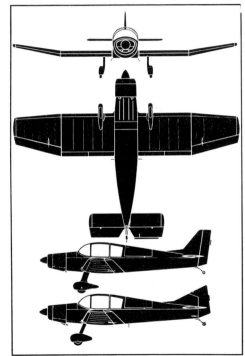

The Mousquetaire was developed by SAN as an economical four-seat light touring aircraft. It first flew in 1958 and sported a distinctive triangular fin, replaced in later aircraft with a conventional swept assembly. Five versions of the D.140 Mousquetaire were built, the sixth, the D.140R, being designated the Abeille. First flown in 1965, this aircraft was exclusively developed for glider towing and featured an extensively glazed cabin. The D.150 Mascaret is a two-seat light aircraft with a 100hp Continental or 105hp Potez. It is outwardly similar to the D.140 series but slightly smaller. Performance figures for the Mousquetaire include a maximum cruising speed at 7,000ft (2,300m) and 75 per cent power of 149 mph (240km/hr); maximum sea-level rate of climb of 750ft/min (230m/min); and maximum-fuel range of 870 miles (1,400km). *Country of origin:* France. *Main silhouette:* D.140; *lower side view:* D.140B. *Picture:* D.140.

 **Rollason D.62 Condor** *Confusion:* Zlin Z 50L

Power: 1 × Rolls-Royce Continental piston engine   *Span:* 27ft 6in (8.38m)   *Length:* 22ft 6in (6.86m)

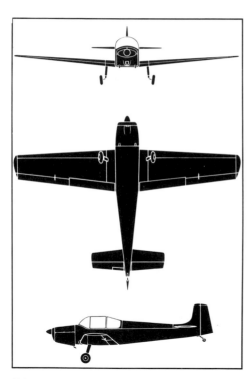

The side-by-side two-seat Condor, essentially a much improved version of the amateur-built tandem two-seat Turbi, was built under licence in Britain by Rollason, the first production aircraft flying in 1961. The all-wood Condor is similar in some respects to the Jodel D.112 Club but has a slightly tapered wing without the Jodel's characteristic upturned outer panels. Total production by Rollason reached 51 by early 1974. Powered by a 100hp Rolls-Royce Continental piston engine, the Condor cruises at about 115 mph (185km/hr). *Country of origin:* France/UK.

Power: 1 × Lycoming piston engine   *Span:* 28ft 2in (8.58m)   *Length:* 21ft 9in (6.62m)

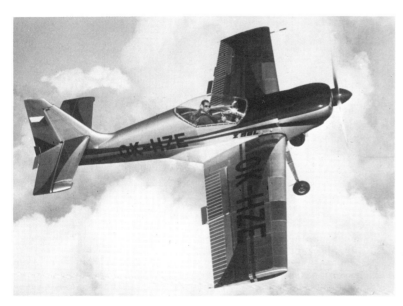

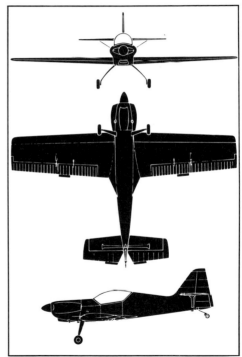

The Zlin Z 50L single-seat fully aerobatic competition aircraft first flew in 1975. The broad wings are of almost constant chord and are symmetrical in section, while the tailplane is braced on the underside. Current production version is the Z 50 LS, fitted with a more powerful 300hp Lycoming. *Country of origin:* Czechoslovakia.

ICA-Brasov IAR-822/IAR-826/IAR-827

Confusion: Pawnee, Ipanema

Power: 1 × Lycoming piston engine   *Span:* 42ft (12.8m)   *Length:* 30ft 10in (9.4m)

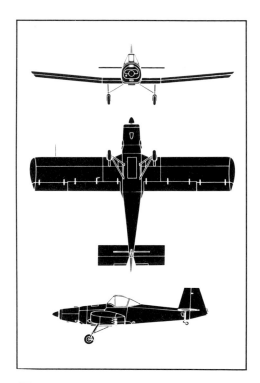

Prototype of the IAR-822 single/two-seat agricultural aircraft first flew in 1970, with series production of the first batch of 200 aircraft commencing the following year. Early aircraft were of mixed construction, but in 1973 an all-metal version was introduced, designated IAR-826. Powered by a 290hp Lycoming engine, the IAR-826 has an operating speed of about 75–100 mph (120–160km/hr). The IAR-827A is a developed version of the all-metal IAR-826 with increased payload, a Polish radial engine and improved flying characteristics. Performance figures for the IAR-827 include a cruising speed (agricultural version at maximum take-off weight) of 121 mph (195km/hr), and maximum rate of climb at sea level of 885ft/min (270m/min). *Country of origin:* Romania. *Silhouette:* IAR-826. *Picture:* IAR-827 Turbo.

Power: 1 × Lycoming piston engine   *Span* (**Pawnee**): 36ft 2in (11.02)   *Length* (**Pawnee**): 24ft 8½in (7.53m)

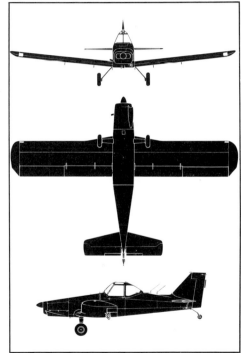

The original Pawnee single-seat agricultural aircraft first flew in 1959. The type has become one of the most used of all agricultural aircraft until production was suspended in 1982. Last production aircraft were the PA-25 Pawnee D, powered by a 235hp Lycoming engine, and the PA-36 Brave, previously known as the Pawnee Brave. Two versions of the Brave were built: the basic Brave 300 powered by a 300hp Lycoming engine and the Brave 375 with 375hp Lycoming. The Brave is externally identifiable by its swept tail assembly, lack of wing bracing and simple sprung-steel undercarriage. *Country of origin:* USA. *Silhouette:* **Brave.** *Picture:* **Pawnee D.**

EMBRAER EMB-201 Ipanema

Confusion: Pawnee, IAR-822

Power: 1 × Lycoming piston engine   *Span:* 38ft 4in (11.69m)   *Length:* 24ft 4½in (7.43m)

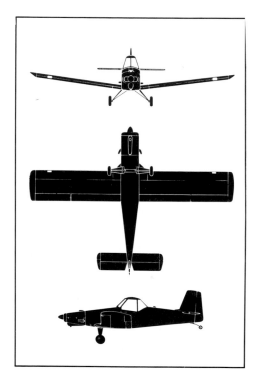

The original version of this single-seat agricultural aircraft was designed to a specification laid down by the Brazilian Ministry of Agriculture and first flew in 1970. The following versions have been built: EMB-200 and EMB-200A, of which 73 were built between 1970 and 1974; EMB-201, the developed version with new wing leading edge and wingtips, of which 188 were built; the current-production EMB-201A, first flown in 1977 with several minor aerodynamic refinements. More than 500 Ipanemas of all versions have been sold. A glider-tug version has also been built, designated EMB-201R. Three examples have been delivered to the Brazilian Air Force. *Country of origin:* Brazil. *Silhouette:* EMB-200. *Picture:* EMB-201.

Power: 1 × Continental piston engine   *Span:* 40ft 8½in (12.41m)   *Length:* 26ft 3in (8m)

The original Model 188 Ag Wagon first flew in 1965, powered by a 230hp Continental, and incorporated a number of components common to the Model 180 high-wing aircraft of that vintage. In late 1971 Cessna introduced a new range of agricultural types, three of which were based on the earlier aircraft. One of them, the Ag Pickup, was discontinued in 1976. The Ag Wagon and Ag Truck are in current production. The Ag Wagon is powered by a 300hp Continental engine and is a conventional agricultural aircraft with strut-braced wings and enclosed cockpit with all-round vision. The Ag Truck is similar to the Ag Wagon, but has a slightly longer wing, a larger hopper and other equipment refinements. Ag Wagon production has now ceased. A turbocharged version of the Ag Truck is called the Ag Husky. *Country of origin:* USA. *Silhouette:* Ag Wagon. *Picture:* Ag Truck.

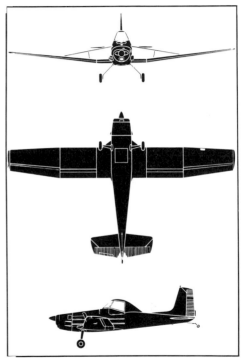

HAL HA-31 Basant

Confusion: Ag Wagon, Privrednik

Power: 1 × Lycoming piston engine   *Span:* 39ft 4½in (12m)   *Length:* 29ft 6¼in (9m)

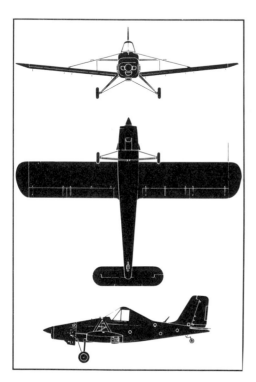

The HAL HA-31 Basant (Spring) was originally powered by a 250hp Rolls-Royce Continental but was subsequently completely redesigned as the HA-31 Mk II and re-engined with a 400hp Lycoming; it first flew in this form in 1972. A pre-production batch of 20 was built, the first eight of which were handed over to the Indian Ministry of Food and Agriculture in 1974. Series production finished in 1980 after 40 aircraft had been built. The Basant is of conventional design and construction for an agricultural aircraft, with strut-braced wings and a swept fin and rudder. Cruising speed is about 115 mph (185km/hr). *Country of origin:* India.

Power: 1 × Lycoming piston engine   *Span:* 34ft 9in (10.59m)   *Length:* 24ft (7.32m)

In the 1970s the Mexican AAMSA company took over production of the Aero Commander Quail and Sparrow Commander from Rockwell in the USA. The Sparrow Commander is no longer on the line but the Quail continues in production under the designation A9B-M. The Quail has a normal operating speed of 90–100 mph (145–161km/hr) and has a 795lit fertiliser/insecticide hopper. *Country of origin:* Mexico.

UTVA UTVA-65 Privrednik

Confusion: Basant, Quail, Ag Wagon

Power: 1 × Lycoming piston engine   *Span:* 40ft 1in (12.22m)   *Length:* 27ft 9in (8.46m)

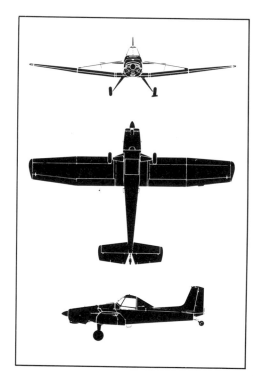

The single-seat UTVA-65 agricultural aircraft first flew in 1965 and combines the basic wings, tail assembly and undercarriage of the four-seat high-wing UTVA-60 with a new all-metal fuselage. In common with most low-winged agricultural aircraft, the UTVA-65 has a high-set, well-protected cockpit located approximately halfway along the fuselage, with a 26.5ft³ hopper forward of the cockpit. Powered by a 295hp Lycoming piston engine, the UTVA-65 has a maximum speed of about 125 mph (200km/hr). *Country of origin:* Yugoslavia.

WSK-PZL Mielec M-18 Dromader

Power: 1 × PZL piston engine *Span:* 58ft 1in (17.7m) *Length:* 31ft 1in (9.47m)

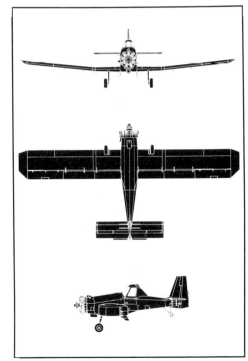

Significantly larger than the Kruk, which is also made in Poland, the M-18 Dromader first flew in 1976 and 230 had been built by early 1984. A two-seat version, designated M-18A, is also available, and a reduced capacity version known as the M-21 is being tested. The Dromader has an operating speed of 106–118 mph (170–190km/hr) and a maximum range of 323 miles (520km). *Country of origin:* **Poland.**

PZL-Warszawa PZL-106 Kruk *Confusion:* Tauro

Power: 1 × PZL piston engine   *Span:* 48ft 6½in (14.8m)   *Length:* 29ft 10in (9.1m)

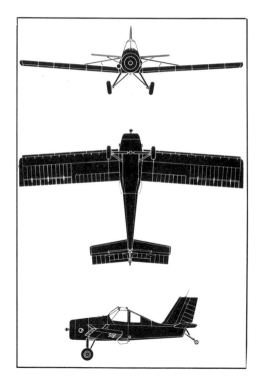

Intended as a replacement for the PZL-101 Gawron, the PZL-101M Kruk (Raven) was designed in the early 1960s. Initially powered by a 260hp Ivchenko engine, the aircraft was progressively refined into the current production version, the PZL-106A. The PZL-106 first flew in 1973, powered by a 400hp Lycoming engine; production aircraft are fitted with a 600hp PZL-35 seven-cylinder radial. Production commenced in 1976, with an anticipated total requirement of some 600 aircraft for the CMEA (Council for Mutual Economic Aid) member countries. The Kruk can carry its maximum chemical payload of 2,205lb (1,000kg) at an operating speed of 75–100 mph (120–160km/hr). A further development is the PZL-106AT Turbo-Kruk, fitted with a PT6A turboprop engine and a Hartzell fully feathering three-blade propeller. The Turbo-Kruk made its first flight in July 1981. *Country of origin:* Poland. *Silhouette:* PZL-106A. *Picture:* PZL-106.

Power: 1 × R-1340 or 1 × R-1300 piston engine or 1 × PT6A turboprop   *Span:* **44ft 4in (13.51m)**   *Length:* **29ft 4½in (8.95m)**

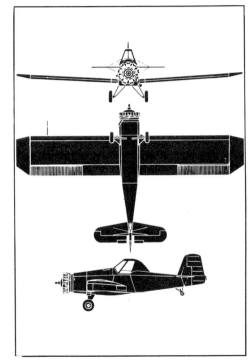

Ayres Corporation acquired the manufacturing rights to the Rockwell Thrush Commander 600 in 1977 and has the following versions in production: Thrush-600 with 600hp Pratt & Whitney Wasp radial and the Turbo-Thrush S-2R, similar to the Model 600 but powered by a 750shp Pratt & Whitney turboprop. The Pezetel Thrush has a 600hp Polish radial, and the Bull Thrush is powered by a 1,200hp Wright Cyclone. Working speed of the Model 600 is 105–115 mph (170–185km/hr), that of the Turbo-Thrush S-2R 95–150 mph (153–241km/hr). Both the Thrush and the Turbo-Thrush have as standard a 53 cu ft (1.5m³) hopper capable of holding up to 400 US gal (1,514 lit) of liquid or 3,280lb (1,487kg) of dry chemicals, while the Turbo-Thrush offers a 500 US gal (1,893lit) hopper as an option. *Country of origin:* USA. *Silhouette and picture:* Thrush-600.

 **Let Z-37 Cmelak** *Confusion:* —

Power: 1 × M462 piston engine *Span:* 40ft 1¼in (12.22m) *Length:* 28ft 0½in (8.55m)

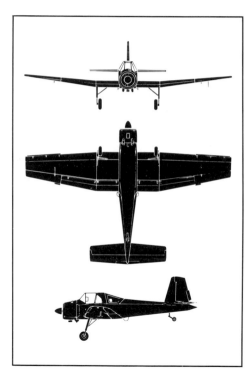

First flown in 1963, this agricultural and light utility aircraft entered series production in 1965. An improved version, the Z-37A, was introduced in 1971. It features some structural reinforcement and incorporates corrosion-resistant materials. A total of more than 700 Cmelaks were delivered, and operators include Bulgaria, Czechoslovakia, Finland, East Germany, Hungary, India, Iraq, Poland, UK and Yugoslavia. Let has also built some 27 examples of a two-seat training version, the Z-37A-2. Powered by a 315hp nine-cylinder radial engine, the Cmelak cruises at about 115 mph (185km/hr) and operates between 68 and 74 mph (109–119km/hr). *Country of origin:* Czechoslovakia. *Silhouette:* Z-37A. *Picture:* Z-37.

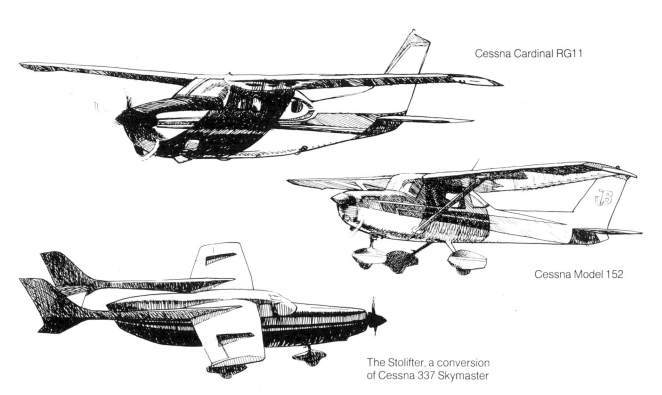

Cessna Cardinal RG11

Cessna Model 152

The Stolifter, a conversion
of Cessna 337 Skymaster

Piper PA-18 Super Cub

Confusion: Autocrat

Power: 1 × Lycoming piston engine   *Span:* 35ft 2½in (10.73m)   *Length:* 22ft 7in (6.88m)

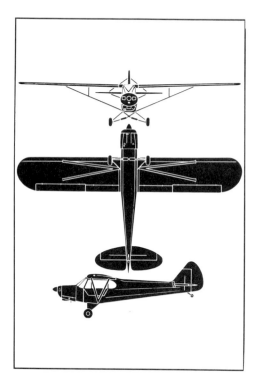

The original Super Cub, powered by a 90hp Continental, was first certificated in 1949 and was itself the successor to a long line of Piper light aircraft which began with the Taylor E-2 Cub of 1931. Later aircraft include the J-3 Cub of 1938, the PA-12 Super Cruiser of 1940 and the Vagabond, which was the forerunner of the Tri-Pacer line. Retaining the tandem two-seat arrangement, the current Super Cub is powered by a 150hp Lycoming, giving it a cruising speed of about 105 mph (169km/hr). Most Super Cubs are used for agricultural purposes. By the beginning of 1978 more than 40,000 Cubs of all types had been delivered and large numbers are still flying throughout the world, though most are concentrated in the USA. *Country of origin:* USA. *Silhouette and picture:* Super Cub.

Power: 1 × de Havilland or 1 × Blackburn piston engine   *Span:* 36ft (10.97m)   *Length:* 23ft 8in (7.21m)

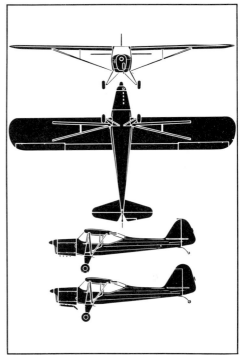

The Auster range embraces several types which can still be seen flying throughout the world. The J/1 Autocrat was the first post-war product of the Auster company and was derived from the Taylorcraft Model D spotter aircraft. Most of the range are externally similar and can be recognised by engine differences and by slight variations in the size of the vertical tail. All have V-strut wing bracing and parallel-chord wings. The Beagle A.61 Terrier is a civil conversion of the Auster AOP.6. Early conversions were also known as the Tugmaster. Introduced in 1961, the Terrier has a larger vertical tail and long exhaust pipe and silencer. *Country of origin:* UK. *Main silhouette:* AOP.6; *lower side view:* Terrier. *Picture:* Autocrat.

Aero Boero 95/115/180 *Confusion:* Citabria

Power: 1 × Continental or 1 × Lycoming piston engine   *Span:* 34ft 2½in (10.42m)   *Length:* 22ft 7½in (6.90m)

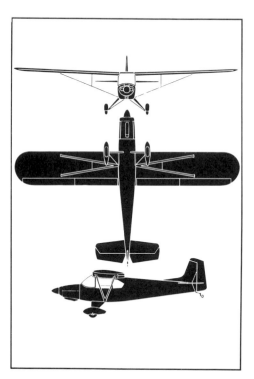

This family of three and four-seat light aircraft consists of some eleven different types: the basic AB 95 Standard with 95hp Continental; the AB 95A De Lujo with 100hp Continental; AB 95A Fumigador agricultural version; AB 95B with 150hp engine; AB 95/115 with 115hp engine, wheel fairings and streamlined engine cowling; AB 115 BS with swept-back fin and rudder; AB 180 four-seat version with 180hp Lycoming; AB 180 RV three-seat version with swept-back fin and rudder; AB 180 Condor high-altitude version with modified wingtips. Two lower-powered versions of the AB 180, the AB 150 RV and the RB 150 Ag, have also been built. *Country of origin:* Argentina. *Silhouette:* AB 95/115. *Picture:* AB 180.

Power: 1 × Lycoming piston engine   *Span* (Citabria): 33ft 5in (10.19m)   *Length* (Citabria): 22ft 8in (6.91m)

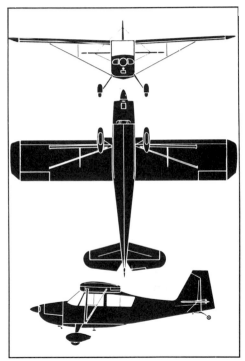

This series of high-wing light aircraft embraces several models of broadly similar appearance but widely differing powerplants and performances. Derived from the Aeronca Champion and Sedan light aircraft of the late 1940s, via the Champion Traveller and Challenger of the 1950s, current aircraft have a squared-off vertical tail and angular fuselage but retain the tandem seating of earlier aircraft. Three versions of the Citabria have been built. Production ceased in 1980. *Country of origin:* USA. *Silhouette:* Citabria. *Picture:* Decathlon.

Maule M-4 Rocket/M-5 Lunar Rocket   *Confusion:* Citabria

Power: 1 × Continental or 1 × Lycoming piston engine   *Span:* 30ft 10in (9.4m)   *Length:* 22ft (6.71m)

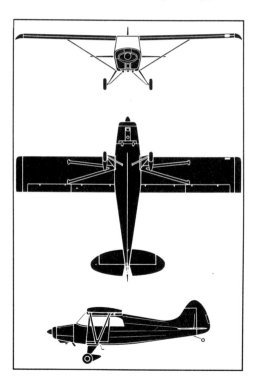

Production of the basic Maule M-4 began in 1963. This design was a conventional four-seat light aircraft with V-strut wing bracing and a rounded vertical tail. Four versions were available: the M-4 Astro-Rocket with 180hp Franklin engine; the M-4 Rocket with 210hp Continental, which was available also as a seaplane; and the M-4 Strato Rocket, generally similar to the Rocket but powered by a 220hp Franklin engine. The M-5 Lunar Rocket has 30% more flap area and enlarged tail surfaces. The five-seat M-6 Super Rocket was introduced in 1984. Powered by a 210hp Avco Lycoming, the M-5 cruises at 190 mph (304km/hr). *Country of origin:* USA. *Silhouette:* M-4. *Picture:* M-5.

HAL HAOP-27 Krishak

Power: 1 × Continental piston engine   *Span:* 37ft 6in (11.43m)   *Length:* 27ft 7in (8.41m)

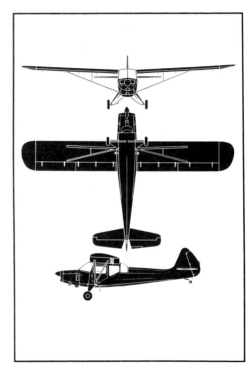

The Krishak was designed to meet an operational requirement of the Indian Air Force for an air observation post (AOP) light aircraft. It first flew in late 1959 and a total of 68 were ordered, all of which had been delivered by 1969. The Krishak normally carries a crew of two, but there is a swivelling seat for a third person in the rear of the cabin. Evolved from the HUL-26 Pushpak, the Krishak has a similar wing, with the addition of flaps, and has a more pointed vertical tail. Powered by a 225hp Rolls-Royce Continental, it has a cruising speed of about 130 mph (209km/hr). *Country of origin:* India.

Cessna Model 180/Model 185 Skywagon

Confusion: Krishak, UTVA-60

Power: 1 × Continental piston engine   *Span:* 35ft 10in (10.92m)   *Length:* 25ft 9in (7.85m)

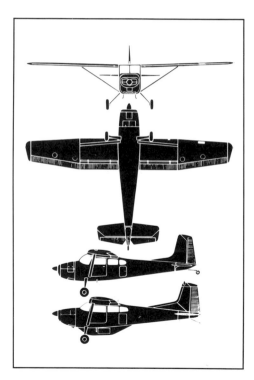

This six-seat utility aircraft first flew in 1952 as a four-seater. Throughout its production life the type has retained the tailwheel undercarriage and the upright vertical tail. Two versions are currently in production: the basic Model 185 Skywagon and the Model 185 Skywagon II, which includes a factory-installed avionics package. Production had exceeded 5,800 by the beginning of 1978. The Model 185 Skywagon has been developed from the Model 180 and first flew in 1960. It features a strengthened fuselage and is fitted with a 300hp Continental in place of the Model 180's 230hp unit. A military version, designated U-17 in the US, is also available. A total of 4,323 Model 185 Skywagons had been built by April 1984. *Country of origin:* USA. *Main silhouette:* Model 180; *lower side view:* U-17. *Picture:* Model 180.

Power: 1 × Lycoming piston engine *Span:* 37ft 5in (11.4m) *Length:* 27ft 6in (8.38m)

Derived from the UTVA-56 four-seat utility aircraft of 1959, the UTVA-60 is essentially the production version of the earlier aircraft. Five basic versions have been built, differing in the type of equipment carried for the various roles, which include light transport, air ambulance, agricultural spraying and float-plane. The UTVA-66 was developed from the UTVA-60 and first flew in 1967. Powered by a 270hp Lycoming engine, the UTVA-66 cruises at 143 mph (230km/hr). Both types are in service with the Yugoslav Air Force. *Country of origin:* Yugoslavia. *Silhouette:* UTVA-60. *Picture:* UTVA-66.

Cessna O-1 Bird Dog *Confusion:* SM.1019

Power: 1 × Continental piston engine   *Span:* 36ft (10.97m)   *Length:* 25ft 10in (7.89m)

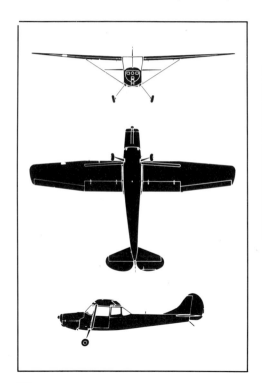

The Bird Dog was developed for the US Army as a light reconnaissance and observation aircraft which could also be used for liaison and training duties. It first flew in 1950 and remained in continuous production until late 1958, by which time more than 3,300 had been built. It briefly re-entered production in 1962 and a further 100 were built. The type is still in large-scale service in many countries throughout the world. The Bird God has a tailwheel undercarriage, and nearly all variants have the characteristic rounded fin and rudder. The exception is the O-1C, some 25 of which were built for the US Marine Corps, which has the old-style squared-off tail of the early Cessna 180s and 185s. *Country of origin:* USA.

Power: 1 × Allison turboprop   *Span:* 36ft (10.97m)   *Length:* 27ft 11½in (8.52m)

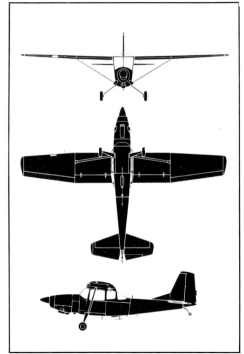

This tandem two-seat Stol light aircraft is based on the Cessna O-1 Bird Dog but has an extensively modified airframe to meet present-day operational requirements. First flown in 1969, it was put into production for the Italian Army, powered by a 400hp Allison 250-B17 turboprop. Total order was for 100 aircraft. The SM.1019E is stressed for two underwing hardpoints and can carry a variety of operational equipment. Cruising speed is about 185 mph (300km/hr). Other performance figures include a maximum rate of climb at sea level of 1,810ft/min (551m/min); operational ceiling of 25,000ft (7,620m); and a typical operational radius with two rocket launchers of 69 miles (111km). *Country of origin:* Italy.

Aeritalia AM-3C

Confusion: SM.1019

Power: 1 × Piaggio/Lycoming piston engine   *Span:* 41ft 5½in (12.64m)   *Length:* 29ft 4in (8.93m)

The three/four-seat AM.3C was originally designated MB.335 and first flew in 1967. Suitable for forward air control, observation, liaison, passenger and freight transport, casualty evacuation and tactical support, the type has been built in quantity for the Rwanda Air Force and the South African Air Force, in which service it is known as the Bosbok. The AM-3C is stressed to carry a variety of armaments on two underwing pylons. Powered by a Piaggio-built 340hp Lycoming, the AM-3C cruises at about 150 mph (245km/hr). *Country of origin:* Italy.

Power: 1 × Praga Doris piston engine   *Span:* 45ft 9½in (13.96m)   *Length:* 28ft (8.54m)

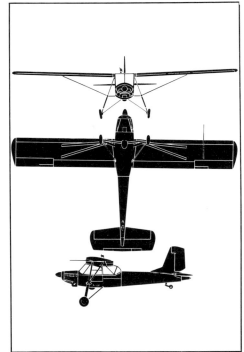

The L-60 Brigadyr three/four-seat general-purpose aircraft first flew in 1955 and by the time production ended in 1960 more than 400 had been built. Bearing a slight resemblance to the wartime Fieseler Storch, with its long, stalky undercarriage and generous expanse of cabin glazing, the Brigadyr has been used for air observation by the Czech Air Force as well as for agricultural duties. Powered by a 220hp Praga Doris M 208B engine, the L-60 cruises at about 110 mph (177km/hr). *Country of origin:* Czechoslovakia.

DHC DHC-2 Beaver   *Confusion:* Otter, Do 27

Power: 1 × R-985 piston engine or/1 × PT6A turboprop   *Span:* 48ft (14.64m)   *Length:* 30ft 4in (9.24m)

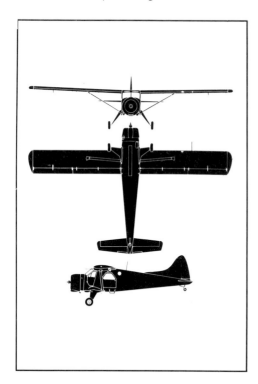

Nearly 1,700 DHC-2 Beaver light utility transports were built, the first flying in 1947. Carrying either seven passengers or freight, the Beaver has proved capable of operating in very rough, remote areas. The Beaver Mk I was produced in both civil and military forms, some 968 of the latter variant going to the US Army/USAF as the U-6A. Beavers have been fitted with floats and skis. A later development is the Turbo-Beaver Mk III, which has the Pratt & Whitney radial engine replaced by a PT6A turboprop. This changes the nose shape significantly. The Mk III can carry 10 passengers, cruises at 157 mph (252km/hr) and has a range of 677 miles (1,090km). *Country of origin:* Canada. *Silhouette and picture:* Mk I.

Power: 1 × R-1340 piston engine   *Span:* 58ft (17.69m)   *Length:* 41ft 10in (12.80m)

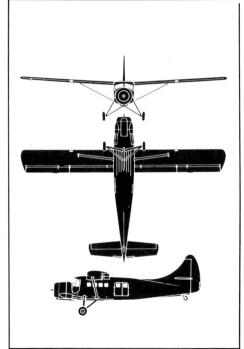

First flown in 1951, the 10-seat Otter has been extensively used by the armed forces of USA, Canada, Australia, Ghana and India, and in smaller numbers by several South American nations. A truly utility type, the Otter can be used for carrying passengers or freight, photographic survey or search and rescue. The Otter can be fitted with floats and skis, and has been used in Antarctica. Powered by a 600hp Pratt & Whitney radial engine, the Otter has a cruising speed of about 130 mph (209km/hr) and a maximum level speed of 160 mph (257km/hr). A turboprop conversion of the Otter, powered by a single Pratt & Whitney Aircraft of Canada PT6A-27, has been produced by Cox Air Resources of Edmonton, Canada. Main advantages of the conversion are a reduced empty weight, increased fuel and payload capacity, and a slight improvement in performance. Some 270 piston-engined Otters are still in service. *Country of origin:* Canada.

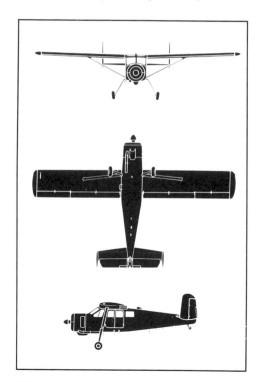

Max Holste Broussard   *Confusion:* Beaver

Power: 1 × R-985 piston engine   *Span:* 45ft 1in (13.75m)   *Length:* 28ft 4½in (8.65m)

The twin-finned Broussard light utility aircraft was developed from the MH 152 experimental observation type and first flew in 1952. Production aircraft were designated MH 1521 and MH 1521A. Total production of the Broussard exceeded 330 aircraft. About 40 remain in military service worldwide with France, Cameroun, Chad, Congo, Mali, Mauritania, Niger, Senegambia and Togo. A small number are civilian registered. Powered by a 450hp Pratt and Whitney Wasp radial, the Broussard cruises at about 150mph (245km/hr) and has a maximum range of 745 miles (1,200km). *Country of origin:* France. *Silhouette and picture:* MH 1521.

Power: 1 × AI-14R piston engine   *Span:* 41ft 7½in (12.68m)   *Length:* 29ft 6½in (9m)

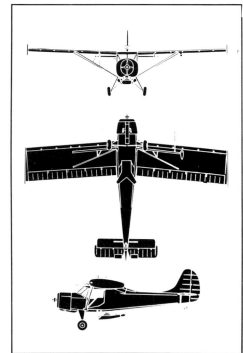

The PZL-101A Gawron (Rook) single-engined agricultural, ambulance and utility light aircraft was developed from the Russian Yak-12M and first flew in 1958. From 1961 the type was approved by a number of Eastern bloc countries as their standard agricultural aircraft, and more than 330 had been built when production ended in 1973. The Gawron has also been sold in Austria, Finland, India, Spain, Turkey and Vietnam. The aircraft is conventional in all major respects, with V-braced high wing and braced tail assembly. Powered by a 260hp AI-14R nine-cylinder radial engine, the Gawron cruises at about 80 mph (130km/hr). *Country of origin:* Poland.

Pilatus/Fairchild PC-6 Porter   *Confusion:* Wilga

Power: 1 × Lycoming piston engine or 1 × Astazou turboprop   *Span:* 49ft 8in (15.14m)   *Length:* 36ft 10in (11.23m)

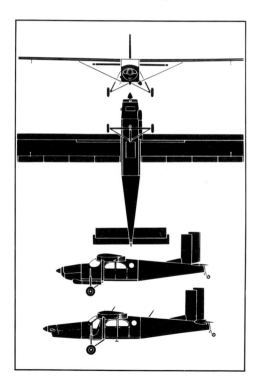

The Pilatus Porter Stol utility aircraft was first flown in 1959 and some 50 production aircraft had been delivered by mid-1965, by which time the Turbo-Porter was in quantity production. The Turbo-Porter first flew in 1961 and several variants have been built over the last few years. Current production version is the PC-6/B-2-H2 Turbo-Porter, powered by a 550shp Pratt & Whitney PT6A turboprop. The type was also manufactured under licence in the USA by Fairchild Industries, the first US-built aircraft flying in 1966. A militarised version with underwing hardpoints is called the AU-23A Peacemaker. The US Army designation for the Turbo-Porter is the UV-20A Chiricahua. By early 1984 more than 440 PC-6s of all types had been ordered by operators in over 50 countries. *Country of origin:* Switzerland/USA. *Main silhouette:* Porter; *lower side view:* Turbo-Porter. *Picture:* Turbo-Porter.

Power: 1 × Ivchenko piston engine   *Span:* 36ft 5¾in (11.12m)   *Length:* 26ft 6¾in (8.1m)

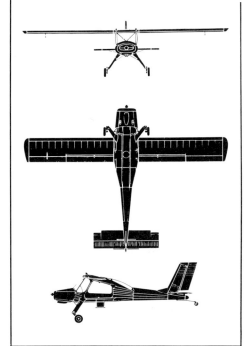

The Wilga (Thrush) was designed as a successor to the Czechoslovakian L-60 Brigadyr in the agricultural role and first flew in 1962 as the Wilga 1. The design was modified in 1967 and designated the Wilga 35. Current production versions are the Wilga 35A for club flying, the Wilga 35P light transport, the agricultural 35R and the float-equipped 35H. The Wilga 80, identified by a carburettor intake mounted further aft, conforms to US requirements. More than 800 Wilgas of all versions have been built. *Country of origin:* Poland. *Silhouette:* Wilga 2. *Picture:* Wilga 35.

Dornier Do 27

Confusion: Super Courier

Power: 1 × Lycoming piston engine   *Span:* 39ft 4½in (12m)   *Length:* 31ft 6in (9.6m)

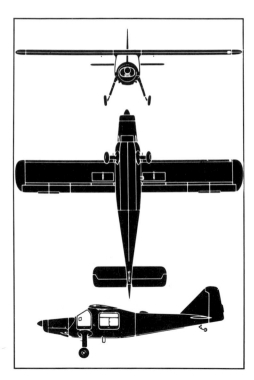

The Dornier Do 27 six/eight-seat utility aircraft first flew in 1955 in Spain, with large-scale production being undertaken in Germany from 1956. When production ended a total of 680 had been built, including 428 for the West German armed forces and 50 manufactured under licence by CASA in Spain as the CASA C.127. Several versions of the German-built aircraft have been manufactured, the principal differences between variants being engine type and internal fittings for different roles. Powered by a 340hp Lycoming, the Do 27H-2 cruises at about 130 mph (209km/hr). Other performance figures include a maximum rate of climb at sea level of 650ft/min (198m/min); service ceiling of 10,825ft (3,300m); and a range with maximum fuel, no allowances, of 685 miles (1,100km). *Country of origin:* West Germany. *Silhouette:* Do 27. *Picture:* C.127.

Helio Super Courier/Trigear Courier

Power: 1 × Lycoming piston engine   *Span:* 39ft (11.89m)   *Length:* 31ft (9.45m)

Evolved from the two-seat Koppen-Bollinger Helioplane, which first flew in 1949, the original Courier appeared in 1952. The main production version was the H-295 Super Courier, which made its maiden flight in 1958. Current production versions are the six-seat Courier 700, and the more powerful Courier 800. Both are available with wheel, amphibious float or ski undercarriages. All versions have an unbraced cantilever wing and characteristic tall fin. Powered by a 295hp Lycoming, the H-295 has a cruising speed of 150 mph (241km/hr). *Country of origin:* USA. *Silhouette and picture:* H-295.

 **Helio AU-24A Stallion** *Confusion:* Super Courier

Power: 1 × PT6A turboprop *Span:* 41ft (12.5m) *Length:* 39ft 7in (12m)

Designed as a successor to the Helio Super Courier, the turboprop Stallion first flew in 1964 and has been developed in both civil and military versions. The civil version can carry up to ten people in a high-density layout or up to six passengers in individual seats. The US Air Force acquired 15 of an armed version designated AU-24, 14 of which were subsequently supplied to the Khmer Air Force. The Stallion is easily recognisable by its swept-back main undercarriage legs and long nose accommodating the 680shp Pratt & Whitney PT6A turboprop. Cruising speed is 198 mph (319km/hr). A total of 600 Couriers, Super Couriers and Stallions were built. There are plans to put the Stallion back into production under the designation H-550A *Country of origin:* USA. *Silhouette:* AU-24. *Picture:* Model H-600B.

Power: 1 × Lycoming piston engine   *Span:* 42ft 10¾in (13.08m)   *Length:* 30ft 6½in (9.31m)

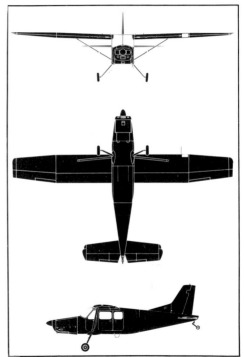

The C4M Kudu is a six/eight-seat light transport which is capable of operating from unprepared surfaces. The type first flew in 1974. The first military prototype flew in 1975 but no details of production figures are available. The type is a development of the Aermacchi-Lockheed AL.60 Conestoga, which was built in both tricycle and tailwheel forms. The Kudu cruises at 124 mph (200km/hr) and is in civil and military use in South Africa. *Country of origin:* South Africa. *Silhouete and picture:* Kudu.

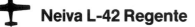

Neiva L-42 Regente *Confusion:* Oscar

Power: 1 × Continental piston engine   *Span:* 29ft 11½in (9.13m)   *Length:* 23ft 1in (7.04m)

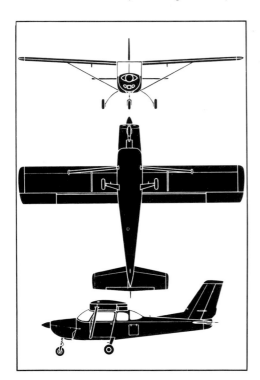

The four-seat Regente was first flown in 1961 and entered service with the Brazilian Air Force in 1963. Two versions have been built: the Regente 360C, designated C-42 in Brazilian Air Force service; and the Regente 420L, designated L-42 by the BAF. Main difference between the two is that the L-42 has a stepped-down cabin rear window for improved all-round visibility. When production ended in 1971, 80 C-42s and 40 L-42s had been built. Powered by a 210hp Continental, the L-42 cruises at about 140 mph (236km/hr). The company also developed a civil version of the Regente, the Lanceiro, which first flew in 1970 but did not enter full-scale production. *Country of origin:* Brazil. *Silhouette and picture:* L-42.

Power: 1 × Lycoming piston engine   *Span:* 32ft 9in (9.99m)   *Length:* 23ft 9in (7.23m)

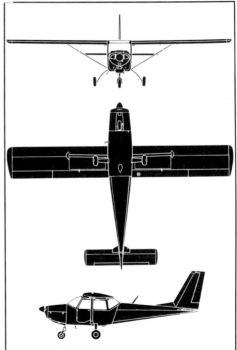

The four-seat P.64 Oscar was first flown in 1965, powered by a 180hp Lycoming engine. The following year saw the introduction of an improved version with cut-down rear fuselage decking to improve all-round visibility. A small number of aircraft were built by AFIC in South Africa as the RSA 200 Falcon. The P.66B Oscar 100 and Oscar 150 are two- and three-seat developments of the P.64. In 1976 the P-66C-160 Charlie was introduced. Powered by a 160hp Lycoming, the P-66C-160 cruises at 135 mph (216km/hr). *Country of origin:* Italy. *Silhouette:* P.64. *Picture:* P.66C-160 Charlie.

Beagle A.109 Airedale *Confusion:* Skyhawk

Power: 1 × Lycoming piston engine   *Span:* 36ft 4in (11.07m)   *Length:* 26ft 4in (8.02m)

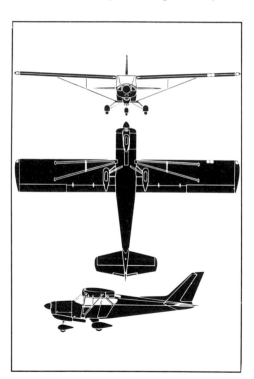

The four-seat Airedale light touring aircraft, first flown in 1961, was a successor to the famous Auster line of light aircraft. Powered by a 180hp (185km/hr) Lycoming, it cruises at about 115 mph (185km/hr). The Airedale was an unsuccessful attempt at producing a British competitor to the American light aircraft that were beginning to swamp the UK market, and production totalled little more than 40. About 20 remain on the British register, with a handful elsewhere in the world. The Airedale has typically Auster-style parallel-chord wings with squared-off tips and V-type wing bracing struts. *Country of origin:* UK.

Power: 1 × Lycoming or 1 × Continental piston engine   *Span:* 35ft 10in (10.92m)   *Length:* 26ft 11in (8.2m)

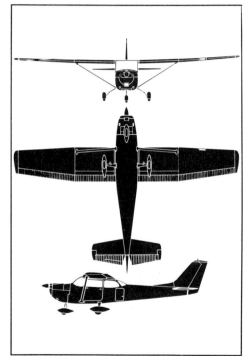

First introduced in 1955, the Model 172 was essentially a Model 170 with tricycle undercarriage and revised tail surfaces. The swept-tail 172A was introduced in 1960. Current versions are powered by a 160hp engine giving a cruising speed of about 140 mph (225km/hr). The Model 172E is a more powerful version with a 210hp Continental. Known in the US Army and Air Force as the T-41 Mescalero, the type is used for basic training. It has also been bought by a few South American air forces. Top of the line is the Model R-172 Hawk XP, which is also in production in France by Reims Aviation. Power is provided by a 195hp Continental. More than 35,300 Model 172 Skyhawks had been produced by 1984, including more than 2,100 French-built F172s. In addition 807 military Mescaleros were built. *Country of origin:* USA. *Silhouette:* **Skyhawk**. *Picture:* **T-41**.

Cessna Model 150/152 Aerobat

Confusion: Skylane

Power: 1 × Continental or 1 × Lycoming piston engine   *Span:* 32ft 8½in (9.97m)   *Length:* 24ft 1in (7.34m)

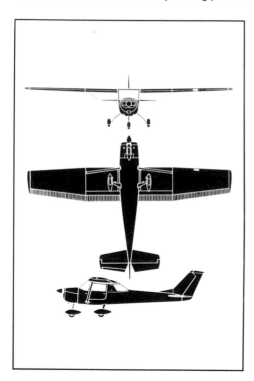

This two-seater, first flown in 1957, was intended as a successor to Cessna's earlier tailwheel Models 120 and 140. Several versions of the 150 have been built, the first major change being the introduction of the swept-tail Model 150F in 1966. Production of the basic aircraft ended in 1977 after almost 24,000 had been built, including 1,500 in France by Reims Aviation. Current production type is the Model 152, which has a more powerful engine than the Model 150 but is otherwise externally similar. The Model 152 Aerobat has certain interior modifications as well as some structural beefing-up to permit simple aerobatics. Maximum cruising speed is 117 mph (188km/hr). *Country of origin:* USA. *Silhouette:* Model 150F. *Picture:* Model 152.

Power: 1 × Continental or 1 × Lycoming piston engine   *Span:* 35ft 10in (10.92m)   *Length:* 28ft 1½in (8.57m)

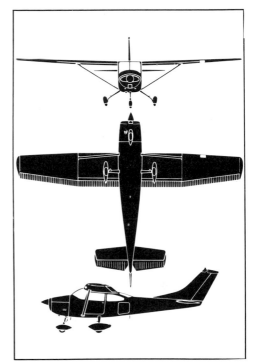

Derived from the Model 180 utility light aircraft, the Model 182 was introduced in 1956. The swept tail was introduced on 1960 aircraft. Production of the Model 182 was discontinued in 1976 and current production aircraft are the standard Skylane and Skylane II; the latter embodies a factory-installed avionics package. In 1977 Cessna introduced a new retractable-undercarriage version designated Skylane RG (and the Skylane RG II with factory-installed avionics). The RG aircraft were also fitted with the more powerful 235hp Lycoming engine. Total production of all variants exceeds 19,000, including a number built in France by Reims Aviation as the Rocket. Cruising speed is 157 mph (253km/hr). Retractable-undercarriage versions are known as the Skylane RG and Turbo-Skylane RG. *Country of origin:* USA. *Silhouette:* Model 182G. *Picture:* Skylane II.

Cessna Cardinal/Cardinal RG *Confusion:* Skylane

Power: 1 × Lycoming piston engine *Span:* 35ft 6in (10.82m) *Length:* 27ft 3in (8.31m)

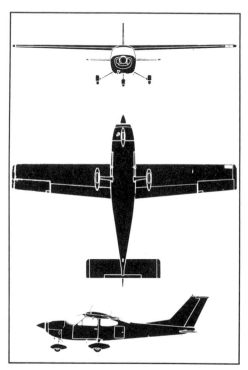

The original Model 177 four-seat light aircraft, introduced in 1967, was powered by a 150hp engine, later increased to 180hp. The 1978 aircraft were re-designated Cardinal Classic and incorporated many improvements to cabin comfort and basic equipment. The Cardinal RG series was introduced in 1970 and featured hydraulically retractable undercarriage and 200hp Lycoming engine. Cruising speed of the Cardinal Classic is about 150 mph (241km/hr) and that of the Cardinal RG about 170 mph (273km/hr). Other performance figures for the RG include a maximum sea-level speed of 180 mph (290km/hr); economical cruising speed at 10,000ft (3,050m) of 139 mph (233km/hr); maximum rate of climb at sea level of 925ft/min (282m/min); service ceiling of 17,100ft (5,210m); and flaps-down stalling speed of 57 mph (92km/hr). Total production had exceeded 4,000 by early 1978, of which about half were RGs. *Country of origin:* USA. *Silhouette:* **Cardinal**. *Picture:* Cardinal RG II.

Power: 1 × Continental piston engine   *Span:* 35ft 10in (10.92m)   *Length:* 28ft 3in (8.61m)

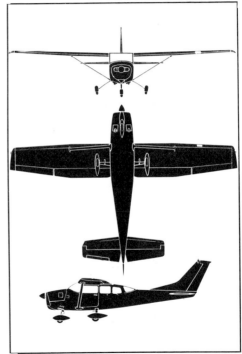

This six-seat light aircraft was introduced in 1962 as the Model 205 powered by a 285hp Continental engine. In 1964 this was superseded by the Model 206 Super Skywagon with more powerful engine and double cargo doors on the starboard side. The aircraft has since been renamed Stationair and Turbo-Stationair. 1978 aircraft were designated Stationair 6 and Turbo-Stationair 6, fitted with the 300hp Continental and 310hp turbocharged Continental respectively. The line also includes the de luxe Super Skylane, and a utility version with a single seat and no wheel fairings. By 1984 production of all variants had exceeded 7,400. *Country of origin:* USA. *Silhouette:* Stationair. *Picture:* Stationair 6.

Cessna Stationair 7/Stationair 8   *Confusion:* Stationair 6, Centurion

Power: 1 × Continental piston engine   *Span:* 35ft 10in (10.92m)   *Length:* 31ft 9in (9.68m)

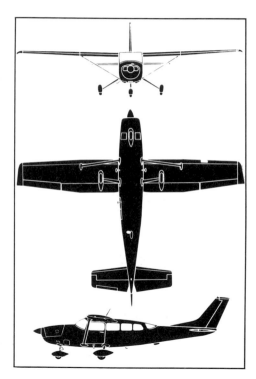

This seven-seat utility aircraft, first announced in 1969, is a stretched version of the Model 206 Super Skywagon. In addition to the longer fuselage, new features included a door for the co-pilot on the starboard side and a separate baggage compartment forward of the cabin. The basic aircraft is powered by a 300hp Continental and cruises at about 165 mph (265km/hr), while the turbocharged aircraft with a 310hp Continental cruises at 185 mph (297km/hr). Production of Model 207s had exceeded 360 by early 1977. The designation was changed to Stationair 7 and Turbo-Stationair 7 for the 1978 aircraft. In 1980 production switched to the eight-seat, slightly longer Stationair 8/Turbo Stationair 8. *Country of origin:* USA. *Silhouette:* Skywagon 207. *Picture:* Stationair 8.

Power: 1 × **PT6A turboprop**   *Span:* **51ft 10in (15.8m)**   *Length:* **37ft 7in (11.46m)**

The turboprop Model 208 Caravan 1 is a completely new Cessna design. Intended to serve as a transport from unprepared strips, the Caravan can carry up to 13 passengers. Wheel, ski and float undercarriages are available and the Caravan is also designed to perform a variety of military and civilian utility duties. Federal Express has ordered 30 of a freight carrying model known as the 208A which has an underfuselage pannier and no passenger windows. Maximum cruising speed is 231 mph (342km/hr). *Country of origin:* USA. *Silhouette and picture:* **Caravan 1.**

Cessna Model 210/Centurion   *Confusion:* Stationair 6/7

Power: 1 × Continental piston engine   *Span:* 36ft 9in (11.2m)   *Length:* 28ft 2in (8.59m)

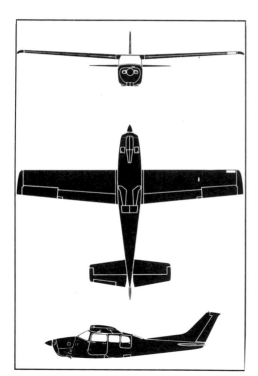

The original Model 210 first flew in 1957 and was the first of the Cessna high-wing range of light aircraft to feature a retractable undercarriage. Later versions also featured an unbraced cantilever wing, as on the Cardinal series. Successive models have introduced enlarged cabin windows. The T210 is now known as Turbo Centurion with two additional rear windows and increased cabin headroom. In late 1977 Cessna introduced the Pressurised Centurion, generally similar to the standard aircraft but powered by a 310hp Continental engine and with four small windows on each side in place of the panoramic windows. Maximum cruising speed is 188 mph (303km/hr). *Country of origin:* USA. *Silhouette:* Model 210H. *Picture:* Pressurised Centurion.

Power: 1 × Continental piston engine   *Span:* 24ft 4in (7.43m)   *Length:* 19ft 2in (5.85m)

The MFI-9B Trainer and MFI-9 Junior are both derivatives of the BA-7 built in the USA by Bjorn Andreasson and first flown in 1958. A total of 25 were built by MFI at Malmo in Sweden. In 1962 Bölkow in West Germany began producing the type under licence from MFI, and by late 1969 production had reached 200 aircraft. Fully aerobatic, the Junior seats two people side-by-side and has a cruising speed of about 125 mph (201km/hr) on its 100hp Rolls-Royce Continental. Other performance figures include a maximum speed of 140 mph (225km/hr); economical cruising speed of 121 mph (195km/hr); and a range of 465 miles (748km). Certified in the normal, utility and glider-towing categories, the MFI-9 is of all-metal construction. The number of Juniors remaining airworthy is dwindling steadily. *Country of origin:* Sweden/West Germany. *Silhouette:* MFI-9B. *Picture:* BO 208.

Saab/Safari/Supporter *Confusion:* Junior

Power: 1 × Lycoming piston engine   *Span:* 29ft 0½in (8.85m)   *Length:* 22ft 11½in (7m)

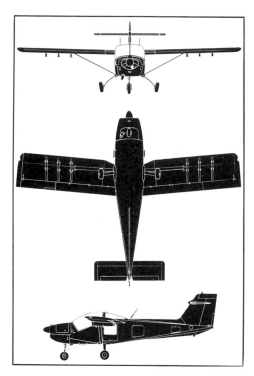

The two-seat Saab Safari (formerly known as the MFI-15) basic trainer and utility aircraft first flew in 1969, powered by a 160hp engine. Originally flown with a low-set tailplane, the type now has a near T-tail. Although designed with a tricycle undercarriage, the type may be seen with an optional tailwheel arrangement. A military version is also available, known as the Supporter. Externally similar to the Safari, the Supporter is stressed to carry stores on six underwing stations. Supporters have been delivered to Denmark, Pakistan and Zambia. Powered by a 200hp Lycoming, both versions cruise at about 130 mph (210km/hr). *Country of origin:* **Sweden**. *Silhouette and picture:* Supporter.

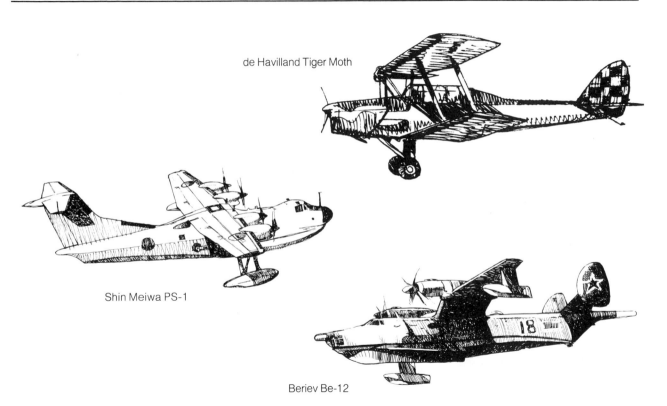

de Havilland Tiger Moth

Shin Meiwa PS-1

Beriev Be-12

Lake LA4 Buccaneer *Confusion:* Teal

Power: 1 × Lycoming piston engine   *Span:* 38ft (11.58m)   *Length:* 24ft 11in (7.6m)

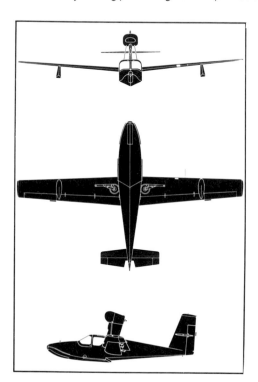

The LA4 Buccaneer four-seat light amphibian is the production development of the C-1 Skimmer, which first flew in 1948. The first Lake-built aircraft, designated LA4, first flew in 1960. Two versions are currently built, the standard LA4-200 EP, and the LA4-200 EPR with a reversible pitch propeller. A six-seat development, the LA-250 Renegade, with a longer fuselage and more powerful engine, is now in production. Over 1,085 LA4s of all versions have been built. Powered by a 200hp Lycoming, the standard LA4-200 has a cruising speed of 154mph (248km/hr) and range with maximum fuel at maximum cruising speed is 650 miles (1,046km). *Country of origin:* USA. *Silhouette and picture:* LA4-200.

Power: 1 × Lycoming piston engine   *Span:* 31ft 11in (9.73m)   *Length:* 23ft 7in (7.19m)

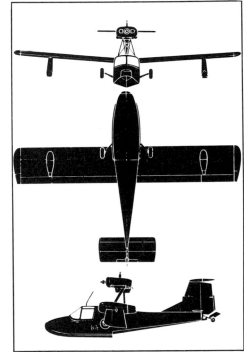

The two-seat all-metal Teal amphibian was developed originally by Thurston Aircraft and first flown in 1968. Design and production rights were acquired by Schweizer in 1972. Production of the Teal I ran to 15 aircraft. The Teal II incorporates several minor design changes. The entire Teal programme was transferred to Teal Aircraft Corporation at St Augustine, Florida, in the spring of 1976. Last production versions were the Teal II and the improved Teal III, which has a more powerful Lycoming engine and can accommodate up to four people. The standard Teal II cruises at about 115 mph (185km/hr). *Country of origin:* **USA**. *Silhouette and picture:* Teal II.

McKinnon G-21 Turbo-Goose   *Confusion:* Super Widgeon

Power: 2 × PT6A turboprops   *Span:* 50ft 10in (15.49m)   *Length:* 39ft 7in (12.07m)

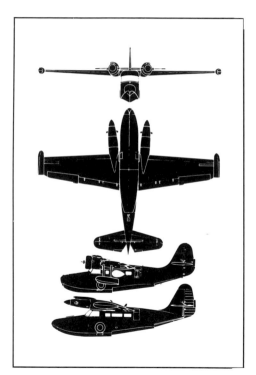

The original six/seven-seat Grumman G-21 first flew in 1937, powered by a pair of 450hp Wasp Junior radials. In the conversion, carried out by McKinnon Enterprises of Oregon, the radial engines are replaced by a pair of 680shp turboprops giving a maximum speed of about 220 mph (354km/hr). Other changes include the fitting of retractable wingtip floats, longer nose, dorsal fin and larger cabin windows as well as numerous interior and equipment changes. The first Turbo-Goose conversion was flown in 1966. There is accommodation for 9 to 12 people. The company subsequently became McKinnon-Viking and moved to Canada. Conversion work has ceased. *Country of origin:* USA. *Main silhouette:* Turbo-Goose; *upper side view:* G-21. *Picture:* Turbo-Goose.

McKinnon Super Widgeon

Power: 2 × Lycoming piston engines   *Span:* 40ft (12.9m)   *Length:* 31ft 1in (9.47m)

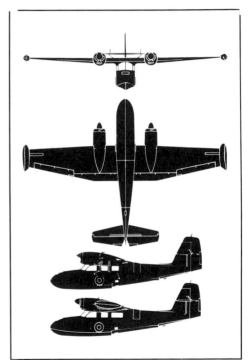

The original G-44 Widgeon was a four-seat light amphibian and first flew in 1940. Although designed as commercial transports the 176 Widgeons built during the Second World War were used as three-seat anti-submarine patrol aircraft. Subsequent civil aircraft were five-seaters, and a number were built in France as the SCAN 30. The McKinnon Super Widgeon is an executive conversion with the original Ranger in-line engines replaced by two 270hp Lycomings, giving a cruising speed of about 180 mph (290km/hr). The company converted more than 70 aircraft, a number of which have retractable wingtip floats. Other features include picture windows, a modern instrument panel, improved soundproofing and an emergency escape hatch. Three or four passengers can be carried over a maximum-fuel range of 1,000 miles (1,600km). *Country of origin:* USA. *Main silhouette:* Super Widgeon; *upper side view:* G-44. *Picture:* Super Widgeon.

Grumman HU-16 Albatross

Confusion: CL-215

Power: 2 × R-1820 piston engines   *Span:* 96ft 8in (29.46m)   *Length:* 63ft 7in (19.38m)

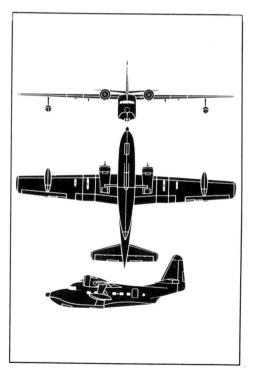

Designed for a US Navy requirement for a utility transport and air-sea rescue amphibian, the HU-16 Albatross first flew in 1947. It was subsequently selected by the US Air Force and a total of more than 300 were built in several versions, including the HU-16D for the US Navy and the HU-16E for the US Coast Guard. Small numbers remain in service with Greece and Indonesia, and 12 aircraft have been converted by Grumman Aerospace to 28-seat configuration for civil use under the designation G-111. Typical cruising speed of the G-111 is 237 mph (382km/hr). *Country of origin:* USA. *Silhouette and picture:* HU-16B.

Power: 2 × R-2800 piston engines   *Span:* 93ft 10in (28.6m)   *Length:* 65ft 0½in (19.82m)

The Canadair CL-215 amphibian first flew in October 1967. Designed primarily for firefighting, the CL-215 serves also in air-sea rescue, coastal patrol and passenger transport roles. For fire-fighting a load of 1,176 gallons (5,346 litres) of water can be carried, and scoops in the hull of CL-215 enable it to pick up a full load from the surface of a lake or ocean in 10 seconds. More than 100 aircraft had been ordered by 1985 by operators in Canada, France, Spain, Greece, Italy, Thailand, Venezuela and Yugoslavia. Powered by two Pratt and Whitney R-1800 radial engines, the CL-215 cruises at 181 mph (291km/hr). *Country of origin:* Canada.

Beriev Be-12 Mail *Confusion:* PS-1/US-1

Power: 2 × Ivchenko turboprops   *Span:* 97ft 6in (29.7m)   *Length:* 107ft 11¼in (32.9m)

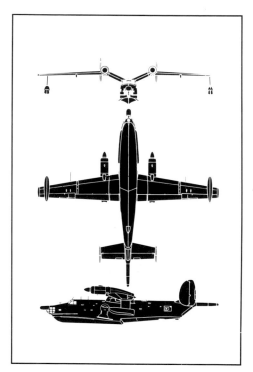

The twin-engined Be-12 maritime patrol amphibian is in current service with the Soviet Naval Air Force. A successor to the Be-6, it was displayed publicly for the first time at Moscow Tushino in 1961. The Mail has a normal operating speed of about 200 mph (322km/hr). Armament is carried in an internal bomb bay and there is provision for two stores pylons underneath each wing. About 100 Be-12s are thought to have been built. The Be-12 holds every one of the FAI world records in its class, no fewer than 38 in all. These marks include an average speed of 343 mph (552km/hr) over a 500km closed circuit, and a closed-circuit distance of 1,592 miles (2,562km). *Country of origin:* USSR.

Power: 4 × T64 turboprops   *Span:* 108ft 9in (33.15m)   *Length:* 109ft 9¼in (33.46m)

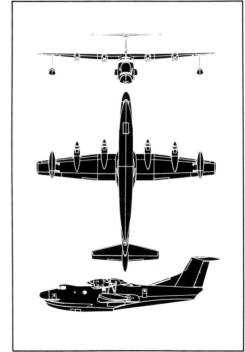

Developed to fill a Japanese Maritime Self-Defence Force requirement for an anti-submarine flying boat (PS-1) and a search and rescue amphibian (US-1), this aircraft, which carries the company designation SS-2 (SS-2A for the amphibious version), first flew in October 1967. Some 23 PS-1s, including two prototypes, were delivered. The first US-1 flew in 1974 and nine had been built by 1985 with a tenth approved for construction. Later aircraft in this series are fitted with more powerful engines and are designated US-1A. Cruising speed of the US-1A is 265 mph (426km/hr). *Country of origin:* Japan. *Silhouette and picture:* SS-2A.

de Havilland D.H.82 Tiger Moth   *Confusion:* SV.4

Power: 1 × de Havilland piston engine   *Span:* 29ft 4in (8.94m)   *Length:* 23ft 11in (7.29m)

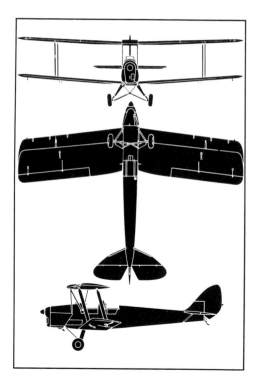

Probably the most famous training aircraft of all, the Tiger Moth first flew in 1931. When production ended more than 7,000 had been built in Britain, Canada, Australia and New Zealand. Relatively few are still airworthy, with only about 120 on the British register, but several of these have been extensively rebuilt and should be flyable for many years to come. Its distinctive de Havilland-style tail and swept-back wings make the Tiger Moth fairly easy to recognise. Powered by a 130hp Gipsy Major engine, the Tiger Moth cruises at about 90 mph (145km/hr) over a range of 300 miles (483km). *Country of origin:* UK.

Power: 1 × Renault or 1 × de Havilland piston engine   *Span:* 27ft 6in (8.38m)   *Length:* 22ft 10in (6.96m)

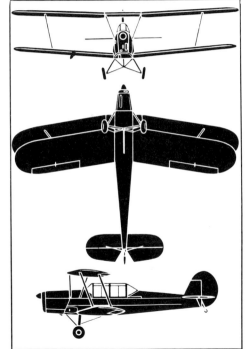

The SV.4 tandem two-seat light biplane was first flown in 1933, powered by a 130hp Gipsy III engine. Used originally as a primary trainer by the Belgian Air Force, it has since been much sought after as a sporting aircraft by virtue of its excellent aerobatic qualities. Before the advent of the Pitts and Zlin the Stampe SV.4 was the mainstay of British competition aerobatics. Bearing a superficial resemblance to the Tiger Moth, the Stampe may be recognised by its rounded fin and rudder, rounded wingtips, and ailerons on both upper and lower wings. Powered by the 130hp Gipsy Major, the SV.4 cruises at about 110 mph (177km/hr). *Country of origin:* Belgium. *Silhouette:* SV.4. *Picture:* Single-seat conversion of SV.4.

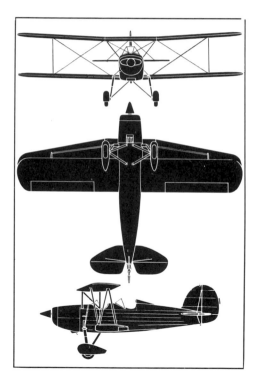

Great Lakes Sports Trainer Model 2T-1A-2 *Confusion:* Pitts Special

Power: 1 × Lycoming piston engine   *Span:* 26ft 8in (8.13m)   *Length:* 20ft 4in (6.2m)

The original Model 2T-1 tandem two-seat light biplane was built in substantial quantities by the Great Lakes Aircraft Co between 1929 and 1932 and was fitted with a variety of engines ranging in power from 95 to 200hp. The company was taken over in 1972 and subsequently the Great Lakes Sports Trainer was put back into production, initially powered by a 140hp Lycoming. Following suspension of production from 1982, the line was restarted in 1984. Current aircraft are fitted with 180hp engines. *Country of origin:* USA. *Silhouette and picture:* Sports Trainer.

Power: 1 × Lycoming piston engine   *Span:* 17ft 4in (5.28m)   *Length:* 15ft 5½in (4.71m)

First flown in single-seat form in 1944, the Pitts Special has become the best-known competition aerobatics aircraft. Now built by Christen Industries, both single seat S-1S and two-seat S-2A versions are manufactured. An advanced single-seat version known as the S-1T special is available. All versions can be purchased in kit form. Powered by a 180hp Lycoming engine, top speed of the S-1S is 176 mph (283km/hr). *Country of origin:* USA. *Main silhouette:* S-1S; *lower side view:* S-2A. *Picture:* S-1S.

Bücker Jungmann/Jungmeister *Confusion:* Pitts Special

Power: 1 × Hirth (Jungmann) or   *Span* (Jungmann): 24ft 3¼in (7.4m)   *Length* (Jungmann): 21ft 8in (6.6m)
1 × Siemans piston engine (Jungmeister)

The tandem two-seat Jungmann was first flown in 1934 and several remain in use in various parts of the world. The type has been licence-built in several countries, including Czechoslovakia, Switzerland and Spain, with production in the latter country resuming in 1956 with the manufacture of 55 aircraft by CASA. The single-seat Jungmeister was introduced in 1935 as an advanced aerobatic biplane and, like the Jungmann, the type was licence-built in Spain and Switzerland. Limited production was restarted in 1968 by Aero Technik Canary in West Germany, the aircraft being standard apart from the wheels and instruments. *Country of origin:* West Germany. *Main silhouette:* Jungmeister; *lower side view:* Jungmann. *Picture:* Jungmeister.

Confusion: Super Ag-Cat **Emair MA-1B Diablo 1200**

Power: 1 × R-1820 piston engine   *Span:* 41ft 8in (12.7m)   *Length:* 30ft (9.14m)

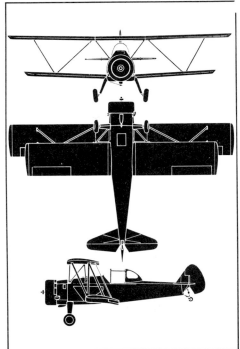

The first Emair MA-1 was built by Air New Zealand engineers under contract to a Hawaiian company and first flew in 1969. Subsequently 25 were produced in Texas by Emair. Production of the MA-1 ended in 1976 and a new version, the MA-1B Diablo 1200, was put into production, 48 being built before the line was closed in 1980. Powerplant is a 1,200hp Wright R-1820 radial derated to 900hp, giving a cruising speed of about 115 mph (185km/hr). As in most agricultural aircraft, the cockpit is raised well above the level of the fuselage top decking and incorporates a hefty roll-bar. The chemical hopper is built into the front fuselage and has two outlets. *Country of origin:* USA. *Silhouette:* MA-1. *Picture:* MA-1B.

Schweizer Super Ag-Cat

Confusion: MA-1B

Power: 1 × R-985 or 1 × R-1340 piston engine   *Span:* 35ft 11in (10.95m)   *Length:* 24ft 4in (7.42m)

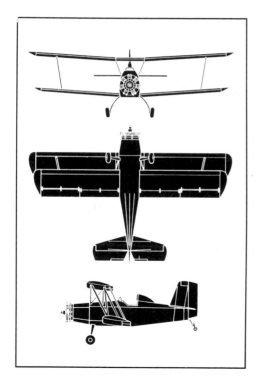

The original Ag-Cat agricultural biplane first flew in 1957 and was manufactured by Schweizer under licence from Grumman; Schweizer has since taken over all rights to the Ag-Cat. The Super Ag-Cat was first certificated in 1966 and was fitted with a 600hp Pratt & Whitney. Several versions of the Super Ag-Cat have been built, with a variety of power options; the B and C versions are also slightly larger. The Turbo Ag-Cat D has a very long nose housing a Pratt & Whitney PT6A turboprop. All Ag-Cats have the distinctive square fin and rudder and are considerably shorter than the other US-built agricultural biplane, the Emair MA-1B. *Country of origin:* USA. *Silhouette:* Ag-Cat. *Picture:* Super Ag-Cat.

Power: 1 × Shvetsov radial   *Span:* 59ft 8½in (18.18m)   *Length:* 41ft 9½in (12.74m)

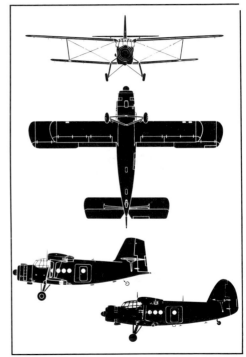

The first An-2 made its maiden flight in 1947. No longer produced in the Soviet Union, the An-2 is manufactured in Poland by the WSK factory at Mielec. Others have been built in China under the designation Y-5, and total production exceeds 14,500. Polish production is scheduled to be phased out in favour of a turboprop-powered version known as the An-3, which is identified by a longer, slimmer nose. Powered by a nine-cylinder radial, the An-2 has a cruising speed of 115 mph (185km/hr). *Country of origin:* Poland/USSR. *Main silhouette:* An-2; *upper side view:* An-2M. *Picture:* An-2R.

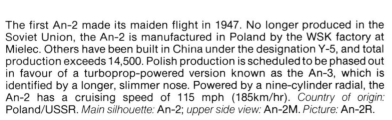

469

 **de Havilland D.H.100/Vampire** *Confusion:* Skymaster

Power: 1 × Goblin turbojet *Span:* 38ft (11.6m) *Length:* 30ft 9in (9.37m)

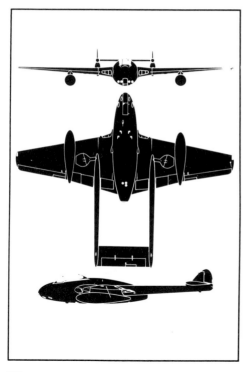

First flown in 1943, the Goblin-powered Vampire was built in large numbers for more than 14 years, but only a handful remain in service. The Dominican Republic still operates about six F1 and FB 50s; Switzerland has 35 T55 two-seat trainers and about 20 FB6s, while Zimbabwe retain a mixed fleet of about ten FB9s, T55s and T11s. Typical maximum speed of the Vampire is 540 mph (870km/hr) and ceiling is 40,000 ft (12,000m). *Country of origin:* UK. *Silhouette and picture:* Vampire FB6.

Power: 2 × Continental piston engines   *Span:* 38ft 2in (11.63m)   *Length:* 29ft 9in (9.07m)

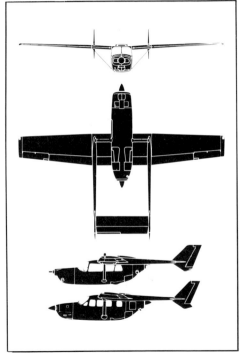

This all-metal four/six-seater is unusual in having a 210hp Continental mounted at each end of the fuselage nacelle. First flown in 1961, it entered series production as the fixed-undercarriage Model 336 Skymaster in May 1963. A military version, designated O-2, has also been delivered to the USAF and Iranian Air Force for forward air controller and psychological warfare missions. Military deliveries totalled 513. The Model P337 is a pressurised version distinguished by having four instead of three fuselage cabin windows. Deliveries of all variants had totalled 2,993 by the time production was terminated in 1980. Performance figures for the P337 include a maximum level speed of 250 mph (402km/hr), maximum cruising speed of 236 mph (380km/hr), and a range at economical cruising speed of 1,330 miles (2,140km). *Country of origin:* USA. *Main silhouette:* Model P337; *upper side view:* O-2. *Picture:* Model P337.

IAI 101/102/201 Arava *Confusion:* Noratlas

Power: 2 × PT6A turboprops   *Span:* 68ft 9in (20.96m)   *Length:* 42ft 9in (13.03m)

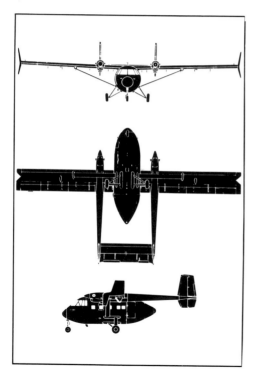

The Arava was designed to fulfil a requirement for a light Stol transport for civil and military use. First flight was in late 1969. Four versions have been announced to date. Three of these are externally similar: the IAI 101, the first civil version; the IAI 102, the second civil version, based on the original 101 and able to accommodate up to 20 passengers; and the IAI 201, the military transport version. Based on the original 101, it first flew in 1972. Latest variant is the IAI 202, distinguished by its wingtip winglets. An electronic-warfare version of the IAI 201 is reported to be in service with the Israeli Air Force. Operators outside Israel are mainly South American armed forces. *Country of origin:* Israel. *Silhouette:* IAI 202. *Picture:* IAI 201.

Power: 2 × Hercules piston engines   *Span:* 106ft 7½in (32.5m)   *Length:* 72ft 0½in (21.96m)

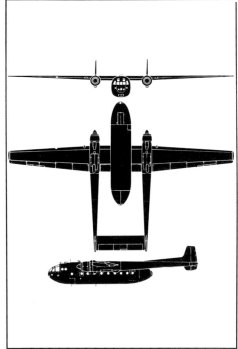

The twin-engined, twin-boom Noratlas was the standard medium tactical transport of both the French and West German air forces, which received 211 and 188 respectively. France retains about 50 in service, and small numbers of surplus aircraft serve with Chad, Greece, Niger, Angola and Djibouti. Five crew and up to 45 troops can be carried, or alternatively, up to 15,000lb of freight. Similar in size to the Fairchild C-119 Flying Boxcar, the Noratlas is identified by squared-off rudders, narrower wings and a distinctive stepless nose. Powered by two 2,090hp Snecma-built Bristol Hercules radials, the Noratlas cruises at about 200 mph (322km/hr). *Country of origin:* France.

Fairchild C-119 Flying Boxcar

Confusion: Argosy, Noratlas, Arava

Power: 2 × R-3350 piston engines   *Span:* 109ft 3in (33.3m)   *Length:* 89ft 5in (27.25m)

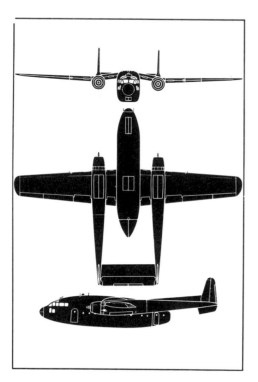

The C-119 is a development of the C-82 Packet, which first flew towards the end of the Second World War. Retaining the twin-engine, twin-boom arrangement of the Packet, the Flying Boxcar has a longer and slimmer fuselage. When production ended in 1955 some 1,100 C-119s had been built. Although no longer used in quantity by US forces, the type is still in limited service with Taiwan, India and Ethiopia. Powered by two 3,400hp Wright R-3350 radials, the C-119 cruises at about 200 mph (320km/hr). Maximum payload is 20,000lb (9,070kg), which can be carried over a range of 990 miles (1,595km). Ferry range with four 500 US gal overload tanks is 3,460 miles (5,570km). Variants currently in service include the AC-119 gunship and the Indian Air Force's C-119 Jet Pack, fitted with an auxiliary Orpheus turbojet. *Country of origin:* USA.

Power: 2 × T76 turboprops   *Span:* 40ft (12.19m)   *Length:* 41ft 7in (12.67m)

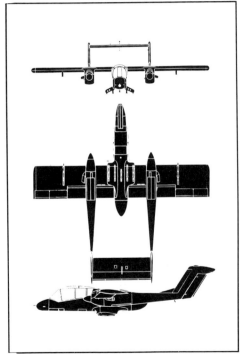

The Bronco was North American's winning entry in the US Navy's Light Armed Reconnaissance Aircraft (LARA) competition and the first prototype flew for the first time in mid-1965. The OV-10A, the basic production aircraft, is in service with the USAF, US Navy and US Marine Corps. This variant has also been delivered to Thailand, Venezuela, Indonesia and South Korea; these aircraft carry the designations OV-10C, E, F, and G respectively. The OV-10B is used for target towing, while the OV-10B(Z) is equipped with an auxiliary turbojet mounted above the fuselage nacelle. The OV-10D is the Night Observation Gunship System (NOGS) with increased armament, including a 20mm gun turret beneath the rear fuselage. *Country of origin:* USA. *Silhouette:* OV-10A. *Picture:* OV-10D.

Edgley EA7 Optica

Confusion: Bronco

Power: 1 × Lycoming piston engine and fan   *Span:* 39ft 4in (12m)   *Length:* 26ft 9in (8.15m)

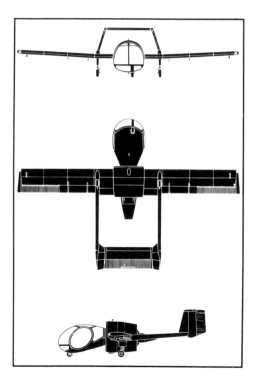

Like the Lear Fan, the Optica is not a jet but it looks line one in the air. A unique design, this three-seater with twin booms and high tail is designed for aerial surveillance of all types and photography. It can loiter at speeds as low as 61 mph (98km/hr) and is much cheaper to operate than a helicopter. The Lycoming piston engine drives a fixed-pitch fan; this combination is known as a ducted propulsion unit. First flown in December 1979, the Optica had attracted 82 orders from 25 countries by September 1984. *Country of origin:* UK.

PZL-Mielec M-15 Belphegor

Power: 1 × Ivchenko turbofan   *Span:* 73ft 6in (22.4m)   *Length:* 41ft 9in (12.72m)

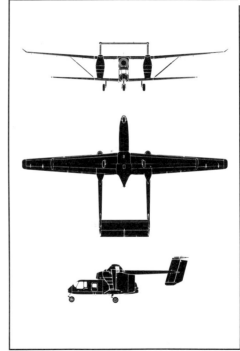

Produced as a result of an anticipated Soviet requirement for up to 3,000 large agricultural aircraft, the Polish-built M-15 Belphegor first flew in 1973. The full-chord interplane struts are used as streamlined chemical hoppers, while the 3,306lb-thrust turbofan is mounted in a pod on top of the fuselage. The single pilot is accommodated in the extreme nose of the aircraft and there is a cabin to the rear of the cockpit for two extra people during ferry flights. A tandem two-seat trainer version has been built. Production ended in 1981 after 180 aircraft had been built. *Country of origin:* Poland.

Power: 1 × Continental piston engine   *Span:* 39ft 3½in (11.98m)   *Length:* 20ft 10in (6.35m)

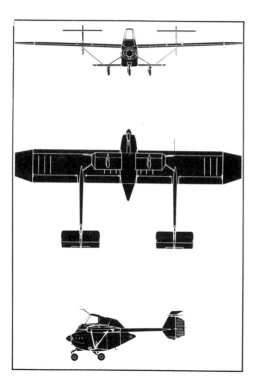

This single-engined agricultural aircraft has one of the most distinctive layouts imaginable, the twin-boom arrangement having been adopted to keep the tails clear of chemicals and also to permit rapid loading from a vehicle. After a first flight in 1966, production had reached 120 by the beginning of 1984 for customers in Australia, Denmark, India, Malaysia, New Zealand, Thailand and Africa. A utility version designated the PL-12-U has also been built. This variant can carry one passenger on the upper deck behind the pilot's position and another four on the lower deck. The T-320 Airtruk differs principally in having a 325hp Continental Tiara in place of the PL-12's 300hp Rolls-Royce Continental. A development is the T-300 Skyfarmer with an Avco Lycoming engine. Cruising speed ranges from about 110 mph (177km/hr) for the PL-12 to 130 mph (209km/hr) for the T-320. *Country of origin:* Australia. *Silhouette and picture:* PL-12.

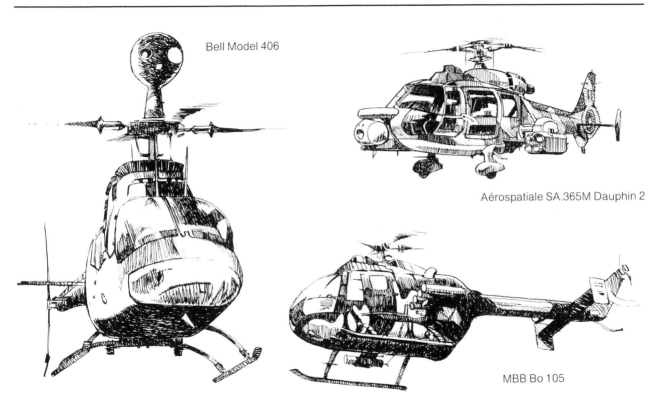

Bell Model 406

Aérospatiale SA.365M Dauphin 2

MBB Bo 105

Hiller UH-12/Model 360/H-23 Raven *Confusion:* Bell 47, Alouette II, R22

Power: 1 × Franklin or 1 × Lycoming piston engine   *Rotor dia:* 35ft 5in (10.8m)   *Length:* 28ft 6in (8.69m)

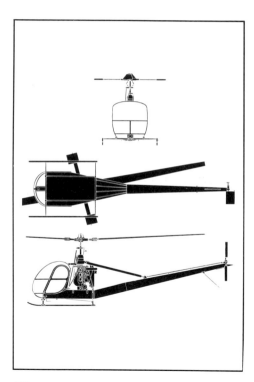

The UH-12 was first produced in 1948 and was followed in 1950 by the UH-12A with a semi-enclosed cockpit. The UH-12B was the military variant and the UH-12C introduced the "goldfish bowl" cabin. The Models A, B and C were all powered by 200hp or 210hp Franklin engines. The Model 12E was powered by the 305hp Lycoming engine. Hiller Aviation was reformed in 1973 and was taken over by Rogerson Aircraft in 1984, the current designation being UH-12E for the basic three-seat version and UH-12E-4 for the four-seat version powered by a 400shp Allison turboshaft engine. The H-23 Raven is a military version of the Hiller 12. Performance figures for the Model 12E/Raven include a maximum speed of 96 mph (154km/hr), cruising speed of 90 mph (145km/hr) and sea-level range of 225 miles (362km). Deliveries of the UH-12 were resumed in 1984. *Country of origin:* USA. *Silhouette and picture:* Hiller 12E.

Bell Model 47/H-13 Sioux/AH.1 Sioux

Power: 1 × Lycoming piston engine   *Rotor dia:* 37ft 1½in (11.32m)   *Length:* 31ft 7in (9.63m)

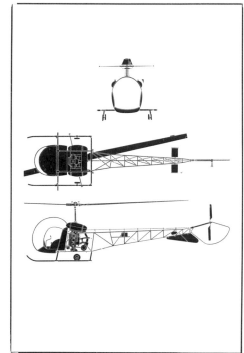

The basic Bell Model 47 first flew in 1945, and the first production models were ordered for service with the US Army and Navy. Many versions have subsequently been built for military service in a variety of countries, and a large number used by civil operators. The Model 47 has also been built under licence in Italy as the Agusta-Bell 47 series, and in Britain by Westland as the Sioux AH.1. All models from the 47D onwards have the familiar "goldfish bowl" cabin and open tail-boom. Subsequent variants had engines of differing powers, but the main design change came with the Model 47H and Model 47J Ranger, which had a fully enclosed fuselage and cabin. These changes apply also to Agusta-built aircraft. *Country of origin:* Italy/UK/USA. *Silhouette:* Bell 47G2. *Picture:* Sioux AH.1.

Robinson R22 Alpha *Confusion:* Raven

Power: 1 × Lycoming piston engine   *Rotor dia:* 25ft 2in (7.67m)   *Length:* 28ft 9in (8.76m)

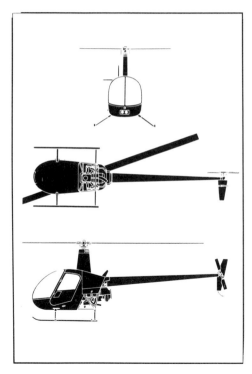

Over 400 Robinson R22 light utility helicopters had been built by January 1984, largely for civil pilot training. One of the cheapest two-seaters on the market, the R22 has a top speed of 116 mph (187km/hr) and cruises at 108 mph (174km/hr). Maximum range is 240 miles (386km). The prototype R22 first flew in 1975. The current production model has a higher-powered Lycoming 0-320-B2C engine. *Country of origin:* USA.

Confusion: Bell 47, Alouette III   # Aérospatiale Alouette II

Power: 1 × Artouste or 1 × Astazou turboshaft   *Rotor dia:* 36ft 1¾in (11.02m)   *Length:* 33ft 8in (10.26m)

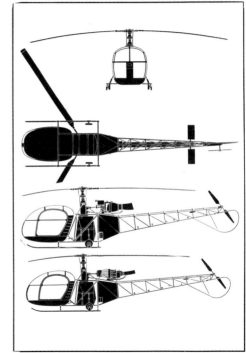

All the helicopters in this family are basically similar and differ principally in their powerplants. The prototypes were built as SE.3120s and powered by a Salmson 9 engine; production types were designated SE.3130 and subsequently SE.313B Alouette II. Production totalled more than 900. The Astazou-powered SA.318C first flew in 1961 and when production ended in 1975 more than 350 had been built. The SA.315B Lama is an Artouste-powered version built to an Indian requirement, while the Cheetah is a licence-built version produced by HAL for the Indian Army. The Lama has been sold to operators in more than 20 countries. *Country of origin:* France. *Main silhouette:* SA.318C; *lower side view:* SE.313B. *Picture:* SA.318C.

 **Aérospatiale Alouette III** *Confusion:* Alouette II, Gazelle

Power: 1 × Artouste or 1 × Astazou turboshaft   *Rotor dia:* 36ft 1¾in (11.02m)   *Length:* 32ft 10¾in (10.03m)

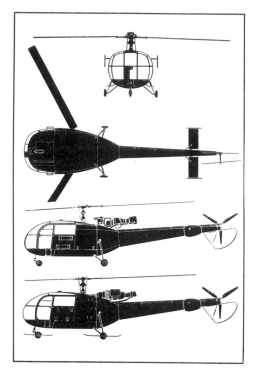

The Alouette III series was derived from the Alouette II, offering a larger cabin, more powerful engine and improved performance. The type first flew in 1959 as the SE.3160, and later production aircraft were designated SA.316B. Some 1,450 Alouette IIIs of all versions had been delivered to a number of operators in more than 70 countries by early 1984. The SA.316B has also been built under licence in India as the Chetak, and in both Switzerland and Romania. The SA.319B, a direct development of the SA.316B, is powered by a 870shp Turboméca Astazou engine. First flown in 1967, the type is still in production in Romania. Powered by an 870shp Turboméca Artouste turboshaft, the SA.316B cruises at 115 mph (185km/hr), while the SA.319B cruises at about 120 mph (190km/hr). *Country of origin:* France. *Main silhouette:* SA.316B; *lower side view:* SA.319B.

Power: 1 × **Astazou turboshaft**   *Rotor dia:* **34ft 5½in (10.5m)**   *Length:* **39ft 3½in (11.97m)**

This five-seat light helicopter first flew in 1967, powered by an Astazou III engine. The first production aircraft flew in 1971, differing from the prototype in having a longer cabin, larger tail unit and uprated Astazou IIIA. Ten versions of the Gazelle have been built to date: the SA.341B, 341C, 341D and 341E for the British armed forces; the SA.341F for the French Army; the SA.341G and SA.342J for civil operators; SA.341H military export version; and the SA.342K, 342L and 342M military versions. Under an Anglo-French agreement signed in 1967, Gazelles were produced jointly with Westland Helicopters and are also built under licence in Yugoslavia and Egypt. Total sales have exceeded 1,200. *Country of origin:* **France.** *Silhouette:* SA.341. *Picture:* Gazelle HT.2.

Aérospatiale SA.360 and SA.361H Dauphin *Confusion:* Gazelle

Power: 1 × Astazou turboshaft (SA.360 and SA.361) or   *Rotor dia:* 37ft 8¾in (11.5m)   *Length:* 43ft 3½in (13.2m)
2 × Arriel turboshafts (SA.365)

Developed as a replacement for the Alouette III, the SA.360 Dauphin first flew in 1972 powered by a 980shp Turboméca Astazou XVI turboshaft. Production aircraft are powered by the 1,050shp Astazou XVIIIA. The SA.361H Dauphin is similar in most respects to the SA.360 but is powered by a 1,400shp Astazou XXB. The SA.365C Dauphin 2 is marginally larger than the standard Dauphin and differs principally in having two 650shp Turboméca Arriel engines and accommodation for up to 13 persons. Cruising speed for both versions is about 170 mph (275km/hr). *Country of origin:* France. *Silhouette:* Dauphin 2. *Picture:* SA.360

Power: 2 × Arriel turboshafts   *Rotor dia:* 39ft 1in (11.93m)   *Length:* 37ft 6in (11.44m)

Confusing because it is also called Dauphin 2, the 365N is in fact a major redesign compared with the 365C, with extensive use of composite materials and a retractable undercarriage. The 365N is a 10–14-seat transport, 365M a military utility vehicle and 365F a maritime version for anti-shipping and search and rescue. The SA.366, with two Avco Lycoming turboshafts, has been ordered by the US Coast Guard for short-range recovery. In this form it has the US designation HH-65A Dolphin. The 365N is being produced under licence in China and several hundred of the variants have been built. *Country of origin:* France. *Silhouette and picture:* SA.365F.

Power: 1 × Nimbus turboshaft   *Rotor dia:* **32ft 3in (9.83m)**   *Length:* **30ft 4in (9.24m)**

Derived from the Saunders-Roe P.531, which first flew in 1958, the Scout army helicopter is fitted with a skid undercarriage. The British Army took delivery of about 150 Scouts and the type is also in service with Australia. The Wasp naval version, distinguished by its wheeled undercarriage, was first delivered to the Royal Navy in 1963. Wasps are also operational in Brazil, New Zealand and South Africa. Powered by a 710shp Rolls-Royce Nimbus turboshaft, the Scout cruises at about 120 mph (210km/hr) and the Wasp at about 110 mph (175km/hr). *Country of origin:* UK. *Main silhouette:* Scout; *lower side view:* Wasp. *Picture:* Scout.

Power: 1 × T53 turboshaft   Rotor dia: **44ft (13.41m)**   Length: **38ft 5in (11.7m)**

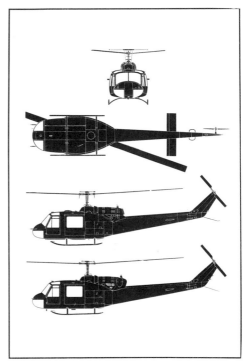

The Model 204 and UH-1 Iroquois belong to a family of commercial utility and military general-purpose helicopters derived from the XH-40, which first flew in 1956. The civil and military versions are essentially similar in external appearance and differ principally in their internal equipment. A licence-built version, the Agusta-Bell 204B, was in production in Italy between 1961 and 1974. Italian-built aircraft were fitted with the Rolls-Royce Gnome turboshaft. *Country of origin:* USA/Italy. *Main silhouette:* Bell 204; *lower side view:* Agusta-Bell 204B. *Picture:* Agusta-Bell 204B.

Bell Model 212/Model 212ASW *Confusion:* Bell 204, Bell 205

Power: 1 × PT6T turboshaft   *Rotor dia:* 48ft 2¼in (14.69m)   *Length:* 42ft 4¾in (12.92m)

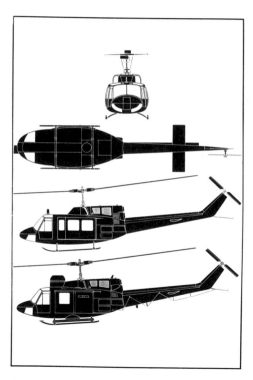

The Model 212 Twin Two-Twelve 15-seat military/civil utility helicopter first flew in 1968. Military aircraft are designated UH-1N in the USA and CH-135 in Canada. Powerplant is a 1,290shp Pratt & Whitney of Canada PT6T-3 Turbo Twin-Pac, comprising two PT6 turboshafts coupled to a combining gearbox. The Agusta-Bell Model 212 is produced in Italy by Agusta, the 212ASW being for the Italian Navy, Turkey, Iran and a number of other countries, including Peru and Venezuela. Main external difference is the large cylindrical radome mounted on top of the forward cabin roof. Armament options include two homing torpedoes or depth charges for the anti-submarine role, and up to four AS.12 air-to-surface wire-guided missiles for use against ships. *Country of origin:* USA/Italy. *Main silhouette:* Bell 212; *lower side view:* 212ASW. *Picture:* 212ASW.

Bell Model 205/UH-1 Iroquois/Model 205A-1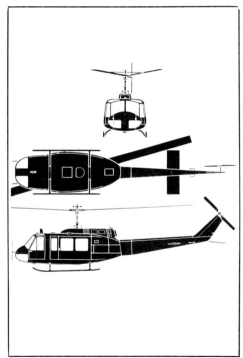

Power: 1 × T53 turboshaft   *Rotor dia:* 48ft (14.63m)   *Length:* 41ft 10¾in (12.77m)

The Model 205 military general-purpose helicopter first flew in 1961. Basically similar to the earlier Model 204 Iroquois, it has a longer fuselage, an additional cabin window and equipment improvements. The Model 205A-1 15-seat commercial utility version of the Model 205 is powered by a 1,250shp Lycoming turboshaft. Both versions are also built under licence in Italy by Agusta. Licence production has also been undertaken in Japan (HU-1H) and Taiwan. Cruising speed for all versions is about 125 mph (200km/hr). *Country of origin:* USA. *Main silhouette:* UH-1D. *Picture:* Model 205A.

Bell Model 214A/214B/214ST *Confusion:* Bell 205

Power: 1 × T55 turboshaft, 2 × CT7   *Rotor dia:* 50ft (15.24m)   *Length:* 42ft 4¾in (12.92m)

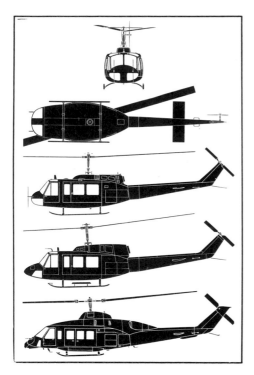

Initially produced in quantity for Iran as the Isfahan, the Bell 214A military utility helicopter was developed from the Bell 205 and first flew in 1974. Iran also ordered the 214C version for search and rescue. The civil version is the 214B BigLifter, which carries 14 passengers or can be used for cropspraying or firefighting. The latter version is known as the BigFighter. Typical 214 internal load is 4,000lb (1,814kg), while up to 7,000lb (3,175kg) can be slung externally. The BigLifter differs from the 214A in having a fire-extinguishing system, push-out escape windows and commercial avionics. Agusta has also built the 214A. Cruising speed is 161 mph (259km/hr) and range 300 miles (483km). Also produced in quantity is the 214ST Supertransport with two GE CT7 engines, longer fuselage and accommodation for up to 18 passengers. *Country of origin:* USA. *Main silhouette:* Model 214; *middle side view:* Model 214B; *lower side view:* Model 214ST. *Picture:* Model 214A.

492

Power: 1 × Allison 250 turboshaft   *Rotor dia:* 33ft 4in (10.16m)   *Length:* 31ft 2in (9.5m)

This general-purpose and light observation helicopter first flew in 1962. The original Model 206A JetRanger remained in production until 1972, when 660 had been built. Deliveries of the Model 206B JetRanger II, powered by a 400shp Allison turboshaft, began in 1971. A total of 1,619 were delivered. Current production model is the Model 206B JetRanger III, which has an uprated engine of 420shp, and enlarged tail rotor mast. The Kiowa is the military variant of the JetRanger, from which it differs in having a main rotor of slightly greater diameter and equipment changes for its military role. Bell is converting US Army Kiowas to OH-58D standard with mast-mounted sight. A new development is the light, simplified combat helicopter, the Model 406CS Combat Scout. *Country of origin:* USA. *Silhouette and picture:* **Kiowa.**

MBB-Kawasaki BK 117 *Confusion:* JetRanger

Power: 2 × LTS101 turboshafts   *Rotor dia:* 36ft 1in (11m)   *Length:* 42ft 8in (13m)

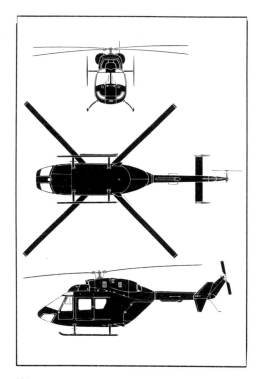

A joint development by West Germany and Japan, the BK 117 seats seven passengers in executive form and up to eleven in high-density transport form. With a range of 339 miles (545km), the BK 117 has a cruising speed of 145 mph (234km/hr). The first prototype flew in Germany in May 1979, followed by a second in Japan. There are two production centres, at Gifu in Japan and Munich in Germany. The BK117 is also being built in Indonesia. *Country of origin:* Japan/West Germany.

Power: 2 × Gem turboshafts   *Rotor dia:* 42ft (12.8m)   *Length:* 39ft 6¾in (12.06m)

One of the three helicopters covered by the Anglo-French agreement of 1967, the Lynx first flew in 1971. Two main versions have been built, one for naval use and the second for the British Army. Equipped with a skid undercarriage, the Lynx AH.1 entered British Army service in 1977. Naval versions are the Lynx HAS.2, 60 of which have been ordered for the Royal Navy, and variants for the French Navy, the Royal Netherlands Navy and the navies of Argentina, West Germany and Brazil. The type has also been ordered by Qatar, Denmark and Norway. All naval aircraft are equipped with a wheeled undercarriage. Powered by two Rolls-Royce Gem turboshafts, the Lynx has a cruising speed of about 130 mph (210km/hr). *Country of origin:* UK/France. *Main silhouette:* AH.1; *lower side view:* HAS2. *Picture:* HAS2.

Bell Model 206L LongRanger

Confusion: Bell 206, Lynx

Power: 1 × Allison turboshaft   *Rotor dia:* 37ft (11.28m)   *Length:* 33ft 3in (10.13m)

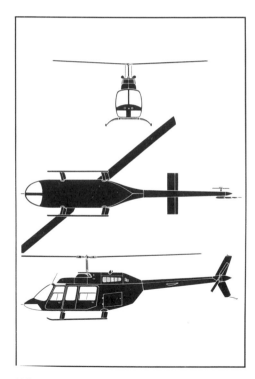

The Model 206L LongRanger seven-seat general-purpose helicopter first flew in 1974. Developed from the Model 206B JetRanger II, it has a longer fuselage with an additional pair of cabin windows. First deliveries were in 1975. Current production version is the LongRanger II. Double doors on the port side of the cabin provide an opening 5ft (1.52m) in width, permitting the straight-in loading of stretchers or cargo. Two stretchers and two walking patients can be carried in the ambulance role, while an optional executive interior accommodates four passengers. Powered by a 420shp Allison turboshaft, the LongRanger cruises at about 130 mph (210km/hr) over a sea-level range of 342 miles (550km). The type is also being licence-built in Italy by Agusta. Current production version is the Model 206L-3 LongRanger III. *Country of origin:* USA. *Silhouette and picture:* Model 206L.

Power: 2 × Allison 250 turboshafts or 2 Arriel turboshafts   *Rotor dia:* **36ft 1in (11m)**   *Length:* **42ft 10in (13.05m)**

The Agusta A109A high-speed twin-engined helicopter is available in both civil and military versions. First flown in 1971, the type entered production in 1976. The A109 is powered by two 420shp Allison turboshafts and features a fully retractable undercarriage. Military versions, under construction for the armies and navies of several nations, are externally similar to the civil model, varying only in the armament and equipment carried. An improved Mk II version is now on the line. The military Mk II can perform the utility, ECM, ambulance, scout/attack/air defence and anti-tank roles. A new military variant is the A109K with two Arriel engines, fixed undercarriage and longer nose. *Country of origin:* Italy. *Silhouette:* A109A. *Picture:* A109K.

 **Bell Model 222** *Confusion:* A.109

Power: 2 × LTS101 turboshafts   *Rotor dia:* 39ft (11.89m)   *Length:* 36ft 0¼in (10.98m)

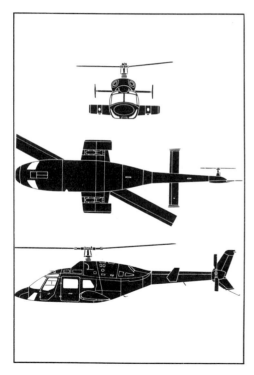

The Model 222 eight-seat light commercial helicopter first flew in 1976. The first commercial light twin-engined helicopter to be built in the USA, the Model 222 has a fully retractable undercarriage accommodated in two short-span sponsons set low on each side of the fuselage. The tailplane, mounted midway along the rear fuselage, is fitted with endplate fins. The type is produced in three versions: the basic Model 222B, the 222B Executive and the 222UT. Externally alike, these variants are distinguished by equipment differences except on the 222UT which has a skid undercarriage. Powered by two 600shp Avco Lycoming turboshafts, the Model 222 cruises at about 165 mph (265km/hr). *Country of origin:* USA.

Confusion: Westland 30 **Kaman H-2 Seasprite**

Power: 2 × T58 turboshafts   *Rotor dia:* 44ft (13.41m)   *Length:* 38ft 4in (11.68m)

The H-2 Seasprite anti-submarine, anti-missile defence, search and rescue, observation and utility helicopter first flew in 1959. The original series was single-engined and, as the UH-2A, entered service with the US Navy in 1963. Few remain in service, although some have been converted to twin-engine standard. Current versions are the HH-2D for coastal and geodetic survey; NHH-2D test aircraft. SH-2D Lamps anti-submarine and utility aircraft; and SH-2F, a developed Lamps version. All SH-2Ds are being upgraded to SH-2F standard. Powered by two 1,350shp General Electric turboshafts, the SH-2F cruises at about 150 mph (240km/hr). *Country of origin:* USA. *Silhouette:* SH-2F. *Picture:* SH-2D.

Westland 30 *Confusion:* BK 117, Bell 222, Seasprite

Power: 2 × Gem turboshafts   *Rotor dia:* 43ft 8in (13.31m)   *Length:* 47ft (14.33m)

A combination of the Lynx rotor and powerplant with a new transport fuselage, the Westland 30 seats 17 passengers to airliner standards and up to 22 in high-density layout. The type is also available as a multi-role military helicopter. First flown in April 1979, the Westland 30 is in production. The initial production version is the 30 Series 100, the 100-60 has Gem 60 engines and the Series 200 has GE CT7 engines. A projected version is the Series 300. Cruising speed is 150 mph (241km/hr) and range with seven passengers is 426 miles (686km). *Country of origin:* UK.

Power: 1 × Allison 250 turboshaft   *Rotor dia:* 26ft 4in (8.03m)   *Length:* 23ft (7.01m)

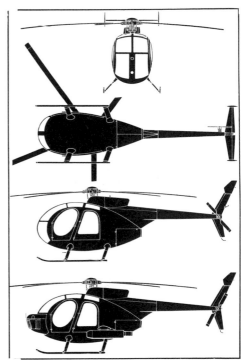

The Model 500 series is the commercial and foreign military counterpart of the US Army's OH-6 Cayuse. The Model 500 and Model 500C are identical apart from the installation of the uprated 400shp Allison turboshaft in the Model 500C. The Model 500D and Model M-D are fitted with the 420shp Allison turboshaft and are distinguished by a small T-tail and five-blade rotor. The Model 500D is the basic commercial version, while the 500M-D Defender is the multi-role military variant. The 500E has a longer and more streamlined nose while the 530F is for high temperature/high altitude operations. Latest model is the 530MG with mast-mounted sight. The basic Model 500 cruises at about 145 mph (235km/hr). *Country of origin:* USA. *Main silhouette:* Model 500D; *lower side view:* Defender. *Picture:* 530MG.

 **MBB BO 105** *Confusion:* Hughes 500

Power: 2 × Allison 250 turboshafts   *Rotor dia:* 32ft 3½in (9.84m)   *Length:* 38ft 11in (11.86m)

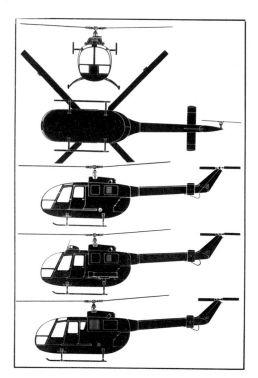

The MBB BO 105 five-seat light utility helicopter first flew in 1967. A number of different versions have been built, but all are essentially similar in external appearance. Original standard production model was the BO 105C, powered by two 400shp Allison turboshaft engines. This was succeeded in 1975 by the BO 105CB, powered by two 420shp Allison turboshaft engines and incorporating strengthened rotor gearing. Other versions currently in production are the BO 105CBS with longer fuselage and increased seating capacity; BO 105D for the UK market; BO 105M (PAH 1) military version armed with six Hot missiles; the BO 105M (VBH) light observation helicopter and the 105 (PAH-1) anti-tank variant. Cruising speed is about 145 mph (235km/hr). *Country of origin:* **West Germany.** *Main silhouette:* BO 105CB; *middle side view:* BO 105M; *bottom side view:* BO 105CBS. *Picture:* BO 105C.

Power: 1 × Arriel or 1 × LTS101   *Rotor dia:* 35ft (10.69m)   *Length:* 35ft 9in (10.91m)
or 2 × Allison 250 turboshafts

Intended as a successor to the Alouette II, the Ecureuil (Squirrel) first flew in 1975 as the Arriel-powered AS350B. The Lycoming-powered AS.350C Astar was intended for the US market alone, with the AS350B available elsewhere. Accommodation is provided for six people in bucket seats in the front of the cabin and two rows of bench seats behind. Performance of the two versions is similar, cruising speed being about 145 mph (235km/hr). A twin-engined version is known as the Twinstar (AS355E) in the USA and the Ecureuil 2 (AS355F) elsewhere. A further military version is the A5355M. *Country of origin:* France. *Silhouette:* Ecureuil. *Picture:* AS355M.

Fairchild FH-1100 *Confusion:* Ecureuil

Power: 1 × T63 turboshaft   *Rotor dia:* 35ft 4¾in (10.79m)   *Length:* 39ft 9½in (9.08m)

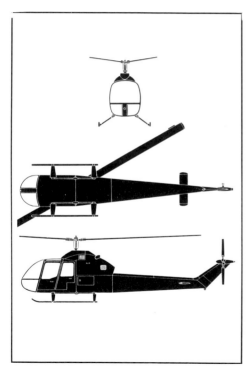

The Hiller FH-1100 utility helicopter, the first American light turbine-powered helicopter to enter the market, evolved from the Hiller OH-5A, which first flew in 1963. The FH-1100 was developed by Fairchild Industries, which had taken over Hiller and has in turn been taken over by Rogerson Aircraft Corp. Production eventually reached about 250, for both civil and military operators, and the type remains in small-scale service with the armed forces of a number of South American nations. Powered by a 317hp Allison turboshaft, the FH-1100 cruises at about 120 mph (195km/hr). *Country of origin:* USA.

Power: 1 × Lycoming piston engine *Rotor dia:* 23ft 9in (7.24m) *Length:* 21ft 9in (6.62m)

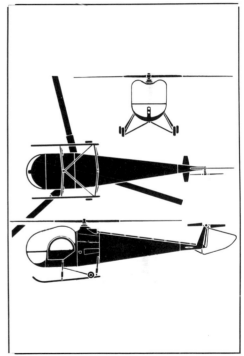

The Model B-2 two-seat light helicopter was first flown in 1953, though deliveries did not begin until 1959. The B-2A is an updated version with redesigned cabin and improved equipment. Main production version is the B-2B, which differs in having a fuel-injected engine for improved performance. Powered by a 180hp Lycoming piston engine, the B-2B has a cruising speed of about 90 mph (145km/hr). Hynes Helicopter Inc has now put the H-12 (formerly B-2B) back into production as the Hynes H-2; and maximum-fuel range is 250 miles (400km). *Country of origin:* USA. *Silhouette:* B-2B. *Picture:* B-2.

Power: 1 × Lycoming piston engine   *Rotor dia:* 28ft 8in (8.74m)   *Length:* 24ft 5in (7.44m)

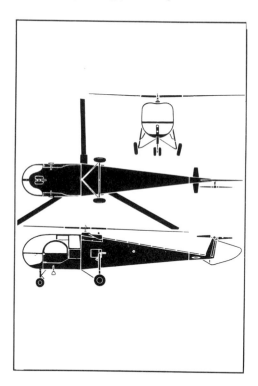

The Model 305 five-seat light helicopter first flew in 1964. Similar in configuration to the Model B-2B, the Model 305 is larger in all respects. Accommodation consists of two front seats side-by-side, with a rear bench seat for three persons. The Model 305 can be fitted with skid, wheel or float undercarriage. Powered by a 305hp Lycoming flat-six piston engine, the Model 305 cruises at about 110 mph (175km/hr). Other performance figures include a maximum speed at sea level of 120 mph (193km/hr) and maximum sea-level rate of climb of 975ft/min (297m/min). Hynes Helicopter Inc hoped to put the 305 – re-designated H-5 – into production in 1985. *Country of origin:* USA.

Power: 1 × Lycoming piston engine   *Rotor dia:* 32ft (9.75m)   *Length:* 29ft 4in (8.94m)

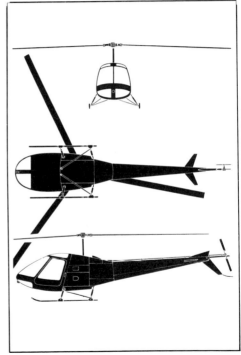

The original three-seat F-28 first flew in 1962 and entered production in 1965. During 1973 an advanced version of the basic Model F-28A was developed. Known as the Model 280 Shark, it is generally similar to the F-28A but has improved cabin contours and some small modifications to the tail area. There are a number of production versions: the F-28A powered by a 205hp Lycoming; Model 280 Shark; F-28C with turbocharged 205hp Lycoming; Model 280C; F-28C-2; and Models 280C, 280F and 280FX Hawk. *Country of origin:* USA. *Silhouette and picture:* Model 280.

 **Silvercraft SH-4**   *Confusion:* Shark

Power: 1 × Franklin piston engine   *Rotor dia:* 29ft 7½in (9.03m)   *Length:* 25ft 1¼in (7.65m)

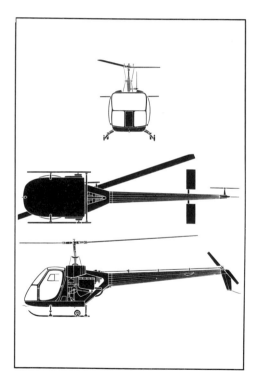

The SH-4 is a three-seat light helicopter designed for pilot training, utility, agricultural and similar roles. First flown in 1965, the type entered full-scale production in 1967 and a total of 50 were completed. Two versions were built: the standard SH-4 and the SH-4A agricultural version fitted with spraybars and two chemical tanks. Powered by a 235hp Franklin engine derated to 170hp, the SH-4 cruises at about 81 mph (130km/hr). Other performance figures include a maximum level speed at sea level of 100 mph (161km/hr); economical cruising speed of 73 mph (117km/hr); maximum sea-level rate of climb of 1,180ft/min) (360m/min); and a range of 200 miles (320km). *Country of origin:* Italy. *Silhouette:* SH-4. *Picture:* SH-4A.

Power: 1 × Ivchenko piston engine   *Rotor dia:* 47ft 1in (14.35m)   *Length:* 39ft 8½in (12.1m)

The first helicopter to enter series production in the USSR, the Mi-1 first flew in 1948 under the designation GM-1; delivery of production aircraft began in 1951. The type remained in production until 1964 and several versions were built. A version built in Poland by WSK-Swidnik is designated SM-1. Powered by a 575hp Ivchenko radial engine, the Mi-1 has a cruising speed of about 90 mph (145km/hr). Maximum level speed at sea level is 106 mph (170km/hr), and maximum range at economical cruising speed and 3,280ft (1,000m) altitude is 370 miles (600km). Maximum climb rate at 5,070lb (2,300kg) all-up weight is 1,043ft/min (318m/min). Built in both civil and military versions, the type is still in service, particularly in Third World countries. *Country of origin:* USSR. *Silhouette and picture:* Mi-1.

Bell AH-1 HueyCobra *Confusion:* Hind

Power: 1 × T53 or 1 × T400 turboshaft *Rotor dia:* 44ft (13.41m) *Length:* 44ft 7in (13.59m)

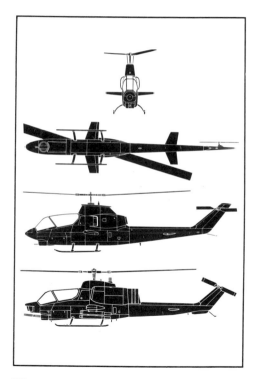

The Model 209 HueyCobra armed attack helicopter first flew in 1965. Four single-engined versions have been built to date: AH-1G, the original version for the US Army; AH-1Q anti-armour version with eight Tow missiles; AH-1R, as AH-1G but with a more powerful engine; and the AH-1S advanced version equipped with Tow missiles and featuring a flat-plate canopy. Some 690 AH-1Gs will ultimately be modified to AH-1S standard. AH-1S has a cruising speed of about 140 mph (225km/hr). The twin-engined versions of the HueyCobra are the AH-1J SeaCobra, operated by the US Marine Corps, and the AH-1T Improved SeaCobra. Latest version is the AH-1T+ SuperCobra with GE T700 engines and extended nacelles for use by the US Marine Corps. *Country of origin:* USA. *Main silhouette:* AH-1G; *lower side view:* AH-1T+. *Picture:* AH-1J.

Power: 2 × Gem turboshafts   *Rotor dia:* 39ft (11.9m)   *Length:* 46ft 10in (14.29m)

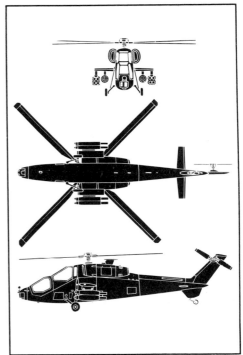

Deliveries of the A129 Mangusta light anti-armour helicopter to the Italian Army are due to begin in 1986. Powered by two Rolls-Royce Gem engines, the A129 is a two-seater with a maximum speed of 196 mph (315km/hr) and a maximum endurance of 3 hours. Armament is carried on four underwing mountings and can consist of eight TOW or six Hellfire anti-tank missiles. Other weapons include HOT missiles, two gun pods or rocket projectiles. The A129 first flew in September 1983. *Country of origin:* Italy.

Power: 1 × Lycoming piston engine   *Rotor dia:* 25ft 3½in (7.71m)   *Length:* 21ft 11¾in (6.8m)

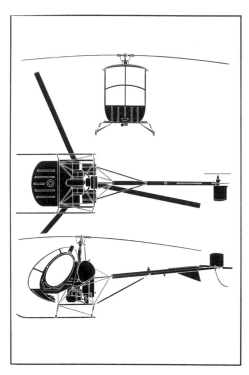

Design and development of the original Model 269 two-seat light helicopter began in 1955, with the first aircraft flying the following year. Production aircraft were designated Model 269A and by early 1968 nearly 1,200 had been built for both civil and military operators. The Model 300 was developed under the designation Model 269B, with production commencing in 1964. In 1964 the Model 269A was selected by the US Army as a light helicopter primary trainer and designated TH-55A Osage. Nearly 800 were built, with deliveries completed by the end of 1969. *Country of origin:* USA. *Silhouette:* Model 300. *Picture:* TH-55A.

Power: 2 × Isotov turboshafts   *Rotor dia:* 47ft 6¾in (14.5m)   *Length:* 57ft 2in (17.42m)

The Mi-2 twin-engined development of the Mi-1 was first announced in late 1961. Under an agreement signed in 1964, production and marketing were assigned to WSK-PZL Swidnik in Poland. Several thousand have since been built, mainly for export, with more than 2,000 being delivered to the USSR. The type is used by both civil and military operators and can be fitted out for a variety of roles, including ambulance, search and rescue, agricultural work, freight and transport of up to eight passengers. The agricultural version is called the Bazant. Mi-2s of the Polish Air Force have been fitted with unguided rocket pods and air-to-surface missiles on pylons on each side of the fuselage. *Country of origin:* USSR/Poland.

Mil Mi-14 Haze

Boeing Vertol CH-47 Chinook

Kamov Ka-25 Hormone

Power: 1 × Shvetsov piston engine   *Rotor dia:* 68ft 11in (21m)   *Length:* 55ft 1in (16.8m)

The Mi-4, code-named Hound, was first put into production in 1952 and several thousand examples have been built for military and civil work. Exports have been widespread throughout the Soviet sphere of influence and to countries such as Egypt and India. Fourteen troops can be carried in the military version, while freight can be loaded through the rear clamshell doors. A military close-support variant is armed with a machine gun in an underfuselage pod, plus air-to-surface rockets. The anti-submarine version is fitted with magnetic anomaly detection gear and an undernose search radar. The civil version is the 11-passenger Mi-4P and the agricultural variant is the Mi-4S. China built the type under licence. Economical cruising speed is 99 mph (160km/hr) and maximum range is 370 miles (595km). *Country of origin:* USSR. *Silhouette:* Mi-4P. *Picture:* Mi-4 (military).

Power: 1 × Gnome turboshaft   *Rotor dia:* 53ft (16.15m)   *Length:* 44ft 2in (13.46m)

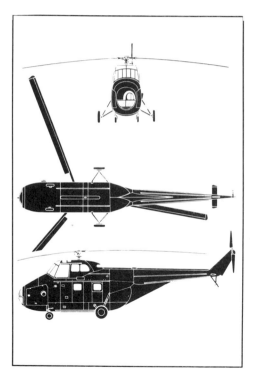

The Whirlwind, a licence-built version of the Sikorsky S-55, first flew in 1952. Series 1 and 2 aircraft were powered by piston engines; only a few remain in service (with Cuba and Yugoslavia). The Series 3 Whirlwind was extensively modified, the installation of a 1,050shp Rolls-Royce Gnome turboshaft necessitating a change in the nose shape. The type is still in limited service in Brazil, Qatar and Yugoslavia. *Country of origin:* UK. *Silhouette:* Series 3. *Picture:* Whirlwind HAR10.

Power: 1 × R-1300 piston engine   *Rotor dia:* 53ft (16.15m)   *Length:* 42ft 3in (12.88m)

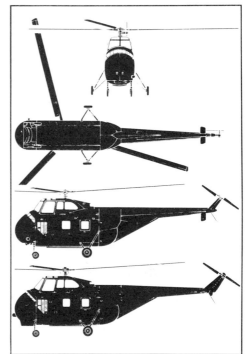

The S-55, the first American helicopter to be certificated for commercial operation, first flew in 1949. The type has been sold to civil and military operators all over the world and has also been licence-built in Japan by Mitsubishi and in Britain by Westland as the Whirlwind. The military version is designated H-19 Chickasaw in US service use and is still operated by a number of South American countries as well as Greece and Turkey. More than 1,200 were built. Powered by an 800hp Wright R-1300 piston engine, the S-55 has a cruising speed of about 90 mph (145km/hr). US company Helitec has produced a turbine-powered version, the S-55T. *Country of origin:* USA. *Main silhouette:* S-55; *lower side view:* S-55T. *Picture:* S-55T.

Sikorsky S-58/S-58T

Confusion: Whirlwind, S-55, Wessex

Power: 1 × R-1820 piston engine or 1 × PT6T turboshaft

Rotor dia (S-58T): 62ft (18.9m)   *Length* (S-58T): 54ft 9in (16.69m)

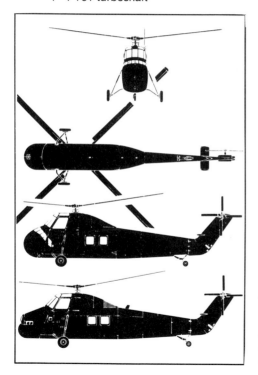

A general-purpose 18-passenger piston-engined military/civil helicopter, the S-58 has been operated all over the world and production totalled 1,821. US Army designations are CH-34A to CH-34D Choctaw. In marinised form the type is known as the UH-34D, VH-34D and UH-34E Seahorse, and the name Seabat is used for anti-submarine variants (SH-34G and SH-34J). The S-58B, C and D are civil transports. First flown in 1970 with two PT6 turboshaft engines, the S-58T was eventually offered as new or in the form of a conversion from the piston-engined version. *Country of origin:* USA. *Main silhouette:* S-58; *lower side view:* S-58T. *Picture:* S-58T.

Power: 2 × Gnome turboshafts   *Rotor dia:* 56ft (17.07m)   *Length:* 48ft 4½in (14.74m)

A general-purpose and anti-submarine helicopter first flown in 1958, the Wessex was originally powered by a Gazelle engine but was later fitted with Rolls-Royce Gnomes. Used by the RAF and Royal Navy, the Wessex has been built in various versions, including the HC2 transport/ambulance for the RAF and the HAS1 anti-submarine and HU5 commando assault transport for the Royal Navy. The Wessex carries a crew of two and ten passengers. Range is 334 miles (538km). *Country of origin:* UK. *Silhouette:* HAS1. *Picture:* HU5.

Power: 2 × Turmo turboshafts   *Rotor dia:* **49ft 2½in (15m)**   *Length:* **46ft 1½in (14m)**

Originally a French product which first flew in 1965, the SA.330 Puma was later adopted as part of a joint Franco-British programme under which production was shared between the two countries. The RAF and the French Army use the type as a transport and some 700 have been sold for military and civil applications in many countries. Early versions were the 330B (French Army), 330C (export), 330E (RAF), 330F and G (civil) and 330H (military). Current models are the 330J (civil) and 330L (military). Sixteen troops or up to 20 passengers can be carried at a cruising speed of 159 mph (257km/hr). The Puma has been licence-built in Romania. *Country of origin:* France/UK. *Silhouette:* SA.330. *Picture:* Puma HC1 (SA.330E).

Aérospatiale SA.332 Super Puma

Power: 2 × Makila turboshafts   *Rotor dia:* 49ft 6in (15.08m)   *Length:* 48ft 8in (14.82m)

A much modified version of the Puma, the 332 Super Puma has a lengthened nose, new undercarriage and higher-powered engines. The five versions of the 332 on offer are the military 332B seating 20 troops; civil 332C seating 17; 332F for ASW/search and rescue and other naval duties; 332L with 2ft 6in (0.76m) fuselage extension, four more seats and two extra windows; and 332M with the same extension for military use. More than 190 Super Pumas had been ordered by mid-1984. Thirty-five 332Ls for Bristow Helicopters are known as Tigers. The 332L has a maximum speed of 184 mph (296km/hr) and range at cruising speed of 527 miles (848km). *Country of origin:* France. *Picture:* 332F with Exocet missiles.

Aérospatiale SA.321 Super Frelon *Confusion:* Puma, Super Puma, S-61L/N

Power: 3 × Turmo turboshafts   *Rotor dia:* 62ft (18.9m)   *Length:* 75ft 7in (23m)

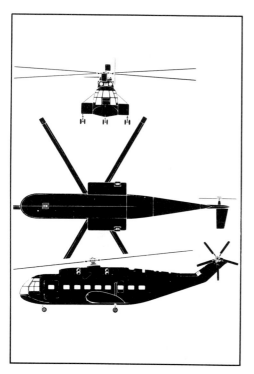

First flown in 1962, the three-engined SA.321 Super Frelon is used as a military and civil transport and for anti-submarine work. Civil versions are the 321F and 321J, the former designed to carry 34/37 passengers. The 321G for the French Navy is amphibious, has radar and carries torpedoes and other military equipment. The 321H army/air force variant accommodates 27–30 troops or cargo. The Super Frelon has been built in large numbers and sold to eight countries, including Israel. Cruising speed is 155 mph (250km/hr) and range 509 miles (820km). *Country of origin:* France. *Silhouette:* SA.321F. *Picture:* SA.321K.

Power: 2 × CT58 turboshafts   *Rotor dia:* 62ft (18.9m)   *Length:* 72ft 10in (22.2m)

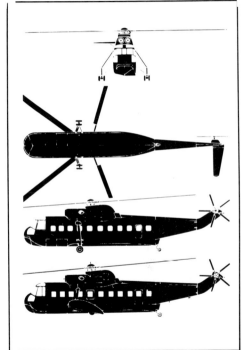

A widely used helicopter airliner, the S-61L/N can seat up to 28 passengers. The S-61L is non-amphibious, while the N has stabilising floats and a sealed hull for use on water. British Airways Helicopters is the largest single operator of this type. The S-61L first flew in 1960 and the S-61N in 1962. The undercarriage is retractable and the nose carries a thimble radome containing weather radar. S-61N production rights are now held by Agusta. This company has now produced the AS-61N1 Silver 50in (1.27m) longer fuselage, re-arranged windows and smaller sponsons. Range is 495 miles (796km) and cruising speed 138 mph (222km/hr). *Country of origin:* USA. *Main silhouette:* S-61L; *lower side view:* S-61B. *Picture:* AS-61N1 Silver.

Power: 1 × T58 turboshaft   *Rotor dia:* 53ft (16.16m)   *Length:* 44ft 6½in (13.58m)

The first amphibious helicopter to be built by Sikorsky, the S-62 first flew in 1958 and has been used in both military and civil forms. As an airliner it carries 12 passengers or cargo. The original S-62A was licence-built by Mitsubishi in Japan, the S-62B had the main rotor system of the S-58 instead of that of the S-55, and the S-62C was the last commercial version. The US Coast Guard took delivery of 99 S-62s, designating them HH-52A. Maximum cruising speed is 98 mph (158km/hr) and range 474 miles (764km). *Country of origin:* USA. *Silhouette and picture:* HH-52A.

Power: 2 × T58 turboshafts   *Rotor dia:* 62ft (18.9m)   *Length:* 54ft 9in (16.69m)

The multi-purpose S-61 is used for anti-submarine work, transport and search and rescue. As the S-61 the type can carry 26 troops. In the anti-submarine role it is known as the Sea King and carries weapons, including homing torpedoes. US Navy designation is SH-3 and there are a number of variants, from SH-3A through to SH-3H. The SH-3 is known as the CH-124 in the Canadian Armed Forces. The SH-3 has been widely exported and is standard equipment in Japan and Italy, where it is built by Agusta. The SH-3 first flew in 1959. Range is 625 miles (1,005km) and cruising speed 136 mph (219km/hr). *Country of origin:* USA. *Silhouette:* SH-3H. *Picture:* SH-3D.

Westland Sea King/Commando *Confusion:* SH-3/S-61, S-61R

Power: 2 × Gnome turboshafts   *Rotor dia:* 62ft (18.9m)   *Length:* 55ft 10in (17.01m)

Developed under licence from the American S-61D, the Sea King is the Royal Navy's standard anti-submarine helicopter under the designations HAS1 and 2. The HAR3 is used by the RAF for search and rescue. The Sea King has been exported widely. The Commando military transport version can seat 30 troops and has no amphibious capability. Commando Mks 1 and 2 are in service. The Commando Mk 1 differs minimally from the Sea King, while the Mk 2, the main production version, can be used for tactical troop transport, logistic support, casualty evacuation, air-to-surface strike, and search and rescue. The Mk 42 is for India, the HAS Mk 5 for the Royal Navy and several have been fitted with Searchwater radar as the Sea King AEW. Sea King cruising speed is 131 mph (211km/hr) and range 937 miles (1,507km). *Country of origin:* UK. *Silhouette:* HAS2. *Picture:* Sea King AEW.

Sikorsky S-61R/CH-3E/HH-3F Pelican

Power: 2 × T58 turboshafts   *Rotor dia:* 62ft (18.9m)   *Length:* 57ft 3in (17.45m)

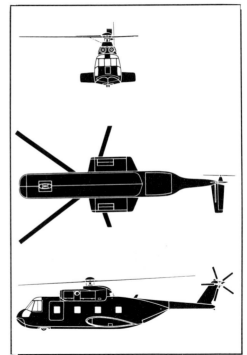

Developed from the S-61 Sea King, the S-61R has a rear loading ramp and retractable undercarriage. It is used for transport, assault and search and rescue. The first S-61R flew in 1963 and the type is used by the USAF as the CH-3E and HH-3E and by the US Coast Guard as the HH-3F Pelican, with a nose radome. The HH-3E has armour, defensive armament and an in-flight refuelling probe on the starboard side. Up to 30 troops can be carried and a hoist is fitted. Agusta in Italy has built a version of the Pelican for the Italian Air Force. Cruising speed is 144 mph (232km/hr) and range 465 miles (748km). *Country of origin:* USA. *Silhouette:* HH-3F. *Picture:* HH-3E.

 **Mil Mi-8/Mi-17 Hip** *Confusion:* S-61L/N, S-62, S-61R, Haze

Power: 2 × Isotov turboshafts *Rotor dia:* 69ft 10in (21.29m) *Length:* 61ft (18.3m)

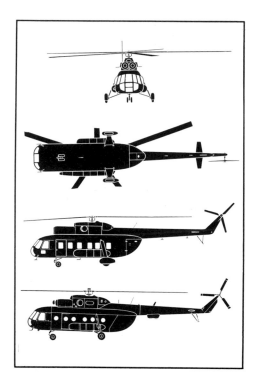

A replacement for the Mi-4 Hound, the Mi-8 is a twin-turbine helicopter seating up to 32 passengers. As with other Soviet medium helicopters, the Hip is used by both the Soviet services and Aeroflot. The military versions have round windows and are code-named Hip-C to Hip-K, this version being used for ECM work. Hip-E carries a gun and massive rocket-projectile armament. The transport has rectangular windows and no radome. With up-rated engines and other modifications a variant of the Mi-8 is known as the M-17, code-named Hip-H. Range is 232 miles (375km) and maximum cruising speed 140 mph (225km/hr). *Country of origin:* USSR. *Main silhouette:* Hip-C; *lower side view:* Hip-H. *Picture:* Hip-K.

Power: 2 × Isotov turboshafts   *Rotor dia:* **69ft 10in (21.29m)**   *Length of fuselage:* **59ft 7in (18.15m)**

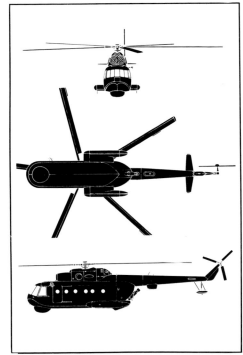

Developed from the Mi-8, the Mi-14 Haze is a shore-based Soviet Navy anti-submarine helicopter. A boat hull is incorporated, there is a radome under the nose, and a magnetic anomaly detector is mounted under the tailboom. The undercarriage is fully retractable. Haze is in full production and in large-scale service with the Soviet Naval Air Force. Over 100 have been delivered. Dimensions and dynamic components are generally similar to those of the Mi-8, while the powerplant is a pair of Isotov TV3-117 turboshafts of the kind fitted to the Mi-24 gunship. There are two versions, Haze-A for ASW and Haze-B for mine countermeasures. Maximum speed is approximately 142 mph (230km/hr). *Country of origin:* USSR. *Silhouette:* Haze-A. *Picture:* Haze-B.

 **Mil Mi-24 Hind** *Confusion:* HueyCobra

Power: 2 × Isotov turboshafts   *Rotor dia:* 55ft (16.76m)   *Length:* 55ft 6in (16.9m)

A heavily armed assault and gunship helicopter, the Mi-24, code-named Hind, is in service in the Soviet Union in very large numbers. Hind-A carries eight troops and has stub-wing-mounted missiles and a nose gun, while Hind-D has separate cockpits for pilot and weapon operator and a four-barrel machine gun in a chin mounting. Hind-C has no nose gun or under-nose sighting system. Hind-E carries tube-launched anti-tank missiles. Early Hinds had the tail rotor on the starboard side, while later versions have it on the port side. Cruising speed is 140 mph (225km/hr) and range 300 miles (480km). *Country of origin:* USSR. *Silhouette and picture:* Hind-D.

Power: 2 × Allison 250 or PT6B turboshafts   *Rotor dia:* **44ft (13.41m)**   *Length:* **44ft 1in (13.44m)**

A commercial transport seating 14 passengers, the Sikorsky S-76 first flew in 1977. The S-76 is classified as an all-weather helicopter. Maximum cruising speed at a gross weight of 8,400lb (3,810kg) is 178 mph (286km/hr). Range with eight passengers, auxiliary fuel and offshore equipment is 691 miles (1,112km). Current production version is the S-76 Mk II. In addition there are the S-76 Utility, the S-76B with PT6B engines, the AUH-76 armed utility model and the H-76N naval variant. *Country of origin:* USA. *Silhouette:* S-76. *Picture:* S-76B.

 **Hughes AH-64A Apache** *Confusion:* Black Hawk

Power: 2 × T700 turbofans   *Rotor dia:* 48ft (14.63m)   *Length:* 48ft 2in (14.68m)

The US Army is to acquire a total of 675 AH-64A Apache tandem two-seat all-weather attack helicopters. Powered by two 1696shp GE T700 engines, the Apache is capable of a maximum speed of 186 mph (300km/hr) and has an endurance of 1hr 50min. The helicopter mounts a 30mm Chain Gun automatic cannon under the fuselage and can carry rockets or 16 Hellfire missiles. An advanced sighting and fire control system is fitted. The first prototype flew in September 1975. *Country of origin:* USA.

Sikorsky S-70/UH-60A Black Hawk

Power: 2 × T700 turboshafts   *Rotor dia:* 53ft 8in (16.23m)   *Length:* 51ft 1in (15.26m)

First flown in 1974, the Sikorsky S-70 Black Hawk, military designation UH-60A, was the winner of the US Army's Utility Tactical Transport Aircraft System (Uttas) competition and is in full-scale production. Ultimately over 1,000 Black Hawks will be acquired. Eleven fully equipped troops can be carried, and alternative loads include cargo and stretchers. Up to 8,000lb (3,629kg) can be carried externally on a hook. The HH-60A Night Hawk is a combat rescue version for the US Air Force, while the EH-60A is equipped for electronic countermeasures. Endurance is up to three hours and maximum cruising speed 169 mph (272km/hr). *Country of origin:* USA. *Silhouette and picture:* UH-60A.

Sikorsky SH-60B Seahawk

Confusion: Black Hawk, S-76

Power: 2 × T700 turboshafts   *Rotor dia:* 53ft 8in (16.36m)   *Length:* 50ft 1in (15.26m)

Developed from the Black Hawk, the three-crew SH-60B Seahawk was the winner in the US Navy's Light Airborne Multi-Purpose System (LAMPS) Mk III competition. The Seahawk will be used for anti-submarine warfare and ship surveillance/ship targeting from cruisers, destroyers and frigates. Sophisticated detection and processing equipment and anti-submarine torpedoes are carried. Deliveries started in 1983 and the US Navy requirement is for 204. The Seahawk has also been purchased by Japan and Australia. *Country of origin:* USA.

Power: 2 × T64 turboshafts   *Rotor dia:* 72ft 3in (22.02m)   *Length:* 67ft 2in (20.47m)

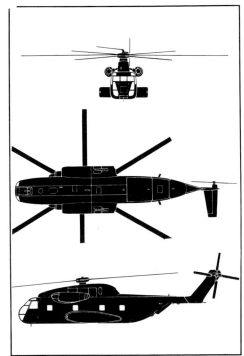

A heavy assault transport, the S-65A first flew in 1964 and incorporates many S-64 components. Fitted with rear loading doors, the type can carry vehicles, guns or 55 troops. The US Marines and Iran use the CH-53A Sea Stallion, while the USAF has the HH-53B/C. An improved US Marine Corps version is the CH-53D, and the CH-53G is licence-built in Germany. The S-65 (MCM), designated RH-53D in the US Navy, is used for mine countermeasures and has a tow boom. Austria bought two S-65-Oes for rescue work in the Alps. Range is 257 miles (410km) and maximum cruising speed 173 mph (278km/hr). *Country of origin:* USA. *Silhouette:* CH-53G. *Picture:* S-65.

Power: 3 × T64 turboshafts   *Rotor dia:* 79ft (24m)   *Length:* 73ft 5in (22.38m)

Developed from the S-65/CH-53A/B/D Sea Stallion, the CH-53E Super Stallion three-engined amphibious assault transport helicopter is used by both the US Navy and US Marines. Up to 56 troops can be accommodated, and very large loads, such as aircraft, can be slung externally. The first prototype flew in 1974 and production is expected to exceed 200. An airborne mine countermeasures version is the MH-53E, of which 57 are to be delivered to US Navy. These have larger sponsons. Maximum cruising speed is 173 mph (278km/hr). *Country of origin:* USA. *Silhouette:* CH-53E. *Picture:* MH-53E.

Power: 2 × Soloviev turboshafts   *Rotor dia:* 114ft 10in (35m)   *Length:* 108ft 10½in (33.18m)

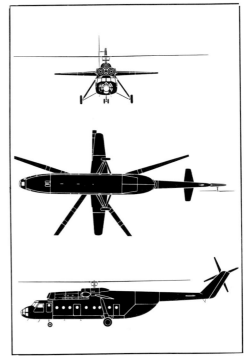

When it first appeared in 1957 the Mi-6, code-named Hook, was the world's largest helicopter. Basically a military design, of which over 800 have been built, the type has also been employed by Aeroflot as a specialised civil transport. Military Hooks have been exported to Egypt, Bulgaria and Vietnam. Equipment, including missiles, can be loaded through the rear clamshell doors and heavy loads can be carried externally. A total of 65 passengers can be accommodated. Maximum cruising speed is 155 mph (250km/hr) and range 404 miles (650km). At one time the Mi-6 held a total of 14 FAI-recognised records. Those still standing include a speed of 211 mph (340km/hr) over a 100km closed circuit; a speed of 186 mph (300km/hr) with payloads of 1,000kg and 2,000kg over a 1,000km circuit; and a speed of 176 mph (284km/hr) with a payload of 5,000kg over a 1,000km closed circuit. *Country of origin:* USSR.

Mil Mi-26 Halo *Confusion:* Hook

Power: 2 × Lotarev turboshafts   *Rotor dia:* 105ft (32m)   *Length:* 110ft 8in (33.7m)

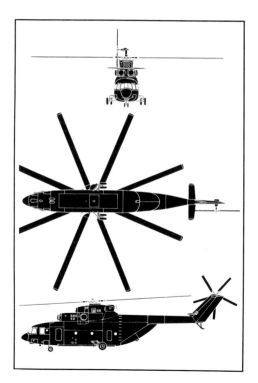

The heaviest helicopter built anywhere in the world, the Mi-26, NATO code-named Halo, is the first to have an eight-blade rotor. Initially flown in 1977 and now in full-scale production, the Mi-26 can carry 44,090lb (20,000kg) of internal payload or up to 70 troops. Capable of operating in extreme winter conditions in the Soviet Union in the civil role, the Mi-26 also has a variety of military applications. The Mi-26 made its first public appearance at the 1981 Paris Show, where it aroused major interest. The Mi-26's top speed is 183 mph (295km/hr) and range 497 miles (800km). *Country of origin:* USSR.

Power: 2 × Soloviev turboshafts   *Rotor dia:* 114ft 10in (35m)   *Length:* 107ft 10in (32.86m)

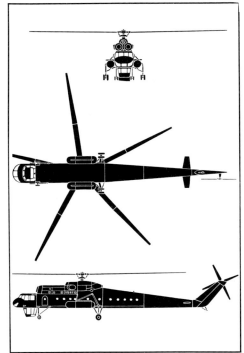

Developed from the Mi-6, the Mi-10 Harke is a very large flying crane which first flew in 1960. Bulky loads can be carried between the long main undercarriage legs and the cabin accommodates up to 28 passengers. The Mi-10 is used by both the Soviet armed forces and Aeroflot. The Mi-10K has the same fuselage but a short undercarriage and a gondola under the nose housing a second pilot. A closed-circuit television system, with cameras scanning forwards from under the rear fuselage and downwards through the sling hatch, is used to monitor Mi-10 payloads. The pilot also uses this system as a touchdown reference. The Mi-10K was first publicly demonstrated in 1966. Range of the Mi-10 is 155 miles (250km) and cruising speed 112 mph (180km/hr). *Country of origin:* USSR. *Silhouette:* Mi-10K. *Picture:* Mi-10.

Power: 2 × JTFD 12 turboshafts   *Rotor dia:* 72ft (21.9m)   *Length:* 70ft 3in (21.41m)

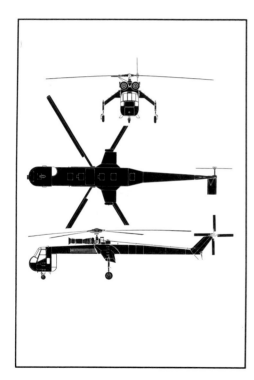

A flying crane designed to lift heavy bulk loads, the S-64 first flew in 1962 and was adopted by the US Army as the CH-54A Tarhe. Special standardised containers can be slung under the fuselage boom. With a maximum loaded weight of 20,000lb (9,072kg), these pods can accommodate 45 combat-equipped troops, 24 stretchers, cargo or other equipment. They can also be adapted in the field to act as surgical units or command and communications posts. A variant with more power and modified rotor system is known as the CH-54B. Civil versions are designated S-64E and S-64F. Range is 230 miles (370km) and maximum cruising speed 127 mph (204km/hr). Production has now ceased. *Country of origin:* USA. *Silhouette and picture:* S-64.

Power: 2 × Glushenkov turboshafts   *Rotor dia:* 51ft 8in (15.74m)   *Length:* 32ft (9.75m)

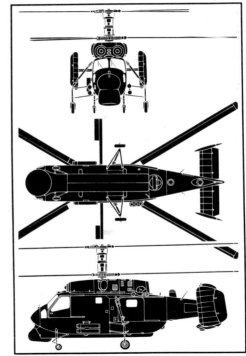

Produced in large numbers, the Ka-25 Hormone is the Soviet Navy's standard shipborne anti-submarine helicopter. Distinguished by a large chin radome, it carries depth charges, torpedoes and guided missiles. Twin main rotors are mounted on a single shaft. A transport version seats 12, while Hormone-B carries special electronics equipment and Hormone-C is a utility search and rescue model. The Ka-25K, with the radome replaced by a glazed gondola, is a commercial version for crane and general duties. Cruising speed is 120 mph (193km/hr) and range 250 miles (402km). *Country of origin:* USSR. *Silhouette and picture:* Hormone-A.

 **Kamov Ka-27 Helix** *Confusion:* Hormone, Hoodlum

Power: 2 × turboshafts   *Rotor dia:* 54ft 10in (16.75m)   *Length:* 39ft 5in (12m)

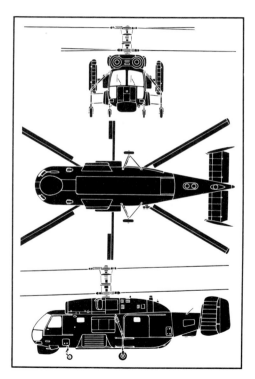

First observed aboard a Soviet cruiser in 1981, this latest Kamov helicopter is designated Ka-27 and is NATO code-named Helix. The layout of Helix is similar to that of Hormone but the former is significantly larger and heavier, with a longer fuselage, increased rotor diameter and two instead of three fins. Helix is basically an anti-submarine helicopter, with two pilots and three sensor operators. Helix-A is the ASW version, while Helix-B is used for assisting with guidance and target acquisition for missiles. A search and rescue variant has been observed and the civil version is known as Ka-32. *Country of origin:* USSR.

Power: 2 × **Vedeneev** piston engines   *Rotor dia:* **42ft 8in (13m)**   *Length:* **24ft 5in (7.75m)**

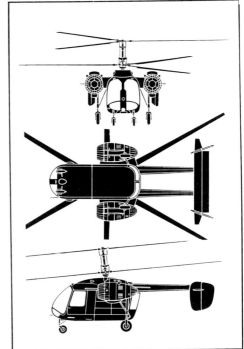

First flown in 1956, the Ka-26, NATO code-named Hoodlum, is a light transport and agricultural helicopter in large-scale service in the Eastern Bloc and exported to such countries as West Germany, Sweden and Sri Lanka. Payloads are interchangeable by the use of specialised fuselage pods designed for the transport, ambulance, cropdusting/spraying and geophysical survey roles. A lifting hook can be fitted. Some Hoodlums are employed on military work. Carrying seven passengers, Hoodlum has a range of 248 miles (400km). A turboshaft-engined version is the Ka-126. *Country of origin:* USSR.

Kaman H-43 Huskie *Confusion:* Hormone

Power: 1 × T53 turboshaft   *Rotor dia:* 47ft (14.33m)   *Length:* 25ft 2in (7.67m)

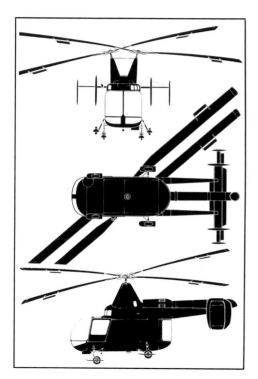

Originally piston-engine-powered, the Huskie was first used by the US Navy and USAF in the 1950s. The initial turbine-powered version was the HH-43B, first flown in 1956 and ordered by the USAF, Burma, Colombia, Morocco, Pakistan and Thailand. A later development was the HH-43F, built for the USAF and Iran. Up to ten passengers, a firefighting/rescue team, or stretchers and medical personnel can be carried. Range is 504 miles (811km) and cruising speed 110 mph (117km/hr). The US Navy uses a drone version designated QH-43G. The Huskie is unusual in having twin rotor masts and intermeshing rotors. *Country of origin:* USA. *Silhouette and picture:* HH-34F.

Power: **2 × T55 turboshafts**   Rotor dia: **60ft (18.29m)**   Length: **51ft (15.54m)**

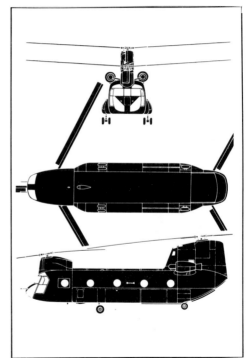

Many hundreds of tandem-rotor Chinook helicopters have been built. In addition to US production, the type is made under licence in Italy. Initial variant was the CH-47A, followed by the uprated CH-47B. The current production model is the CH-47C with more range and better performance. The US Army is upgrading all its Chinooks to a new -47D standard. The RAF operates the Chinook designated HC Mk1 and there have been exports to other countries. Up to 44 troops can be carried in the cabin and large loads can be slung. The international military version is the Model 414. The commercial passenger version, the Model 234, is in service with British Airways Helicopters and other civil operators. Mission radius of action is 115 miles (185km) and cruising speed 158 mph (254km/hr). *Country of origin:* USA. *Silhouette and picture:* CH-47C.

545

Boeing-Vertol H-46 Sea Knight/Model 107 *Confusion:* Chinook

Power: 2 × T58 turboshafts   *Rotor dia:* 51ft (15.54m)   *Length:* 44ft 10in (13.66m)

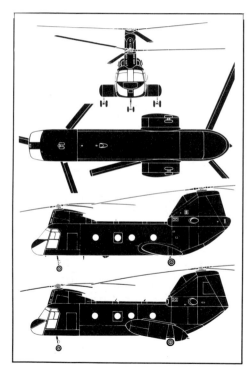

The Sea Knight operates as a shipboard and land-based assault transport carrying 25 troops or freight. First flown in 1958, the Sea Knight has been built in a variety of versions: the CH-46A, -46D, -46E and -46F for the US Marines, and the UH-46A and -46D for the US Navy. Canada operates the type under the designations CH-113 and CH-113A, while Sweden bought some Rolls-Royce Gnome-powered HKP-4s. The commercial version is the Model 107, now solely built by Kawasaki, which also supplies a military KV-107 to the Japanese forces. Range is 633 miles (1,022km) and cruising speed 154 mph (248km/hr). *Country of origin:* USA/Japan. *Main silhouette:* H-46; *lower side view:* Kawasaki KV-107. *Picture:* KV-107/II-5.

Republic RF-84F Thunderflash/F-84F
Thunderstreak

VFW 614

Consolidated PBY-5A Catalina

Handley Page Herald

Bristol Britannia

Convair 990

Hawker Siddeley Argosy

Shorts Belfast

GLOSSARY OF RECOGNITION TERMS

aerofoil section Cross-section through an aircraft wing or helicopter rotor blade.

afterburner Gives a jet engine greatly increased thrust by burning fuel in the exhaust gas stream. Also called reheat.

aileron Wing-mounted lateral control surface.

airbrake Retractable "door" mounted on the fuselage or wing and used to slow the aircraft down or steepen descent angle.

AI Airborne intercept radar.

all-up weight Fully loaded weight of an aircraft or helicopter.

amphibian Aircraft capable of alighting on both land and water.

anhedral Angle at which a wing slopes down from the horizontal in the head-on view. Opposite of dihedral.

antenna Any form of aerial for the transmission/reception of radio/radar signals.

arrester hook Underfuselage hook designed to engage wires on an airfield or a carrier deck in order to stop the aircraft.

aspect ratio The ratio between the span and chord of a wing. Derived by dividing span by chord.

ASV Air-to-surface-vessel radar. Used by maritime aircraft.

balance tab Part of an aileron, elevator or rudder which moves into the opposite sense to the main control surface.

bank/banking Manoeuvre in which the aircraft is rolled to left or right.

bicycle undercarriage Two main wheels in tandem under the fuselage. Usually with outrigger wheels on the wings.

bogie undercarriage Four or more wheels on each undercarriage leg.

camber Curvature of an aerofoil section.

canard Aircraft with its tailplane mounted forward of the wing.

canopy Transparent cockpit cover.

cantilever Wing or undercarriage without bracing struts.

c of g Centre of gravity.

chord Measurement from the leading edge to the trailing edge of a wing or rotor blade, parallel with the fuselage centreline.

contrail White vapour trail caused by the condensation of the water in engine exhaust gases at certain altitudes.

contra-rotating propellers Two propellers mounted on one shaft and rotating in opposite directions.

crescent wing Sweptback wing with varying degrees of sweep on the leading edge.

delta Triangular wing or tailplane.

dihedral Angle at which a wing slopes up from the horizontal in the head-on view. Some wings have dihedral on the outer sections only. Opposite of anhedral.

dogtooth Notch in a wing leading edge, visible in the plan view. Also known as a sawtooth.

dorsal fin Extension of the main fin along the top of the fuselage.

drag The resistance offered by the air to an aircraft or part of an aircraft passing through it.

drone Pilotless aircraft used for reconnaissance, electronic warfare or as a target. Also known as a remotely piloted vehicle (RPV).

droop Means of increasing the camber and therefore the lifting capacity of a wing by mechanically extending and lowering the leading edge.

ECM Electronic countermeasures. Means of jamming or distorting radio or radar signals.

ECCM Electronic counter-countermeasures. Means of overcoming ECM.

ejection seat Seat designed to fire aircrew clear of the aircraft in an emergency.

elevator Tailplane-mounted surface used to control an aircraft in the vertical plane.

elevon Combined elevator and aileron; used on delta-wing aircraft.

fence Vertical metal strips mounted chordwise on a wing upper surface to contain spanwise airflow.

fenestron Multi-blade tail rotor mounted in a duct.

fin Fixed part of a vertical tail.

flap Surface mounted at the wing trailing edge and deployed to increase lift for take-off and landing.

flaperon Trailing-edge surface combining the functions of flap and aileron.

flat four Horizontally opposed four-cylinder piston engine. Also flat twin and flat six.

flight refuelling Means of passing fuel from one aircraft to another in the air. Under the British system the "tanker" aircraft trails a hose with a drogue at the end, into which a probe on the receiving aircraft is inserted. The American system is based on a "flying boom" which can be directed to a receiving point on the aircraft which is being refuelled.

flying tail Tailplane which has no fixed portion and moves in its entirety to give vertical control.

foreplane Forward control surface on a canard aircraft.

fuselage Main body of an aircraft or helicopter.

gull wing A wing with dihedral on the inner sections only. An inverted gull wing has an hedral on the inner sections.

hardpoint Reinforced point, usually on the wings, to which external stores can be attached.

JATO Jet-assisted take-off. Technique under which auxiliary rocket packs are mounted on the aircraft to shorten the take-off run. Also known as RATO (rocket-assisted take-off).

leading edge The front edge of a wing, tail or rotor blade.

lift The upward force which keeps an aircraft flying.

Mach number The ratio between the speed of an aircraft and the speed of sound at a particular height. At sea level the speed of sound is 720 mph, so that an aircraft travelling at 720 mph would be flying at Mach 1; 576 mph under the same conditions would be equivalent to Mach 0.8. The speed of sound decreases with altitude up to 36,600ft; thereafter it stays constant at 660.6 mph.

mass balance Weight mounted internally or externally on a control surface to prevent damaging oscillation.

monocoque Aircraft structure in which the outer skin takes most of the load.

nacelle Streamlined structure housing engines, radar or other equipment.

parasol Monoplane with wings mounted on struts above the fuselage.

payload Paying load of a transport, i.e. passengers or freight.

pitot tube Instrument which detects ram air pressure. This is compared with static pressure to find airspeed.

pod Separate nacelle attached to fuselage or wing and carrying an engine, radar or other equipment.

pressurisation The maintenance of pressure inside an aircraft so that passengers and crew can breathe without personal oxygen supplies at high altitude.

pylon Wing or fuselage-mounted structure carrying engine pods, auxiliary fuel tanks or weapons.

radome Dome-shaped fairing over a radar aerial.

refuelling probe Used to receive fuel from an airborne tanker.

reheat See *Afterburner.*

rotor blade Helicopter lifting and control surfaces. A rotor is made up of two or more blades. The main rotor generates lift and creates propulsive thrust. The vertically mounted tail rotor balances out the torque which makes the fuselage tend to rotate in the opposite direction to the main rotor.

rudder A fin-mounted vertical surface which provides directional control.

servo tab Moving surface on aileron, elevator or rudder which when moved causes the main control surface to deflect in the opposite direction.

slat Section of wing leading edge which moves forward to produce a slot between itself and the wing. Increases lift and improves control at low speeds.

slot Spanwise gap at the wing leading edge (see slat).

slotted flap Flap which creates a slot between itself and the wing trailing edge.

sonobuoy Listening device dropped from an aircraft to detect submarines.

split flap Flap which is hinged forward of the wing trailing edge, so that the wing upper surface is unchanged when the flap is lowered.

spoiler Retractable wing-mounted surface deployed to create drag and reduce lift. Used to slow the aircraft and control its descent path.

sponson Stub wing carrying undercarriage or other equipment.

spring tab Small control surface which acts as both balance tab and servo tab.

stabiliser Tailplane (US).

STOL Short take-off and landing.

subsonic Speeds below that of sound, i.e. less than Mach 1.

supercharger Compressor used to boost the power of a piston engine. Also called a turbocharger.

supersonic Speeds in excess of sound, i.e. above Mach 1.

sweepback Plan-view angle between the wing and the fuselage centreline.

taileron Tailplane used as a primary control surface in both pitch and roll.

tailplane Horizontal surface at the rear of an aircraft which normally carries the elevators.

taper The decrease in wing chord from root to tip.

thickness/chord ratio Ratio of the thickness of the wing section to the chord at a given point. Usually expressed as a percentage.

thrust The force that moves an aircraft forward. Also used to express the power of a jet engine.

thrust reverser System which turns the thrust of a jet engine forwards for braking purposes.

transonic Speeds just above and below Mach 1.

trim tab Adjustable tab on a control surface.

turbofan A jet engine with a large fan on the front which passes air round the core of the engine and also gives more impetus to the compressor.

turbojet An engine in which the hot gases expelled at the rear provide all the propulsive thrust.

turboprop A gas turbine engine in which the shaft is geared to drive a propeller.

turboshaft A gas turbine in which the power is transmitted to a shaft, usually to drive a helicopter rotor.

vortex generators Small protruding plates fitted to wing, tail or fuselage to change the airflow pattern.

wing loading Aircraft loaded weight divided by wing area.

SILLOGRAPH PROFICIENCY TEST

Test your aircraft-recognition skill by identifying these sillograph outlines of well known aircraft. Tackle the whole test in one go, and write down your answers. The solution is on page 572.

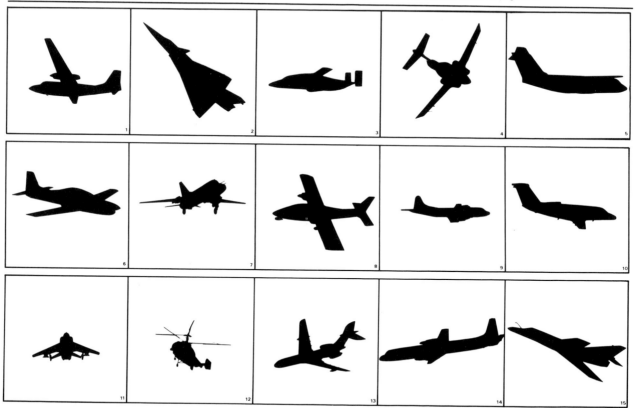

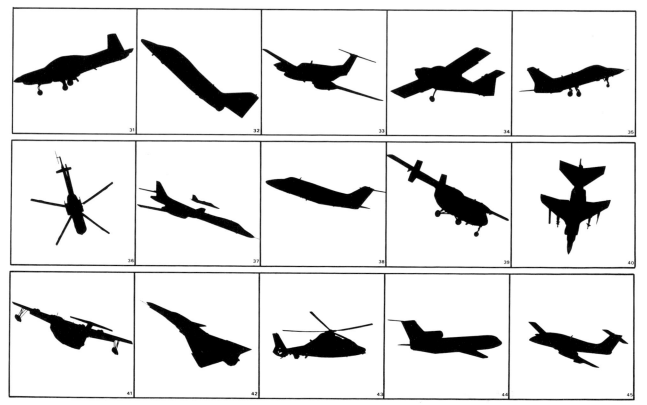

INDEX

INDEX

INDEX

INDEX

INDEX

Test answers (see page 554)

1 Aero Commander 1000
2 Mirage 3NG
3 Shorts 330
4 Buccaneer
5 BAe 146
6 Shorts EMBRAER Tucano
7 Su-17 Fitter-H
8 Partenavia P-68
9 Lockheed P-3C
10 Cessna Citation 111
11 Q-5 Fantan-A (China)
12 Ka-27 Helix
13 VC-10 Tanker
14 Il-18 Coot
15 Super Etendard
16 RFB Fantrainer
17 BAe One-Eleven
18 Saab-Fairchild SF 340
19 Canadair CL-215
20 An-26 Curl
21 Su-25 Frogfoot
22 EMBRAER Bandeirante
23 Aero L-39 Albatros
24 Boeing 737-300
25 Alpha Jet
26 C-141 StarLifter
27 Stampe SV.4
28 Super Galeb
29 Il-76 Candid
30 Dornier 228
31 BAe-Pilatus PC-9
32 CASA C-101 Aviojet
33 Beech C-12F Huron
34 Saab T-17 Supporter
35 AM-X
36 Mi-14 Haze
37 B-1B and F-111
38 Mitsubishi MU-300 Diamond 1
39 IAI Arava
40 Jaguar
41 Shin Meiwa PS-1/US-1
42 IAI Kfir
43 SA365N Dauphin 2
44 Yak-42 Clobber
45 Pucara